Edwin Everton
1949
General Theological Seminary
1976

ST. MARTIN'S CHURCH, CANTERBURY.

This ancient structure, built by British Christians probably in the fifth century, is one of the several existing monumental proofs that Rome did not plant Christianity in England. Here the Christian Queen, Bertha, and the Bishop and Clergy whom she had brought from her home in Gaul, now France, were daily worshipping when the first Roman Missionaries with St. Augustine at their head arrived in A. D. 597.

THE CHURCH FOR AMERICANS

By the Rt. Rev. WILLIAM MONT-
GOMERY BROWN, D.D., Bishop
of Arkansas; Formerly Archdeacon
of the Diocese of Ohio and Lecturer
at Bexley Hall, the Theological Seminary of Kenyon College.

Ἐγὼ δὲ λέγω εἰς Χριστὸν καὶ εἰς τὴν ἐκκλησίαν.
—EPHESIANS, V : 32 ● ● ● ● ● ● ● ● ● ●

REVISED AND ENLARGED.   EIGHTEENTH EDITION.

NEW YORK:
THOMAS WHITTAKER, 2 and 3 Bible House
1909

MADE BY
THE WERNER COMPANY,
AKRON, OHIO.

TO

MY BELOVED WIFE,

ELLA BRADFORD BROWN,

AND HER MOTHER,

MARY SCRANTON BRADFORD,

TRUE AND INSPIRING HELPERS OF THE AUTHOR IN HIS LIFE'S WORK,

THIS VOLUME IS

AFFECTIONATELY AND GRATEFULLY

DEDICATED.

"The Time Will Come When Three Words Uttered with Charity and Meekness Shall Receive a Far More Blessed Reward Than Three Thousand Volumes Written with Disdainful Sharpness of Wit."

—*Hooker.*

PREFACE.

A S the origin of a book is often of interest to the reader, I will explain that this work is along lines, which, as a Missionary, I have followed for many years in my addresses and conversations concerning the Church. I was first induced by the request of the Rt. Rev. Dr. Leonard, Bishop of Ohio, to elaborate my talks into formal lectures, in the hope that they might contribute in some degree to the excellent preparation which our Missionary recruits are receiving at the Divinity School of Kenyon College. After their delivery to the Theological students, it was thought that they would not be without interest to Sunday School teachers and others who now and then are called upon to commend or defend our beloved Church. Accordingly they have been made the basis of Lenten discourses to general congregations in Trinity Church, Toledo, and the Cathedral Parish, Cleveland. Finally, I have been persuaded by the representations of many who heard them that, if published, they would make a useful book for distribution among those who have been reared under Denominational or Roman influences, and supply the need, often felt by Lay readers and young missionaries, of a course of Confirmation instructions about the Church.

The concern which this book manifests for the Ecclesiastical side of Christianity and the little it has to say about its spiritual and practical aspects, is due to what the writer considers to be, just now, the special religious need of our time and country. This is not instruction in the moral requirements of Christianity so much as the establishment of the fact that Christ founded a Church which has come down to us, and with some branch of which it is the privilege and duty of all to identify themselves. The idea that "one Church is as good as another" and that consequently "it practically makes no difference to which we belong," is responsible for the enormous non-church element of the United States, which, according to the last census, amounted to more than half of the whole population, and for the loose hold which all bodies of Christians have upon their constituency.

Under such circumstances it becomes a matter of first importance that the duty of belonging to the National branch of the one Apostolic Church of Christ, and the evil of separation from it, should be set forth in season and out of season. In proportion as this is done, the Episcopal Church will be built up and held together. Our incomparable Liturgy, impressive Services, and attractive yearly round of varied Holy Seasons, are indeed annually drawing thousands to this fold; but others in great numbers who care comparatively little for these things, come because they believe this Church to be historically and canonically the American as well as our racial branch of Christ's Church, and that, therefore, she possesses exclusive claims to allegiance. Every one who is influenced by this conviction, is worth ten of such as are attracted only by æsthetic considerations. Those who are in the Church simply because of natural ties, or on account of her attractive features, are often drawn away by counter influences and alienated the moment that all does not go on according to their liking. But Episcopalians who are such from principle rather than preference— and, thank God, this class is rapidly increasing—stand by the Church through all the changes and chances of parochial life.

I have an instance in mind of a person who, upon coming to a village where our Mission was weak and the Presbyterians and Methodists were strong both socially and numerically, was asked by a caller: "What Church do you and your husband expect to attend?" Upon replying that they were members of the Episcopal Church, her interrogator said: "But that Church is so new and small and has no standing in the community. I think you will find it much more to your taste to be identified with one of the big churches where the other members of the social circle to which you will belong all go. Mrs. B., an estimable lady who recently came to town, was an Episcopalian but, after going once or twice to the little Chapel, she left and joined the Presbyterian Church where she is now a leading member. We like her very much and should be glad if you and Mr. C. would follow her example." To this the self-respecting and consistent answer was made: "We are not that kind of Episcopalians. We became members of the Episcopal Church rather than of any other Christian body because, after studying into the matter, we believed it our duty to do so. I am sorry to hear of the feeble condition of my Church and of the infrequent Services by a Lay reader instead of by a Clergyman. But this is all the more reason why we should be true to our colors and lend a helping hand." This consistency on the part of an influential new-coming family was the making of the mission.

I am under great obligation to some ten or twelve learned and judicious Clergymen of the Diocese of Ohio for their painstaking and helpful criticisms. Especially am I indebted to the Very Rev. Francis M. Hall, M.A., for invaluable assistance in preparing the manuscript for the printer, and to Canon D. F. Davies, M.A., for some exceptionally important suggestions and a careful reading of the proofs. I desire also to thank the Rev. A. E. Oldroyd, M.A., of Oundle, England, for kind permission to use some of the excellent charts in his able pamphlet on "The Continuity of the English Church through Eighteen Centuries," and the Rt. Rev. William Stevens Perry, D.D., LL.D., D.C.L., Bishop of Iowa, and other experts in special branches of learning who were good enough to answer my letters of inquiry and to send me some of their valuable publications, and last, but not least, my printers, THE WERNER COMPANY, of Akron, Ohio, and their efficient and obliging employees who have been uniformly courteous and patient.

I shall feel amply repaid for the time and labor expended upon this work, if, by God's blessing, it shall prove, to any degree, instrumental in persuading non church members to make a profession of Christ by identifying themselves with His Church, in adding to the number of well-instructed persons who come to us from the Denominational and Roman communions because fully convinced of this Church's Divine and superior claims to their allegiance, and in increasing the appreciation, love, and zeal of Episcopalians for their pure branch of the Catholic and Apostolic Church.

W. M. B.

TRINITY CATHEDRAL, CLEVELAND, OHIO,
St. Luke's Day, 1895.

PREFACE TO THE FOURTH EDITION.

Owing to the urgent recommendation of friends, my humble effort to set forth the superior claims of the Anglican Communion to the exclusive allegiance of English speaking people, written especially for Americans, was published a year earlier than was intended and, accordingly, the First Edition lacked a great many finishing touches. When it became manifest that the demand for the book would greatly exceed my expectation, every spare moment that could be commanded was given to the work of revision. A few corrections and changes were made in the Second Edition, but there was no time between it and the Third for further alterations in the plates. It was then determined that the Fourth Edition should be as free from blemishes and points for cavil as possible. Fortunately the summer vacation gave me the necessary leisure for the carrying out of this resolve.

The many letters of warm commendation and friendly criticism received from Clergymen and Laymen have been a great encouragement and help to me. Those to whom I am most indebted are: the Rt. Rev. Thomas Underwood Dudley, D.D., LL.D., D.C.L., Bishop of Kentucky and Chancellor of the University of the South; the Rt. Rev. Hugh Miller Thompson, S.T.D., LL.D., Bishop of Mississippi; the Rev. W. C. Hopkins, D.D., City Missionary of Toledo; the Rev. Wm. Jones Seabury, D.D., Charles-and-Elizabeth-Ludlow Professor of Ecclesiastical Polity and Law in the General Theological Seminary, New York; the Rev. Wm. C. McCracken, M.A., Rector of St. Martin's Church, Fairmont, Minne-

sota; the Rev. G. H. H. Butler, B.A., Curate of the
Church of the Ascension, Mount Vernon, New York;
and some unknown critic and friend of great learning
who signed his several most important communications with the nom-de-plume, "A Layman."

One of the most scholarly and conservative Clergymen
of this country accompanied his valuable corrections
and suggestions with the gratifying assurance that the
First Edition of the Church for Americans "brings out
the whole case so that no one can be seriously misled by
any of its statements; and so that in point of principle
and historical fact the reader who gets his first impressions from it must inevitably be started in the right
direction. He would never feel himself to have been
misled or obliged to deny the substance of what you
have taught him." Many others have given expression
to the same comforting opinion. If this is true of the
first three editions it will be much more so of the fourth.

It is believed that the value of the book has been
materially increased by the addition of the last nineteen sections to the Appendices and an Index of References to Quotations.

I desire to record here my gratitude to God for the
blessing of strength and the grace of perseverance which
have enabled me, notwithstanding the constant traveling and the many engrossing duties of a General Missionary of an extensive and populous Diocese, to
complete a book that has required so much more work
than was at first anticipated.   W. M. B.

TRINITY CATHEDRAL, CLEVELAND, OHIO,
    Feast of St. Michael and All Angels, 1896.

CONTENTS.

LECTURE V.

LECTURE VI.

LECTURE VII.

"Thus Saith the Lord, Stand Ye in the Ways, and See, and Ask for the Old Paths, Where Is the Good Way, and Walk Therein, and Ye Shall Find Rest for Your Souls."

—Jeremiah vi : 16

ILLUSTRATIONS.

"THE SEARCH FOR TRUTH IS NOT HALF SO PLEASANT
AS STICKING TO THE VIEWS WE HOLD AT PRESENT."

INTRODUCTORY.

❖ ❖ ❖

IN our day and country there is, as everybody
knows, a vast non church membership population.
Judging from a somewhat extended personal observation, I should say that at least one-half of the
men and a third of the women are not identified with
any form of organized Christianity. This is not because Americans, at the close of the nineteenth century, are preëminently skeptical and irreligious, but
because the opinion so widely prevails that a person
can be as good a Christian outside of the Church and
without the use of the Sacraments and means of grace
as with them.

The neglect of institutional religion is accounted for
by the exaggerated importance which was attached to
it by Catholic Christendom in the Mediæval Ages, and
is still attributed to it by Romanism. When we consider the tendency of human nature to go from one
extreme to another, we shall not wonder that the
Reformation, in which Wickliffe, Huss, Luther, Calvin
and Knox took such prominent parts, has manifested a
disposition to depreciate the Church with her Priesthood and Sacraments, and to magnify certain Evangelical doctrines and the preaching of them. Romanists
made salvation to depend upon belonging to the
Church; therefore, Protestants hinged it upon belief in
a dogma. Then the pendulum of human opinion, which

C. A.—1

never continueth in one stay, began to swing away from both Romanism and Protestantism towards what is called practical religion, and has gone on in that direction until many in every community, having renounced both ecclesiasticism and dogmatism, are relying wholly upon moral living and good works for salvation. The representatives of institutional, doctrinal and practical Christianity are now widely separated, and between them, apparently, a great and bridgeless gulf is fixed. And, what at first sight seems surpassingly strange and even inexplicable, they are strongly fortified in their respective positions by walls, the stones of which are hewn from the rock of Holy Scripture. And so impregnable are these fortifications that, notwithstanding each has been bombarded for these many years by ponderous controversial artillery, no practicable breach has been effected.

Now, how shall we account for this? Does the Bible, out of which the contending hosts have constructed their defenses, contradict itself? God forbid! It does nothing of the kind. The solution is rather in the fact that the Divine quarry contains more than one stratum of truth. There is an institutional, a doctrinal and a practical stratum. Christ founded a Church to be entered; He appointed Sacraments to be received; He taught doctrines to be believed, and He set an example of good works to be followed. Salvation depends in due proportion upon all of these, not upon one of them alone. These have been joined together by God; therefore, "let no man put them asunder."

If in this book a great deal is said about Church membership and comparatively little concerning the necessity of right living or believing, it is because we have written chiefly for those who, whether as Doctrinalists or Practicalists, have either quite divorced themselves from the Church, or else have learned to esteem her altogether too little. We would not have any reader make less of doctrinal, certainly not of practical Christianity, but would persuade many to attach more importance to the institutional side of our religion. Accordingly, we have endeavored to promote the conviction that every person is in duty bound to identify himself with some branch of the Church of Christ.

It may as well be confessed here that our object is not only to persuade non church members to unite with some one of the many organizations of Christians, but particularly with the Episcopal Church. Moreover, we have been guilty of keeping in mind our Denominational and Roman brethren, in the hope that what we have to say will induce some of them to come over to us. Many condemn such efforts as betokening a want of broadmindedness and charity towards other Christian bodies. Those who pride themselves upon their "non-sectarianism"—and there are multitudes of such in every community—characterize as bigots all who do not acknowledge that one Denomination is as good as another, and contend that it makes practically no difference to which of them one belongs, since all will lead us to the same Heaven if we but trust in Christ and follow Him.

So plausible and pleasing is this representation to people generally, that the assertion of convictions which run counter to it is usually listened to with impatience. And yet no observing and reflecting person can fail to discover the hollowness of the pretensions of those who affect this liberality. Nothing can be plainer than that they regard the Denomination with which they have cast their lot as being, at least in some respects, better than any other. The evidence of this is found in the very existence and continuance of their sect.

It would never have been organized if its charter members had not regarded their creation as superior to others of the kind; and it would soon have died out but for the conviction of its superiority which continued to possess its adherents. Sects, like political parties, originate and perpetuate their existence because their peculiar principles attract men and hold them together. This being the case, no one who is governed by conviction and principle, can be "non-sectarian." All such must feel it a duty to assert and prove superior claims to allegiance for the Denomination with which they are connected. Hence, though the writer may have had some hesitancy arising from the dread of adverse criticism, he has had no qualms of conscience in trying to make it appear that the Episcopal Church can establish superior claims to the allegiance of Americans.

But this work is not prepared exclusively with reference to non church members and the members of other Christian bodies. Indeed, it was primarily intended for the instruction of our own people. The accessions to the Episcopal Church from the various Denominations have been increasing until they constitute a large percentage, often the principal part, of our Confirmation classes. These converts are, as a rule, good, enthusiastic Episcopalians. But in many cases there is reason to fear that the change of Church relationship may be accounted for upon the ground of superficial preferences rather than deep-rooted conviction. It is highly desirable, both on the convert's and the Church's account, that he should be able to justify his course on the score of principle. Those who cannot do this, and there are many such in nearly all of our congregations, have been, we think, insufficiently instructed.

The Archbishop of Canterbury is doubtless correct in the supposition that "there is perhaps not even now

one Churchman in ten who is as well instructed in the
reason why he is a Churchman as Dissenters or Roman
Catholics are instructed in the arguments whereby their
position is defended. This should surely be remedied."
For those who are not well grounded in Church principles are apt to be more or less disturbed by the assertions and objections of Denominationalists on the
one hand and of Romanists on the other. And in defending their transfer of allegiance they are seldom able
to do themselves or their Church justice. In fact they
not infrequently do more harm than good to all concerned. It is believed that the facts and arguments of
these pages will enable those who have come into the
Church from Denominationalism and Romanism, or are
about to do so, to justify their action upon principle as
well as from preference.

Throughout this work the isolated and neglected
brethren, of whom there are many in the rural communities of almost every part of the United States, have
also been kept in view. Such are strongly tempted to
turn their back upon the Church of their birth or adoption. After living for some time without her Services,
and becoming convinced that there is no immediate
prospect of their establishment, in the majority of cases,
they finally yield to the pressing solicitations of the
representatives of one or another of the established Denominations to cast in their lot with them. In this way
it has come about that in some Dioceses the Church has
lost the allegiance of as many communicants as she
now possesses. The writer could mention several towns
in Ohio, in which the "bone and sinew" of some
strong Denomination is composed of lapsed Church
people.

This leakage is largely accounted for by the lack of the missionary spirit on the part of our great city congregations. From every point of view the failure of city Churchmen to minister to their country brethren, by taking the Church to out-of-the-way places and helping to maintain it, has been a mistake. Not only have we lost the nucleus for a congregation that at one time or another has existed in almost every village, but also all the multitudes that would have been added to them, had we been wise enough to plant and nourish missions before the ground was preoccupied and our constituency alienated.

Moreover, the Church in our cities, though usually strong and often the dominant body of Christians, is much weaker than it would have been, had the city Churchman not refused to be his country and village brother's keeper. The drift in this country has been and is from the smaller towards the larger centers of population. The operation of this law of centralization has constantly weakened the rural and strengthened the city Churches. In the Diocese of Ohio many of our congregations in the large cities and towns are greatly indebted to more or less obscure villages and hamlets, where the Apostolic Chase, Searle, Hall, and others, had the wisdom to plant the Church in the early days. Had their policy of strengthening the weak things that remain, by establishing Services wherever two or three of our people could be found and a congregation assembled, been continued, the Church would now be probably two or three times stronger than it is. If the expectation that this book will tend to make the Episcopalian reader a Churchman from conviction is not disappointed, it will also make him a missionary. Nothing extraordinary in the way of gifts or work for the cause of Church extension can be expected of those who are

Episcopalians rather than Denominationalists from
preference only.

And if what we have to say promotes the missionary
spirit among the favored Church people of our cities, it
will at the same time tend to restrain "the neglected
sheep of the wilderness" from wandering away from
this fold of Christ, the Church of their fathers. There
are scattered here and there through Ohio, and no
doubt the same is true of every undeveloped Diocese,
men and women who have been without the Services of
the Church for as many as thirty, forty, and even fifty
years, and yet have remained her faithful children during all this time. These, as a rule, have gone regularly
to some Denominational place of worship and contributed their proportion towards its support, but such
spiritual privileges have never induced them to allow
their Prayer Books to grow dusty. One of the objects
of this book is to increase the number of such by promoting the conviction that nothing will justify the
abandonment of the ancient Catholic Church of the
English-speaking race for membership in any of the
modern Denominations.

Because a person finds himself to be one of only
two or three representatives of the Church in a community, he is not justified in transferring his allegiance
to any of the Denominations. Let him rather constitute himself a missionary. He can persuade his brethren, if there be any, and other well-disposed persons, to
join him in the establishment perhaps of a Sunday
afternoon Lay Service; he can distribute Prayer Books
and tracts in which the claims and ways of the Church
are explained and justified, and he can be instrumental
in an organized effort to secure at least the occasional
visit of a Clergyman. Some of the most prosperous
parishes and promising missions of Ohio have grown

out of the zealous efforts of a very few persons. One of our largest and best equipped Churches and Sunday Schools owes its origin to a discreet Churchwoman. She assembled her numerous family and as many of her neighbors as she could persuade to join them on each Lord's Day, and after she had conducted the Service, her husband, who was not a communicant, read a sermon which she had selected.

Thus, the fact that it has pleased God to call a Churchman to live in a place where he is deprived of priestly ministrations, affords no reason why he should forsake the spiritual mother and guide of his youth by joining himself with those whose ancestors, in their self-will or mistaken zeal, went out from her, and by the forming of rival sects did all in their power to realize the mad cry, "down with her, down with her, even to the ground." On the contrary, such persons have all the more cause for extraordinary faithfulness, since, by such a course, they may become the honored instruments of planting the Catholic Church of the English race and establishing "the Faith once delivered to the Saints" in a region where otherwise these might remain unknown or obscured for generations to come. Think of the inestimable privilege of thus becoming instrumental in establishing a mission or parish of the Church of Christ. It falls to the lot of but few in any other way to erect such a fair, enduring monument to the glory of God and their own memory. The isolated sons and daughters of the Church may in many cases at least have their names inscribed upon such a monument as the charter members of the Church of the place in which their lot has been cast.

It is often very easy to secure this imperishable fame. The truth of this observation might be abundantly illustrated out of the experience of all who have been long engaged in Church extension work. The writer could mention a village where six years ago the only person interested in the Episcopal Church, if not indeed the only one who knew of her existence, was a child who, while attending a seminary, had occasionally accompanied two or three companions to the Services of a neighboring Church. Now the little village boasts of a flourishing mission with a centrally located lot and a picturesque Chapel, paid for, and in all time to come, whenever the history of this Church shall be rehearsed, the name of the school-girl to whom it owes its origin will be mentioned.

If, then, this book should fall into the hands of some isolated member of the Church, let me exhort him to remember that "though a sentinel on the outposts, he is still a member of that vast army with its two hundred Bishops, forty thousand other Clergy, and millions of privates." He is not alone. Though few of his faith are near him, there are, in every portion of the globe, millions of intelligent, godly men and women who think as he thinks, love the same worship and hold the same truths. God has placed him where he is for a purpose, perhaps to be the nucleus of some future Church, in which hundreds will learn her sacred ways. Stand firm, then, as a pioneer. Be true to your trust. Teach your children to love your Church. That Church is doing a work at once great and glorious. She is marching to victory. Be faithful at your post, and watch unto prayer!

It will appear, from an examination of the table of contents, that it was impossible to cover the ground marked out for this book without instituting comparisons between the Episcopal Church and other bodies of Christians. Where we are found to differ radically in matters of doctrine and government, an uncompromising effort has been made to justify our position. But the uniform endeavor has been to speak the truth as Episcopalians understand it, in a spirit of love and fairness, and it is hoped that we have nowhere been so unfortunate in our expression as to wound the feelings of any who differ from us, or to leave the impression that we are so narrow and bigoted as not to perceive that the various Denominations of Christians have done and are doing a great amount of good. If it was said of one who followed not the "twelve," with Jesus personally amongst them, "Forbid him not, for he that is not against us is for us," we must surely say it with far more emphasis with respect to those who follow not the American successors of the Apostles. "No one of the Apostolic band upheld the unity of Christ's mystical body, the Church, as St. Paul did, and he also could say, and let us say it with him, 'Notwithstanding, every way, Christ is preached, and I therein do rejoice, yea, and will rejoice.'" We believe that countless millions will be in Heaven who followed not with us.

But though we are aware of the Christian graces, the good works, and the bright heavenly prospects of tens of thousands of the representatives of the Roman Church and Dissenting Protestants, yet this glad conviction does not justify us in forgetting our prolonged, causeless, hurtful, and, therefore, sinful divisions, and the consequent obligation to do what we can to restore the visible organic unity of the primitive Church. We are indeed all journeying toward the Promised Land; but how much better it would be for us and for the world if we were going together in the straight and narrow way of God's appointment. The fallacy of those who argue that "we are all engaged in the same work and seeking the same Heaven, and after all it does not matter much which way we take," has been illustrated by the Mississippi River at a flood time. The water which remains in the channel, and that which breaks through the dikes and tears its destructive course along, alike make their way to the Gulf; but it does make some difference how they get there. The Church of God is often compared to an army, and the various Denominations are likened to so many regiments in that army. But, as has frequently been pointed out, an army the regiments of which held little or no communication, recognized no common orders or officers, and had no concerted plan of campaign, would be helpless and ineffective. Such an undisciplined horde could only court defeat.

"Let us suppose," says Bishop Coxe, "that General Moltke had said, before crossing the Rhine, to his brave men in arms, 'Soldiers, we are acting on a very false system of war. I observe you all seem to be thoroughly organized as one grand army, and that you are anxious to preserve, however you may be distributed in various corps, one discipline, one common plan of campaign, and one recognized system of drill, of instructions, of subordination, and of organic force. All this is mere delusion. You have different tastes, and are intelligent enough to have each your own ideas of what it is best to do. Break up, then, this vast clumsy organization, and let us have, at least, five or six different armies, each pursuing its own way, and occasionally firing into each other, or pausing for skirmishes between different generals. If these skirmishes should promote subdivisions, and end in producing thirty or forty armies and guerrilla gangs, obviously we should all be the stronger. We want nothing but unity of heart. Be good Germans, and act for the one object of

humbling the enemies of Fatherland. Yes, I hear your
cheers. Your hearts are all right; now then, break up
into your several gangs, act with your favorite officers;
agree to differ; scatter, scatter, scatter! That is the
best plan, if the heart is only true to the cause. Be sure
to shake hands with one another before and after a free
fight among yourselves; then keep to your personal
ideas of a campaign, and follow no leader that will not
gratify these convictions. This will insure success.
Huzzah, boys! Now, begone! Helter-Skelter! be your
war cry.'"

No separations among Christians are lawful, though
they may be divinely overruled for good, except such as
come from the mere national divisions of humanity.
All Americans should be in an American Church. There
should be a "United Church of the United States"—"a
Church with wide freedom in all minor matters, but
with Apostolic succession for its ministry, Ecumenical
indorsement for its Creed, and reverent celebration of
the two Sacraments."

In view of the fact that our blessed Lord fervently
prayed that we might be one, and that He hinged the
Christianization of the world upon a united Church, we
feel in conscience bound to do what we can to convince
all with whom, in any way, we come into contact, and
over whom we have the least influence, that the Anglican
Communion, of which the American Episcopal Church
is a part, offers the only ground upon which the reunion
of divided Christendom can take place. It has been
well said: "We have not, as a communion, such a
monopoly of either piety or learning in this land that
we can afford to be contemptuous, even if that temper
were ever permissible in a Christian Church. But we
have, through the blessing of God, the title deeds of the
old homestead in our hands; we sit by the hearthstone

of the English-speaking race; and ought we to be blamed for thinking that if the family can be gathered anywhere in peace, it must be here?"

> "O Thou who didst on that last night,
> Ere death had paled Thy brow,
> Speak sweetly of love's power and might,
> As none could speak but Thou,
> Remind Thy little flock, alas!
> So prone to disagree,
> That Thy desire and last prayer was
> For Christian Unity."

I must conclude these introductory remarks with a little further justification of our Clergy and a large percentage of the Laity who have no hesitancy in doing what they can to persuade the adherents of other Christian bodies to come into the Episcopal Church. To this end we write and disseminate books such as this, preach sermons, converse, and invite people to the Services. Romanists do not blame us for this because, as a rule, they are also avowed proselyters. But Denominationalists often represent that we are guilty of something akin to robbery, in fact they plainly call it "sheep stealing." They represent our conduct as being, if not absolutely sinful, at least unworthy of any Christian man or woman. We protest that this representation is wholly unjustified. Bodies of Christians have just as much right to proselyte as political parties. If a Prohibitionist has no hesitancy in winning over a Republican or Democrat we do not see why Methodists should have any scruples about taking in Presbyterians or Baptists when they have an opportunity. And if they can win back the adherents of the numerous bodies who at one time or another went out from themselves, it is even harder to conceive upon what grounds they can be justly condemned.

But whether the making of inroads one upon the other by rival Denominations is justifiable or not, we cannot allow those who fault us to forget that if they and their ancestors had all along been guiltless, the great majority of Denominationalists would now be in the Episcopal Church. When the tide was flowing from the Church, Congregationalists, Presbyterians and Methodists did not condemn proselyting, but now that the reaction has set in and the returning waves are bringing tens of thousands from them to our shores, they have suddenly discovered that it is a very discreditable business. We contend, however, that if the law of charity and comity be observed, an Episcopalian has a perfect right to make as many converts to his Church as possible. In fact the majority of us are obliged by our convictions to do so, for we believe that there is only one Catholic and Apostolic Church of Christ, and that the various branches of the Anglican Communion in their respective countries are entitled to the exclusive allegiance and support of the English speaking population. Moreover, we hold that sectarianism is a great evil. This being the case, an Episcopalian who is not a proselyter would be as inconsistent as a Denominationalist who is such.

> "I will not cease from mental strife,
>   Nor shall my sword sleep in my hand,
> Till we have built Jerusalem
>   In this our green and pleasant land."

THE CHURCH FOR AMERICANS.

LECTURE I.

CHURCH MEMBERSHIP.

  I. OBLIGATIONS TO BELONG TO CHURCH.
  II. THE CHOICE OF A CHURCH.

AUTHORITIES.

CHAPIN, Primitive Church.
CHAPMAN, Sermons on the Church.
CHURTON, BP., The Missionary's Foundation of Doctrine.
CUSHMAN, Doctrine and Duty.
GARNIER, CANON, A First Book on Church Principles.
GLADSTONE, Church Principles Considered in Their Results.
GOULBURN, DEAN, The Holy Catholic Church.
HUNTINGTON, The Church Idea.
LABAGH, Theoklesia.
LAY, BP., Studies in the Church.
LEONARD, BP., A Brief History of the Christian Church.
OXONIENSIS, Romanism, Protestantism, Anglicanism.
PALMER, Treatise on the Church. (2 vols.)
Row, Apostolic Christianity.
SADLER, Church Doctrine, Bible Truth.
WEST, Tracts on Church Principles.
WILSON, The Church Identified.

PAMPHLETS.

DRUMMOND, The City Without a Church.
DRUMMOND, The Programme of Christianity.
EWER, What Is the Anglican Church ?
MILLER, My Parish Note-Book.
THOMPSON, BP., First Principles.
WOODHOUSE, What Is the Church ?

CHURCH MEMBERSHIP.

I.

OBLIGATIONS TO CHURCH MEMBERSHIP.

THERE are three principal reasons why every person who hears the Gospel of Christ should belong to His Church. The first grows out of the duty of obedience. The Church is the Kingdom of Christ, and all outside of it is the Kingdom of Satan. We must, in the long run, give our undivided allegiance to either one or the other of these princes. We cannot adhere to both. "No man can serve two masters, for either he will hate the one and love the other; or else he will hold to the one, and despise the other. Ye cannot serve God and Mammon." Those who remain out of the Church, and yet try to follow the example and precepts of Christ, are trying to please two masters. As a rule which holds, notwithstanding the comparatively few exceptions that we may know of, such men fail. The majority of non church members are not the servants of Christ. Speaking generally, men out of His Church do no more serve Him than they who fight in the enemies' ranks help their country. The Kingdom of Christ and the world are in deadly conflict for the mastery. How then can anyone who professes to be a loyal servant of Christ, stand aloof from His Church, which is His Kingdom?

In our day a great many people acknowledge the duty of making the example and precepts of Christ their rule of life, but deny that they are under any obligation to become Church members. They fail to see that this is required of them. "Millions in America," says Bishop Coxe, "live and die in the easy persuasion, from which no trumpet of united testimony rouses them, that they are rather the better for 'reading their Bibles' and 'leading moral lives,' while not 'making any profession of religion,' as they term it. Inverted Pharisaism of American inorganic Christianity! They make a merit of not obeying, and of being so good without the means of grace." Surely such have not asked themselves the question: Why did Christ found a Church, and why did He say so much about it? Was it not manifestly that men might be separated from the Kingdom of Satan, and be identified with Him?

It is well known that all great prophets and reformers have had some particular message which has, by constant reiteration, crystallized into a word or phrase. With Moses it was law; with Confucius, morality; with Buddha, renunciation; with Mohammed, God; with Socrates, soul. With the Master it was "the Kingdom of God." Says Professor Drummond: "Christ's great word was 'the Kingdom of God.' One hundred times it occurs in the Gospels. When He preached He had almost always this for a text. His sermons were explanations of the aims of His society, of the different things it was like, of whom its membership consisted, what they were to do or to be or not to do or to be. And even when He does not use the word, it is easy to see that all He said and did had reference to this."

A little reflection, therefore, must convince all that the founding of the Church by Christ, or by His representatives, the Apostles, and the importance which He attaches to it, make identification with it of universal obligation. The prevailing demand is for a preaching of the Gospel with the Church left out, or at least put far in the background. Surely the many who, in deference to popular sentiment, have tried to preach such a Gospel, have not preached Christ's Gospel, for it dwells more on the Church than upon any other subject.

Though the duty of membership may be clearly inferred from the fact that Christ founded a Church and made it the burden of His discourses, we are not left without explicit injunctions requiring identification with His Kingdom. For every command to receive Christian Baptism is really a positive injunction to belong to the Church. Baptism is the door to the Church. It is the Sacrament of initiation. A person cannot receive it without becoming a member of the Church. Therefore, when our Lord said, "Go ye and teach all nations, baptizing them in the name of the Father and of the Son and of the Holy Ghost," it is as if He had said, Go ye into all the world and preach the Gospel, making whosoever accepts it a member of My Church. Nothing can be clearer than that in Apostolic days none who stood aloof from the Church were regarded as having received the Gospel. Non church members were looked upon as heathen. The unbaptized stood in the same relation to Christianity as the uncircumcised did to Judaism. It must be evident to all that if others are commanded to see to it that we are identified with the Kingdom of Christ by Baptism, it is equivalent to a command that we should become Church members.

The first and most important step in the way of obedience to Christ is, therefore, Church membership. No man, who has heard the Gospel and acknowledges the claims of Christ to his allegiance, can discharge his duty while remaining outside the Church. The first thing to be done by him who would follow Christ is to transfer his allegiance from the prince of this world to the Divine Lord of the Kingdom of Heaven. It is the height of absurdity for a man to claim that he can be as good a Christian while outside of the Church as he could be within it. As well might a foreigner pretend that he can be as good an American citizen without naturalization as with it. Such a man is not an American at all. Neither is a non church member, strictly speaking, a Christian.

A good story is told by a distinguished Presbyterian clergyman, about a little girl who was talking to her grandfather. The old gentleman had been imparting some advice, suitable to the tender years of his grandchild. Finally the latter put the question: "Grandpa, are you a Christian?" "Yes, my dear, I hope I am." "What Church do you belong to, grandpa?" "Oh, I belong to the Church of Christ." "But what is that? Are you a member of the same Church that mamma and I are—the Episcopal Church?" "No, my dear, I am not an Episcopalian." "Are you a Presbyterian, then?" "No, I am not a Presbyterian." "Are you a Baptist, then?" "No." "Are you a Methodist?" "No, dear; I don't belong to any of the churches." After a pause, in which the little one was thinking it all over, she turned her face up to her grandfather's and said: "Well, grandpapa, if I were you, I would try and get in *somewhere*." Until modern times no one claimed to be a Christian, or was regarded as such, who did not "get in somewhere."

Again, those who are standing aloof from the Church should enter out of consideration for their own highest welfare. Salvation is made by our Lord Himself to depend upon the confession of Him. "Whosoever shall confess me before men, him will I confess also before my Father, which is in heaven; but whosoever shall deny me before men, him will I also deny before my Father, which is in heaven." Now there is no way in which a person can make an open unreserved confession of Christ except by the renunciation of the world for the Church. This, according to our Lord's own appointment, must be done in Holy Baptism. "Except a man be born of water and of the Spirit, he cannot enter into the Kingdom of God." And the Kingdom of God here does not mean that Heaven which we hope to attain after this life, but the Church which Christ founded when upon earth. It is, therefore, the same as if He had said, Unless you belong to the Church, you cannot attain unto covenanted Salvation.

I cannot do better than to quote in this connection the weighty words of Bishop Pearson: "We read at the first that the Lord added daily to the Church such as should be saved; and what was then daily done hath been done since continually. Christ never appointed two ways to Heaven, nor did He build a Church to save some and make another institution for other men's salvation. There is none other name under Heaven given among men, whereby we must be saved, but the name of Jesus, and that name is no otherwise given under Heaven than in the Church. As none were saved from the deluge but such as were within the ark of Noah, framed for their reception by the command of God; as none of the firstborn of Egypt lived, but such as were within those habitations whose doorposts were sprinkled with blood by the appointment of

God for their preservation; as none of the inhabitants of Jericho could escape the fire or sword but such as were within the house of Rahab, for whose protection a covenant was made, so none shall ever escape the anger of God which belong not to the Church of God."

As some one has pointed out, "The nineteenth century needs to be told, as by another John Baptist, crying, not in the wilderness, but throughout all the American continent, that not to confess Christ openly, that is, not to accept His covenant in the institution He has provided, is virtually to deny Him. How very comfortable it would have been had this American gospel been taught in the first century: 'Be good, read your Bibles, and God will not ask you whether or not you belong to Church.' That would just have suited Demas, who loved this present world and had no idea of coming out of it and being separate. He would have lived and died, 'respecting religion,' as the phrase is, but chiefly consoled by that blessed doctrine, 'It makes no difference about externals, provided only the heart is right.' 'Precisely so,' brother Demas would have said; 'I trust my heart is all right, but I've no trust in ordinances.' To come out and be baptized and to receive the laying on of hands, and to frequent the Lord's Supper, he would have argued, 'are well enough for those who are so superstitious. But stoning by the Jews is uncomfortable; beheading and other tortures of the Romans involve great personal sacrifices. I can believe in my heart, you know, without confessing with my mouth, or submitting to those outward things which carnal minds make so much of. Yes, I've always been consoled by those spiritual views of the Gospel which teach me to be a good Christian in my heart, without submitting to any formal system, subversive as such systems must be of our Christian liberty.' "

Moreover, the good of others should move non church members to identify themselves with the Church. The continuation and development of our civilization depend upon the Church which gave it birth, and has brought it to its present stage of perfection. It is wrong for any man or woman to pursue a course which if universally adopted would make the world worse instead of better. If all were from this time on to follow the example of the non church members who are to be found in every community, the Christian civilization, in every respect, even in its present imperfect state, the best that the world has ever seen, would rapidly decline, and a generation or two would suffice to bring about its extinction. History plainly teaches that no civilization long survives the abandonment of the religion upon which it is founded. Up to this time all civilizations have had some religion for their basis. Christianity is the foundation of our civilization.

So long as the Greeks and Romans were faithful in the service of their gods, their magnificent civilizations advanced to higher stages of perfection, but when they began to forsake their temples a retrogression commenced which in its degree kept pace almost exactly with the progress of the national apostasy. History would certainly repeat itself in the case of our civilization, if all were to imitate the example of non church members. In addition, therefore, to the duty of obedience to Christ and consideration for your own highest welfare, the good of the world, in so far as it depends upon the perpetuity and development of our civilization, requires you to identify yourself with the Church. Duty to Christ, to yourself, and to every human being in the world, makes it incumbent upon you to belong to the Church. "If," to borrow the burning words of another, "you know anything better, live for it; if not, in the name of God and of humanity, carry out Christ's plan" by the identification of yourself with his Kingdom.

It is impossible for the non church member to justify his position. It is not sufficient that he should be able to say truthfully: "I follow the example and precepts of Christ as closely as the majority of Church members who are within the circle of my acquaintance." The Church, which was founded for the salvation of the world, would cease to exist if all followed your example, and but for the Church and its imperfect, sinful members, towards whom you are ever pointing the finger of criticism, you would know little, and care less, about Christ.

To quote Professor Drummond again: "Here and there an unchurched soul may stir the multitudes to lofty deeds; isolated men, strong enough to preserve their souls apart from the Church, but shortsighted enough perhaps to fail to see that others cannot, may set high examples and stimulate to national reforms. But for the rank and file of us, made of such stuff as we are made of, the steady pressure of fixed institutions, the regular diet of a common worship, and the education of public Christian teaching, are too obvious safeguards of scriptural culture to be set aside."

Even Rénan, one of the most gifted of modern French skeptics, declares it to be his conviction that, "beyond the family and outside the state man has need of the Church. Civil society, whether it calls itself a commune, a canton, or a province, a state or a fatherland, has many duties towards the improvement of the individual; but what it does is necessarily limited. The family ought to do much more, but often it is insufficient. Sometimes it is wanting altogether. The association created in the name of moral principle can alone give to every man coming into this world, a bond which unites him to the past, duties as to the future, examples to follow, a heritage to receive and to transmit, and a tradition of devotion to continue."

Nor can a non church member justify his position by the opposite plea, so frequently urged—"I am not good enough to belong to Church." Christ came to save sinners. He said: "They that be whole have no need of a physician." The Church would collapse to-day if goodness and worthiness were made conditions of membership. In the Litany all, even those who have attained the greatest degree of Christlikeness, are taught to pray, "Have mercy upon us miserable sinners." Whether in or out of the Church every member of the human race is a sinner. We are of course aware that some deny that they are sinners. My attention has recently been called to an instance. In a sermon preached at one of our mission stations I had occasion to refer to the fact that the Church teaches all, not excepting the most venerable and godly, to look upon themselves as sinful men and women. The lay reader afterwards told me that he was glad for that passage in my sermon, because on the Sunday before, during the reading of the Litany, a woman had abruptly left the Church in manifest displeasure and that one who afterward made inquiry concerning the ground of her exception to the Service was told: "I will have nothing to do with a Church that obliges all her worshipers, without distinction, to confess and acknowledge that they are sinners. I was converted only a few weeks ago, and am not a sinner." Of course such a person cannot be an Episcopalian nor a member of any branch of the Catholic Church of Christ, which is exclusively for sinners.

The man of whom one of our missionary Bishops tells had a truer appreciation of his real condition. Upon going to a mining village of his jurisdiction, where the Services of the Church had never been held, the Bishop inquired of a person whom he met at the boarding house whether or not there were any members of the Episcopal Church in the camp. "Why, yes," said he, "that is my Church, and I am glad you have come." The Bishop expressed his gratification at running across an interested person so soon and requested his help in securing a hall and making the arrangements for the initiatory Service. He found the miner to be a cheerful and efficient helper, taking everything into his own hands. When the hour of Service arrived he conducted the Bishop to a billiard hall, where a good sized congregation of miners had assembled. The Service was quite satisfactory, considering the incongruous surroundings, there being some half dozen Churchmen present who read the responses. But the Bishop noticed with surprise that his zealous helper could not handle the Prayer Book, and did not even conform to the customary postures. So, after returning to the house, he naturally made some inquiries of his friend. "Did you, Mr. ——, say that you are an Episcopalian?" "Yes, sir, that is my religion." "Where were you confirmed?" He did not seem to understand what was meant. After the Bishop's explanation of the rite he replied: "Oh, I never had that done to me." "Where were you baptized?" "I never was baptized." "Indeed," said the astonished Bishop. "How is it then that you told me that you were a member of the Episcopal Church?" "Well, parson, when I was at ——" naming a mining camp in an adjoining Territory, "one of your kind of preachers came along and held a meeting in the billiard hall. I was there, and when I heard

them say, ' We have left undone those things which we
ought to have done and we have done those things which
we ought not to have done,' I said, 'that hits me exactly, I am one of them kind of Christians,' and that is
why I say that I am an 'Episcopal;' and parson, if
you think it necessary, I want them things that you
were a telling about done to me when you come again."

Strange as it may seem to many, this man rather
than that deluded woman had the true idea. His only
title to Church membership was the recognition of the
fact that he was a sinner, both by commission and
omission, and a manifest desire to do better. Of course
the Bishop, after due instruction, would baptize, confirm and admit him to the Holy Communion. It is surpassingly strange that men and women who have heard
the Gospel all their lives, should still suppose that none
ought to come to Baptism or Confirmation or the Holy
Communion who are not prepared to stand and make
the Pharisee's profession of religion—"God, I thank
Thee that I am not as other men are. I am converted.
I am not a sinner." But, as all are sinners, and those
who say they are not, deceive themselves and the truth
is not in them, the salvation of the world depends upon
the sinners that are in the Church. They are the salt of
the earth without which all would perish. Not that a
bad man in the Church is more pleasing to God and has
brighter prospects of heaven than a good man outside,
but that the place for all who would serve Christ is
inside.

Some imagine that by remaining non church members they escape the responsibilities of professing Christians. But this is by no means the case. The Gospel makes identification with the Kingdom of Christ

obligatory upon every man and woman, and refusal to
fulfill this obligation in no degree lessens responsibility;
for the Gospel rule of life is binding upon all alike. In
Christian lands, such as ours, Church members and non
church members are under one and the same law. In
that great day when all must give a strict account of
the deeds done in the body, we shall not be judged by
different standards.

As Bishop Hugh Miller Thompson says: "It is one
of the prevailing delusions and one, we fear, which the
common pulpit seldom reaches, to suppose that a man
is free to accept or refuse the responsibilities of the
Christian life—that ' the professing of Christianity' is the
taking up of new and quite voluntary duties. We distinctly write it down a delusion; and such a shallow delusion that it will stand no test. It is a flat contradiction of human life, and of the facts of human life that
stare us all in the face. The profession of Christ is not
the taking up of a single duty which is not binding on
every man already, at least in lands like this. The
baptized man has bound himself to nothing which is
not on the unbaptized man as well. The communicant
is measured by no rule which is not used righteously
also for the noncommunicant. There are not two
classes of people in a Christian country, under two different laws—the ' professors' under one, and the ' non-
professors' under another. By God's divine ordering
of human life, we are elected to Christianity. Why, we
cannot tell. It is His ' good pleasure.' It is the fact,
that is all we know about it, and all that, as sensible
people, we should care to know. Our plain business is
to ' make the election sure.'"

Let none, therefore, stand aloof from the Church,
either upon the pharisaical plea of righteousness, or
upon the publican's plea of sinfulness, but let all do

their duty to Christ, to themselves and to the world, by becoming faithful, humble, unostentatious, and, so far as possible, consistent members of the Church.

II.

THE CHOICE OF A CHURCH.

"IF we only get to Heaven," says a dear old lady, in her arm-chair, her face beaming with good nature and kindly Christian feeling, which we would not rudely violate for the world: "If we only get to Heaven, it will never be asked by what road we came." We trust that the tranquillity and radiancy of the lovely creatures, of whom this good woman is a representative, will not be too much disturbed or obscured if, in accordance with our sense of duty, we try to make it appear that more thought and care than is customary should be exercised in the selection of a Church in which to become a member. Usually a person when he has perceived the duty of confessing Christ by identification with His Church and has made up his mind to discharge it, feels at liberty to unite with that Denomination which may chance to be his preference. This in the majority of cases is determined by some accident of circumstances and environment, as, for instance, the Church relationship of parents and friends, the size of the Denomination, its social status in that particular place, or its advantages from a business point of view.

Now there is nothing wrong about this, if the assumption that we are free to follow natural preference in the matter of Church membership can be supported; for taking this freedom for granted, why should not a man in the choice of a Church, as in other affairs of life, act with reference to those who are near and dear to him and to the furtherance of his social and commercial interests? But a moment's reflection will convince all thoughtful persons that we are not in the enjoyment of this assumed liberty. We are under a law that requires us in this, as in all matters of importance, to be guided by principle, not by preference. The conscience of all will bear witness to the truth of the assertion that a man, in the choice of a profession or business, should be influenced not by his inclinations, but by the prospect of service to God and man. We may imagine a young man with life before him strongly inclined to the profession of the law or of medicine, although he is thoroughly convinced that the need for him is greater, and that he would be more useful, in the ministry. In such and all analogous cases, a person is not at liberty to follow his preference. Duty to God and man lays upon him the obligation of denying himself and of taking up his cross and following Jesus.

The duty of such a course is quite as apparent in the choice of Church relationship. If God were equally pleased, and if our opportunities for usefulness were the same, no matter what body of Christians we join, then indeed we might follow preference, for there would be no principle at stake. But would God be equally pleased, and would our opportunities for usefulness be the same? These are questions which should be candidly and conscientiously considered by every non church member who has made up his mind to do his duty, and equally so by any who, without a proper understanding of the claims of this subject upon his thoughtful attention, has already united with some one of the numerous religious bodies about us.

There is a great advantage in the choosing of a Church from principle rather than preference; for, besides promoting self-respect and contentment, it enables one to give a manly and thoughtful reason for his choice.

A person who is known to entertain a deep-seated and rational conviction that the Church with which he is identified has superior claims to his allegiance, will always have an influence over those who have been guided by mere preference or circumstances in the choice of their Church relationship. This is illustrated by an anecdote told of a parishioner by one of our Clergy. A well-instructed young woman of his Parish married a Denominationalist. Upon returning home for a visit a year or so later, her old pastor inquired, "How about Church attendance? You go with your husband, I presume?" "Oh, no, he goes with me," was her reply. "His Church, he said, was the Church of his choice. But mine, said I, of my principle. 'Preference must yield to principle,' said my good man; and he always goes to Church with me."

We believe that it is God's will that we should belong to a branch of the One, Holy, Catholic and Apostolic Church of Christ, spoken of in the ancient Creeds. No other organization can make good a Divine claim to the allegiance of any man or woman. We contend also, that not only are we under no moral obligation to belong to an un-Catholic and un-Apostolic Christian body, but rather obliged not to belong to such, since our doing so would tend to destroy the unity of Christ's Kingdom, and hinder His holy conquest of the world. It may be a good thing for a man to found a new fraternity, or to become a member of human societies, such as the Masons, Odd Fellows, or Knights of Pythias, but it is wrong for him to establish, or to identify himself with, a human church.

But since there are many bodies of Christians, each claiming to be a little more according to the mind of Christ and the Apostles than any of its rivals, it becomes necessary to investigate the several grounds upon which this claim is based, in order that we may be able to make an intelligent choice among them. Then, if, in the end, we yet fail of reaching the truth, we at least shall have done our best to discover the will of God in regard to our Church affiliation; and although we may join a schismatical body instead of a true Church, we nevertheless shall not be held to have been thoughtlessly or willfully guilty of the great sin of schism. It is quite likely that some will never be able to decide among "the churches," and that they may make this inability an excuse for remaining non church members. To such I would say: At least put yourself in a state of safety by being baptized. "Except a man be born of water and of the Spirit he cannot enter into the Kingdom of God." Baptism in the Name of the Father and of the Son and of the Holy Ghost, by whomsoever administered, will make you "a member of Christ, the child of God and an inheritor of the Kingdom of Heaven." The fact that Baptism does not make us members of a Denomination, and that all duly baptized persons are members of one universal Church of Christ, is not generally known and appreciated as it should be.

There are three conceptions of what is necessary to constitute an organization of Christians a true branch of the Catholic Church of Christ.

1. According to the Roman conception of the Church, there are, properly speaking, no branches; for the Church of Rome, so widely diffused throughout the world, is the only Catholic and Apostolic Church that has ever existed, or ever can exist. It is claimed that the Pope is the sole representative of Christ on earth, and that only by allegiance to him can a person be identified with Christ and His true Church. These are sweeping

pretensions. Their very boldness and magnitude are well calculated to awe and fascinate the minds of the unsophisticated. "As," says Mr. Gladstone, "advertising houses find custom in proportion, not so much to the solidity of their resources, as to the magniloquence of their promises and assurances, so theological boldness in the extension of such claims is sure to pay, by widening certain circles of devoted adherents, however it may repel the mass of mankind."

There are, however, unanswerable objections to the Roman claims, a full consideration of which will require a separate lecture.† For the present it must suffice simply to observe that they were unknown in the earliest and purest ages of the Church. The peculiar position of Rome as the chief city of the world early tended to the undue exaltation of her Bishops or Popes, but they are on record as repudiating any exclusive right or claim to lordship over other Bishops and Churches. Even so late and great a Pope as Gregory I., Bishop of Rome from A.D. 590 to A.D. 604, rebuked John IV., Patriarch of Constantinople, who, it is interesting to note, was the first to style himself the "Ecumenical Patriarch" or "Universal Pope." "This title," wrote Gregory, "is profane, superstitious, haughty, and invented by the first apostate. St. Peter is not called universal Apostle. No one of my predecessors ever consented to use so profane a title. Far from Christian hearts be that blasphemous name. I confidently affirm that he who calls himself, or wishes to be called, universal Priest, is in his pride a forerunner of Antichrist."

2. A satisfactory discussion of the Denominational conception of the Church also will require a lecture devoted exclusively to its consideration.§ What we say at this time must necessarily be prefatory. By

---

† Lecture II. § Lecture III.

the Denominations we mean all the Protestant bodies, except those that are comprised within the Anglican Communion. The chief of the Denominations, in the order of their organization, are the Lutherans, A.D. 1517; Congregationalists, A.D. 1571; Presbyterians, A.D. 1592; Baptists, A.D. 1644; and Methodists, A.D. 1739. According to the conception which prevails among these and all Denominations of later origin, any Christian is at liberty to collect about him persons of like mind with himself, and to form a society for the preaching of the Gospel and the administration of the Sacraments. Such societies are mutually acknowledged to be so many true Churches. In theory, at least, these Churches are admitted to be one as good as the other.

We are aware that Presbyterians, Methodists and Lutherans might protest, with some show of reason, that this is not a correct statement of their position. "We," they may say, "believe in Ordination as firmly as do Episcopalians, but contend that Bishops and Presbyters are the same Order." But the force of this objection is turned aside by the consideration that those who make so much of the Presbytery when arguing against Episcopacy, show little or no regard for it when dealing with societies of Christians which confessedly have a self-constituted ministry. Such are recognized as standing upon the same footing with themselves. They freely exchange with their ministers and even receive them into fellowship, and give them pastorates without reordination. This they could not do if the Presbyterian régime were held to be by Divine appointment essential to the constitution of a valid ministry. Mr. MacLean, a writer who has given considerable space to this subject, speaking of Scotch and English Presbyterians, says that they, "and the other bodies which are separated from the ancient Church, are now agreed in saying that it does not matter whether there is any succession or none at all. The Nonconformist bodies do not claim to have any succession going back to the Apostles, or going back at all more than a few generations at most. They all really derive the authority of their ministry from the congregation, that is, from below instead of from above. They mostly hold that any assembly of 'believers' may appoint a man, either with or without the laying on of hands, to the Holy Ministry. For this is the way in which the ministry of all Nonconformist bodies, or almost all, first began." Elsewhere he writes: "Scarcely anyone now holds the belief that a succession of sacred ministers must be passed on through an unbroken line of Presbyters. The Presbyterians have almost entirely ceased to hold it, and most of them hold, with the other nonchurchmen, that the Christian congregation can appoint its own ministers."

It is said that there are above three hundred Denominations. According to their principles a man can have his choice among them; or, if none of them accord with his ideas, he may start one to suit himself. This is doubtless the prevailing view with professing Christians in America; but, taking the world at large, there are probably not more than one-tenth who hold it. And there is an increasing number of the adherents of the Denominational system who have more or less serious misgivings as to whether or not a church which they might see fit to found upon their preferences in regard to doctrine or government, would really be a true branch of the One, Holy, Catholic and Apostolic Church of Christ. They realize that it is not lawful for men to make new books written since the

Apostles' day and to pretend for them that they should be received as of Divine authority. And, they inquire, if the most learned, gifted and best men who have lived since the Apostolic age cannot make a New Testament, or add so much as a syllable to it, how can any found a new Church? Moreover, they perceive that the principles of Denominationalism would be rejected by human organizations such as the Masons, Odd Fellows and Knights of Pythias, and ask themselves, if I cannot found a new and independent lodge, how can I found a new and independent Church? And if I, in my day, cannot start such a Church, how is it that Luther and Brown and Calvin and Knox and Williams and Wesley and Campbell could do so in their days? In the estimation of all such as have regard to law and order and perceive the force of the historical argument, these questions can never be satisfactorily answered on behalf of Denominationalism.

Take for example Mr. Wesley's Society. What is true of this, the largest of modern Denominations, is true of all. Is it a Church? If the Denominational reader insists that "yes" must be the answer to this question, let me ask him, is Mr. Booth's Society, known as the Salvation Army, also a Church? As I understand it, the founder and adherents of this organization do not regard it as such; nor have I met with any Denominationalists who do. But if Mr. Wesley's Society is a Church, why is not Mr. Booth's? They were both founded for the same purpose, and their methods, though differing in external details, are in principle essentially the same. The brass band, street parades, and services are, after all, only another form of the old-fashioned revival system. I am not here pronouncing upon this way of bringing men and women to Christ. For the purpose of my argument it is only necessary to point out that according to all reports Mr. Booth and his army are using it quite as successfully as Mr. Wesley and his followers. Now, if the Methodists constitute a Church, why do not the Salvationists? True the latter do not claim to be a Church, but neither did the former at first. Indeed, I have seen it stated that in England the Wesleyans have not up to date formally claimed to be a Church, though they have gradually adopted the name. Their founder to the day of his death insisted that they were not such, but only a society. Will the Denominational reader occupy himself in trying to give a satisfactory answer to the following questions: When did Methodism change from the state of a society to that of a Church? What were the steps in the transition? Why is the Salvation Army not a Church? What will it have to do to become one? An observing traveler in New England sees over the doorway of primitive places of worship the original inscription "Meeting House," while, at the side, on the modern bulletin board he reads "Congregational Church." What has happened in the interval represented by these designations to justify the change? Whoever attempts to answer these inquiries will ultimately abandon the Denominational conception of the Church and conclude that, in the nature of things, mortal men cannot organize a new Church any more than they can create a new Bible or place a new star in the heavens.

Bishops of regular and canonical descent from the Apostles are the perpetuators of the Church. As a true lodge, through its legally executed charter, must be historically connected with its founder, so a true Church, through its lawful Bishop-successors of the Apostles, must be able to show an uninterrupted continuity back through the ages to Christ. One of the earliest of the Christian Fathers and Doctors tersely gave expression to the conviction which prevailed universally during the first fifteen hundred years when he said, "No Bishop, no Church."

The oldest of the Denominations, and in many respects the most dignified and justifiable of them, the Lutherans, started about fifteen hundred years too late to make good its claim to be a regular and legitimate branch of the Church of Christ. There will ever remain, after all that can be said in justification of the sixteenth century and later organizations of Christians, room for reasonable and serious doubt concerning their Catholicity. Such organizations, it will be perceived, would not have been recognized as true Churches in the earlier and purer, or indeed in any preceding, ages of the Church. They are not so regarded even now, and in all probability never will be, by the vast majority of Christians. All Churches whose claim to Catholicity cannot be gainsaid were founded by the Apostles, or by those who "continued steadfastly in the Apostles' doctrine and fellowship, and in the breaking of bread and in *the* prayers." But the founders of modern Denominations were not Apostles nor did any of them, except the Wesleys, remain in communion with any undoubted branch of the Apostolic Church. John and Charles Wesley lived and died in the communion of our Mother Church of England. Would to God that Coke and Asbury had done the same!

Those who perceive the difference between a Divine and a human Church, and realize their obligation to belong to the former rather than to the latter, can never be quite satisfied in any body of Christians which traces its origin to uninspired men, and is not the recognized offspring of any undisputed branch of the ancient Catholic Church.

3. Finally, we have the Greek and Anglican conception of the Church, which is held by all Christians outside

the Roman and Denominational Communions. The Greek Church is the Church of Western Asia and Eastern Europe. It embraces nearly all Christians in Turkey, Servia, Roumania, Greece, Russia, and is strongly represented in Austria. The Anglican or English Communion includes all Christians in full fellowship with the Church of England, and is composed of these parts: The Church of England, the Episcopal Church in the United States, the Church of Ireland, the Church of Wales, the Church in Canada, the Church in Asia, the Church in Africa, the Church in Australia, the Church in Scotland, and in nine scattered Dioceses.

The Greek and Anglican Churches are in practical communion with each other; at least, they agree perfectly in regard to their conception of what is necessary to constitute a Catholic Church. According to their view there are as many branches of the true Church of Christ as there are nations in which there is an independent Church that can trace its origin to the Apostles. Each such Church has a right to self-government, having respect only to the general regulations of the great Councils in which the whole of Catholic Christendom was represented.

The Church, according to the Greek and Anglican conception, may be compared to a fruitful vine which, having been planted by the Apostles at Jerusalem, not Rome, overran, even in their lifetime, almost all of the then known world, pushing its tendrils into the several political divisions of Western Asia, Northern Africa and Eastern Europe. These branches were in many cases carried over by the Apostles themselves, and through their planting took independent root. The successors of the Apostles, whom we call Bishops, have been going on with this work ever since, and they will continue to do so until the vine has taken root in every nation of

the earth. Thus the one vine of the Church of Christ has
as many roots as there are National Churches. If the
parent root of any branch should wither and die, the
offspring would flourish nevertheless, and if in future
ages the surviving offshoot should send a branch back to
the native land to take new root there, the second Church
of that country would be essentially the same as the first.
This makes it impossible that the gates of hell should
permanently prevail against any branch of the Church.
According to the Roman theory there is only one vine
having its root in Christ through only one Bishop, who
is the representative of only one Apostle. The branches
of this vine overrun other countries, but they do not
take root, and thus have no independent national life.
There is, therefore, according to this view, no such thing
as a National Church. Of course, if Romanists are right
Anglicans and Greeks are wrong.

An argument for the Scripturalness of independent
National Churches, as well as for the equality of Bishops,
might be built upon our Lord's commission to the
Apostles, "Go ye therefore and teach all nations." "Go
ye," not go thou, St. Peter, and all thy successors in
the See of Rome, but "go ye," all the Apostles and all
their successors, and make disciples of "all nations,"
not make missions of Rome. Obedience to this command, especially in the early days of Christianity, when
the animosity between nations and the difficulties of
intercommunication were much greater than at present, made the establishment of independent National
Churches unavoidable. Take England for illustration.
In obedience to Christ's command some early successor
of one of the Apostles, not St. Peter—many think it was
St. Paul himself—preached the Gospel and established
the Church there. But even as late and intelligent a
Pope as Gregory I. did not appear to know of the exist-

ence of the British Church until informed of it by St. Augustine about the year 600. Nor can this ignorance be accounted for by supposing that the Church was insignificant. Hundreds of years before, the British Church had been represented in great Councils by a delegation of Bishops and other Clergy. This was the case at Arles, A. D. 314, and Ariminum, A. D. 359, and probably at Nice, A. D. 325, and Sardica, A. D. 347. And though the Church had undoubtedly suffered severely from the northern invasions, there still remained many Bishops, Priests and Deacons who congregated from all parts to the monasteries in the region of Wales, Scotland and Ireland. The number of Bishops at that time we do not know. Bede says that seven were present at a conference with Augustine. According to a widely received tradition there were twenty-five Bishops and three Archbishops.

The Anglican idea concerning self-governing National Churches is confirmed by the parable of the vine. At least the Roman doctrine in regard to St. Peter and the necessity to Catholicity of communion with the Popes, is irreconcilable with our Lord's teaching in this passage: "I am the Vine, ye are the branches." Note that Christ is here represented as the stem and root, that the Apostles are only branches, that there is no indication that the branch represented by St. Peter should, by Divine right, overshadow the rest, and that there is not the faintest allusion to his successors in the See of Rome. In order to harmonize the parable with the Ultramontane conception it would have to be recast so as to read: While in the world I am the Vine, but after My ascension Peter and the Bishops of Rome, one after the other, until the end of the world, will take My place. Therefore, in all time to come, he that abideth in the Pope, and the Pope in him, the same will bring forth much fruit, for without the Pope you can do nothing.

If a man abide not in the Pope, he is cast forth as a branch and is withered. But since Romans interpret the Scriptures one way and we another, let us turn to the history of the earliest and purest ages for the purpose of ascertaining who are right.

The very name of the Roman Church proves the National Church theory, and shows that originally she was regarded as one of the state Churches. Her official name is "The Holy Catholic Apostolic Roman Church." Before the Council of Trent it was "The Holy Roman Church." The word "Roman" in this title is inexplicable upon the hypothesis that the Papal Communion comprised the whole of Catholic Christendom.

Again, the phrase "The Catholic Churches," which occurs so frequently in the writings of both the Latin and Greek Fathers, cannot be explained in harmony with the Roman theory of Catholicity, for how could they speak of more than one Catholic Church, if "The Holy Roman Church" could make good its exclusive pretensions? St. Irenæus bears witness to the National Church idea when he says: "and neither do the Churches founded in Germany, nor those of Spain, in Gaul, in the East, in Egypt, in Africa, nor in the regions in the middle of the earth, believe or deliver a different Faith."

The Church is compared by the Fathers to the sea, as being diffused throughout all the world; as being, like it, one; as having one name, that of the Catholic Church; and as containing within it many Churches with various names, as the ocean has many bays within it.

The so-called "Canons or laws of the Apostles," which were compiled about the end of the second century, distinctly mention the existence of independent state or national Churches. "It is necessary," runs the thirty-fourth canon, "that the Bishops of every nation should know who is first among them, recognize him as such, and do nothing important without his assent." How unfortunate it is for the Papal claims that this celebrated canon was not worded something like this: It is necessary that every Bishop throughout the world should know that he is subject to the Pope of Rome, and that he should do nothing of importance without first securing his consent.

The local character of "The Holy Roman Church" was recognized by Pope Innocent III., A.D. 1198–1216, who, though given to the most unwarrantable efforts towards the aggrandizement of his position, says, in a letter to the Patriarch of Constantinople: "That is called the Church universal which consists of all the Churches and is named from the Greek word Catholic. And in this sense of the word the Roman Church is not the Church universal, but a part of the Church universal." Gregory IX., A.D. 1227–41, admitted that the Eastern Church was a part of the universal Church. Even as late as the middle of the sixteenth century, the Council of Trent, presided over by Pius IV., tacitly acknowledged the existence of National Churches; for the creed which it formulated declared that Rome was "the Mother and Mistress of all Churches." It is impossible to escape the logical conclusion that there must have been more than one Church in the minds of the Pope and theologians; for otherwise that of Rome could not be regarded as a mother.

But if there be any room for doubt as to the opinion of Innocent III. and Pius IV., upon this subject, there is none whatever when we go back to the time of Pope Gregory I. Bede records that among the questions submitted to this Pontiff by St. Augustine, who, in A.D. 596, had been sent by him to England, was the following: "When there is but one Faith, why are there different customs of Churches, and why is one custom of Masses observed in the Holy Roman Church, and another in the Church of Gaul?" To which Pope Gregory made this answer: "You, my brother, know the custom of the Roman Church, in which you remember that you your-self were brought up. But my sentence is, that whether in the Roman, or the Gallican, or in any Church, you have found anything which may be more pleasing to Omnipotent God, you carefully select, and with special instruction impart to the Church of the English, which, as yet, is new to the Faith, what things you have been able to collect from many Churches. For things are not to be loved for the sake of places, but places for the sake of things. From each individual Church, therefore, choose the things which are pious, which are religious, which are right, and deposit these things—when you have collected them, as it were, into a bundle—in the minds of the English for their use."

It cannot, therefore, be disputed, by any who acknowledge the infallibility of the Popes, that there were, at least in England and Gaul, National Churches which were separate and distinct from the Church of Rome. Until the Council of Trent, Roman writers, like those of the rest of the world, speak of the Churches of these countries, and of Germany and Spain, and, in fact, of every nation, in such a way as to show conclusively that the idea of the Church's being one universal communion with Rome and her Bishop as its indispensable center, had not been conceived, or at least did not obtain, even among Ultramontanists, until after the middle of the sixteenth century.

If the present Roman theory and the interpretation given to the texts by which it is supported be correct, we ought to find that during the first three or four hundred years, all Churches were subject to the Bishop of Rome, and that there was no such thing to be found in all the world as an independent Provincial or National Church. On the other hand, if the Anglican theory be tenable, it will appear that during this period the Churches of the several political divisions throughout the vast Roman Empire governed themselves without practically any reference to the Bishops of the capital city, or to any other external authority except the decrees of the General Councils. Those who have not taken the pains to investigate the truth of the representations of modern Romanists respecting their universal sway in primitive times, will be surprised when they learn the real extent of the original Diocese presided over by the Bishops of the Imperial city, and of the comparatively little influence and power that they exercised abroad during the first four or five centuries. The limits of the original Papal See were those of the city of Rome. Even after the development of the Patriarchal system the region in which the Bishop of Rome was first among equals was by no means co-extensive with Italy. "Italy," says an Ecclesiastical geographer, "from very early times was divided into two great Provinces. First, the Italic Diocese, which comprehended the present Kingdom of Lombardy, and the other countries subject to the Empire south of the Danube, of which Milan was the metropolis; and, second, that of Rome, which comprised Tuscany, the recent States of the Church, Naples, Sicily and the Mediterranean Islands of Sardinia and Corsica, usually known as the Loca Suburbicaria."

Now, in the early times, the primacy of the Bishop of Rome was confined to the limits of the Suburbicarian Churches, and his jurisdiction to the city. He had nothing whatever to do with the great Italian Churches of Ravenna, Aquileia or Milan. Ravenna was

only about a hundred and eighty miles northeast of
Rome; Aquileia was three hundred miles in that direction, and Milan about the same distance to the north-
west. Since the jurisdiction of the Pope was originally
confined to Rome, and his primacy was so far from being coextensive with Italy itself, we might regard it safe
to conclude that he had nothing to say about the government of the Church in remoter parts of Christendom.
But we are not left to conjecture on this point. There
is abundant evidence, known to all readers of Ecclesiastical History, that the Churches of Palestine, Asia Minor,
Africa, France, Spain and England were all for the first
six centuries, and some of them during the first thousand years, quite independent of Roman, or any other
foreign, domination. In fact, such of these Churches as
compose the great Greek Communion have never submitted in the least degree to Papal dominion.

"Janus"* says: "There are many National Churches
which were never under Rome, and never even had any
intercourse by letter with Rome, without this being considered a defect, or causing any difficulty about Church
Communion. Such an autonomous Church, always independent of Rome, was the most ancient of those

---

*"Janus" was a mythological deity of the Latins who had the power of
looking both ways at once. It was therefore, not without significance, assumed
as the pen name by the profoundly learned German authors of "The Pope and
the Council," a powerful protest against the proposition to declare the infallibility of the Papacy. It looked at the question from both the standpoint of
history and expediency. Professor Schaff speaks of this work as "a book which
will be memorable in the history of literature as one of the most crushing
blows ever struck in any controversy. It is the work of more than one learned
theologian of the Roman Catholic Church and deals with the question of infallibility from the root. It shows that the theological opinion in favor of Papal
infallibility, as it has been held by many in other ages, was the offspring of
sheer imposture and wholesale forgery sustained and repeated from generation to generation, and that many other claims of the Papacy rest on like
foundation." There is considerable uncertainty about its authorship. It is
supposed to be the joint work of Professors Von Döllinger, Friedrich and Hu-
ber of the University of Munich. There seems to be little room for doubt that
the famous Dr. Von Döllinger was the chief writer and the editor of the whole.

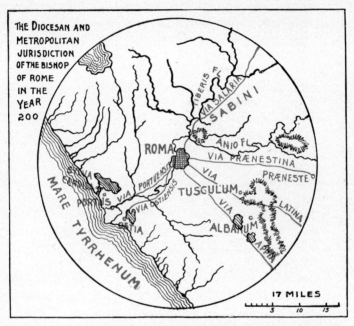

THE DIOCESAN AND METROPOLITAN JURISDICTION OF THE BISHOP OF ROME IN THE YEAR 200

17 MILES

The author is greatly indebted to the Rev. Greenough White, M.A., Professor of Ecclesiastical History in the University of the South, for the critical and artistic work connected with the production of the above map and its companion on the next page. By the aid of these maps the reader will see at a glance just what was the territorial jurisdiction of the Bishop of Rome up to the Nicene age, which commenced in the year 325. Those portions of Christendom which were not recognized as belonging to his jurisdiction before that age could not legitimately be claimed by him at any subsequent period. In view of the modern claims of the Papacy to universal rulership, it will be observed with surprise the little authority which the Roman Bishop had outside of his own Diocese, was territorially so very limited its boundaries being the City limits.

About A.D. 150 the Metropolitan or Archiepiscopal system sprang up in the Church. The Roman Metropolitanate comprised the seven Sees, which, a thousand years later, gave titles to the first Cardinals. The most remote of these Sees was Præneste, only twenty-three miles from the City. The Bishop of Rome could convene in Council the Bishops and Clergy of his Metropolitanate, which was much smaller than Rhode Island. He presided over the Council but, without its sanction, he could not make laws. Some of the Bishops of his Province, for example, St. Hippolytus, Bishop of Portus, who flourished at the beginning of the third century, manifested a great deal of independence.

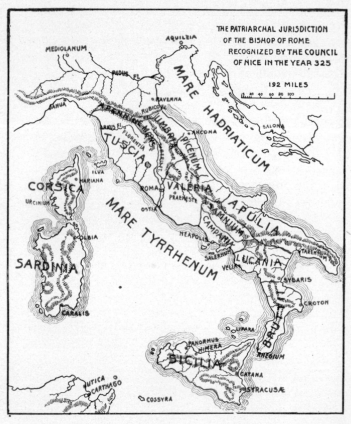

The map shows:

MEDIOLANUM
AQUILEIA
THE PATRIARCHAL JURISDICTION
OF THE BISHOP OF ROME
RECOGNIZED BY THE COUNCIL
OF NICE IN THE YEAR 325

192 MILES
20 40 60 80 100

GENUA
PADUS FL.
RAVENNA
RUBICON
ARNUS FL.
APENNINES
FLORENTIA
UMBRIA
LIGURIA
PICENUM
ANCONA
MARE HADRIATICUM
SALONÆ
TUSCIA
ILVA
MARIANA
ROMA
VALERIA
PRAENESTE
OSTIA
SAMNIUM
APULIA
CORSICA
URCINIUM
MARE TYRRHENUM
NEAPOLIS
CAMPANIA
SALERNUM
VELI
LUCANIA
TARENTUM
OLBIA
SARDINIA
SYBARIS
CROTON
CARALIS
BRUTII
LIPARA
PANORMUS
HIMERA
RHEGIUM
SICILIA
CATANA
UTICA
CARTHAGO
COSSYRA
SYRACUSÆ

When, in the course of the third century, the Patriarchal system was developed, Rome was the centre of one of the five Patriarchates into which Christendom was divided. Her Bishop was consequently recognized as the first among equals by the Bishops of the central and lower parts of Italy and the Islands of Sicily, Sardinia, and Corsica.

Ravenna and Milan, it must be remembered, were centres of separate and quite independent Provinces. In the Nicene age they did not even belong to the Roman Patriarchate, the limits of which are traced by the blue line on the map facing page 47. It should be remembered also that the oath of allegiance to the Pope, taken by Latin Bishops, was first invented in a Council at Rome under Gregory VII. in 1079, wherein the words of the older oath, binding them to obey the Canons and to maintain "*regulas Sanctorum Patrum*," were cleverly altered into "*regalia Sancti Petri*."

founded beyond the limits of the Empire, the Armenian, wherein the primatial dignity descended for a long time in the family of the national Apostle, Gregory the Illuminator. The great Syro-Persian Church in Mesopotamia and the western part of the Kingdom of the Sassanidæ, with its thousands of Martyrs, was from the first, and always remained, equally free from any influence of Rome. In its records and its rich literature we find no trace of the arm of Rome having reached there. The same holds good of the Ethiopian or Abyssinian Church, which was indeed united to the See of Alexandria, but wherein nothing, except perhaps a distant echo, was heard of the claims of Rome. In the West, the Irish and the ancient British Church remained for centuries autonomous, and under no sort of influence of Rome."

This being notoriously the case, what becomes of the assertion of Romanists that the Church of England and the American Episcopal Church are not true branches of the Catholic Church of Christ, because they are not under the dominion of St. Peter's successor in the See of Rome? May we not effectually answer that if obedience to the Bishop of Rome is essential to Catholicity, the Church did not exist anywhere in all the world during the first six centuries after the Ascension, except in the little Diocese of Rome? Roman Catholics feel the weakness of their cause when pleaded at the bar of antiquity; hence, in the person of one of their most representative Cardinals, Manning, they have proclaimed that to appeal to history instead of the Pope is a sin no less heinous than "treason" and "heresy."

Though the Roman view differs widely and fundamentally from the Anglican and Greek conception, there is manifest agreement in the belief that there can be no such thing as a valid Church of Christ, to which it is the duty of non church members to belong, unless there be an historical connection with Him through Bishops in unbroken succession from the Apostles. We also agree that the Church is a Divine institution with a human mission. Denominationalists think that it is a human institution with a Divine mission. We hold that the Church is the Kingdom of Heaven seeking men on earth; they that it is a society on earth seeking the Kingdom of Heaven. We think that it is an organization for dispensing Christianity; they that it is for the attainment of Christianity. On these points Romans, Greeks and Anglicans, who constitute about nine-tenths of Christendom, are agreed.

It may as well be observed here as elsewhere that our argument in many places throughout this book is on behalf of the whole of the great ancient Catholic Church. If we were to contend thus for some nonessential feature of the Anglican Communion, however admirable in itself, what we say might apparently for good reason be disregarded as an ebullition of the sectarian spirit; but as we speak for the whole of Christendom during the first fifteen centuries, and for the overwhelming majority in our own time, it will surely be conceded that we are entitled to a respectful hearing.

Even the small minority who maintain that connection with Christ through Bishops of the Apostolic succession is not necessary to the existence of a true Church, did not originally reject the Historic Episcopate because they thought it to be unscriptural, but because of the force of circumstances. Luther intended that his followers should be governed by regularly consecrated Bishops as soon as they could be obtained. Calvin applied to the Church of England for Consecration; Wesley to a Greek Bishop; and Dr. Coke first to the American and then to the English Episcopate. The hopes and schemes of these were in each case frustrated, but their advice and efforts should deter any of their admirers, who cannot like them plead necessity, from choosing a non-Episcopal Church for membership, and, also, their example should turn the face of all Lutherans, Presbyterians and Methodists towards Episcopacy.

Of course Anglicans, Romanists, and Denominationalists each cite Holy Scripture in support of the claim that their respective organizations are true branches of Christ's Church. In view of our wide differences, outsiders cannot decide which is right, and what Church to join, unless they can determine which is the best interpreter of the New Testament teaching. Now it so happens that we are all able to refer such to an interpreter, which we severally regard as eminently trustworthy. Romans direct us to the Pope, and Denominationalists to their founders and bright lights, but the Episcopal Church has no modern Pope or founder; so, instead of referring to personal interpreters, we have always asked inquirers to examine our claims in the light of the early Fathers and the history of the Church. We think that those who lived nearest the time of our Lord and the Apostles knew more concerning their teaching than the Christians of subsequent ages, and that consequently what they said and did must be taken into account by those who would conscientiously and intelligently choose between the Anglican and Roman Churches or amongst the various Protestant bodies of Christians.

We are well aware that with tens of thousands of the representatives of the Denominations which have sprung up in the course of the last three hundred and fifty years, the historical argument will be without influence. They contend that a Church, which it is

C. A.—4

quite within the power of a half dozen Christians to organize at any time, may have a much greater claim upon the allegiance of non church members than some undoubted branch of the Historic Church of Christ. But as time goes on, the test of history is sure to be applied more and more by the educated and reflecting who are guided by principle rather than by preference in the choice of their Church relationship. Even now the experience of our Clergy shows that of all those whom they are able to induce really to investigate the subject at least one-half of them come into the Episcopal Church. This is because it appears from history as clear as the sun on a cloudless noonday that originally each nation of Christendom had a self-governing Church, that the Church of England is the Apostolic, Catholic Church of our race, and that, therefore, her American daughter, the Episcopal Church, is the only body of Christians which can establish a Divine claim to the allegiance of Americans.

The Church for Americans.

LECTURE II.

OUR CONTROVERSY WITH ROMANISTS.

AUTHORITIES.

BACON, The Vatican Council.

BARROW, The Papal Supremacy.

BENNETT, The Distinctive Errors of Romanism.

BRIGHTMAN, What Objections Have Been Made to English Orders

COLLETTE, The Papacy.

COXE, BP., Institutes of Christian History.

COURAYER, On English Ordinations.

DENNY, Anglican Orders and Jurisdiction.

GAYER, Papal Infallibility and Supremacy.

GIBBONS, CARDINAL, Our Christian Heritage.

GORE, CANON, Roman Catholic Claims.

GUETTE, ABBE, The Papacy.

HADDAN, Apostolic Succession in the Church of England.

HUSSEY, On the Rise of the Papal Power.

"JANUS," The Pope and the Council.

JENKINS, Romanism: An Examination of the Creed of Pope
Pius the IV.

INGRAM, England and Rome.

LEE, The Validity of the Holy Orders of the Church of England.

LETO, Rome During the Vatican Council.

LITTLEDALE, Plain Reasons Against Joining the Church of Rome.

LITTLEDALE, The Petrine Claims.

MOORE AND BRINCKMAN, The Anglican Brief Against Roman
Claims.

NEWMAN, Apologia Pro Vita Sua.

PATON, British History and Papal Claims.   (2 Vols.)

PULLER, The Primitive Saints and the See of Rome.

RAMSAY, PROF., The Church in the Roman Empire.

ROBERTSON, The Growth of the Papal Power.

ROBINS, On the Claims of the Roman Church.

SALMON, Infallibility of the Church.

SEYMOUR, BP., What Is Modern Romanism?

SMITH, English Orders.

SPENCER, Papalism versus Catholic Truth.

STEARNS, The Faith of Our Forefathers.

TREAT, The Catholic Faith.

WILSON, The Papal Supremacy and Provincial System.

PAMPHLETS.

BUTLER, Rome's Tribute to Anglican Orders.

HOPKINS, JOHN HENRY, Monsignor Capel.

LITTLEDALE, Words for Truth.

OUR CONTROVERSY WITH ROMANISTS.

THE object of this lecture is to correct two widely spread, mistaken impressions concerning the Episcopal Church, namely, that her sympathy is, upon the whole, with Romanism rather than with Protestantism, and that she is not Catholic because she does not form a part of the Papal Communion.

Here and there is to be found a person who, having heard the claims of Rome, is possessed with the uncomfortable misgiving that perhaps, after all, they are true, and that in standing aloof from the Pope he is living in disobedience to the will of God. The number of such among Protestants of every name is probably greater than is generally supposed. Certainly there are multitudes who are more or less disconcerted whenever they enter into an argument with Romanists, or read any of their controversial books. So far as non-Episcopalians are concerned their embarrassment is easily accounted for. They rest their whole case upon "the Bible and the Bible only." Owing to the many-sided character of Revelation, Romanists are able to cite as many texts in support of their position as Protestants are. If exception be taken to their interpretations, they reply: "We have as good a right to our opinion in such matters as you have to yours."

In the Roman controversy, Episcopalians have this advantage over other Protestants that, being connected in unbroken continuity with the Apostolic Church, and having rid themselves of erroneous doctrines, and superstitious ceremonies which grew up in the Dark Ages, they are able to wield the two-edged sword of Scripture and history. With this weapon in hand, and standing on the vantage ground of the Reformation, we are, indeed, weak Anglo-Catholics, if unable to vanquish the most powerful champion of the Papacy. Any person of average intelligence, who has attentively read one of our Reformation fathers, or such writers of this generation as Littledale, Salmon, Puller, Hopkins, Kip, Little, Ingram, and many others whose books are easily procured, is more than a match for all the accomplished controversialists that Rome can produce. An Episcopalian who has any hesitancy in meeting an intelligent Roman Catholic Layman, or even Priest, in debate, should request his Rector to deliver a course of lectures on the points of difference between Romanists and ourselves, or at least to lend him a book upon the subject.

I.

PAPAL INFALLIBILITY.

SINCE the year 1870, belief in the inerrancy of the Pope, as the guide of mankind in the way of truth and life, has been made the condition of membership in the Roman Church and of salvation. Of all the articles which Rome has added to "the Faith once delivered to the Saints," this is the most remarkable, both for its presumptuousness and for its irreconcilableness to Scripture and Church history. No wonder that its promulgation caused even the Ultramontane Communion fairly to reel with astonishment, and that it set on foot a reformatory movement headed by Döllinger, the greatest theologian of the Roman obedience if not indeed of modern times, who with other scarcely less distinguished scholars restored the "Old Catholic Church" to parts of Europe. Nor was this all. The knowledge that the Jesuits were bent upon having the Pope declared infallible gave a great impetus to the Liberal School of Romanists. Many, representing almost every country of Christendom, who could not quite justify separation even from a heretical Church, felt, nevertheless, in conscience bound to identify them. selves with this movement in ringing protests.

There is little room for doubt that the resolution to make the dogma of infallibility an article of faith would have been voted down, if free and full discussion had been allowed and if the vote had been at all representa-tive of the whole communion. But the well-known pol-icy of Rome, which from the beginning has been to give the Italian Prelates the balance of power, defeated the ma-jority. As there was some reason to fear that the num-ber of these among the legitimate Cardinals and Bishops might fall short of an overwhelming majority, a host of native titular, or merely nominal, Ecclesiastical digni-taries had been created. By this desperate expedient, Italy had an altogether disproportionate representation of two hundred and seventy-six delegates. France, with a much larger Roman Catholic population, had only eighty-four, Germany, nineteen and the United States, forty-eight. By one means and another Pius IX. made sure of the enormous majority of 576 votes out of 770, for the dogma of infallibility. All whose attitude was in the least doubtful were, as far as possible, persuaded to accept his lavish hospitality. The Pope himself had his good-humored jokes about the numbers who com-promised themselves by living like princes at his ex-pense. "If they do not," said he, "make me *infallible*, they will render me *fallire*," that is, bankrupt.

After the resourceful Pontiff and Jesuits had done all they could to minimize the opposition, what little remained was, by one means and another, coerced so that only the most fearless could summon sufficient courage to raise their voices in debate; and even these were prevented by strategy from speaking at length and by the notoriously bad acoustics, inexcusably so, of the hall erected for the meeting, were not heard except by a few in the region of the platform. The wary infallibilists instinctively felt that it would not do to give such Germans as the authors of "Janus," or Frenchmen as the Archbishop of Paris, or Americans as Archbishop Kenrick, the floor for extended speeches. The proceedings were, of course, in the official language of the Roman Church, which all Prelates could understand and speak, though very few of them with sufficient ease to do justice to themselves and their subjects. "Quirinus" asserts that nine-tenths of the Prelates were condemned to silence simply from being unable to speak Latin readily and coherently through want of regular practice. And to this must be added the embarrassment occasioned by diversities of pronunciation. It was impossible, for example, for Frenchmen or Italians to understand an Englishman's Latin.

The rules of order provided that the chairman, who, of course, was the Pope's appointee and trusted representative, might call any speaker to order for wandering from the question and deny him liberty to proceed. No appeal from the decision of the chair was allowed. The working of this rule is illustrated by the experience of Monsignor Haynald, one of the most prominent Bishops in the opposition. In proof of a statement in his address he made some historical quotation, which showed that on the occasion of the reform of the Roman Breviary, a Pope had expressed an opinion contrary to that of the present majority in the Council. Thereupon, the president immediately requested him to stop, and to descend from the tribune. Anything like debate was precluded. Offhand remarks were out of order. The speakers were required to give notice some days in advance of their wish to be heard. They had to speak in the order of their rank, without refer- ence to the relevancy of any speaker's remarks to those of his predecessors. No reply was permitted. When, on the 3rd day of June, 1870, the debates of the Coun- cil on the main question were suddenly silenced, there remained on the list of those who had signified their in- tention to speak, the names of some forty Bishops who were still unheard. They were forbidden, by the rules of the Council, to print their views for private circulation among the Bishops; and the spiritual prohibition was reënforced by police arrangements which locked every printing office in Rome against them. But while noth- ing derogatory to the dogma of infallibility could be printed, the organs of the Pope had full freedom to publish what they pleased.

However, an American Prelate, Archbishop Kenrick, of St. Louis, refused to be thus gagged. Claiming a "Divine right to express his convictions, on this most important question, to his fellow-Bishops," he sent the carefully prepared manuscript of his Latin speech to a printer in Naples, where, under the flag of an excom- municated king, might be found that liberty for the Bishops of the Church which was denied them in the States of the Church itself. A copy of this remarkable document afterwards fell into the hands of the author of "An Inside View of the Vatican Council," by whom it was translated, and made an appendix to his excellent volume. We shall have occasion frequently to quote from it, and from the other notable protests of German

and French Romanists against the Scheme which had
been prepared for the Council by the Pope and the
Jesuits.

Another expedient that was resorted to, for the purpose of making sure of the end in view, was the post-
ponement of the voting upon the dogma of infallibility
until the intolerable Summer heat of Rome had driven
two hundred and thirty-five Bishops from the Council.
Of the delegates from foreign countries who were in the
city when the vote was finally taken, many were de-
tained from the session by sickness, and others would
not attend because of their disgust at the way in which
the council had been manipulated.   A private vote was
taken on July 13, 1870, only five days before the promulgation of the doctrine of infallibility, which resulted
in four hundred and fifty-one affirmative and eighty-
eight negative votes; sixty-two Bishops giving a qualified affirmative, and ninety-one abstaining from voting,
although present in Rome.   "Among the negative votes
were the Prelates most distinguished for learning and
position, as Schwarzenberg, Cardinal Prince-Archbishop
of Prague; Rauscher, Cardinal Prince-Archbishop of
Vienna; Darboy, Archbishop of Paris; Matthieu, Cardi-
nal-Archbishop of Besancon; Ginoulhiac, Archbishop of
Lyons; Dupanloup, Bishop of Orleans; Maret, Bishop of
Sura; Simor, Archbishop of Gran and Primate of Hun-
gary; Haynald, Archbishop of Kalocsa; Forster, Prince-
Archbishop of Breslau; Scherr, Archbishop of Munich;
Ketteler, Bishop of Mayence; Hefele, Bishop of Rotten-
burg; Strossmayer, Bishop of Bosnia and Sirmium;
MacHale, Archbishop of Tuam; Connolly, Archbishop
of Halifax; Kenrick, Archbishop of St. Louis."   If
scholarship instead of votes had counted, the minority
would have been found to have overbalanced the majority
by as much as a giant outweighs a pigmy.   Thus the

article of infallibility was added to the Ultramontane creed by the scheming Jesuits and Italians and not by the Roman Church as a whole.

All accounts of the Vatican Council contain references to a remarkable coincidence. Its two most important days were December 8, 1869, when the magnificent opening session was held, and July 18, 1870, when the vote upon the momentous question, whether or not the Pope should be declared infallible, was taken Both of these events occurred during the most terrific storms of which the oldest inhabitants of Rome had any recollection. The thunder and lightning were appalling, and the darkness was so great at midday that the ceremonies and business could not proceed without artificial light. A candle had to be brought in order that Pius IX. might see to read his decree of Papal infallibility. All this made a profound and lasting impression upon the members of the Council and the whole city. It was universally regarded as a manifestation either of Divine approval or disapproval of that which was commenced on the first day and consummated on the last. Of course Infallibilists took one view of it and Anti-Infallibilists the other. But the untoward events which followed in quick succession abundantly justified the opinion to which the latter adhered. For "behold," says Professor Schaff, "the day after the proclamation of the dogma, Napoleon III., the political ally and supporter of Pius IX., unchained the furies of war, which in a few weeks swept away the Empire of France and the temporal throne of the infallible Pope. His own subjects forsook him, and almost unanimously voted for a new sovereign, whom he had excommunicated as the worst enemy of the Church. History records no more striking example of swift retribution of criminal ambition."

As Romanists speak of the doctrine of Papal infallibility so as to create the impression that the difficulties
in the way of its acceptance are not nearly so insuperable as is popularly supposed among Protestants, we will
here quote the decree and explain the qualifying clauses
behind which they take refuge when we press them too
hard. After the introduction, which is too long for
quotation, this declaration follows:

"Therefore, faithfully adhering to the tradition received from the beginning of the Christian Faith, for the
glory of God our Saviour, the exaltation of the Catholic religion, and the salvation of Christian people, the
sacred Council approving, we teach and define that it is
a dogma divinely revealed: that the Roman Pontiff,
when he speaks ex-cathedra, that is, when in discharge
of the office of pastor and doctor of all Christians, by
virtue of his supreme Apostolic authority, he defines a
doctrine regarding faith or morals to be held by the
universal Church, by the Divine assistance promised to
him in blessed Peter, is possessed of that infallibility
with which the Divine Redeemer willed that His Church
should be endowed for defining doctrine regarding faith
or morals; and that, therefore, such definitions of the
Roman Pontiff are irreformable of themselves and not
from the consent of the Church. But if anyone—which
may God avert—presume to contradict this our defini-
tion, let him be anathema."

The Pope's infallibility is limited indeed to his *ex-
cathedra* pronunciamentoes affecting the *universal
Church*. But these phrases cannot be so explained as
to exclude anything except his informal conversations
without making it impossible to determine when his
words are infallible truth. Certainly all his allocutions,
encyclicals, bulls and decrees are ex-cathedra proclama-
tions, and as such they must necessarily, to the Roman

mind, affect the "universal Church." In short, if the
Pope is ever infallible, he is always so whenever he seriously assumes the character of a teacher, even though
it be in the preaching of an ordinary sermon.

The almost blasphemous doctrine of Papal infallibility is partly accounted for (1) by the deep-seated desire
of mankind for certitude in matters of religion, and (2)
by the comparative freedom of the early Roman Church
from theological error.

But, before proceeding to consider the causes which
led to the decree, let me observe, by way of self-justifica-
tion, that I am not the first to make use of strong language in its condemnation.   Professor Schaff, who as an
historian enjoyed an enviable reputation for sobriety of
judgment, did not hesitate to say that, "if the dogma
is false, it involves a blasphemous assumption, and
makes the nearest approach to the fulfillment of St.
Paul's prophecy of the man of sin, who 'as God sitteth
in the temple of God, showing himself off that he is God.'"
"The fundamental error of Rome," says the same author, "is that she identifies the true ideal Church of
Christ with the empirical Church, and the empirical
Church with the Romish Church, and the Romish Church
with the Papacy, and the Papacy with the Pope, and at
last substitutes a mortal man for the living Christ." Before the Vatican Council many Romanists took this
view. "Janus" prophesied that if the Jesuits had their
way, "In Rome itself the saying will be verified, 'Thou
wilt shudder thyself at thy likeness to God.'" And an
anonymous writer of great learning and eloquence, in a
"Pretended Speech of a Bishop in the Council," thus expresses his horror at what was contemplated: "Ah, if
He who sitteth in the heavens is disposed to make heavy

His hand upon us, as once on Pharaoh, he has no need
to suffer the troops of Garibaldi to drive us out of the
Eternal City; he need only let us go on to make Pius IX.
a God, as we have made the blessed Virgin a goddess."

Nor is blasphemy the only evil that grows out of the
doctrine of infallibility. For, if on the one hand it tends
to idolatry, its opposite tendency is towards infidelity.
As some one has pointed out, it is a very short way
from the doctrine that Pius IX. and Leo XIII. were as
much inspired as Peter and Paul, to the doctrine that
the Apostles were no more inspired than the Popes.

1. There can be no doubt that men generally have
felt the need of a Supreme and Omniscient Ruler who
would authoritatively say, "This is the way; walk ye in
it." Romanists appeal to this well nigh universal crav-
ing in their efforts to commend the doctrine of Papal
infallibility to Anglicans and other Protestants. They
contrast the divisions of Protestantism with the unity
of Romanism, and account for our unhappy condition
by assuming that, because we are not in communion with
the Pope, we are without a reliable guiding star, compass or pilot. Hence, in their opinion, we are like a ship
tossed about by every wind of doctrine, wrecked and
buffeted to pieces upon the rocks of heresy and schism.
We shall see how much there is in this representation later.
For the present, let us examine the claim to definiteness
of teaching in matters of faith and morals with which
Ultramontanists claim to be blessed in their Pontiff.

They have the canonical Scriptures. When Protestants accuse them of rejecting or ignoring the Bible,
Romanists contend that it is either an ignorant or a
malicious misrepresentation. They say that they consider themselves just as much bound as we do to make

its revelations and precepts their rule of life, and cite a decree of the Council of Trent in proof of this. Not only are they obliged to have reference to all the books which we recognize as canonically forming a part of Holy Scripture, but also to those called the apocrypha which we regard as uncanonical. So far, therefore, as the Bible is concerned, Romanists have less of definiteness by fourteen books than Protestants.

The Denominational wing of Protestantism does not acknowledge the binding force of Ecumenical enactments, but Romanists and Anglicans do. We do not, however, make belief in them, except as they pertain to the Creeds, necessary to salvation. Here again Episcopalians have a decided advantage over Ultramontanists; we recognize only four, or at most six, General Councils, because these are all in which the whole of Christendom can be said to have been fairly represented, or that received universal acceptance for their enactments; but there are fourteen or fifteen other synods, chiefly Italian, which are equally binding upon members of the Roman Communion. The fullest and most reliable collection of the Conciliary decrees is said to be a French work in twenty-one large folio volumes. It is perhaps not too much to say that every page of this huge collection contains, on an average, at least some one doctrine upon which salvation is hinged. And, even if every Romanist could read French, and it were possible for him to go through all the ponderous tomes for the purpose of making sure that he observes every precept, the dread of damnation would nevertheless still haunt him, because many of the canons which were doubtless coupled with the usual anathema upon those who should disregard them, have been lost beyond recovery.

But we have really only begun to show the hollowness of Rome's pretension to satisfy our desire for

definiteness. There remain the decrees, which no man
can number, of the two hundred and fifty-six Popes. As
the infallibility of the Bishops of Rome did not suggest
itself to anyone until about fifty of them were in their
graves, and as it was not officially proclaimed to be
a verity before the lapse of more than eighteen hundred
years, no great care was taken to preserve their official
utterances, and hundreds and thousands of these,
unquestionably, have perished. During the Avignon
Schism, which commenced in A. D. 1379 and continued
until A. D. 1409, two and sometimes three rivals disputed the fictitious "chair of St. Peter." It is impossible to decide between their respective claims. Even
the great Councils held at Pisa and Constance could
not do this. Accordingly they deposed all the Popes
in turn, and elected a new one. Now this is the predica-
ment in which Romanists find themselves. They do
not know which of the claimants was the true Pontiff,
and so of course cannot tell whose decrees to obey.
Moreover, as if for the very purpose of creating as
much confusion and uncertainty as possible, Papal
decretals are said to be infallible only when spoken
ex-cathedra. There are no less than eleven theories
as to when the Pope so speaks.

Finally, to cap the climax of Roman indefiniteness,
after the Bible, the Councils, and the Popes, come the
writings of the Saints and Doctors of both the West and
the East. Even the number of these cannot be accu-
rately ascertained without laborious research, and
what remains of their writings could scarcely be thoroughly read in a long lifetime by one who was at liberty to devote himself wholly to the task. It has been
facetiously said of Duns Scotus, one of the Doctors who
flourished in the thirteenth century, that "he wrote
more than ten men could read in a generation and

more than a hundred could understand!" Those whom Romanists reckon as Latin Fathers form two hundred and twenty-two thick volumes; the Greek, one hundred and sixty-seven; total, three hundred and eighty-nine.

The only reply that Ultramontanists can make to our representation of indefiniteness, is that the common people are not expected to concern themselves about all this. They look to the Priests for guidance. But the Priests are not infallible. Besides, in nine cases out of ten, yes, in nine hundred and ninety-nine out of a thousand, they are practically no better off than the Layman, for, if the doctrine of Papal infallibility be true, they do not, and no man can, know the millionth part of that which is necessary to salvation.

Nor is there more of doctrinal stability than of certitude in the Papal Communion. Since the time of the illustrious Bossuet a staple argument of Romanists against Protestants has been based upon the variations of belief among us. There is no denying the fact that there is a great deal of truth in this charge, in so far as the non-liturgical and non-Episcopal bodies of Christians are concerned. But however this may be with respect to them, we are safe in making the assertion that the Anglican Communion, in the course of the last three hundred years, has manifested less of instability than the Church of Rome. In fact, it cannot be shown that we have departed in any important particular from the position which we occupied immediately after the Reformation. Our Prayer Book, which includes the Creeds and Catechism, has remained essentially the same. It certainly will not be pretended that this can be said of the Roman book of worship and standards of doctrine. Some of these have been materially changed within the present generation. For example, thirty years ago "Keenan's Catechism" was

C. A.—5

recognized by the Romanists of Scotland, Ireland, England and America as an eminently orthodox exposition
of the things most surely believed among them. It
was highly recommended by many Bishops, including
Cardinal Manning. All the editions of this popular
manual of instruction and controversy which appeared
before the year 1870, contained the following question
and answer: "Q. Must not Catholics believe the Pope
in himself to be infallible?" "A. This is a Protestant
invention: It is no article of the Catholic Faith: No
Papal decision can bind under pain of heresy, unless it
be received and prescribed by the teaching body; that is,
by the Bishops of the Church." Of course this with all of
the same import has been omitted and exactly the contrary doctrine substituted in the post-Vatican editions.

It is remarkable that the very history of Bossuet's
great work on the *Variations among Protestants*, illustrates how little advantage can be gained for the
Roman Church by the arguments which it contains. It
was approved by one Pope and disapproved by another; applauded by the Archbishop of Rheims, and
condemned by the university of Louvain; censured by
the Sorbonne in the year 1671, and in the next century
declared by the same learned body to be a true exposition of the Catholic Faith. And whatever may have
been the success of this great controversialist against
those who rejected the Papal Communion, it is beyond
denial that, during the controversy concerning Papal
infallibility, he proved at least as formidable against
the Italian section of his own Church.

The bare list of the heretical changes in the Roman
creed is enough to show that the faith of the Anglican
Communion is by comparison like the Rock of Gibraltar beside a sand heap. In A. D. 754 the Church of
Rome introduced the worship of Saints; in A. D. 787

she authorized the use of images and relics in religious worship; in A. D. 1123 she forbade the Clergy to marry; in A. D. 1215 she proclaimed the supremacy of the Pope and the doctrine of transubstantiation; in A. D. 1414 she withheld the Cup from the Laity; in A. D. 1438 the lucrative doctrines of purgatory and indulgences were invented; in A. D. 1439 it was first officially declared that Christ instituted seven Sacraments; in A. D. 1854 the Immaculate Conception of the Blessed Virgin Mary was promulgated; and in A. D. 1870 the infallibility of the Pope was asserted. "Janus" calls attention to the fact that "the very names the Popes assumed or accepted, mark the broad division between the earlier and new Gregorian Papacy. To the end of the twelfth century they had called themselves Vicars of Peter, but since Innocent III. this title was superseded by Vicar of Christ. In fact, the gulf between the position and rights of a Gregory I., and the pretensions and plenary power of a Gregory IX., or between A. D. 600 and A. D. 1230, is as wide as from Peter to Christ." Surely, of all Christians our Roman brethren have the least of doctrinal certitude and stability.

The author of an able article in one of our magazines is right when he says: "There is no royal road to certainty; no organon for the summary extinction of doubts. As much in the sphere of religion, as in the social and political domains, infallibility and perfection are mere dreams of the imagination." And, after all, it is questionable whether the definiteness of which Romanists make so much and have so little, would be desirable, even if it were attainable. "It would," as Bishop Hall says, "have saved the Church much perplexity, much discussion, if she had been able to refer her questions and doubts as to points of faith and morals to an infallible guide and teacher. But she did not. And we can see what she would have lost had she been able to do so. Out of all the discussion, debate, and controversy, in Council and in treatise, the weighing of evidence, the pondering of arguments, through much perplexity, in spite of some mistakes and blunders, the Church advances, like the individual, in the knowledge of God, and in an intelligent apprehension of His mind and will. We gain first a practical working assurance, then a growing certainty. God, who surely hates sin more than He hates error, wills us to be freed from both; but as He has not made sin impossible, so neither error."

But Anglicans are not left quite so hopelessly adrift as Ultramontanists represent. For the Bible is our guiding star, history our compass, and conscience our pilot. If these be faithfully followed there can be no doubt that, though for one reason and another we may now and then deviate more or less widely from the true course, we shall nevertheless drop anchor at the last in the haven where we would be.

2. The development of the doctrine of Papal infallibility is also due in part to the fact that, during the first centuries, the Bishops of Rome, though by no means exempt from error, were singularly free from heresy. The great majority of the Popes held unswervingly to the Faith as it had been handed down to them in succession from the Apostles or defined by the Ecumenical synods. As compared with the other chief Sees, Rome certainly had a well-earned and enviable reputation for orthodoxy. It is therefore not surprising that the impression early began to prevail that the Faith, though it should come to be everywhere else corrupted, would always be kept whole and undefiled at Rome. Some of

the early Fathers who lived at a distance from Rome, gave expression to this conviction. Ultramontanists make a great deal of such well-merited compliments. They see in them an evidence that the infallibility of the Pope was recognized from the beginning. But this is far from having been true. For long centuries, no one dreamed of accounting for the comparative immunity of the Roman Church from error, upon the hypothesis of infallibility. The reason they uniformly gave for her good fortune was the fact that Rome, being the capital of the empire, was the rendezvous of Christians from every part of the world who bore testimony to the Faith, as it was taught in their respective Churches. Hence, if any error of doctrine arose, it was promptly detected and protested against.

The comparative freedom of the Church of Rome from heresy is also accounted for by the fact that she was so far removed from the scenes of battle between the orthodox and heterodox. It is one thing to stand off at a safe distance looking on, and quite another to take part in the fray. The Faith was formulated and defended by the Greeks. The Latins accepted the Creeds and preserved them as they came from the Councils, but they had practically nothing to do with the making of them. If the Bishops of Rome are really the Divinely appointed infallible teachers of mankind in the Christian Faith, the fact that they had so little to do with the formulation and promulgation of the Catholic Creeds, is inexplicable. Nor can the absence of any reference in the universally accepted Creeds to the doctrine in question, be satisfactorily explained upon the Roman hypothesis. If it were correct, after the article on the "One Catholic and Apostolic Church," this would have followed: "And I believe in the Pope of Rome, the successor of Peter and infallible Vicar of Christ."

But though the Popes were really exceptionally orthodox, nevertheless their doctrinal errors were numerous and serious enough clearly to disprove the infallibility which in our generation has been decreed of them. In fact, the dogma will not at all stand the test of history. The occupants of the so-called "chair of Peter" have all along been guilty of as many errors, follies and sins as ordinary mortals would have been under similar circumstances. Even in their doctrinal decisions, which were certainly "ex-cathedra" utterances, they have frequently contradicted each other; and some of them have taught downright heresy.

(1) Innocent I. and Gelasius I., who occupied the Papal chair in the fifth century, dogmatically maintained that infants who died without receiving the Holy Communion, were without doubt damned. The Council of Trent, which assembled A. D. 1545, about a thousand years after their time, with a Pope at its head, rightly condemned and anathematized this monstrous teaching.

(2) Pope Victor, A. D. 192, approved of Montanism, and afterwards condemned it. This heresy consisted in the belief that its promoter, Montanus, by virtue of a revelation, was to introduce a new dispensation of the Spirit superior to that of Christ and his Apostles.

(3) Zephyrinus, A. D. 201–19, and Callistus, A. D. 219–23, two Bishops of Rome, held and taught the Patripassian heresy, which is that God the Father became incarnate, and suffered on the cross.

(4) Marcellinus, A. D. 296–303, was an idolater. He entered the temple of Vesta and offered incense to that goddess. Romanists excuse him on the ground of intimidation and human infirmity. To this Protestants reply that if this Pope had been really the Vicar of Christ, he might have died, but could not have apostatized.

(5) Liberius, A. D. 352, for the sake of being recalled from exile, and reinstated in his See, consented to the condemnation of Athanasius, and openly professed Arianism. This heresy consisted in the denial of the Divinity of Christ. The apostasy of Liberius sufficed, through the whole of the Middle Ages, for a proof that Popes as well as other people could fall into heresy.

(6) Zosimus, A. D. 417, at first indorsed as orthodox Pelagius and Celestius, who denied the fall and the necessity of Divine help in order to attain salvation. Afterwards Augustine and the African Bishops compelled Zosimus to follow the example of his predecessor, Innocent I., in condemning these heretics.

(7) Gregory I., A. D. 540–604, condemned as antichrist anyone who assumed the title Universal Bishop; Boniface III., A. D. 607, obtained this title from the parricide Emperor, Phocas.

(8) Pelagius, in the sixth century, and Nicholas, in the ninth, made contradictory decisions upon the form of words necessary to valid Baptism. The earlier Pope declared that it is essential that the Sacrament should be administed in the name of the Father and of the Son and of the Holy Ghost; and the later, that in the name of Christ alone is sufficient.

(9) Stephen, about the year A. D. 750, officially declared that a marriage with a slave girl might be dissolved and another contracted. In this he contradicted his predecessors, who had uniformly decreed such marriages indissoluble.

(10) In A. D. 826, the Bishops assembled in synod at Paris spoke without hesitation of the "absurdities" of Pope Adrian, who, they said, had commanded an heretical worship of images.

(11) Adrian II., A. D. 867–72, declared civil marriages valid; Pius VII., A. D. 1800–23, condemned them.

(12) Celestine III., A. D. 1191, pronounced the marriage tie broken when either party became heretical. Innocent III., A. D. 1198, annulled this decree, and Adrian VI., A. D. 1522, declared that it was a pernicious heresy.

(13) Stephen VI., A. D. 885, caused the body of Formosus to be disentombed, clothed with Pontifical robes, and cast into the Tiber, after he had cut off from it the fingers with which he had given the benediction, pronouncing him perjured and illegitimate. Stephen himself was afterwards imprisoned by the people, poisoned and strangled. His successor restored the body of Formosus to Christian burial, and, at a council presided over by John IX., A. D. 898, the Pontificate of Formosus was declared valid and all his acts confirmed.

(14) The doctrine that Christ's body is sensibly touched by the hands and broken by the teeth, in the Eucharist—an error rejected by the whole Church—was affirmed by Nicholas II., at the Synod of Rome, in A. D. 1059.

(15) Paschal II., A. D. 1088-99, and Eugenius III., A. D. 1145-52, authorized dueling; Julius II., A. D. 1509, and Pius IV., A. D. 1560, forbade it.

(16) Eugenius IV., A. D. 1383-1447, approved the Council of Basle and the restoration of the Chalice to the Bohemian Church; Pius II., A. D. 1458, revoked this concession.

(17) Coming down to the time when the doctrine of Papal infallibility had been quite fully developed, and had become the shibboleth of the Jesuits and of the dominant school in the Roman Communion, we have the amusing experience of Sixtus V., A. D. 1585-90, in connection with the issue of his revised edition of the Latin translation of the Holy Scriptures. Imagining that the immunity from error which he believed he had inherited as Pope from St. Peter, would enable him to produce an abso-

lutely correct rendering, he undertook, with much enthusiasm, the task of doing the world this invaluable
service. In due time his revision of the Latin Bible
came forth from the press with a great flourish of
trumpets. The bull by which it was introduced, declared
that, inasmuch as it had been corrected from beginning
to end by his own infallible hand, it was absolutely faultless, and must supersede all imperfect renderings as rapidly as copies could be supplied, and that in reprints
the greatest care must be taken to prevent the slightest
deviation from the edition bearing his *imprimatur.*
Printers and editors who should be either so careless or
presumptuous as to change so much as a syllable,
were then and there excommunicated. Surely no one
will pretend that the Pontiff was not speaking *ex-cathedra* when he issued his version of the Holy Scriptures,
and anathematized all who would not recognize and admit its absolute perfection. In view of all this, the surprise and chagrin of His Holiness may be imagined
when the scholars about his court represented that,
after a somewhat hasty examination of his work, they
felt obliged to call his attention to more than two
thousand glaring errors which, upon reference to the
compositor's copy, were found to be in his handwriting,
and to say that, unless the whole edition could be called
in and suppressed, it would undoubtedly prove fatal to
the doctrine of Papal infallibility. Of course some way
out of the difficulty had to be found. Among the suggested schemes, the one adopted was to ask for the return of the copies which had been sent out, upon the
ground of the discovery of some mistakes which had
crept in through the carelessness of the printers. This
apology appeared in the Pope's preface to the new
edition, in which the errors of this infallible successor of
St. Peter were corrected. That Sixtus was guilty of the

multitudinous inaccuracies and base deceit of which we have spoken, we know on the authority of no less a personage than the learned Bellarmine, upon whom the Pope chiefly relied for extrication from the embarrassing situation in which he found himself. In his autobiography the great Cardinal congratulates himself on having thus requited the Pontiff with good for evil; for he had put Bellarmine's work concerning controversies on the Index, because he had not maintained the direct, but only the indirect, dominion of the Pope over the whole world. "And now," says one of the Roman Catholic authors of the Pope and the Council, "followed a fresh mishap. The autobiography, which was kept in the archives of the Roman Jesuits, got known in Rome through several transcripts. Hereupon Cardinal Azzolini urged that, as Bellarmine had insulted three Popes and exhibited two as liars, namely, Gregory XIV., and Clement VIII., his work should be suppressed and burnt, and the strictest secrecy inculcated about it." I have dwelt somewhat at length upon this instance of Papal fallibility, because it seems to me that in itself it is sufficient to explode the Vatican dogma of infallibility.

(18) But this unfortunate Bible, which as we have seen had already scored above two thousand points against the Papal doctrine, was destined to make still another. For in his bull announcing its publication, Sixtus strongly recommended the general study of the Holy Scriptures; but Pius VII., A. D. 1800, severely condemns the reading of them by any except the Clergy.

(19) Perhaps, after all, nothing can show the absurdity of the Papal claims to infallibility quite so well as the spuriousness of the relics, which, from time to time, the Popes, directly or indirectly, pronounced to be genuine. Even the gravest enumeration of those which

have been preserved at Rome, sounds like profane jesting. Among them are:

"The sponge tinged with the blood of our Lord.

"The spearhead which pierced His side.

"The pillar at which He was scourged.

"Thorns from His crown.

"Nails from His cross.

"The Infant Saviour's cradle.

"The table at which the Last Supper was eaten.

"The cloth with which Christ wiped His disciples' feet.

"Blood from Christ's side and the drops which fell from His brow." Among miscellaneous treasures of the same sort are showed:

"A stone cast at St. Stephen.

"Part of Aaron's rod.

"Manna from the wilderness.

"The espousal ring of the Blessed Virgin.

"A piece of money received by Judas." Absurd as all this is, it is really no more so than the relics of which an extended account is given in the New York "Times" of Friday, September 20, 1895. Under the head-line "Relics of Many Saints" are described the achievements of a Brooklyn lady, who organized a pilgrimage to Lourdes, where, at the famous grotto of Massavievelle, the Virgin Mary is believed by Romanists to have revealed herself repeatedly to a peasant girl in A. D. 1858. The spot at which this occurred is now resorted to by multitudes of pilgrims from all parts of the world. It is marked by a large Church, consecrated A. D. 1876 in the presence of thirty-five Cardinals and other high representatives of the Pope. The Holy Father was so much pleased with the number and zeal of the American pilgrims that he favored their fair leader with a "reliquary." "In appearance," says the "Times" correspondent, "it is a silver frame, measuring five or six

inches from top to bottom. In the oval opening are
exposed the relics, each very tiny and marked with its
Latin name. The back of the oval can be removed, and
underneath it is the seal of the Holy See, firmly affixed
in red wax, to show that the contents remain intact as
first arranged. A paper accompanies the reliquary,
giving the names of the relics and vouching for their
genuineness. This is the list given in order:

"Veil of the Blessed Virgin.

"Cloak of St. Joseph.

"Bone of St. Peter and St. Paul.

"Bone of St. John and St. Andrew.

"Bone of St. Philip Neri.

"Bone of St. Augustine.

"Bone of St. Dominick.

"Bone of St. Francis de Sales.

"Bone of St. Alphonsus.

"Habit of St. Francis of Assisi. "Other valuable
relics which were given to ———— in Rome were:

"A piece of the true cross.

"A piece of thorn from the crown of thorns.

"A piece of the Saviour's winding sheet.

"A bone of St. Francis Assisi.

"A bone of St. Clair of Assisi.

"A relic of the habit of St. Cecilia. The first three
were in one reliquary. The piece of the cross is in the
form of a tiny cross, and the other relics are on either
side below it. The two bone relics are in still another
reliquary, and the piece of the habit of St. Cecilia on a
sheet of paper and stamped with a seal. Proper papers
accompanied them all."

(20) But passing over the above mentioned relics we
fix upon the famous house of the Blessed Virgin in Loretto, because, upon the whole, it may fairly be said to
put the finishing touches to this class of Roman absurd-

ities. In order to escape the accusation of drawing upon my imagination, I shall give the story in the words of Professor Salmon, whose reputation for learning and candor will shield him from suspicion. "You have all, I dare say, heard the story of the holy house at Loretto. The Virgin Mary's house at Nazareth, when the land fell into the possession of unbelievers, and worshipers could no longer resort to it, was carried by the angels across the seas on the 9th of May, 1291—for I like to be exact—and, after taking three temporary resting places, finally settled down at Loretto in the year 1295. There, on the credit of so great a miracle, it attracted many pilgrims, and was by them enriched with abundant gifts. *Several Popes pledged their credit to the proof of the story*, and rewarded pious visitors with indulgences. I possess a history of the holy house, written by Tursellinus, a Jesuit, and printed at Loretto itself in 1837, from which I find that the story is proved by such irrefragable evidence that no one can doubt it who is not prepared to deny the power and Providence of God, and to remove all faith in the testimony of man. Mr. Ffoulkes, whose turn of mind was such that he seemed to find it as hard as the holy house itself to find a resting place, either among Protestants or Roman Catholics, neither accepted this story without inquiry, as might a thorough-going Roman Catholic, nor rejected it without inquiry, as might a thorough-going Protestant. He took the trouble of going both to Loretto and to Nazareth, and making laborious investigations on the spot; and the result of his inquiry was, that he came back thoroughly convinced of the fictitious character of the Santa Casa *notwithstanding the privileges bestowed by so many Popes*."

(21) In the eighth century, Virgil, Bishop of Salzburg, was condemned by Pope Zachary, because he maintained

the spherical form of the earth, and the existence of the
antipodes; he is now a saint of the Roman calendar.
In the thirteenth century, Roger Bacon was imprisoned
as an astrologer, and dealer in unlawful arts; his appeal to Nicholas IV. only procured him a closer captivity. A hundred years later it was still the same. Several Popes and their representatives in the infamous
Inquisition condemned Galileo's system of astronomy,
and in contradiction to it asserted that the sun goes
round the world every twenty-four hours. Every good
Roman Catholic was forbidden even to read a book
which taught the mobility of the earth. The poor
astronomer escaped the stake by confessing, through
extreme fear of a horrible death, what he never believed,
that the Church was right and he wrong. It is needless
to say that the Popes and Doctors have long since
abandoned the ground which their predecessors occupied, and have come over to Galileo's way of thinking.
Kepler would have fared no better than his friend
Galileo, had he lived at Pisa instead of Gratz; nor
Newton, if his lot had not been fortunately cast in England, and a little too late for such interference.

(22) Adrian I., A. D., 772-95, sent a long letter to
the Council in defense of the use of images. It contains
the following story in support of his argument: Constantine was at first a persecutor of the Christians, and
put many of them to death—among others his own wife
—for refusing to sacrifice to the gods of Rome. He
was struck with leprosy, and, in order to effect a cure, it
was prescribed that he should bathe in infant's blood.
The mothers of the children who were destined to fur-
nish this very uninviting bath, however, prevailed on
him by their tears to give up the idea, and he was
warned in a heavenly vision by St. Peter and St. Paul
to apply to the Bishop of Rome, Sylvester, who had

been driven by the persecution to take refuge on Mount Soracte. Constantine accordingly sent for Sylvester, found him as described, and in short carried out the whole programme of the dream with the happy result of a complete cure. He then asked, who those gods, Peter and Paul, might be. Sylvester replied, they were not gods, but the servants of Christ. Constantine then asked, whether there were any images of them preserved; and when the Pope sent for paintings of the two Apostles, and showed them, the emperor at once recognized them as the persons who had appeared to him in the vision. This was one of Pope Adrian's authorities for the use of images. Now it is to be observed that Sylvester was not Pope until the persecution was ended; that Constantine never persecuted in Italy; that, on the contrary, his coming to Italy put a stop to the persecution; that he was not baptized by Sylvester, nor baptized at all until his last illness, and then at Nicomedia, most probably by Eusebius; that there is no notice in history of his ever having been afflicted by leprosy, and it is most incredible that he ever was. The infallibility of Adrian, which ought to be the voucher for this story, involves here the veracity of the two Apostles, who are both made to assert in the vision what was not true. The ridiculous legend was probably taken from some spurious biography of the Popes. Did Adrian know the worth of his authority or not? The answer either way is fatal to the dogma of Papal Infallibility.

(23) A number of the Popes have proved themselves incompetent to distinguish spurious from genuine documents. Adrian I. and others cited the donation of Constantine; Nicholas I. the acts of the apocryphal Council of Sinuessa; and his successors for ages the decretal letters. The work of Gratian, which was corrected by a

commission appointed by Pius IV., and published with
confirmation by Gregory XIII., is full of coarse and
stupid forgeries, which needed no supernatural gift to
detect. Sometimes they mistook one writing for another,
as when Zosimus and others produced the Sardican
canons for the Nicene, which Baronius, Bellarmine, and
others ascribe to ignorance, as a less injurious imputa-
tion than fraud. Innocent III. quoted for Holy Scripture a passage written by Augustine. Books to which
the Papal sanction is pledged as fully as possible contain undeniable misstatements. Thus the Roman Catechism, after describing the ceremonies used in Baptism,
such as the use of salt and the chrism, adds that they
were instituted by the Holy Apostles.

(24) But the case of Pope Honorius, A. D. 625–38, is
generally regarded as affording the most conclusive and
unanswerable historical evidence against this decree of
the Vatican Council. The facts which historians, having access to orginal sources of information, tell us with
practical unanimity are the following: (1) Honorius
taught in two *ex-cathedra* letters the Monothelite
heresy, that is, that the human will was wanting in
Christ, and that therefore He was wholly possessed and
influenced by the Divine will. (2) The doctrine, which
was a denial of our Lord's perfect manhood, was condemned; and Pope Honorius, as one of the chief heresiarchs, was excommunicated by the generally accepted
sixth Ecumenical Council assembled at Constantinople in
A. D. 680. "Not a single voice was raised in his defense.
Even the Papal Legates had nothing to say." The
anathema which accompanied the excommunication
of the Pontiff, was repeated at the seventh and eighth
Councils, which were held respectively in A. D. 787,
and A. D. 869. (3) All the successors of Honorius down
to the eleventh century, included him in the eternal

anathema which they pronounced upon the authors and abettors of the Monothelite heresy. They undertook to see that he was condemned in the West as well as throughout the East and that his name was struck out of the Liturgy. Pope Leo II., in a letter to the emperor, strongly confirmed the decree of the Council, and denounced his predecessor Honorius as one who endeavored by profane treason to overthrow the immaculate Faith of the Roman Church. The same Pope says, in a letter to the Spanish Bishops: "With eternal damnation have we punished Theodore, Cyrus, Sergius, together with Honorius, who did not extinguish at the very beginning the flame of heretical doctrine." Thus, after A. D. 680, for three hundred years the Popes formally and publicly recognized the right of General Councils to condemn and depose any of them that might fall into error of doctrine. There is, therefore, no getting around the fact that during the first one thousand years both Councils and Popes believed in the fallibility of the Bishops of Rome, in flat contradiction to the dogma promulgated at the Vatican in A. D. 1870. As was said in one of the many able protests by Romanists against the Scheme of the Pope and the Jesuits: "This one fact, that a Great Council, universally received afterwards without hesitation throughout the Church, and presided over by Papal legates, pronounced the dogmatic decision of a Pope heretical, and anathematized him by name as a heretic, is a proof, clear as the sun at noonday, that the notion of any peculiar enlightenment or inerrancy of the Popes was then utterly unknown to the whole Church."

(25) Finally, we have what in itself should settle the question, namely, the confession of three of the Popes. John XXII., A. D. 1316–34, and Gregory XI., A. D. 1370–78, when dying, confessed their liability to error, and submitted all their statements, whether spoken or written,

C. A.—6

to the judgment of the Church. Pius IV., A. D. 1559–65, declared, in consistory, that he himself, like his predecessors, was fallible. Perhaps the most remarkable case was that of Adrian VI., A. D. 1522–23, who, while he was a professor at Louvain, maintained that the Pope might err in questions of faith, and support heresy by decisions and decretal letters. This is his declaration: "It is certain that the Pope can err even in matters of faith, asserting heresy in his determination or decree; for many of the Roman Pontiffs were heretics." He did not retract these words after becoming Pope, but reprinted them at Rome in the year 1522. There were certain Cardinals to whom this was a "hard saying," and, as the book had been published and republished in Rome itself, and had become extremely popular, they urged the Pope to reconsider his judgment. This he nobly refused to do. "His opinion," he said, "had always been this in the case of other Popes, and he could not hold the contrary in his own case."

My chief authorities for the above twenty-five paragraphs, any one of which is sufficient to disprove the doctrine of Papal Infallibility, are Salmon, Coxe, Robins, Hussey, Robertson, Littledale, Schaff, Gore, Gladstone, Puller, Von Döllinger, Hefele, and the unknown brilliant author of the "Pretended Speech of a Bishop in the Council."* If the reader desires to pursue the subject further, he will find all that I have said in expanded form in the works of these unexceptionable authors, and much more of the same tenor which I am obliged to pass over for the want of space.

* Before the Vatican Council there was a large school of "Liberal Catholics," composed chiefly of Frenchmen, Germans and Americans, many of whom were scholars of the first rank, who expressed their opinions freely about the grosser errors and corruptions of their Church and the schemes of their bitter enemies, the Jesuits, for the aggrandizement of the Pope and their order. Our quotations from Roman authorities are chiefly from the writings of representatives of this School.

II.

JURISDICTION OF THE POPE.

INNOCENT III., A. D. 1198–1216, wrote to the Patriarch of Constantinople that "Christ has committed the whole world to the government of the Popes." In the famous Bull, *Unam Sanctam*, promulgated about the year 1300, by Pope Boniface VIII., occurs this passage: "We therefore declare, assert, and define that for every human creature it is altogether necessary to salvation that he be subject to the Roman Pontiff." The closing words of the third chapter of the dogmatic decrees of the Vatican Council, of A. D. 1870, are to the same effect: "If, then, any shall say that the Roman Pontiff has the office merely of inspection or direction, and not full and supreme power of jurisdiction over the universal Church, not only in things which belong to faith and morals, but also in those which relate to the discipline and government of the Church spread throughout the world, or assert that he possesses merely the principal part, and not all the fullness of this supreme power, or that this power which he enjoys is not ordinary and immediate, both over each and all the Churches, and over each and all the pastors and the faithful, let him be anathema."

As the interpretation which Protestants put upon the above quotations is as a rule warmly repudiated by American Roman Catholics, it will be well to quote two or three passages from their own highest authorities. "No man can deny," says Archbishop Kenrick, in his

(83)

undelivered speech at the Vatican Council, "that the purpose of Boniface in that bull was to claim for himself temporal power, and to propound this opinion to the faithful, to be held under pain of damnation." Turrecremata says that "the power of the keys committed to the Pope reaches all places, persons, and cases, and that in the authority of his jurisdiction he is superior to all the remainder of the Church;" Becan, that "the Pope has the same power of making Ecclesiastical laws, to bind the whole Church, as a secular prince for a kingdom or empire;" De Castro, that "the denial of the Papal supremacy has been the great source of heresies;" Duval, that "the power of Bishops and Patriarchs in the Church is derived from the supreme monarch, the Vicar of Christ, just as the great offices in France are held of the king;" Bellarmine, that "no man can have Christ for his Master, who is not a subject of the Pope." Cardinal Manning, speaking in the Pope's name, says: "I claim to be the supreme judge and director of the consciences of men; of the peasant that tills the field, and the prince that sits on the throne; of the household that lives in the shade of privacy, and the legislature that makes laws for kingdoms—I am the sole last supreme judge of what is right and wrong." The following is from the Pope's official organ, the *Civilita Cattolica*, of March 18, 1871: "The Pope is the supreme judge of the law of the land. In him, the two powers, the spiritual and the secular, meet as in their apex; for he is the Vicegerent of Christ, who is not only a Priest forever, but also King of kings and Lord of lords. The Pope, by virtue of his high dignity, is at the summit of both powers." Pope Innocent III. described himself as "the Vicar of Jesus Christ, the successor of Peter, the anointed of the Lord, the God of Pharaoh, short of God, beyond man, less than God, greater than man, who judges all men, and is judged by no man."

Of course, if the Popes were really all this, no man who has reference to the will of God in the choice of a Church, can either become or remain a member of any branch of the Anglican Communion, because the Churches of which it is composed, not being in subjection to the Bishop of Rome, would form no part of the Catholic and Apostolic Church. Episcopalians contend, however, that neither Boniface VIII., nor any one of his predecessors or successors, was endowed with infallibility, and that the Episcopal Church, by proofs drawn from both Holy Scripture and Ecclesiastical History, can be shown to be not a whit less Catholic because of her independence of Papal government. Which of the parties in this contention is right? This is a question which we shall now proceed to answer. Though we shall confine ourselves as much as possible to the dispute concerning the jurisdiction of the Pope, it will be clearly impossible to lose sight altogether of the controversy about his infallibility. For in showing that the universal authority claimed by him has no foundation in Scripture or history, we necessarily undermine his pretension to exemption from error.

Romanists base the Papal claim to universal dominion upon the following texts: "Thou art Peter, and upon this rock I will build my Church, and the gates of hell shall not prevail against it. And I will give unto thee the keys of the Kingdom of Heaven: and whatsoever thou shalt bind on earth shalt be bound in heaven; and whatsoever thou shalt loose on earth shall be loosed in heaven." (St. Matthew, 16:18-19). "I have prayed for thee that thy faith fail not, and when thou

art converted, strengthen thy brethren." (St. Luke,
22:32.) "Feed my sheep." (St. John, 21:17.)

From these texts it is argued that St. Peter was constituted prince of the Apostles and Vicar of Christ; "that
all the power and office that was communicable from his
Lord to him who should stand in His place as the head
and center of the Apostles, was communicated to Peter,
and to him was given the undivided pastoral care of the
whole flock upon earth." This conclusion reached, it is
further claimed that the successors of St. Peter in the
See of Rome are Christ's sole representatives in the
world, and that there can be no such thing as a true
Church unless it be presided over by the Pope and in
communion with him.

Learned Anglicans have repeatedly shown, by Scriptural and historical arguments, which the Romanists
have never been able to answer, that the texts referred
to do not give the slightest support to these conclusions,
and have proved that the Church is built on the foundation of the Apostles and Prophets, not of St. Peter alone;
Jesus Christ Himself, not St. Peter, being the chief corner-
stone. There is no intimation in the New Testament that
St. Peter based any claims to authority upon Christ's
words; nor is there one recorded instance of his exercis-
ing any primacy or presidency, or even claiming it. The
most that can with any show of reason be inferred from
the texts under consideration, is a kind of personal
leadership among the Apostles. But granting, for the
sake of argument, that he was distinguished by such
primacy, there is not the slightest ground for the claim
that his successors in the See of Rome were to enjoy a
similar distinction. The words of Bishop Barrow are
true: "In all Divine Revelation the Bishop of Rome is
not so much as once mentioned, either by name, or by
character, or by probable intimation."

The great majority of the Fathers and Doctors understood the chief of these texts, "Thou art Peter, and upon this rock I will build my Church," to refer to St. Peter's confession of Christ's Divinity. The venerable and learned Roman Catholic Archbishop of St. Louis, in his famous discourse against the proposition to declare the Pope infallible, contends that, because the creed of Pope Pius IV. makes it obligatory upon them to interpret the Holy Scriptures according to the unanimous consent of the Fathers, Roman Catholics cannot make good their claim of supremacy for St. Peter. "If we are bound," says he, "to follow the great number of the Fathers in this matter, then we must hold for certain that the word Peter means, not Peter professing the Faith, but the Faith professed by Peter. In a remarkable pamphlet, printed in the fac-simile of the manuscript, and presented to the fathers almost two months ago, we find five different interpretations of the word 'rock,' in the place cited.

"The first of these declares that the Church was built on Peter; and this interpretation is followed by seventeen fathers, among them, by Jerome, and Cyril of Alexandria. The second interpretation understands from these words, 'On this rock will I build my Church,' that the Church was built on all the Apostles, whom Peter represented by virtue of the primacy. And this opinion is followed by eight fathers—among them, Origen, Cyprian, Theodoret. The third interpretation asserts that the words, 'On this rock,' are to be understood of the faith which Peter had professed—that this faith, this profession of faith, by which we believe Christ to be the Son of the living God, is the everlasting and immovable foundation of the Church. This interpretation is the weightiest of all, since it is followed by fifty-four Fathers and Doctors; among them, from the

East, are Gregory of Nyssa, Chrysostom, Theophylact; from the West, Hilary, Ambrose, Leo the Great; from Africa, Augustine. The fourth interpretation declares that the words, 'On this rock,' are to be understood of that rock which Peter had confessed, that is, Christ— that the Church was built upon Christ. This interpretation is followed by sixteen Fathers and Doctors. The fifth interpretation of the Fathers understands by the name of the rock, the faithful themselves, who, believing Christ to be the Son of God, are constituted living stones out of which the Church is built."

"I suppose," says Professor Salmon, "there is no text on which the Fathers have given greater variety of interpretation than 'Thou art Peter;' and we have to go down far indeed before we find one who discovered the Bishop of Rome in it."

In their Collect for the Vigil of St. Peter and St. Paul, Romanists are taught to pray: "Grant, we beseech Thee, Almighty God, that thou wouldst not suffer us, whom Thou hast established on the Rock of the Apostolic Confession, to be shaken by any disturbances."

The remaining part of the text contains, indeed, a notable promise, and, if it were all that our Lord had said upon the subject, the supremacy of St. Peter over the rest of the Apostles could hardly be questioned. "I will give unto thee the keys of the Kingdom of Heaven; and whatsoever thou shalt bind on earth shall be bound in heaven; and whatsoever thou shalt loose on earth shall be loosed in heaven."

But what was here promised before the Crucifixion to one Apostle, was, after the Resurrection, actually bestowed upon each of them, without distinction, as a part of their common commission. "Then said Jesus unto them again, Peace be unto you: as my Father hath sent me, even so send I you. And when He had said this He breathed on them, and saith unto them, Receive ye the Holy Ghost: ,Whosesoever sins ye remit, they are remitted unto them, and whosesoever sins ye retain, they are retained." By interpreting these texts in the light of each other, it is clear that the promise was made to St. Peter as the representative of his fellow Apostles. This was the view of the great St. Augustine, Bishop of Hippo, A. D. 391–430. He says: "Peter, in many places of the Scriptures, appears as representing the Church, but especially where it is said of him, 'I will give you the keys.' Has Peter received these keys, and has not Paul received them? Has Peter received them, and not James and John, and the rest of the Apostles?"

The context shows how St. Peter came to be representatively addressed. It was not because he was to be the first Bishop of Rome, St. Paul, or more probably Linus, was this, but because he was the first to give expression to the growing conviction among the twelve that Jesus was none other than the promised Messiah, the Divine Saviour of the world. As he was the spokesman for the rest in this glorious confession, it was natural that they should through him receive the promise of stewardship—that is what the keys signify —in the Church or Kingdom which Christ would found on the rock of faith in His Divinity. "I do not think," says Canon Gore, "we can make it too plain how exclusively Western in growth is the Papal claim, as Rome understands it. Thus it does not appear that a single Greek Father of the first six centuries recognizes the connection, which Rome supposes to exist, between the promise to St. Peter and the position of the Pope. 'In the writings of the Greek Doctors,' says 'Janus,' 'Eusebius, St. Athanasius, St. Basil the Great, the two Gregories, and St. Epiphanius, there is not one word of any prerogatives of the Roman Bishop. The most copious of the Greek Fathers, St. Chrysostom, is wholly silent on the subject.' Universal negatives are somewhat dangerous, but I do not think that this can be disputed."

But owing to the fact that the promise was made through St. Peter, and because we see in the Acts of the Apostles that he was the first to exercise the power of the keys by opening the door of the Church to both the Jewish and Gentile world, Anglican scholars, following the early Christian writers, very generally grant that Christ may have intended to reward him for his courageous avowal, by making him the first among his equals, that is to say, the chairman or official head of his brethren. There is no serious dispute between Romanists and Anglicans on this point. We part company, however, when they pretend, upon the ground of the primacy, which we are willing to admit, that St. Peter was the Vicar of the ascended Master to the Apostolic Church, and that, therefore, his successors in the See of Rome are Divinely commissioned to lord it over the rest of Christendom.

Moreover, it has been settled almost conclusively that the Roman Succession is due quite as much to St. Paul as to St. Peter and that the Church of Rome does not owe her origin, except perhaps indirectly, to the latter of these Apostles, and that he was not the first resident Bishop of "the Eternal City." Such authors as Professor Salmon on the one side and Dr. Döllinger on the other substantially agree in this conclusion. The former of these great authorities in his chapter on "Peter's Alleged Roman Episcopate," says: "I am justified in thinking that candid inquirers need not differ very much on these questions, because I find that the results at which I had arrived independently are, on several points, in agreement with those obtained by von Döllinger in his *First Age of the Church*, a book published while he was still in full communion with the Church of Rome, and was regarded as its ablest champion." Scaliger, the greatest scholar of the sixteenth century, says that "no moderately learned man can believe Peter's journey to Rome, his session for twenty-five years, or his capital punishment there." Ranke says cautiously and truly: "Historical criticism has shown that it is a matter of doubt whether the Apostle ever was at Rome at all." But however this may be, Wycliffe expressed the whole truth of the matter in a few words when he said: "As it does not follow, because Peter was personally called 'Satan' by our Lord, that, therefore, he was made lower than any of the Apostles, so it does not follow, because certain privileges were given him personally in the words: 'Thou art Peter,' that, therefore, he was made Pope and head of the Church after our Lord's ascension."

According to the understanding of the Fathers, the second text relied upon by Romanists, "I have prayed for thee that thy faith fail not, and when thou art converted strengthen thy brethren," was intended to warn St. Peter of his pitiable weakness which manifested itself in the base denials of his Lord recorded in the same chapter, and to prevent him from falling away altogether. It is claimed by Roman divines that this prayer and precept of our Lord extends to all the Bishops of Rome, as St. Peter's successors, and that in speaking to St. Peter our Lord spoke to them. "Would they," asks Dr. Wordsworth, late Bishop of Lincoln, "be willing to complete the parallel and say that the Bishops of Rome especially need prayer because they deny Christ? Let them not take a part of it and deny the rest."

The third text, "Feed my sheep," was regarded as Christ's gracious absolution of Peter upon his sorrowful repentance, and the restoration of him to the Apostolic office which had been forfeited. True, our Lord, in commanding St. Peter to feed his sheep, uses, as Roman Catholic controversialists point out, a word which conveys the idea of ruling as well as feeding. But if they argue from this that to St. Peter alone was given the fullness of authority to feed the lambs and the sheep—the whole flock of Christ—how will they explain St. Paul's injunction to the elders of Ephesus, "Feed the Church of God?" It is the same Greek word. Manifestly the Roman argument, if consistently adhered to, would prove that the Ephesian elders and their successors were, by the use of this word, all created universal Popes. "Indeed, St. Paul expressly tells them that the Holy Ghost has made them overseers to all the flock, which is more than the Lord said to St. Peter himself." St. Peter received no more power from Christ than the other Apostles, for nothing was said to him which was not also said to them. All the Apostles were therefore equal to St. Peter in power.

An exhaustive consideration of all the passages of Scripture which are irreconcilable with the Papal pretensions would be wearisome. It is therefore fortunate that the texts, as a rule, are so clear and conclusive that only a few need to be cited or alluded to, with but little comment. Upon two or three occasions our Lord refused to grant the request of His disciples to indicate which of them was to be chief. The last was on the night before His Crucifixion. His refusals will at once be seen to be unaccountable upon the Roman hypothesis. For, surely, if that were correct, the supremacy of

St. Peter would have been clearly proclaimed and recognized.

Again, the claim of Ultramontanists cannot be reconciled with the fact that St. Paul received neither his commission as an Apostle nor his doctrine from St. Peter individually, or from the college of Apostles, and that yet they gave him the right hand of fellowship and intrusted him with the leadership in the evangelization of the Gentiles. As he himself tells us, he labored more abundantly than any of his colleagues, and this he did quite independently of St. Peter. "This fact," says one, "seems to have been Divinely intended to bar, from the very first, the Papal claim as false and untenable."

When St. Peter dissembled with the Jews, St. Paul not only rebuked him, but rebuked him publicly, showing that if St. Paul was not his superior, he was at least his equal.

After Samaria had received the gospel from Philip, the Deacon, and converts needed Confirmation, and the subject came before the Apostles, did St. Peter direct who should perform the duty? On the contrary, the Apostles sent him, together with St. John; and Christ says, "A servant is not greater than his lord; nor he that is sent greater than he that sent him."

St. Paul speaks of: "That which comes upon me daily, the care of all the Churches." How fortunate it would have been for the Roman claims if St. Peter had said this of himself.

"The same Apostle Paul," says a Roman Catholic writer, "enumerating the offices of the Church, mentions Apostles, Prophets, Evangelists, pastors and teachers. Is it credible that St. Paul, the great teacher of the Gentiles, would have left out the greatest of all the offices, the Papacy, if the Papacy had been founded by

Divine institution? It seems to me that this omission would have been no more possible than a history of the Vatican Council that should make no mention of His Holiness, Pius IX."

"But," says the same author, "the thing which astounds me beyond all expression is the silence of St. Peter himself. If he had been what we say—the Vicar of Christ upon earth—he must have known it. If he knew it, how does it happen that he never once, not one solitary time, acted as Pope? He might have done it on the Day of Pentecost, when he pronounced his first discourse; but he did not. He might have done it at Antioch; but he did not. He might have done it at the Council of Jerusalem; but he did not. He might have done it in his two epistles to the Churches; but he did not. Can you imagine such a Pope as this?"

Of St. Paul it is said that to him the uncircumcision were committed; that is, all but Jews were put under his headship. Hence, it is clear that if we Gentiles have a spiritual monarch, he is St. Paul, not St. Peter. [Please read Galatians II: 7-9.]

The claims of Rome respecting St. Peter's superiority will appear in their right light if, as Dr. Littledale suggests, we ask these questions: Suppose the rest of the Apostles decided one way and St. Peter separately decided the other way, which decision would stand? When St. Paul withstood St. Peter to the face, which of the two actually yielded? See Galatians II: 11-14.

The silence of our Lord is hard to explain on the Roman hypothesis. As a candid author of the Roman Communion observes: "Not only is Christ silent upon this point, but He has so little thought of giving the Church a chief, that when He is promising thrones to His Apostles, to judge the twelve tribes of Israel, He promises twelve of them, without saying that one is to be higher than the rest, and is to belong to Peter. Surely, if he had wished Peter to occupy a throne that should overshadow the rest, He would have said so. What must we infer from this silence? Logic tells us: Christ did not intend to make Peter the chief of the Apostolic college."

The following golden words of a Franciscan monk show how utterly out of accord the Papal claim to sovereignty is, with not only the letter but the spirit of the New Testament: "If the Bishop of Rome possessed a plenitude of power, such as the Popes falsely lay claim to, and such as many, through mistake, or in the spirit of adulation, concede to them, all men would be slaves; and this is plainly contrary to the liberty of the Gospel law."

The hollowness of the Papal pretensions to supreme authority appears also from the history of the early Ecclesiastical Councils. If the Bishops of Rome were really by Divine appointment and inspiration the universal sovereigns and unerring guides of Christendom, it is impossible to explain the obscure and subordinate position which some of them occupied in these deliberative assemblies and the condemnation which was passed upon others. Indeed, upon the Ultramontane hypothesis, it is difficult to account for the great Councils at all. If the infallibility of the Bishop of Rome had been recognized during the Conciliary period which embraces the five hundred years from the fourth to the ninth centuries, there would have been no need of the expense and trouble of bringing a host of fallible Bishops from distant parts to pass upon matters that might have been disposed of by a stroke of the Pope's pen. Under such circumstances, the only imaginable reasons for a Council would have been to give an opportunity of explaining to the heads of Dioceses, Provinces, and Patriarchates the decrees upon which His Holiness had resolved, and to add dignity and solemnity to the occasion of their promulgation. But if these had been the ends in view, the Popes would have called each of the Councils which are recognized by the Greek and Latin Churches as Ecumenical, and their resolutions or decrees, passed not infrequently after many months of debate, would have served no purpose but to provide the delegates with an exciting pastime. At best their action could have had no other effect than that of a recommendation to the Pope, whose approval and signature would have been required to make it a law. But it has been admitted by the greatest Roman scholars that "the Popes took no part in convoking Councils. All Great Councils, to which Bishops came from different countries, were convoked by the emperors." The same authorities also admit that "neither the dogmatic nor the disciplinary decisions of these Councils required Papal confirmation."

Even St. Peter himself, as we have seen, did not preside at the Council of the Church held at Jerusalem to settle the dispute which had arisen between the Jewish and Gentile converts. Nor were the so-called successors of St. Peter in the See of Rome the conveners, or *ex officio* presidents, of any of the General Councils. These were all called by the reigning emperor. They were predominantly, and some of them exclusively, Oriental. From the year 325, in which the first Council of Nicæa was held, to the year 680, the date of the third Council of Constantinople, out of the one thousand one hundred and nine Bishops who attended the six great Councils, only nineteen were from Western Europe. They were "presided over," says Dr. Kurtz, "either by the monarch in person, or by a prelate chosen by the Council."

Hosius, Bishop of Cordova, a province of Spain, was elected president of the first Nicene Council. The third Council, A. D. 431, which met at Ephesus, was presided over by St. Cyril of Alexandria. It was convened to consider a matter which had already been passed upon by the Pope, in a Roman Synod, whose judgment was not regarded as conclusive. The Pope's legates, together with the Patriarch of Constantinople, presided at the fourth Council, A. D. 451, which also acted upon matters that had already been considered by the Roman Bishop and Synod. The fifth Council, A. D. 553, contradicted with anathemas a doctrinal statement of Pope Vigilius, and compelled him to retract it, as well as to conform to its own contrary decision. The sixth Council, A. D. 680, as we have observed elsewhere, formally anathematized Pope Honorius I. as a heretic — a condemnation which was submitted to by the Roman Church, and for nearly a thousand years afterward was renewed by every one of her Popes at his coronation. In view of the simple truth in regard to the Popes and the Councils which may be read in the Church histories of reliable Roman, as well as Protestant, authors, what becomes of the Papal claims?

In addition to the abundant evidence which has already been given in support of the Anglican and Greek contention, that the Bishops of Rome, during the first centuries, did not claim or exercise jurisdiction outside of their own Diocese, may be mentioned the correspondence which they had with their brethren of the Episcopate. If by Divine appointment they stood in the same relation to the rest of the Bishops as our Lord did to the Apostles, the early Church Fathers knew it, and their

C. A.—7

knowledge of this vitally important fact would be manifest in their communications with them, and they themselves would be evidently mindful of their unique position while inditing letters. But there is nothing in the epistolary remains of the first three or four hundred years to indicate that it ever occurred to any of the Popes, or to their contemporary Bishops, that they were not, in respect to their commission, on the same footing. They addressed each other just as the Bishops of the United States and our Primate do. On the one hand there was no assumption of superiority, and on the other no acknowledgment of inferiority, even by the occupants of the most out-of-the-way and obscure Dioceses.

For example, St. Cyprian, Bishop of Carthage from A. D. 248–57, corresponds with the various Popes with whom he was contemporary, on terms of complete equality. He speaks of them, and addresses them, as his brothers and his colleagues. "What is more notorious than that those, and those only, could be colleagues who enjoyed the same power and the same prerogatives?" Councils used the same form of address. The Fathers of Constantinople inscribed their epistle to their "brethren and colleagues, Damasus of Rome, Ambrose of Milan, and others." The Council of Antioch addressed a synodical letter, about Paul of Samosata, to "Dionysius, Bishop of Rome, and Maximus, Bishop of Alexandria, and to all their fellow-servants, Bishops, Presbyters, Deacons, and to the whole Church." Another Council at Constantinople wrote to "Damasus, Britto, Valerian," and others, uniting their names without any mark of distinction, but calling them alike brothers and fellow-servants. "It must not be supposed," observes Father Puller, "that this familiar style of address was due to the primitive simplicity of the Christians of that age.

On the contrary, when the Priests and Deacons of Rome have occasion to write to St. Cyprian, they conclude their letter thus: 'Most blessed and most glorious Pope, we bid you ever heartily farewell in the Lord.' And again, when the same Priests and Deacons of Rome, writing to the Clergy of Carthage, have occasion to refer to St. Cyprian, they say: 'We have learnt that the blessed Pope Cyprian has, for a certain reason, retired.'"

The equality of the Pope and other Bishops is even more apparent from the disputes which he had with some of them than from his friendly correspondence. Firmilian, Bishop of Cappadocia, applied language of unusual harshness to Stephen, Bishop of Rome. He compares him to Judas; accuses him of "defaming the Apostles;" calls him "blind," "ignorant," "rash," "presumptuous," "a partaker with heretics,"—Stephen had called Cyprian, Bishop of Carthage, whose part Firmilian was taking, "antichrist," "false apostle" and "deceitful worker." "Nothing, indeed, could well be more grievous than the spirit in which the conflict was carried on. Christian meekness and charity were sacrificed by both parties; there was certainly no restraint in the use of reproachful terms through any conscious inferiority to the Roman Bishop. Cyprian maintained his conclusion as strongly against Stephen as he would against any other Bishop; he rebuked him as freely, and condemned him as severely. The anger of Stephen, on the other hand, is a proof of how he understood the conduct of his opponent; yet he does not venture to charge him with rebellion against the See, which is now said to be the center and source of unity. Harsh words he gave abundantly in reply, but he stopped short of the point which is indispensable to the papal argument." An appeal to local synods or General Councils sometimes showed that the Pope was right, and then he had the satisfaction of a victory; but, unfortunately for the Papal claims, quite as frequently he was convicted of error, and so had to bear the chagrin of defeat, and even of rebuke and condemnation.

It should be remarked in this connection that there were times, before the rise of the Papacy, when the Sees of Carthage, Alexandria, Constantinople and Milan in turn temporarily quite overshadowed the See of Rome. This was sometimes owing to political circumstances, but more frequently to the great superiority of the Bishop or Patriarch over the Pope. Gregory Nazianzen, himself one of the Primates of Christendom as Bishop of Constantinople, said truly of his brother Patriarch, "The head of the Alexandrian Church is the head of the world." At a later period, Justinian's rescript also recognizes Constantinople as the head of all the Churches. At another time it was correctly said of the great Cyprian, Bishop of Carthage, that he "presided not only over the Church of Carthage and over Africa, but also over all the countries of the West, and over nearly all the regions of the East and of the South and of the North." It is scarcely necessary to add that the presidency which St. Cyprian exercised was not, outside of Africa, a headship of jurisdiction, but one of love and honor, and, as a consequence, of influence.

But though the Pope of Rome has not, by Divine appointment, any jurisdiction over other Bishops and their Dioceses, yet at an early date the Church of both the East and the West conceded the primacy to him, and in the course of time he began to exercise a more or less universal and absolute supremacy over Western Christendom. An explanation of how this came about will be necessary to show that the Catholicity of the Anglican

Communion is not in the least compromised by its present independent position.

The universal primacy with which the Pope was honored during several centuries, is accounted for by the development of the Patriarchal system. The Apostles were equal in authority, because they all received the same commission. As the authorized representatives of Christ they gave this commission and the authority connected with it to their successors, whom we call Bishops. When the Apostles and Bishops met for consultation and corporate official action, as they did more or less frequently from the beginning, it was necessary that one of them should be the chairman. Before the creation of Diocesan Bishops, this privilege, by common consent, may have been accorded to St. Peter. Whenever a number of men associate themselves together for any purpose, some one of them comes to the front as a leader. In this instance, it would appear from the Acts of the Apostles, and from tradition, that St. Peter was the person who did so. It is probable that he was the oldest of the twelve. If so, this of itself, other things being equal, would single him out for honor. But it would seem that not only was he the senior, but that he was also by nature endowed above his fellows with the qualities of leadership. In order to account for the part which he took after the Ascension, until St. Paul becomes the central figure, there is no need of the Ultramontane hypothesis that he was designated by the Lord as Prince of the Apostles. Even if Romanists could substantiate this view, which is an impossibility, before it would be of service to them in their controversy with the great Greek and Anglican Communions, it would be necessary for them to show con-

clusively that the prerogatives of St. Peter had been
duly made over to the Bishops of Rome in succession.
There is not a scrap of evidence that they ever inherited
anything from him, not even the primacy of natural
leadership, which he appears to have enjoyed for a season,
certainly not the supremacy which he never possessed.

We have conceded that, owing to his age and natural qualifications, St. Peter may have presided at
most of the formal meetings of the Apostolic college.
But as the Diocesan system developed, the Bishop of
the city in which a Council was held, would take
the chair without encroaching upon any known right
of St. Peter. This was illustrated in Jerusalem, the
first See City, by St. James, the first Diocesan. After
his Consecration to be Bishop of the Mother Church,
the Apostles had occasion to meet at their headquarters. As this is the only Council of which we have
any New Testament record, we conclude that it must
have been of exceptional importance. In view of the
claims which Romanists make for St. Peter, the fact that
not he, but St. James, was president, is inexplicable.

In the course of time, when the whole Roman Empire
was divided into Dioceses, the Bishops of each Province
were accustomed to meet for consultation and legislation. The Bishop of the Diocese in which the Provincial
Council met presided, or at least his right to the presidency was for a long time recognized. But the transac-
tion of business in the interim between the Councils required an official head, and this was usually the Bishop
of the chief city or of an Apostolic See. Out of this necessity it was that the Metropolitan system grew. Ultimately the Metropolitans were called Archbishops, and
were generally, by courtesy, conceded the right to preside at all Provincial Councils, whether held in or out of
their own Dioceses. When it was necessary to decide

some question of more general importance, the Arch-bishops and Bishops of two or more Provinces would come together for the purpose. At first the Archbishop of the Province in which the meeting was held presided. But after a time the confederation developed into the Patriarchal system, and its official head for the interim between Councils, who usually occupied the most impor-tant See of the whole confederation, was designated Pa-triarch, and conceded the right of presidency over these assemblies, whether held in his own or in another Arch-episcopal Province.

The whole of Christendom was divided into five Patriarchates, namely, Rome, Constantinople, Anti-och, Alexandria and Jerusalem. Now and then it was found necessary, for the preservation of the Faith and the Unity of the Church, to hold a Council in which all the Patriarchates should be as fully represented as possible. These General Councils created the need of of an official head for the whole Christian world. This high distinction would, of course, fall to one of the five Patriarchs, and naturally to him who occupied the most powerful See, namely, the Pope of Rome.

Every Bishop was originally called Pope, but as time went on the title was more and more restricted to the Patriarchs. Then, owing to various circumstances, the occupant of the Roman See had the distinction of being called "the Pope." In later times the title was appro-priated almost exclusively to the Bishops of Rome, while those of the other Patriarchal Sees were called Patriarchs. Both titles are derived from a Greek word meaning "father." Patriarch is the more dignified of the two, since it is applicable not so much to the head of a family as to the chief or ruler of a clan.

It is worthy of note that England, probably by reason of its isolation and early political obscurity, was

not canonically made a part of the Roman, or of any
other, Patriarchate. Says an able writer on "English
Orders:" "Our contention is that Britain or any part
thereof, as England, was never within any Patriarchate
at any time, and was never assigned by any Ecumenical
Council to any Patriarchate. It was and is outside of all
Patriarchates and therefore was and is independent."
The exceptional position of the Church of England was
recognized by a Pope, in his treatment of one of the Archbishops of Canterbury who, happening to be in Italy
during the meeting of a Provincial Synod, made an
effort to attend its sessions incognito. He did not,
however, escape recognition. The Pope, having been
made aware of his presence, introduced him as "the
Pope of another World" and insisted on his being
seated with him upon the Papal throne.

It was not then on account of any prerogative inherited from St. Peter, but because their See City was the
world's metropolis and seat of government, that the
Bishops of Rome, with the development of the Patriarchal
system, came to be recognized as the first among equals.

That the presidency enjoyed by the Roman Prelates
was of human rather than Divine institution, is also
evident from the legislation upon the subject by several
Councils. It was ordained at Constantinople, in A. D.
381, "That the Bishop of Constantinople shall hold the
first rank after the Bishop of Rome, for Constantinople
is new Rome." This decree was reiterated and more
fully explained at the General Council of Chalcedon, A.
D. 451. The fact that Rome was the only Apostolic See
in the West, and that both St. Peter and St. Paul were supposed to have suffered martyrdom there, also contributed
to exalt its Bishop. "The reverence paid in the East to

Alexandria and Antioch and Ephesus and other Churches was in the West monopolized by Rome." But as Primus he had, of course, no canonical jurisdiction outside of his own Diocese. He had no more authority over his Episcopal brethren than Bishop Williams of Connecticut, the present Primate of the American Episcopal Church, has over Bishop Leonard of Ohio.

Papal supremacy developed much later than the primacy and was limited to the Western Church. As the doctrine of infallibility grew out of the widespread desire for an unerring religious teacher, so that of the Pope's right to universal dominion had at least one of its roots in the felt need of a Supreme Ruler, which has manifested itself in both the Old and the New Dispensations, by the setting aside of the polyarchical for a monarchical regimen. God provided that the government of the Jewish nation and Church should be divided between the elders of the twelve tribes, Himself being Head over all. A similar provision was made by Christ for His Kingdom, which is a continuation and development of the old Church. He was to be its supreme Ruler and center of unity. His administrative representatives were to be the twelve Apostles and their successors. These were invested with equal authority, so that in their respective fields of labor they were quite independent of each other.

We would not be understood to teach that in the early Church every Bishop was a law unto himself, but that none had a right to meddle in the administration of another's Diocese, so long as the Faith and the regulations which the college of Bishops had decreed in Council assembled, were not violated. It was, in the nature of things, necessary that the head of a Diocese under certain circumstances should be called upon by an higher authority to give an account of his stewardship. An authority that should be recognized as final was clearly indispensable to the well being of the Church. During the first one thousand years, this was found in the Ecumenical Councils, which possessed both legislative and judicial functions, and bore much the same relation to the Diocesan and Provincial Synods that the Supreme Court of the United States bears to the other courts of the country. The Scriptural warrant for these Councils and their essential value to the Church may be inferred from the fact that the Apostles, themselves, set the example of convening them for the solution of difficulties which none of them, not even St. Peter, could solve. Western Christians repeated the fault of the Jews in abandoning God's government for one of their own choosing, when they allowed the Popes more and more to supplant the Councils and to lord it over their brethren of the Episcopate.

The circumstances which led to this unfortunate and sinful exchange of the Episcopal polyarchy for a Papal monarchy were very much the same in both cases. It seemed to the worldly wise to be a necessary expedient for self-protection against heathen enemies. Of course, when the Church in the West determined to have a king, it had no difficulty in finding a candidate who was head and shoulders above his rivals for the throne. All eyes naturally turned to the Bishop of Rome, who had long been the Primus of Christendom.

But the exaltation of the Papacy is by no means wholly accounted for by the people's desire for an Ecclesiastical monarch. They were indeed ready to invest the great Bishop of the Imperial City with extraordinary judicial powers and to make him the center of unity in both Church and State, but they had no intention of going beyond this. The greatness which they may be said to have thrust upon him, though much more than the primacy, was far less than the supremacy. But for the ambition of the Popes, and the corrupt methods which the degeneracy and ignorance of the Dark Ages made it possible for them and their aggrandizers to employ in its gratification, they would never have become more than supreme judges in cases which had been carried from the Diocesan to the Archbishop, and from him to the Patriarch, without settlement. The Church always has stood in need of a court from which there is no appeal except to a General Council, but it has never required a king other than the One who ever sits at the right hand of God. Fortunately for the world the Popes have not and never can attain the goal upon which, with astounding presumption, they have fixed their eyes. Nor, as has just been observed, would their efforts to reach it have been crowned with anything like the measure of success which has been achieved, but for the unscrupulous use of the most reprehensible means. We must make a long story as short as is consistent with clearness.

When at length the combination of circumstances to which we have referred began to open a little the door of dominion to the ambitious Popes, they found themselves constantly embarrassed by its rubbing and sticking against the grain of tradition and history and of the ancient Conciliary decrees and Patristic writings. In fact, it was discovered that everything would have to be either planed off a good deal or made over altogether before there could be any freedom of action. Accordingly, work was begun and vigorously continued throughout the Dark Ages.

From first to last, there were a great many more or less systematic efforts to reconstruct history in the interest of the Papacy. One of the most important of these was made as early as the beginning of the third century, in a work of fiction which, however, purports to be the autobiography of Clement, who, at that time, was erroneously supposed to have been the first occupant of the Roman See. The object of the unknown author was to create the impression that the honor of being the first among equals, which had long been conceded to the Bishops of Rome, was not due, as had hitherto been believed, to the political greatness of the city over which he presided, but to the circumstance that St. Peter, who was represented, contrary to fact, to have been the founder and Apostolic head of the See, had, shortly before his death, consecrated Clement to succeed him, and bequeathed to him and his successors forever the headship of the whole Church.

Before the close of the ninth century, the Popes, by the mutual consent of the disputants, had frequently acted as arbitrators and judges in cases that naturally should have come before the other Patriarchs. A record was kept of the decisions rendered in these exceptional instances of appeal to Rome. As this business added greatly to the dignity and revenue of the Roman Bishops, they grew more and more anxious to make it appear that they were, by Divine appointment, the supreme judges of Christendom. So they made a great deal of the romance concerning St. Peter and Clement. But in pushing their claims, at every step they were asked such questions as these: If the right to adjudicate all difficult cases has been inherited from St. Peter by the Popes, why is it that, as the records show, appeals were not made to the Holy See from the beginning; and why do the canons forbid the carrying of cases beyond the Patriarch of the jurisdiction to which the litigants belong, and make it unlawful for all

Bishops, Archbishops, and Patriarchs to exercise any of their functions beyond their canonically defined borders? What are known as the False Decretals of Isidore assisted greatly in getting rid of these embarrassing questions. The work in which they were embodied contained both genuine and forged canons of the Councils and judgments of the Popes. It has been established beyond dispute that they contain ninety-four spurious Papal Decrees, fifty-four of which are attributed to the first thirty-five Bishops of Rome. The rest are distributed along the intervening period to A. D. 851, so as to make the chain of appeals practically continuous from St. Clement to the then reigning Pope. This gross forgery, owing to the uncritical age in which it was perpetrated, was not detected or at least not exposed until the Reformation. Though the Bishops of Rome had very little if anything to do with the authorship of the Pseudo-Clementine literature and the Isidorian Decretals, they are none the less guilty, for they vouched for their authenticity, and made use of them to change the government of the Church from a Divine polyarchy to a human monarchy.

After the appearance of the decretals the canons of the Councils and the writings of the Fathers were rapidly more and more corrupted by additions and suppressions. But by the twelfth century such tinkerings, extensive as they were, having been found to be insufficient, Gratian deliberately undertook the work of recasting the whole canonical code, so as to make it fit in with the new order of things. Thomas Aquinas, the intellectual giant of the thirteenth century, accepted, apparently without misgiving, the whole mass of false Decretals, counterfeit Canons, and corruptions of Patristic writings, which had accumulated during five hundred years, and, after fusing them together into a homogeneous whole, and rounding out the work of fraud by additions from the spurious Cyril of Alexandria, built upon it his system of Papal dominion and infallibility which has continued to this day. "John XXII., in his delight," says "Janus," "uttered his famous saying, that Thomas had worked as many miracles as he had written articles, and could be canonized without any other miracles, and in his Bull he affirmed that Thomas had not written without a special inspiration of the Holy Ghost. Innocent VI. said that whoever assailed his teaching incurred suspicion of heresy."

The world has never witnessed such gross and all pervading literary frauds as those for which the Papacy is responsible. Everything which they and their aggrandizers touched has been modified so as to square with the dogmas of universal dominion and doctrinal infallibility. An old author, in connection with what he has to say about the corruption of the Fathers, gives a list of one hundred and eighty-seven treatises cited by Roman writers, about the spurious character of which no doubt remains; and modern criticism could easily add to the number. He gives also a list of fifty passages corrupted in the genuine writings of the Fathers, and adds: "I have set down only five decades whereby you may conjecture of the rest, which for brevity's sake are omitted."

Not even the Roman Breviary, or Prayer Book, has escaped. An author quoted by Canon Gore says: "The condemnation of Pope Honorius for heresy is recorded in the Roman Breviaries until the sixteenth century, at which period the name of Honorius suddenly disappears. The theory of Papal infallibility was at that time being rapidly developed. A fact opposed it. The evidence for the fact is suppressed." "I have before me," writes Père Gratry, "a Roman Breviary of the year 1520, printed at Turin, in which, on the feast of St. Leo, June 28th, I find the condemnation of Honorius:'In which synod were condemned Sergius, Cyrus, Honorius, Pyrrhus, Paul and Peter who asserted and proclaimed one will and operation in our Lord Jesus Christ. I open the Roman Breviary of to-day,'" he continues, "and there I find in the instruction of St. Leo, June 28th: 'In this Council were condemned Cyrus, Sergius, and Pyrrhus, who preached only one will and operation in Christ.' The trifling incident of a Pope condemned for heresy by an Ecumenical Council is simply omitted by the revisers of the Breviary in the sixteenth century. Father Garnier, in his edition of the Liber Diurnus, says, with a gentle irony, that 'they omitted it for the sake of brevity.'" "One of the enrichments of the Breviary," pointed out by another Roman Catholic writer, "was the putting of Satan's words to our Lord in the Temptation, 'I will give thee all the kingdoms of the world,'into the mouth of Christ, who is made to address them to Peter." These forgeries and mutilations in the interest of the Papal system were so astonishing, that the Venetian Marsiglio thought that in course of time no faith would be reposed in any documents at all, and that so the Church would be undermined. "It is impossible," as Professor Salmon observes, "to think that if Roman prerogatives had rested on any Divine gift, it would have been necessary to bolster up the fabric with so enormous a congeries of fraud and lies."

In cases wherein the light of modern learning and the art of printing have made it impossible to effect the necessary changes, the books have been placed upon the Index of works which may not be read by Romanists. Indeed, the reading of any book or article which contains anything derogatory to Ultramontanism

is forbidden except to a few specially licensed controversialists. The Bible itself is popularly supposed,
not without good reason, to be among such books.
Certain it is that Scripture reading was for ages dis-
couraged, and sometimes absolutely interdicted. For
instance at the Council of Toulouse, A. D. 1229, the Laity
were forbidden to have in their possession any copy of
the books of the Old or New Testament if translated
into the vulgar tongue. This was the first synodical
prohibition; there had been no instance of a law
since the days of the emperors which showed the
same hostility to the Bible. When the Council of
Trent met, A.D. 1562, the first business taken in hand
was to prepare an Index of prohibited books. The
work was intrusted to a committee of Bishops, who
reported, concerning the Scriptures, that as the result
of experience their translation into the vulgar tongues,
and the indiscriminate use of them, has produced
"more evil than good." The report was not made
until there was no time left for its consideration by
the Council; so the matter was committed to Pope
Pius IV., who approved the part in which we are here
interested. It reads as follows: "Since it is manifest
by experience that if the Holy Bible in the vulgar
tongue be suffered to be read everywhere without distinction, more evil than good arises, let the judgment
of the Bishop or inquisitor be abided by in this respect;
so that, after consulting with the parish Priest or the
confessor, they may grant permission to read transla-
tions of the Scriptures made by Catholic writers, to
those whom they understand to be able to receive no
harm, but an increase of faith and piety, from such
readings; which faculty let them have in writing. But
whosoever shall presume to read these Bibles, or have
them in possession without such faculty, shall not be

capable of receiving absolution of their sins, unless they have given up the Bible to the ordinary."

But conclusive as are the foregoing arguments against the claims of the Papacy, the strongest yet remains to be presented. It is based upon the scandalous lives which many of the Popes have lived. For how can they make good the pretension that since the Ascension they stand in the same relation to the Church universal as our Lord did to His Disciples, unless it be shown that, like Him, they have also been a perfect example to the world as well as its light and king? As the claims of Christ could not stand for a moment but for His absolute holiness, so the assertion that the Popes are His infallible and all powerful representatives must fall to the ground if any of them can be convicted of sin. Many of the Bishops of Rome have been in all respects ornaments to the Church and have rendered her inestimable service. I would rather dwell on the virtues of these than upon the heresies, frailties, and immoralities of the unworthy occupants of that illustrious Apostolic See. But as Professor Salmon says: "When Rome is made the hinge on which the whole Church turns—the rock on which it rests—then it is necessary to give proof that Rome has not the strength to bear the weight which it is proposed to lay upon it." The evidence by which her weakness will be made manifest shall, for obvious reasons, be quoted solely from the pages of her own sons. I shall be obliged to suppress some of the passages which have been collected from their books, because they contain accounts of crimes too revolting for mention in a work that is intended for general reading, but not one word will be added from Protestant authors.

The learned Cardinal Baronius, speaking of the Papal Court in the tenth century, says: "What was then the semblance of the Holy Roman Church? As foul as it could be, when harlots, superior in power as in profligacy, governed at Rome, at whose will Sees were transferred, Bishops were appointed, and, what is horrible and awful to say, their paramours were intruded into the See of Peter; false Pontiffs who are set down in the catalogue of Roman Pontiffs merely for chronological purposes; for who can venture to say that persons thus basely intruded by such courtesans were legitimate Roman Pontiffs? No mention can be found of election or subsequent consent on the part of the Clergy; all the canons were buried in oblivion, the decrees of the Popes stifled, the ancient traditions put under ban, and the old customs, sacred rites, and former usages in the election of the chief Pontiff were quite abolished. Mad lust, relying on worldly power, thus claimed all as its own, goaded on by the sting of ambition. Christ was then in a deep sleep in a ship, when the ship itself was covered by the waves and these great tempests were blowing. And what seemed worse, there were no Disciples to wake Him with their cries as He slept, for all were snoring. You can imagine as you please what sort of Presbyters and Deacons were chosen as Cardinals by these monsters."

Genebrardus, Archbishop of Aix, speaking of the duration of the Papal profligacy which Baronius thus describes, says: "This age has been unfortunate, in so far that during nearly a hundred and fifty years, about fifty Popes have fallen away from the virtues of their predecessors, being apostates, or apostatical, rather than Apostolical."

Very sad is the picture drawn in the speeches at the Roman Catholic Councils of the 16th century, when a powerful but unsuccessful effort at reformation was attempted. The speakers made avowals and charges so outspoken and of such overwhelming force that they cannot but amaze us. Their descriptions reproduce in various forms the same idea: "We Cardinals, Italian Bishops, and officials of the Curia, are a tribe of worthless men who have neglected our duties; we have let numberless souls perish through our neglect, we disgrace our Episcopal office, we are not shepherds but wolves, we are the authors of the corruption prevalent throughout the whole Church, and are in a special sense responsible for the decay of religion in Italy." Cardinal Antonio Pucci said publicly, before the assembly of A. D. 1516: "Rome, and the Roman Prelates and Bishops daily sent forth from Rome, are the joint causes of the manifold errors and corruptions in the Church; unless we recover our good fame, which is almost wholly lost, it is all up with us."

"Janus" tells us that: "The means used by the Popes to secure obedience, and break the force of opposition among people, princes, or Clergy, were always violent. The interdict which suddenly robbed millions, the whole population of a country — often for trifling causes which they had nothing to do with themselves — of Divine Worship and Sacraments, was no longer sufficient. The Popes declared families, cities, and states outlawed, and gave them up to plunder and slavery; as, for instance, Clement V. did with Venice; or excommunicated them, like Gregory XI., to the seventh generation; or they had whole cities destroyed from the face of the earth, and the inhabitants transported — the fate that Boniface VIII. determined on for Palestrina."

Macchiavelli says: "The Italians are indebted to the Roman Church and its Priests for our having lost all religion and devotion through their bad examples, and having become an unbelieving and evil people. The nearer a people dwells to a Roman Court the less religion it has. Were that court set down among the Swiss, who still remain more pious, they too would soon be corrupted by its vices." Nor was a more favorable judgment given by Macchiavelli's fellow-citizen, Guicciardini, who for many years served the Medicean Popes in high offices, administering their provinces and commanding their army; he observes, on Macchiavelli's words, that "whatever evil may be said of the Roman Court must fall short of its deserts."

The corruption of the Hierarchy is witnessed to in Rome itself by that triumph of Michael Angelo's genius, the "Last Judgment," which was painted for the Altar of the Sistine Chapel, in A. D. 1541. This magnificent work, according to all accounts, is a thrilling prophetic parable, which the Papal Court, in its stupid debauchery, was incapable of comprehending. It portrays to the eyes, in awful menace, the final reckoning. By including some of them among the damned, the saintly artist, who must have been scandalized at what he constantly beheld of the abomination of desolation in the temple, wrote "Tekel," in vivid and unmistakable characters, on the walls of the Popes and Cardinals. Of course, those who saw their own portraits in this terrible caricature, winced a little, "but they were too torpid to comprehend the length and breadth of such a prophecy. A day of retribution was close at hand. God, in the great Reformation, was arising to shake terribly the earth."

Roman writers have put as good a face as possible upon this unfortunate showing. Of those who have exercised their ingenuity to this end, Baronius has succeeded as well as any. He contends that inasmuch as the Church and Roman Hierarchy were not utterly ruined by the sins of the Popes, their Divine origin and indestructible character are manifest. "If," the ingenious Cardinal asks, "the Papal chair was filled by a succession of monstrous men, most base in life, most abandoned in morals, and in every way most foul, if it had a set of chiefs whose sins would have brought down judgments and utter ruin on any other government, must we not infer, from the fact of the Papacy's having survived such a state of things, that it enjoys the special favor or blessing of Heaven?" But Baronius was not the first to resort to this paradoxical makeshift; in fact, he only restated and lent the weight of his reputation to an explanation which had long exercised a great influence over the illiterate masses, but which, in his time, was fast losing its influence with the educated and thoughtful.

Boccaccio, an Italian writer of the fourteenth century, should have been canonized by the Roman Church for the support which her corrupt Bishops long derived from his account of "Abraham's Conversion to Christianity." If it were not for the age and the context in which the narrative appears, it would seem incredible that a story which cannot now be read or heard without laughter, should ever have been regarded as a satisfactory illustration of the way in which the worst Popes, scarcely less than the best, contributed to the Glory of God in the upbuilding of His Church. As given in the "Decameron," it is briefly this: Abraham was a Parisian Jew, who, being pressed to embrace Christianity, declared his intention of visiting Rome, in order to determine by personal investigation whether the morals of Christ's Vicar and of the Cardinals and Clergy proved the superiority of their Creed over his own. His Christian friend, intensely desiring his conversion, was horrified, knowing too well that the spectacle of sensuality, avarice, and simony which tainted all at Rome, from the least to the greatest, was better calculated to make a Christian turn Jew than to induce a Jew to become a Christian. But Abraham could not be dissuaded from going. However, it turned out better than there was reason to fear, for upon his return he, after all, presented himself for Baptism, declaring himself convinced of the Divinity of a religion which survived, notwithstanding that its chief ministers were doing their very best to destroy it. "The popularity of this tale in pre-Reformation times, shows that, if the Bishop of Rome was then believed to be a guide to truth, he was not imagined to be an example of moral purity."

A brilliant objector against the doctrine of infallibility, after an almost brutal exposure of the monstrous crimes of the Popes, in which special mention is made of the infamous Alexander VI. and John XXII., sums up his argument thus: "If you declare the infallibility of the present Bishop of Rome, you will be held bound to prove the infallibility of all his predecessors, without a single exception. But can you do this, with history lying open and showing as clear as sunshine that the Popes have erred in their teaching? Can you do it, and maintain that Popes who were guilty of avarice, of incest, of murder, of simony, were nevertheless Vicars of Jesus Christ? Oh, venerable brethren, to maintain this monstrous thing would be to betray Christ worse than Judas did. It would be flinging mud in His face! Believe me, venerable brethren, you cannot make history over again. There it stands, and there it will stand forever, to protest mightily against the dogma of Papal infallibility. You may proclaim it unanimously, but you will have to do without one vote, and that is mine."

III.

ANGLICAN ORDERS.

BESIDES the consecration of oneself to the Christian ministry and the spiritual and intellectual preparation necessary for this high calling, two things always have been required in every branch of the Catholic Church, namely, Apostolic and Canonical Ordination to the office of Deacon, Priest or Bishop, and a lawful appointment to a particular field of labor. Upon the first of these depends the validity of Sacramental ministrations, and on the second the exclusive authority and submission which are indispensable to efficiency and harmony. So far, there is no difference of opinion between Romanists and Anglicans. Our controversy is concerning the question, whether or not we have the regular Orders and commission.

Romanists represent that pre-Reformation Bishops in England derived whatever authority they had from the Pope, and that, now that he has withdrawn that authority, they are none the better for this connection with the past. Anglicans reply that the Church of England was, in its origin, independent of Rome and continued so for hundreds of years.* This being the case, Canon VIII., of the General Council of Ephesus, A. D. 431, makes the interference of the Pope in the Ecclesiastical affairs of England unlawful, and annuls his bull of excommunication. This canon restrains all Bishops, not excepting the Popes, from the exercise of Episcopal functions and jurisdiction in any Diocese or Province except their own. Thus, when the Pope excommunicated

---

* Lecture IV.

the Church of England in the reigns of Henry VIII. and Elizabeth, he did no more than cut himself and his Diocese off from a pure branch of the Catholic and Apostolic Church of Christ. His excommunication of the whole Eastern Church some four centuries before had the same effect. St. Firmilian, Metropolitan of Cæsarea in Cappadocia, was right when he said to Stephen, Patriarch of Rome, "Whilst you think it in your power to excommunicate all the world, you have only separated yourself from the communion of the whole Catholic Church."

During the fourth and fifth centuries, the Church was harassed by the rise of many grave heresies. In this period of excited disputation the weapon of excommunication was brandished recklessly, not only by the Popes of Rome, but also by the other heads of Patriarchates, and even by comparatively obscure Diocesans. When there was danger of serious corruption, the best way to guard against it known to the Ecclesiastical authorities of those days, was to cut the offender off from fraternal intercourse with the endangered Diocese and to brand him with the censure called *anathema*. But when one Bishop excommunicated another, it never occurred to the excommunicate that he and the Christians of his Diocese were cast out of the Catholic Church. It required the condemnation of a General Council for this. With but comparatively few exceptions, the cause for the excommunication was too trifling to commend it to the attention of such a body. The dispute was therefore usually settled, and the parties directly concerned reconciled, by arbitration, or by time, that great healer of petty differences and alienations.

It seldom happened that the aggressor in an excommunication procedure enjoyed the undivided support of neighboring Dioceses. As in the case of nearly all disputes about little matters, there were two sides to the question. Often the Bishops far and near were pretty evenly divided. This was frequently so when the Bishop of Rome was the excommunicator. In fact, there is more than one instance on record in which he was so clearly in the wrong as to be obliged, under the pressure of public sentiment, to annul his bull or at least to allow it to become inoperative. This conclusively shows that excommunication by the Bishop of Rome did not, in the early days of Christianity, separate from the Church; and if it did not do so then, there is no reason for believing that it did in the sixteenth century or that it does now. It must be remembered too, in this connection, that the argument by which Romanists would unchurch Anglicans proves too much. We have seen that the power of loosing and binding was given to all the Apostles and their successors, not to St. Peter and his alone, and that in the primitive Church it was exercised by all Bishops. If, therefore, our Orders are to be regarded as invalidated by the fact that the Pope has separated himself from communion with us, their own must be similarly affected by the refusal of the great Greek Church to commune with Rome.

Not only were our Orders thus canonically protected from any invalidating effect of the Pope's excommunication, but, at the time when his final bull was promulgated, it happened, either by chance or, as is more probable, by a Providential election, that there was not one of all the English Bishops who owed either his appointment or his Consecration to the Pope of Rome. None had promised obedience to him, nor derived even a show of authority from him. "They had all been ordained under Edward VI., before Mary's reign, or under Elizabeth, after Mary's reign was over." It is sheer absurdity to pretend that the Bishop of Rome could abrogate what was in no way derived from him. If it were not for the Ephesian Canon, it might be conceivable that Rome could withdraw, by canonical deposition, the Apostolic strand which we have through the Italian succession, but, even then, our Bishops could trace their spiritual descent through two and probably three remaining continuous Apostolic ancestral lines, namely, the English, the Irish, and the Saxon. No allegation of loss of continuity has ever been, with any show of reason, urged against the last two of these. And unless Archbishop Theodore disregarded the precautionary Canon which requires that every Bishop shall have at least three Consecrators, the third has been continued also through Chad, who was elevated to the Bishopric of York in A. D. 664.

But if our Orders were wholly derived through the Roman succession, it would not follow that we must be in subjection to the Pope in order to retain a valid Apostolic ministry. For as has been well said: "The Consecration of a Bishop or Archbishop by the Pope, does not invest him with authority or jurisdiction over the said Bishop or Archbishop, or over their Diocese or Province. Otherwise Virgilius, Bishop of Arles, in France, by consecrating Augustine, would have acquired jurisdiction over him, and over Canterbury likewise; and also Godwin of Lyons by consecrating Brightwald, Theodore's successor, would have done the same. Several Priests in Roman Orders are, it is stated, at this moment incumbents in the English Church, having conformed thereto. Supposing this to be the fact, that would not make their parishes Roman parishes; and, in like manner, a number of Bishops, with an Archbishop at the head of them, would not, because they had received their Consecration from Roman Bishops, turn their Dioceses or Provinces into Roman ones." To argue otherwise would prove too much for Romanists. Many of the Popes were translated to Rome from the French and other National Churches—one from England. Are we, therefore, to conclude that the foreign Church which happens to have a son in the reputed chair of St. Peter is, for the time being, entitled to rule over the Roman Church? If so the "Holy See" must always be subject to some jurisdiction other than that of its occupant, for the Pope never consecrates or appoints his successor.

However, the Roman strand has never been withdrawn from the Anglican succession by any Papal deposition of our Bishops. Though the Pope withdrew from their Communion, neither he nor anybody else ever deposed them. Certainly, without canonical deposition and degradation there can be no such thing as nullification of the right of a Bishop or Priest to officiate. Courayer, in his defense of English Ordinations, points out that "when the Donatists made a schism, the succession of the Episcopate was acknowledged in them. Yet they were guilty of the same intrusion with which the English are reproached. They had erected Altar against Altar; they had put themselves in the place of the Catholic Bishops; their title was altogether faulty, and they were equally excommunicated and irregular. Nevertheless, the Catholic Bishops acknowledged in them the validity of the Priesthood, and, far from disputing their succession, offered to yield them their place, provided they would, by their reunion, terminate the schism. We cannot refuse the English a succession of the same nature, supposing once the validity of their Ordination, which the authors of the objection are willing to admit."

Besides, when Romanists insist upon the necessity of submission to the "Holy See," we can quote the words of a Pope to one of our Archbishops of Canterbury: "By

the authority," said he, "of the blessed Peter, Prince
of the Apostles, to whom power was given by our
Lord to bind and to loose in heaven and on earth,
we, however unworthy, holding the place of that same
blessed Peter, who bears the keys of the kingdom of
heaven, grant to you, Theodore, and your successors,
all that from old time was allowed, forever to remain
unimpaired in that your Metropolitan See in the city
of Canterbury." This grant was made more than a
thousand years ago. Dr. John Henry Hopkins' witty
remarks upon it are to the point: "Our modern controversialists on behalf of the Pope would fain make
us believe that this, the Pope's promise and gift 'forever to remain unimpaired,' is now utterly null and
void. But we think better of 'His Holiness' than that!
It was hardly worth while, indeed, to lug in St. Peter as
having anything to do with conveying to Theodore
'all' that the Archbishops of Canterbury had already
been enjoying from 'old time.' It sounded generous,
and was certainly quite safe, however, to give to the
Archbishop what belonged to his See anyhow. It was a
way the Popes had. But if there was anything at all
in the gift prospectively, we would only call attention to
the fact, that, as the Pope gave the Archbishop of Canterbury all these things, in the name of Blessed Peter, and
to the Archbishop's 'successors,' 'forever to remain unimpaired,' of course, if there is any truth or reality in a
gift from a Pope, the Archbishop of Canterbury must
retain them all to this day. To deny it, and maintain
that they are all gone, is to be guilty of flat blasphemy
against the Pope!"

Romanists also try to discredit the mission of the
Clergy of our Mother Church of England, by disparag-

ing her connection with the state, and the part taken
by the crown and civil authorities in the filling of vacant Bishoprics and benefices. They never tire of representing that Henry VIII., after breaking with Clement
VII., styled himself Supreme Head of the Church, and
usurped the Ecclesiastical government which, up to
that time, by Divine appointment, had devolved upon
the Pope. This notion is entirely erroneous. "We
must not be misled," says the learned Canon Dixon,
"by the term 'supremacy,' which first began to be
applied to the Papal power in England after that
power had been taken away. It was not applied to
the Papal power so long as it existed, while, on the
other hand, it was always applied to the kingly power,
and properly expressed the nature of the same. The
sovereign was at all times the head of the realm, both
of the spirituality and the temporality, whether or not
he had borne a title to express his spiritual supremacy. In the laws of Edward the Confessor, A. D.
1004–66, he was termed the Vicar of Christ, a title which
seems as expressive as that which was taken by Henry
VIII." But in speaking of the king's title, candor should
induce Romanists not to stop short of the important
qualifying clause, "*as far as is permitted by the law of
Christ.*" Perhaps it would be a little too much to expect them to add Henry's official explanation, in which
he disclaimed any intention of usurping the Spiritual
government of the Church. "It were absurd," he says,
"for us to be called Head of the Church, representing
the mystical Body of Christ." He restored the spiritual
headship to the Bishops, convocations and Ecclesiastical courts, to which it canonically and constitution-
ally belonged. There is one more fact bearing upon
this subject to which Romanists of course never refer.
The title which is such a stumbling-block to them was

dropped by Queen Mary, since whose time it has not been assumed by any English sovereign.

Those who have not read both sides might suppose, from the representations of Ultramontanists, that the Bishops of England and her colonies derive their mission from the King or Queen. In reality jurisdiction is given at Ordination. The crown, as represented by the Prime Minister, for the purpose of safeguarding the interests of the state, of which the Church is such a powerful factor, simply reserves the right of nomination. The Bishop elect is then consecrated by order of the Archbishop of the Province. Thus the English Bishops, like those of any other branch of the Church Catholic, owe their Mission to Ecclesiastical Consecration, or, in case of Missionary Jurisdictions, to appointment, by the Metropolitan. "In sum," says Bishop Bramhall, "we hold our benefices from the King, but our offices from Christ; the King doth nominate us, but Bishops do ordain us."

The objection to the mission of the Anglican Episcopate and ministry upon the ground of Erastianism will not stand, therefore, even so far as England is concerned, and, as for the American Episcopal Church, it has no foundation whatever. But even if it were well taken, Romanists could not safely make much of it, as we would not be slow in pointing out that the Popes were for several centuries created by the Emperors. Much of their jurisdiction was derived from the same source. For example, whatever authority they exercised in France was due to a statute of the Emperor Valentinian III., which runs as follows: "We decree, by a perpetual sanction, that nothing shall be attempted against ancient custom by the Bishops of Gaul, or other Provinces, without the authority of the venerable Pope of the Eternal City; but whatever the authority of the

THE EPISCOPAL DESCENT OF PARKER.

PARKER (1559-75)

No Records—BARLOW (1536-69)

COVERDALE (1551-65) SCORY (1551-85) HODGKIN (1537-60)

CRANMER (1533-56) RIDLEY (1547-55) HODGKIN (1537-60) PARFEW (1536-57)

STANDISH (1518-35)

VOYSEY (1519-54)

LONGLAND (1521-47)

HOLBEACH (1537-51)

HODGKIN (1537-60)

No Records—CHETHAM (1585-59)

No Records—STOKESLEY (1530-39)
No Records—HILSEY (1535-39)
PARFEW (1536-57)

CRANMER (1533-56)
No Records—RUGG (1536-50)

CAPON (1534-57)

WARHAM (1503-32)
SHERBURN (1505-36)
YOUNG (1517-26)

WARHAM (1503-32)
FISHER (1504-35)
HALSAY

WARHAM (1503-32)
FISHER (1504-35)
WEST (1515-33)
VOYSEY (1519-54)

HILSEY (1535-39)
LATIMER (1535-55)
PARFEW (1536-57)

STOKESLEY (1530-39)
HILSEY (1535-39)
PARFEW (1536-57)

No Records—CHETHAM (1585-59)

No Records—STOKESLEY (1530-39)
No Records—HILSEY (1535-39)

CRANMER (1533-56)

CHETHAM (1535-59)
CRANMER (1533-56)
LONGLAND (1521-47)

Episcopal descent of Parker traced back four successions. The names in black type were consecrated under the old Latin Ordinal. Names in red type were consecrated under the new Reformed Ordinal. Names underlined with red conformed to the Reformation under Henry VIII., Edward VI., and Elizabeth. Names underlined with black conformed to the Papacy under Mary.

Apostolic Chair ordains, shall be law to them; so that if any Bishop when summoned shall omit to come to the court of the Roman Bishop, he shall be compelled to come by the governor of the province." "Thus," observes Professor Hussey, "the Pope's supremacy was now established, not by the law of Christ, nor by a canon of the Church over the Church, but by the Roman law over the dominions of the Roman emperor of the West."

Roman Catholic controversialists have tried to discredit the English Succession by affirming that the register at Lambeth Palace, recording the Consecration of Archbishop Parker, was a forgery, and that all which really took place was a mock consecration at the Nag's Head tavern in London. It was said that Kitchin and Scory, with Parker and other Bishops elect, met there, that Kitchin, on account of a prohibition by Bonner, refused to consecrate them, that Scory, therefore, ordering them to kneel down, placed the Bible on the head of each and told them to rise up Bishops. But this representation was at once thoroughly exploded by Anglican writers, and has long been repudiated by all respectable Roman authors. One of these, Lingard, says: "Of this tale, concerning which so much has been written, I can find no trace in any author or document of the reign of Elizabeth. I should not hesitate to pronounce in favor of the Consecration, even if all direct and positive evidence respecting it had perished. But there exists such evidence in abundance." And an erudite Roman Catholic Layman writes: "I am unable to understand those who maintain that the Protestant Bishops went through a mock consecration at a tavern in Cheapside. If there is one historical fact for which the existing evidence should render it undisputed, it is the fact of the Consecration of Dr. Parker at Lambeth, on December 17, 1559."

It is further urged that Barlow, the chief Consecrator of Parker, was not a Bishop. To this we reply that, whether he was or not, Dr. Parker was validly consecrated, because three other Bishops, whose Ordination is unquestioned, laid hands upon him and repeated the words of Consecration. But there is no reason, except the fact that the records have been lost, for the assertion that Dr. Barlow had not been duly invested with the Episcopal character. If Romanists foolishly insist that this not unusual circumstance must be regarded as conclusive, we will meet them on their own ground by insisting that all the Popes whose records of Consecration are not extant, and there are many such, were merely Laymen. Ordination papers and records are by no means the only sufficient evidence of canonical ministerial office. In the case of Dr. Barlow there is enough besides to convince Dr. Lingard, one of the greatest of Roman Catholic historians, and many other scholars of the first rank, that he was regularly consecrated. "When," says Lingard, "we find Barlow during ten years, the remainder of Henry's reign, constantly associated, as a brother, with the other consecrated Bishops, discharging with them all the duties, both spiritual and secular, of a consecrated Bishop, summoned equally with them to Parliament and Convocation, taking his seat among them, according to seniority, and voting on all subjects as one of them, it seems most unreasonable to suppose, without direct proof, that he had never received that sacred Rite, without which, according to the laws of both Church and state, he could not have become a member of the Episcopal body."

Finally, it is objected that the Ordinal of the first
Prayer Book of Edward VI., used at the Consecration of
Archbishop Parker and others who continued the
Anglican Succession, was defective in that the word
"Bishop" did not occur in the formula appointed to be
said at the laying on of hands, and that there was
nothing in any part of the Service to make the intention of consecrating to the Episcopate sufficiently clear.
The answer to which is that the only Sacraments tied
to express forms of words and particular matter, by
our Lord's appointment, are Baptism and the Eucharist. Courayer says that "according to a principle now
almost universally received in the schools, and generally by all learned divines, imposition of hands
and prayer are the only essentials of Ordination, and
the Ritual of Edward has preserved both. Therefore,
the Bishops ordained by this new Ritual are truly
Bishops, and this new Ordination would suffice alone to
assure the succession of the Episcopate." The omission
of the word Bishop in the formula repeated at the laying on of hands does not make the purpose of the
Ordination indefinite, when all the circumstances render
the intention unmistakable. The following rubrical
direction, which occurs in the Service used at Dr. Parker's Consecration, puts the intention of those who took
part beyond dispute: "After the Gospel and Credo
ended, first the elected Bishop shall be presented by two
Bishops unto the Archbishop of that Province, or to
some other Bishop appointed by his commission; the
Bishops that present him saying: Most Reverend
Father in God, we present unto you this godly and
well-learned man, to be consecrated Bishop." Further
on we find this rubric: "Then the Archbishop and
Bishops present shall lay their hands upon the head
of the elected Bishop, the Archbishop saying: Take the

Holy Ghost, and remember that thou stir up the grace of God which is in thee by imposition of hands; for God hath not given us the spirit of fear, but of power, and love, and of soberness."

It should be observed in this connection that the Edwardian Ordinal was strictly in accord with the usage which universally prevailed until the twelfth century, and still prevails in the Greek Communion. If, therefore, Archbishop Parker's Consecration is invalidated on account of the form of words used, there was no valid Ordination of a Bishop until after twelve hundred years, when the Latins added certain novelties of ceremony to the ancient usage. But as the Orders of the Greeks are acknowledged, notwithstanding their persistent adherence to the old form, it is difficult to see how those of the English can be objected to on this ground. The difficulty is increased by the fact that Pope Pius IV., by his envoy, offered, in the reign of Elizabeth, to confirm the whole English Prayer Book, of course including the Ordinal, provided the Church of England would be reconciled to the Pope, and acknowledge his supremacy. The Roman Catholic, Father Courayer, calls attention to the report of Lord Camden to this effect, and also to Sir Edward Coke's independent and solemn statement of the same.*

There is, then, not the slightest ground for doubt that the Apostolic Succession has been duly transmitted through Archbishop Parker and the Elizabethan Bishops. But even if the transmission of valid orders through Archbishop Parker were not, in so far as matters of history are capable of mathematical certainty, a demonstrable fact, we have Archbishop Laud to fall back upon. That he received Episcopal Consecration by those whose Orders were valid, has not been and never will be questioned. Through him, quite indepen-

---

* Appendix X.

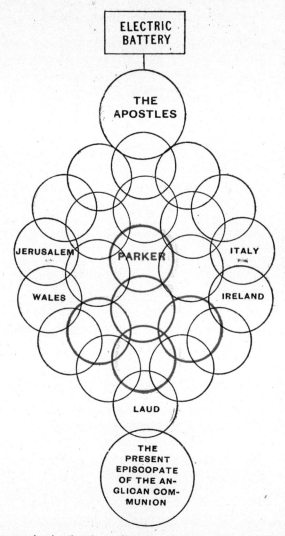

Diagram showing that the Anglican Communion through Archbishop Laud has the Apostolic Succession independently of Archbishop Parker. Each ring represents a Bishop and his interlaced succession from the Apostles. The red illustrates the succession of Archbishop Parker. It will be seen that without it the present Bishops of the Anglican Communion could, nevertheless, trace their succession from the Apostles through Laud, via the Bishops of Jerusalem, Wales, Ireland, and Italy; for it is evident that if the diagram were actually constructed from wire rings, that an electric battery, placed at the ring representing the Apostles, would send a current around that including the present Episcopate of the Anglican Communion; and this it would do through the iron rings representing the Jerusalem and other successions, even if the copper rings representing the Parker succession were removed.

DESCENT OF OUR PRESENT EPISCOPATE TRACED TO ITALIAN, WELSH, IRISH AND EASTERN LINES OF SUCCESSION.

S. PATRICK, 1st Archbishop of Armagh, Ireland, A. D. 432 = CHRISTOPHER HAMPTON, 92nd Abp. Armagh, A. D. 1613.

ABP. CANTERBURY
ABP. ARMAGH, A.D.1613.
BP. LONDON
BP. ROCHESTER
BP. LICHFIELD

ABP. CANTERBURY
THOS. MORTON
{ BP. CHESTER, A.D. 1616. }
{ BP. LICHFIELD, A.D.1618. }
BP. ROCHESTER
BP. BATH-WELLS
BP. LONDON

JOHN HOWSON
BP. OXFORD, A.D.1619.

ABP. CANTERBURY
MARK ANTONY, ABP. of SPALATRO, ITALY.
BP. LONDON
BP. ELY
BP. ROCHESTER
BP. LICHFIELD

GEO. MONTAIGNE
BP. LINCOLN, A. D. 1617.
BP. LONDON, A. D. 1621.

BP. LONDON, A.D.1621.

ABP. SPALATRO, ITALY.

BP. ELY

WILLIAM LAUD
BP. S. DAVID'S, A. D. 1621.
ABP. CANTERBURY, A.D.1633.

ALL THE 8 BISHOPS WHO SURVIVED THE COMMONWEALTH:

SIX OF THEM were personally consecrated by Laud, including

DUPPA
BP. WINCHESTER

THE PRESENT EPISCOPATE OF THE ANGLICAN COMMUNION.

BP. JERUSALEM, PATRIARCH, 6th Century,
S. PATRICK, ABP. 5th Century,

BP. S. DAVID'S, WALES.
BP. DERRY, IRELAND.

BP. LLANDAFF

ENGLAND: { BP. WORCESTER
BP. CHICHESTER }

S. PATRICK, 5th Century,
MURRAY, BP. of KILFERNOA, IRELAND.

LAUD
MORTON
BANCROFT

From the above chart it will be seen at a glance that even if the Succession in black type, which represents the old English Succession through Parker, be omitted, as suggested in the previous chart, we still have the several successions in red type derived from various foreign sources which centred in Laud.

The Records leave no room for doubt that the Anglican Succession, through its chief and co-ordinate Consecrators, has the following strands: Italian, innumerable; Greek, two; French, Irish, Welsh and Scotch, many; Portuguese, one; Spanish, one; Hungarian, two; Savoyard, one; and Dalmatian, one. Though there is no documentary evidence, it is nevertheless almost absolutely certain, that to the above mentioned strands must be added at least one and probably three strands that have come down to us from the British Succession. This can only be questioned by assuming that Theodore and others conducted a series of single-handed consecrations, contrary to Canon law and when there were other Bishops within convenient reach. To get rid of the cumulative proof here indicated Romanists have quite recently invented the theory that co-consecrators do not convey orders, but are only witnesses. This is contrary to Catholic teaching and renders the canonical rule requiring three Consecrators a farce.

dently of Archbishop Parker, we have the English, the Irish and the Italian succession and probably also that of the Saxon. This is clearly shown from the record of Laud's Consecration as Bishop of St. David's, which took place in the reign of King Charles I. He had six Consecrators, of whom Montaigne, Bishop of London, and Felton, Bishop of Ely, had been consecrated on the 14th of December, 1617, by George Abbot, Archbishop of Canterbury, assisted by Mark Antonio de Dominis, an ex-Roman Catholic Archbishop. Laud therefore received, through Montaigne and Felton, both the English and Italian successions. He had also the Irish through three other of his Consecrators, John Thornborough, Bishop of Worcester, translated from Limerick; John Howson, Bishop of Oxford, who had the Irish succession through the Archbishop of Armagh; Theophilus Field, Bishop of Llandaff, one of whose Consecrators was the Bishop of Derry. Nine Bishops survived the rebellion, eight of whom—Juxon, Duppa, Wren, Skinner, King, Warner, Roberts, and Frewen—had the succession from Laud; and from these all the Bishops of the Anglican Communion derive their Orders. They, therefore, have their spiritual descent from Laud, and derive through him, independently of Archbishop Parker, the three successions, English, Irish and Italian.

An able writer calls attention to the interesting fact that Roman controversialists never attack the validity of the Orders of the old Apostolic 'Church of Ireland.' "In fact, there can be no question about them, as they are derived from Connor's Consecration of Archbishop Curwin in Queen Mary's reign. This has a vital bearing upon the question of English Orders since Irish Bishops of this succession took part in the Consecration of Archbishop Laud. Thus, even if it could be for

a moment admitted that there was any doubt of the
validity of Parker's Consecration, it would have to be allowed that the defect was at least in a measure rectified.
A Roman Catholic Archbishop, who had connected himself with the Anglican Church and received an appointment to an English benefice, also took part in Laud's
Consecration. Absolutely certain as the Consecration
of Archbishop Parker is, English orders do not stand
or fall even with that."

IV.

LEO XIII'S DECREE OF INVALIDITY.

Many were deeply concerned when in A. D. 1896 it
was announced that the Pope had entered upon an
investigation of Anglican Orders for the purpose of
making a definite and decisive pronouncement concerning them. His adverse decision will settle the question with the rank and file of Romanists. This is the
decree: "We pronounce and declare that Ordinations
carried out according to the Anglican Rite have been
and are absolutely null and utterly void." But there is
nothing in the long and intricate arguments of the
Bull that will change the mind of a single scholar of
either Communion. It throws no new light upon the subject, and does not raise a single objection that has not
been answered a thousand times. Perhaps some of my
readers will be glad to know that the Pope's arguments are all anticipated and very effectually answered
in a little book, entitled, "What Objections Have Been
Made to English Orders," which is published by the
Society for the Propagation of Christian Knowledge. In
the future Anglican Orders will of course not have so
many outspoken champions among Roman writers, but

> "A man convinced against his will,
>   Is of the same opinion still."

There are many learned Roman Catholics who will
continue in one way or another to make felt their re-
sentment at the scandalous disregard of history and
canon law, which the Jesuits have manifested all along
in their propaganda against the ministry of the Apostolic Church of the English race.

It may turn out that the "Black Pope" and his
followers, by practically forcing Leo XIII. to declare
against Anglican Orders, have done our Communion a
great service.   There have been a considerable number
of both Clergymen and Laymen whose devotion to the
idea of the restoration of intercommunion with the
Roman Church has been so great as, in a few instances,
to compromise their loyalty to the great Historic
Church of their race.   These, as their leader, Lord Halifax, admits, will now be forced to perceive, what their
forbearing Bishops and brethren have seen all along,
that there can be no such thing as the unity upon which
they had set their hearts without a complete and un-
conditional surrender on our part of the liberty which,
according to the Ecclesiastical Canons, belongs to every
National Church.

The Pope's decree will be welcomed cordially by many
Episcopalians, not only because it will turn the faces of
their mistaken brethren away from Rome, but also
because it gives them possession of all the outposts
around which the battle of controversy concerning our
Orders has hitherto raged.   Since the publication a few
months ago of M. Dalbus' work on the validity of Anglican Orders, Ultramontanists have realized that there
was nothing for them to do except to extort a decree
from the "infallible" Pope and take refuge behind it, for
it appears from these publications that the controversial
guns of every other parapet have been silenced by our
relentless artillery, reinforced by many an effective shot

from the enemies' own ranks. Those who are familiar
with the ground upon which the battle between Anglicans and Romanists has been raging for three centuries,
will be greatly surprised that the Bull contains not a
word about the "Nag's Head" or Bishop Barlow. This
gives us a position which our enemies long regarded as
their Gibraltar.

M. Dalbus is the pen name of a distinguished French
Priest and scholar, the Abbé Portal. His work was
honored with a commendatory letter by the learned Cardinal Bourret, and a favorable criticism by the great
Abbé Duchesne. I will, in part, quote Abbé Duchesne's
review of M. Dalbus as condensed in the Literary Digest,
because comparatively few words will thus suffice to show
what both have to say.

Abbé Duchesne says: "M. Dalbus begins by establishing the claim that Bishops Parker and Barlow, from
whom the whole of the Anglican Clergy derives its
Ordinations, were really ordained; or, at least, that
there is no ground for contesting their Ordination. On
the other hand, the Ritual of the Anglican Church is
substantially similar to the Ritual of the Greek Church,
and even to that of the Latin Churches down to the
twelfth century. Conclusion: The Ministers of the Anglican Church are just as rightly ordained as Gregory of
Tours, Hincmar of Rheims, and other Latin Clergy of
ancient times."

It is difficult to see how the Pope could be induced to
take the stand he has in the face of the admissions and
contentions of many of the most scholarly among his
own officers. He passes over what they have to say
with the remark that the validity of Anglican Orders has
been maintained by "some few Catholics, chiefly non-
English," and attributes their mistake to "insufficient
knowledge" concerning certain documentary evidence

relating to the decisions of his predecessors. Such contemptuous references to men who might forget more than Leo XIII. ever knew and still be better furnished than he to pass upon the subject in question, are calculated to provoke both pity and contempt.

As the Pope seems to congratulate himself upon the alleged fact that the Catholics who admit the validity of Anglican Orders are chiefly "non-English," we will here call attention to a remarkable letter by an English Ultramontanist. It is reprinted in full by Dr. Lee in the Appendix to his great work on "The Validity of the Holy Orders of the Church of England." The following is a short extract: "Now, my own conviction has always been, as you are aware, that the probability in favor of English Orders, as gathered from the direct evidence amounts to moral certainty, which is the highest kind of certainty attainable in such questions. I have, therefore, myself, no more doubt of their validity than I have of the validity of the Orders of the Catholic Church or of the Greeks. The Jesuit Missionaries of Elizabeth's reign, and those who have followed in their footsteps since, thought it necessary for Catholic interests to strain every nerve to disprove the Anglican Succession. Hence, first the scandalous invention of the Nag's Head Fable. When that was too much blown upon for any respectable writer to be able to use it, the mare's nest about Barlow's Consecration was thrust to the front, though even if his Consecration could have been disproved it would have had no real bearing on Parker's, for of the Episcopal Orders of his three other Consecrators there can be no doubt. When that broke down, the Doctrine of Intention was attempted to be worked in a way which, if it proved anything, would shake the validity of every Sacrament in Christendom. The whole history of the controversy about Anglican Orders, so far from

tending to shake their validity, very strongly confirms it."

Many of the brightest lights of the Roman Communion have held and are holding these views. The Rev. M.
R. Butler, in his "Rome's Tribute to Anglican Orders,"
has compiled many pages of extracts from the writings
of more than thirty of the most eminent Roman Catholic
authors, who admit the validity of our ministry, and in
some cases even contend for it. Among those who have
done this are such celebrated names as Dr. Nicholas
Sanders, Cardinal Archbishop of Odescalchi, Monseigneur De Dominis, Archbishop of Spalatro, and Primate
of Dalmatia and Croatia; Monseigneur Jacques Benigne
Bossuet, the renowned Bishop of Meaux; Monseigneur
Harlay, Archbishop of Paris; St. Alfonso M. Liguori,
Bishop of Agatha, and founder of the congregation
of the Most Holy Redeemer, and the celebrated Gallican
divine, Le Courayer, who wrote a dissertation in support
of Anglican Orders and afterwards a defense of it, which
together contain perhaps the most thorough refutation
of Roman attacks which has ever been made.

In the verdicts rendered in the case of Dr. Stephen
Gough, we have the deliberate and semi-official pronouncement of the Sorbonne Faculty, upon two occasions, in favor of Anglican Orders. Dr. Gough, before
entering the Church of Rome, had been one of the Chap-
lains of Charles I. His ministrations as a Roman Priest
were in the Diocese of Paris. He insisted that the Ordination which he had received at the hands of an English Bishop was valid, and the Archbishop of Paris holding the same view, gave him a cure without reordination.
The most learned Faculty of the celebrated Theological
Seminary of the Sorbonne was, however, charged with
the thorough investigation of the whole subject of Anglican Orders. After spending several months in research

and conference they pronounced them unquestionably valid. But after a time the misgivings of some influential Ultramontanists induced the Archbishop to re-commit the case to a choice number of the great Sorbonne Doctors. These, after sifting again all the evidence, confirmed the verdict of the preceding committee, and framed a report which had the effect of silencing all opposition to Dr. Gough. This testimony to the validity of English Orders is exceptionally valuable, because it comes from what, during several centuries, was "the most renowned and competent theological school in Latin Christendom."

The "Life of Archbishop Tait" contains an account of a very important communication, received by the late Bishop of Lincoln, Dr. Wordsworth, from some of the Bishops who were attending the Vatican Council, A. D. 1870, in which it was signified that the opposition to the Dogma of Papal Infallibility would be exceedingly grateful for the moral support of the Anglican Episcopate. Thus the validity of our Orders was acknowledged by the Vatican minority, which, so far as learning is concerned, was the flower of the Roman hierarchy.

Moreover, by declaring Anglican Orders to be totally invalid Leo XIII. reverses the decision of Popes Julius III., Paul IV., Pius IV. and Urban VIII., who admitted their validity. The evidence of this statement will be found excellently summarized and well supported by quotations from and references to original authorities in the Rev. Mr. Butler's pamphlet referred to above. Our space will admit of little more than a bare statement of the facts.

Pope Julius III. addressed a brief to Cardinal Pole in the year 1554, desiring him to absolve and reconcile the Bishops and Priests made in Edward VI.'s time, but not directing him to reordain them. Leo XIII.

tries hard to get rid of this embarrassing fact by maintaining that Julius III. at the restoration of the usurped Papal power in England on the accession of Queen Mary reinstated only the Bishops and Clergy who had been ordained by the Roman Ordinal. But the instructions to Cardinal Pole, the Apostolic Legate to England, nowhere discriminate against those who had received the Edwardian Ordination. In order to make it appear to the contrary, the Pope and his advisers conveniently lose sight of the fact that in those days it was not uncommon for Laymen to nominally hold vacant benefices, which were sometimes of considerable duration. The Bull, so far as it relates to this subject, is a restatement of the argument of Canon Moyes, "who, finding a man described in Mary's reign as never ordained or 'no minister' calmly puts him down among those whose Orders were disallowed because conferred by the Edwardian form. Canon Moyes' logic is of the most refreshing type, since to him 'ordained' by the Edwardian form is equivalent to 'not ordained at all.' Therefore, also, 'not ordained at all' is equivalent to 'ordained by the Edwardian Form.'"

Though during Mary's reign many of the Edwardian Clergy were reconciled to the Pope by his representatives and satisfactorily reëstablished in their benefices, there is no instance of the reordination of a single Bishop, Priest or Deacon. Bishop Bonner, who was high in favor at Rome, on the 14th of July, 1554, restored his beloved colleague Scory; the sole ground alleged for the need of such restoration to his Episcopal office being his marriage; and there is no question that Scory was consecrated on the 10th of August, 1551, with the Revised Ordinal.

Pope Paul IV., A. D. 1555-59, "established" and "confirmed" the action of Julius III.

Pope Pius IV., A. D. 1559-65, invited the English Prelates, as Bishops, to join in the deliberations of the Council of Trent. No Bishops were sent from England and the Council expressed amazement that the English Bishops did not even send a letter "to excuse their absence when summoned by the Vicegerent of Christ, for the settlement of religion."

Pope Urban VIII., A. D. 1623-44, twice offered a Cardinal's hat to the Anglican Primate, Archbishop Laud, without questioning his Orders.

An effort to disparage Anglican Orders was made at the Council of Trent, not, however, upon the ground that they were defective, but that our Episcopate was not in subjection to the Roman Pontiff. One of the members maintained without contradiction that it was for "this one reason and no other" that the Roman Church argued against the Bishops of England, "for they prove that they have been called, elected, consecrated and given mission." The Popes regard this Council as Ecumenical, thus giving it their highest sanction.

The Popes did not question our Orders for many years after we had cast off every semblance of allegiance to them. Once and again they signified a willingness to restore us to Communion without re-Baptism, Confirmation or Ordination, providing only that we should return to the partial subjugation of the Dark Ages. And even at this late date there is not the least doubt in the minds of the well instructed that, notwithstanding his recent decree, His Holiness would repeat the overtures, looking to the wholesale restoration made by his predecessors, if there were the slightest chance of their acceptance.

We submit that in view of the above mentioned acknowledgments of his predecessors the dogmatic decree of the present Bishop of Rome tells more against the doctrine of infallibility than against Anglican Ordinations.

The reasons now given by Leo XIII. for declaring Anglican Orders to be invalid are only two: (1) the defectiveness of the Edwardian Ordinal, and (2) the want of the requisite Intention.

1. We have already had occasion to refer at some length to the first of these objections, but we must in this connection quote a few more sentences from what Abbé Duchesne, the most celebrated liturgiologist of the Roman Communion, has to say about it. "The objection drawn from the modifications in the Rituals is no more admissible than the other. The objection concerns the Ordination of Priests. The schoolmen laid down the rule that, for this form of Orders, the essential part of the Rite consists in the delivery of the sacred vessels, and in the words which the Bishop pronounces in giving them. At present, this system is abandoned; it is too clear that, to maintain it, all the Greek and Oriental Ordinations, and even those of the Latin Church before the eleventh or twelfth century, would have to be considered null."

To this we will add the clear statement of a scholarly writer in the English *Church Times:* "Words which the Romans say are essential to a valid Ordination of a Priest were not in the Ordinal of the Western Church till the tenth century. Before that period the words of 'a commission to Consecrate the Holy Eucharist' were never given. Nor was the form 'for conveying the power of absolution' given till a later time. That is completely modern. The actual words, 'Receive ye the Holy Ghost: Whosoever sins ye remit, they are remitted unto them; and whosoever sins ye retain, they are retained,' are first found in a book belonging to the Cathedral of

Mayence, of the thirteenth century. They are not in the early English manuscripts of Egbert or Dunstan or the Winchester Use. They are not in any of the foreign Ordinals printed by Martene before the twelfth century. They are not in the old Sacramentaries of St. Gregory or Gelasius. Such being the case, and as the Roman Bishops and Priests receive their Orders through St. Gregory, according to their present contention that the omission of this form of words invalidates a professed Ordination, they should, to be consistent, conclude that their own Orders are null and void. We, of the purer branch of the Catholic Church, believe our Orders to be valid because of our true and unbroken succession from the Apostles, and because the Ritual used at the time of our Ordination was in accordance with the ancient use of the Church before the Mediæval corruptions set in."

2. We may also answer the Pope's objection to Anglican Orders, so far as it is based upon lack of Intention, by a quotation from the profoundly learned Abbé Duchesne: "Intention must be presumed till the contrary is proved. Baptism may be validly conferred by a person who knows only that it is a sacred rite by which one becomes Christian. In the same way, the Anglican Ordinations have always been performed by persons who wished to make Bishops or Priests, and so on. We ought not to ask more."

As one of the critics of the Bull observes: "The Pope has not the hardihood to say that if he used the Anglican Ordinal it would not make a Priest or a Bishop, and he hardly could, considering how many of his predecessors in primitive times were ordained and consecrated by forms equally elastic and indefinite, but he does say that the excision of everything in the Ordinal referring to sacrifice clearly shows that those who compiled and first used it had no 'intention of making a sacrificing Priest.' The question, then, is one of Intention, and here the Pope gives away his case, for he admits that the Intention of the compilers of the Ordinal, as expressed by themselves, was to return to primitive usage; his words are, 'under a protest of returning to the primitive form;' the Intention of the Ordinal, therefore, was to make Priests of the primitive type, and if the Intention was good, the Pope does not venture to deny that the Orders are valid."

In times gone by when Denominationalists taunted Episcopalians with the fact that the Church of Rome virtually denied Anglican Orders by reordaining Episcopal Clergymen who go over to her, we could retort that nevertheless our Ordinations had at various times been regarded as valid, and that as a whole they never have been officially pronounced invalid. We shall now be reminded that so far as Rome is concerned, we stand on the same footing with the Denominational bodies. To this we will reply that there is no adequately supported statement in the Pope's pronunciamento which goes to show that the status of our Bishops, Priests and Deacons is not historically and Canonically what we have hitherto held it to be. Our arguments will still be strong enough to compel many of the leading ministers of the various Denominations to transfer their allegiance to the Catholic Church of the English speaking race. Ever since Colonial times, when President Cutler of Yale College, with several of the Professors, did this, the procession has been continuous, and there is no probability that it will be interrupted. On the contrary, the statistics show that the number of Denominational ministers who make application for Holy Orders in the Church is increasing steadily. I know the Bishop of Ohio almost always has from one to four of such on his list of candidates, and he might have more if he could accept all who offer themselves. When it is remembered that we have nearly three hundred Bishops in the Anglican Communion, and that most of them have more or less of the same experience, the magnitude of the reaction towards the Mother Church may be imagined. Many of the ministers who have their faces turned homeward are far above the average, and not a few of them rank among the very first in their respective Denominations.

The decree of invalidity, though coming as it does from the infallible successor of St. Peter, will not go very far in the minds of most Protestants towards counteracting the impartial and weighty testimony of such men as Dr. Döllinger. It will be generally recognized that the question respecting Anglican Orders is one to be settled by the facts of history, not by intuition or inspiration. This being the case, Döllinger's utterance will command the respect due to one who speaks or writes with the authority of an expert, and consequently what he says is much more likely to influence intelligent, sensible people than the decree of the good and amiable Italian Ecclesiastic, who enjoys no great reputation for learning, and owes what little weight it will have to his exalted position. At the "Reunion Conference" held at Bonn in A.D. 1874, Dr. Döllinger, who is generally ranked as the first theologian and Ecclesiastical historian that the nineteenth century has produced, said:

"The solution of the question depends solely on an examination of historical evidence, and I must give it, as a result of my investigations, that I have no manner of doubt as to the validity of the Episcopal Succession in the English Church. The Ordinations of the English Bishops since the Reformation were first assailed by a now exploded story, the Nag's Head Fable, and then by sundry objections, some of which rested on utterly unfounded suppositions, while others were quite as applicable, or more so, if any importance were to be attached to them, to the Ordinations of Roman Catholic Bishops and Priests. Circumstances occurred in the Western Church, before the Reformation, calculated to raise far more serious doubts as to the unbroken succession and the validity of many Ordinations than anything which has been alleged against English Orders."

As Anglicans can prove that their Bishops are historically and Canonically in unbroken succession from the Apostles, the Pope's pronunciamento does not disturb us in the least. All that we regret is that it will widen and deepen the gulf between Rome and the rest of Catholic Christendom. There now seems to be no possibility of the reunion of Greeks and Anglicans with Italians for a long time to come. But many are taking comfort in the consideration that what the cause of unity loses in this direction will be compensated for by the accelerated drawing together of the rest of the Christian world. There is much more ground than ever for the hope that the restoration of intercommunion between Greek and Anglican Catholics will take place within the next generation.* The Greeks will not fail to observe, and the observation will produce righteous indignation, that the Pope of Rome is killing two birds with one stone. For, if our Orders are invalid because of the reasons which he gives, theirs are the same, and if there is anything in the proverbial representation that "misery loves company," the decree will tend to bring the great Catholic and Apostolic Communions which it affects together. Henceforth, either Constantinople or Canterbury — more probably the latter, for she is the centre of the race and Church that are rapidly becoming

* Appendix XI.

dominant—will supplant Rome, which, by the indiscretion of the present incumbent of the reputed Chair of St. Peter, has lost the golden opportunity of becoming the reconciler of divided Christendom.

The reconciliation and bringing back to the Catholic fold of our Denominational brethren probably will take much longer than the reunion of Anglicans and Greeks, but the Pope's action will hasten this as well, and, we believe, make its accomplishment for the most part possible within the coming century. Whenever in the providence of God that time comes, the Italian Church will be compelled to give up its preposterous claims and to form one division of the great reunited Catholic army which will then march on to the rapid conquest of the world for Christ.

Although the limits to which I have confined myself will not admit of adding to or expanding the foregoing arguments, it is hoped that enough has been said to leave no room for doubt that if a General Council could be assembled, and be asked to decide whether or not Anglican Orders are valid, the vote would be overwhelmingly in the affirmative.   We should be morally certain of the unanimous vote of every branch of Catholic Christendom,* except the Roman, and there would be many a representative of that Communion, probably the majority, certainly the choicest of them, who would cast their ballot for us.

In conclusion let me say, by way of a general answer to any quibbles which, for the want of space, have necessarily failed to receive attention here, that Romanists urge no objection against the Anglican Ministry and Communion, which will not be found, upon examina-

* See Appendix XXVII.

tion, to apply with more force against themselves than it does against us.   We are quite ready to admit that our branch of the Catholic Church may have some more or less serious defects, for nothing with which imperfect men have anything to do can be altogether faultless; but however great our imperfections can be shown to be, we should much rather be held responsible for them than for those of the Roman Communion.

The original plan of this lecture provided for the taking up of several other points of our controversy with Romanists, namely: Praying to the Virgin Mary and other saints; prayers in an unknown tongue; compulsory auricular confession; transubstantiation, penance, purgatory, image worship and clerical celibacy. However, I pass them over the less reluctantly, because from the most cursory examination of the Prayer Book, which is accessible to all, the Denominational reader may see that none of these Roman corruptions can be fastened upon the Episcopal Church.   Enough has been said to convince any candid person that the Anglican and Roman Communions differ fundamentally, and to show that we are none the less Catholic because we are not under the dominion of the Pope.   If, therefore, anyone would discharge the duty incumbent upon all, of confessing Christ by identification with some branch of His Catholic and Apostolic Church, he can make no mistake if he allow himself to be guided by the Greek and Anglican conception of the Church, for, unlike that of either Denominationalism or Romanism, it is in accord with Holy Scripture, when interpreted in the light of the history of the earliest and purest Christian ages.

The Church for Americans.

LECTURE III.

Our Controversy With Denominationalists.

AUTHORITIES.

Coit, Puritanism.
Cotterill, Bp., Genesis of the Church.
Coxe, Bp., Apollos, or the Way of God.
Eagar, The Christian Ministry in the New Testament.
Gore, Canon, The Church and the Ministry.
Hammond, What Does the Bible Say About the Church?
Hammond, What is Christ's Church?
Hammond, English Nonconformity and Christ's Christianity.
Hammond, The Christian Church: What Is It?
Marshall, Notes on the Catholic Episcopate.
Morse, Apostolical Succession.
Mountfield, The Church and Puritans.
Neal, Puritans. (2 Vols.)
Seabury, Lectures on Haddon's Apostolical Succession.
Seabury, Introduction to the Study of Ecclesiastical Polity.
Shields, The Historic Episcopate.
West, The Kingdom of Heaven upon Earth.

PAMPHLETS.

McIlvaine, Bp., The Origin and Design of the Christian Ministry.
Thompson, Bp., Concerning the Kingdom of God.
Thompson, Bp., The Protestant Episcopal Church and Her Relation to Other Bodies.

MISCELLANEOUS.

Pitt's Street Chapel Lectures.
Library of the Fathers—Oxford Edition.
The Church Defense Institution "Handy Volume."
The Doctrine of the Apostolic Succession.
Tracts for the Times—Apostolic Succession.

OUR CONTROVERSY WITH DENOMINA-
TIONALISTS.

H AVING grown up in one of the many communities
of Ohio in which the Episcopal Church is not
represented, I well remember the astonishment
produced in my mind by the first tractates concerning the Church which fell into my hands. They were
Bishop Randall's "Why I Am a Churchman" and
Bishop Thompson's "First Principles." The idea that
some Churches are Divine Institutions, and others only
human societies was to me altogether new and preposterous; so, also, was the doctrine that the Gospel religion
and covenanted salvation are inseparably connected
with the historic Church of Christ. All I had heard or
read led me to believe that Christianity was essentially
doctrinal and spiritual, and only incidentally institutional. To me religion was a faith, an experience, a life
with which the Church and the Sacraments had nothing to do, except in so far as they contributed to keep
up enthusiasm and to prevent from backsliding.
This is the view of nine-tenths of the people in the
various Denominations. Hence they cannot understand the position of Churchmen, and think that all
that we have to say about the Church and her threefold ministry coming from the days of the Apostles, is
so much trifling.

An editorial in a recent number of a widely circu-
lated religious paper, speaking of the now famous essay

on "The Historic Episcopate," accuses its distinguished Presbyterian author, Professor Shields, of surrendering "the entire Protestant position in the declaration that the institutions of Christianity, its ministry and Sacraments, are revealed in the Scriptures no less than its doctrines." "No Protestant," warmly contends the gifted editor, "if he is Protestant on principle, and understands his Protestant principles, will accept an Historic Episcopate as essential to the Church of Christ; for he holds that the only thing essential to that Church is loyalty to Christ, who is the living and ever-present Head, and therefore needs no Vicar or series of Vicars; and he holds that the true bond of Church Unity is Spiritual and not Ecclesiastical." He then goes on to say in almost so many words that Christ did not, as Episcopalians would have non-Episcopalians believe, organize an Ecclesiastical society, founding it upon the twelve Apostles who had authority to appoint their successors, a society that he intended should be the depository of His special grace and the revelation of His truth. A forcible writer in another popular religious paper says: "Denominationalists think that Christianity is not concerned with Primacies and Apostolic successions, that Christianity is a matter of the heart and loyalty to Jesus Christ and love to God and man; and that all the machinery that goes with the Church is but a greater or lesser convenience or burden. They are satisfied with the Kingdom of God, which is righteousness and peace and joy in the Holy Ghost."

In order to secure further reading from those who thus flatly deny the premises upon which the chief arguments of the remainder of the book are based, it is necessary to turn aside at this point for the purpose of proving four propositions, namely: (1) Christ founded a visible organic society. (2) This society has been perpetuated through duly constituted successors of the Apostles. (3) This Apostolic Church is the appointed ark of Gospel salvation, and only by entering it can a person place himself in assured covenant relationship with God. (4) This Church is also the sole Divinely constituted depository of Sacramental grace.

But, before entering upon the task of establishing these propositions, a preliminary remark is necessary in explanation of the fact that our arguments to a considerable extent, will be based upon inferences drawn from the Scriptures and Patristic writings rather than upon quotations that, in so many words, declare the truth for which we contend. This is because the Church had existed for a number of years before the earliest of these productions were penned. "The Bible," says an author, quoted by Bishop Leonard, of Ohio, "was not put together till the Council of Carthage A. D. 397. When the Nicene Creed was formulated, Scripture was never even appealed to. The three hundred and eighteen Bishops were asked singly concerning each article of the Apostles' Creed, what its meaning was, according to the tradition handed down in his Church. Seventy years afterward it was found that every particular of the Doctrine was registered somewhere or another in the written Code, and thus it became an axiom that whatever claimed to be an article of belief, must also be tested and proved by the written word." So, also, Bishop Thompson: "The Church was already organized, and at her appointed work within a year after the Ascension. Men were admitted into her, and trained and taught within her, heard the Gospel, 'The whole counsel of God,' believed it, and lived and died by it, before the first line of the New

Testament was penned. We cannot expect, therefore, to find in the New Testament a formally drawn up constitution of the Church. The book was not first written, and the Church organized according to a plan laid down on paper beforehand; but the Church was first organized, and then the book was written because the Church needed it—required a written record of the Gospel she was teaching. The Church produced the New Testament, and not the New Testament the Church."

And when, at length, the writings of the Apostles and Fathers began to come forth, they were addressed to congregations or to individuals, who were already familiar with the organization instituted by Christ. It was, therefore, in no case the object of the author of these writings to announce the existence of the Church, or to set forth and explain its constitution. The Gospel writers give fragmentary and supplementary accounts of our Lord's life and works for the purpose of persuading the reader to accept Christ as the promised Messiah, or of building up believers in faith and righteousness. The Epistles are, for the most part, concerned with the correction of irregularities in life and doctrinal errors. Even the Acts of the Apostles, though professedly historical in character, throws only an indirect light upon the questions which we are to discuss. What, in this respect, is true of the New Testament is equally true of the Fathers. They have nothing to say directly on the various points of controversy between the Romanists or the Denominationalists and ourselves, for the simple reason that the Romanism and Denominationalism against which Catholic Christians of both the Greek and Anglican Communions protest, had respectively no existence, for a thousand and fifteen hundred years.

As the Church antedates the Sacred and Patristic writings, and as they were addressed to those who had her constantly before their eyes, it is not to be expected that they will contain a systematic treatise concerning Ecclesiastical polity and other matters about which there was little, if any, dispute, until many centuries later. Under the circumstances we cannot reasonably expect to find much beyond incidental remarks and hints, which, taken in connection with the Christian institution and faith that have come down to us from the earliest times, will enable us to determine, with more or less certainty, what were the original organization and doctrines. The messages of our Presidents do not contain a history of our origin as a nation, nor do they explain our form of government. Nevertheless, if all our histories were to be lost, these documents, if preserved, would enable our descendants to determine whether or not they had departed from the constitution by which we have been governed since the time of Washington. If a thousand years hence it should be pretended by some that up to the year 1896 our form of government was an absolute monarchy, the assumption would be refuted by innumerable quotations from the Presidential messages. The same would be true if, on the other hand, any should maintain that, until our day, there were forty-nine independent nations in the United States.

Now what it is desired that the reader shall clearly perceive is this: though the argument by which it would be shown that the America of the nineteenth century was one nation under a Democratic form of government, would be chiefly inferential, it would notwithstanding be strong enough to convince the great majority of our descendants of, say, the thirtieth century. No doubt the *monarchists* on the one hand and the *multinationalists* on the other, would quote in their support many isolated passages from the messages, but the advocates of Democracy and Unity would insist that such quotations must be interpreted in harmony with the general drift of the utterances of the Presidents and with the fact that the government which had come down to them was unified and representative, and that this inestimable heritage still had the cordial support of nine out of every ten of all the millions of American citizens.

The arguments of Anglican and Greek Christians, so far as they are based upon the New Testament and Patristic writings, are confessedly, to a great extent, inferential. We infer that the extremes of Romanism and Denominationalism are wrong, because in the literary remains of the Apostolic age and first centuries, there is no trace either of the Papacy or of non-Episcopal sectarianism, while what light is indirectly thrown upon the subject reveals the truth of our conception of the Church. Nor does the doctrine concerning the Church for which we contend, stand alone in being largely supported by inferences drawn from the Bible rather than by clear, positive statements. On the contrary some of the chief doctrines set forth in the Creeds and Confessions of Faith are inferred from, rather than expressly taught by, the Scriptures. This, for example, is true even of the fundamental doctrine of the Trinity. Indeed it would seem to be a characteristic of God's revelation, whether through His works or in His Word, that only so much is made manifest as will enable the earnest student to arrive at something like satisfactory conclusions concerning the rest. Both the scientist and the theologian must ascend the ladder of inferences, the one to learn the mysteries of creation, and the other those of redemption. Of course the former must make sure that the lower end of the ladder stands upon some well-ascertained law of nature, and the latter that it is planted upon the sure Word of God, for only so will the upper end lean securely against the truth.

But we by no means rest our case wholly upon Biblical and Patristic inferences. We also appeal to history which we think bears testimony for *us* and against *them*. How far we are right in this has already appeared so far as Romanism is concerned. Unless we are greatly mistaken, it will be seen as we proceed that Denominationalism is equally unable to endure the historical test.

I.

CHRIST FOUNDED A VISIBLE CHURCH.

NO attentive reader of the Holy Scriptures, whether Episcopalian or non-Episcopalian, denies that they are filled with prophecies of, and references to something which is variously denominated "the Kingdom," "the Church," "the Body," and "the Bride of Christ." Moreover, there is no difference of opinion touching the fact that Christ would have all men to be His Disciples, and followers of His precepts and example; and that those who do His will are so united to Him, and stand in such close relationship to each other that they constitute a separate and distinct family, in the world, but not of it. All alike hold that there is a vast invisible society, composed of true believers and the pure in heart, the number of which no man, but God only, can tell. But though all who confess the name of Christ go together thus far in the interpretation of the phrases just mentioned, the Denominational minority separate from the Catholic majority, when the latter contend that the expressions have primary, if not sole, reference to a divinely constituted visible organization, the constituency of which may be determined as certainly as that of the United States or of any civilized commonwealth.

Now which of these views is right? Of all religious questions this is at the present time the one of the most world-wide and intense interest, for upon its answer depends more than upon anything else the reunion of English-speaking Christians. As the writer of one of the editorials quoted above says: "The consummation of Church Unity must wait until Protestant [non-Episcopalian] Christians are convinced that Christ instituted an Ecclesiastical society into which every follower of His should enter." The answer to the question, Did our Lord found such a society? like all the points of dispute between Denominationalists and Episcopalians, must, of course, be determined by a study of the Scriptures in the light of the Primitive Fathers and Ecclesiastical History. I say Scripture in the light of the Fathers and history, because, though the texts which can be quoted in support of the institutional conception of Christianity, are as numerous and conclusive as those that might be cited in proof of almost any of the fundamental articles of the Christian Faith, yet if we confined ourselves to them and to dogmatizing about them, the argument would be comparatively weak and unsatisfactory, because large parts of the Sacred Record which more or less clearly favor our conclusion, would not be taken into the account.

Starting then with the Scriptures as a basis, let us proceed to determine whether or not the mission of Christ, as non-Episcopalians claim, simply was the promulgation of a system of philosophy and doctrine, which, at the Ascension being left to itself, or to such voluntary associations as His Disciples might see fit to form, should leaven and regenerate the human race; or whether, as is claimed by Episcopalians, He made provision through a visible organic society for the preservation and universal dissemination of the knowledge of His revelation, precepts, and example, and for the conveyance of His enabling grace to believers, who, through the instrumentality of the Sacraments, are by the Holy Ghost joined to Him in living union as the husbandman unites the graft to the tree or vine.

That the society instituted by Christ was a visible organization rather than a school of philosophy, may be inferred from the prophecies of the Old Testament relating to the Messiah. According to them one of the chief reasons for His coming was to restore the throne of David and to establish an everlasting kingdom. Now the Davidic Kingdom was an organized visible institution. Indeed, in the nature of things, there could be no such thing as an unorganized kingdom, or an organized kingdom which would be invisible. There can be no question that the Messianic prophecies lend their support to the Episcopalian rather than to the Denominational conception of the Christian society. The same is true of the names by which this society is referred to in the New Testament Scriptures, "the Kingdom of God," "the Church of Christ," "the Body of Christ," "the Bride of Christ." These phrases all refer to a visible organism between which and an undefined school of philosophy there is no possible correspondence. Moreover, in the parabolic teaching of our Lord and the Apostles this society is compared to many things which are visible, and more or less highly organized. It is like "a field," "a vineyard," "a mustard tree," "a net," "leaven," "a city set on a hill," "the human body," "a household," "a sheepfold," and so on. Surely it will be admitted that, if Christ intended simply to preach the Gospel and leave it to spread through all the world without the aid of an institution, His doctrine might have been more aptly illustrated; but, on the other hand, if it was His intention to found a visible society in which the Gospel should be preserved during all the ages and disseminated throughout the world, no better illustrations are conceivable.

It has been held apparently upon good ground, that at least one of the similitudes, the parable of the leaven, favors the Denominational conception of an invisible Church. It is maintained that the leaven works unobserved until the whole lump is leavened. But, though this be true, the leaven itself is visible as are also the meal into which it is put and the woman who kneads the dough. If, therefore, the parable of the leaven illustrates the mysterious secret workings of the Holy Spirit, it nevertheless lends its support to the conclusion that ordinarily His operations are through the visible agencies of the Church and her ministry.

When our Lord said that He would build His Church upon the foundation of faith in His Divinity, He had reference to a visible organization. This is evident from the fulfillment of the promise of which we read in the Acts of the Apostles. On the Day of Pentecost three thousand were added to the Church. This proves that the membership of the society founded by Christ may be known, for it can be numbered, and that, therefore, the society itself is visible.

Again, the Church of Holy Scripture is not, as Denominationalists say, a human organization, founded by the voluntary coming together of Christians; but it is, as Episcopalians and the representatives of every branch of the Catholic Church hold, a Divine institution, membership in which is necessary on the part of all who would become Christians. This appears from its name, *Ecclesia,* which means an assembly of those who have been *called.* Christ established a Church, and made it the duty of its charter members, the Apostles, to go in person, and in the persons of their representatives and successors, into all the world, and by the preaching of the Gospel to call all men into that Church. Those who accepted the good news were to be admitted into the Kingdom by Baptism, and to be retained in it so long as they maintained fellowship with the Apostles by holding their doctrines, joining in the prayers, and partaking of the Eucharistic feast.

"Men speak," says the Bishop of London, "as if Christians came first, and the Church afterwards; as if the origin of the Church was in the wills of the individual Christians who composed it. But, on the contrary, throughout the teaching of the Apostles, we see that it is the Church which comes first, and the members of it afterwards. Men were not brought to Christ, and then determined that they would live in a community. Men were not brought to believe in Christ and in the Cross, and then decided that it would be a great help to their religion that they should join one another in the worship of the Father through His Name. In the New Testament, on the contrary, the Kingdom of Heaven is already in existence, and men are invited into it. The Church takes its origin, not in the will of man, but in the will of the Lord Jesus Christ. Everywhere men are called in; they do not come in, and make the Church by coming. They are called into that which already exists; they are recognized as members when they are within; but their membership depends upon their admission, and not upon their constituting themselves

a body in the sight of the Lord. In the New Testament
the Church flows out from the Lord, not flows into
Him. In the New Testament, the ministers are sent
forth to gather the children of men within the fold, and
are not simply selected by the members of the Church to
help them in their spiritual life.''

"Jesus," says another able writer, "never speaks of
the Kingdom as something which men could constitute
for themselves; it must come to them."   And Dr. Milligan, a distinguished Scotch Presbyterian professor and
author, has brought out this point with perfect clearness. "The true idea of the Church on earth," he writes,
"is, therefore, not that of a body starting from earth
and reaching onwards to a heavenly condition, to be
perfectly attained hereafter. It is rather the idea of a
Body starting from Heaven, and so exhibiting, amidst
the inhabitants and things of time, the graces and
privileges already ideally bestowed upon it, that it may
lead the world either to come to the light or to condemn
itself because it loves the darkness rather than the light,
its deeds being evil. It will follow that the community
thus constituted must be the visible representative of
our Lord, while He is Himself invisible, and that to it
must be committed the work, which, in personal presence with us, He can no longer do. As the Father
sent Me, so send I you — Prophets, Priests, and Kings—
envoys of the Father through the Spirit, proceeding
from the Father and the Son.''

The name given by Gentiles to the followers of Christ
also favors the Anglican, rather than the Denominational, conception of our Lord's mission. "The Disciples
were called Christians first in Antioch." The form of
the word *Christiani* indicates their adherence "not as
Disciples to the founder of a school — in that case
it would have been *Christici*—but rather as partisans

to a leader and commander. The Christians were not merely people of a certain way of thinking, suggested to them by Christ; they were a party who wanted Christ to be King."

Denominationalists endeavor to support their theory of the Church by such texts as "The Kingdom of God is within you." "The Kingdom of God is not meat and drink, but righteousness and peace and joy in the Holy Ghost." "For in Christ Jesus neither circumcision availeth anything nor uncircumcision, but faith which worketh by love." "Christ sent me not to baptize but to preach the Gospel." "The Church of God which he purchased with His blood." "He is the Head of the Body, the Church." "We are come to the Church of the first born who are enrolled in Heaven." "Whenever two or three are gathered together in my name, there am I in the midst of them." "Jesus said, Forbid him not, for there is no man that shall do a miracle in My Name that can lightly speak evil of Me." "For he that is not against us is on our part."

If these texts comprehended all that the New Testament has to say upon the subject, Episcopalians would have decidedly the worst of the argument; but in reality they represent only one side of the truth: the other is expressed in such passages as these: "Thou art Peter, and upon this Rock I will build My Church; and the gates of Hell shall not prevail against it. And I will give unto thee the keys of the Kingdom of Heaven: and whatsoever thou shalt bind on earth shall be bound in Heaven: and whatsoever thou shalt loose on earth shall be loosed in Heaven." "Tell it unto the Church: but if he neglect to hear the Church, let him be unto thee as an heathen man and a publican. Verily I say

C. A.—11

unto you, Whatsoever ye shall bind on earth shall be bound in Heaven: and whatsoever ye shall loose on earth shall be loosed in Heaven." "Then said Jesus to them again, Peace be unto you, as My Father hath sent Me, even so send I you. And when He had said this, He breathed on them, and saith unto them, Receive ye the Holy Ghost: whosesoever sins ye remit, they are remitted unto them; and whosesoever sins ye retain they are retained." "All power is given unto Me in Heaven and in earth. Go ye therefore, and teach all nations, baptizing them in the name of the Father, and of the Son, and of the Holy Ghost; teaching them to observe all things whatsoever I have commanded you: and lo, I am with you alway, even unto the end of the world."

These passages, and many others, including most of our Lord's Parables, and all that the Gospels have to say about the Kingdom of Heaven or of God, and the Epistles about "the Church," "the Body," and "the Bride of Christ," are inexplicable upon the Denominational hypothesis that "Christ did not institute an Ecclesiastical society into which every follower of His should enter." Romanists have made too much of them; but are Denominationalists therefore justified in passing them over altogether? Because they do not teach that the Pope is infallible and that the Papal Communion comprehends the whole of the One, Catholic, and Apostolic Church, must we conclude that they mean nothing at all, or the opposite of what they plainly say?

It is impossible for Denominationalists to explain the texts upon which they rely to prove that the Church of Christ is the unorganized invisible society of true believers, or at most the aggregate of voluntary associations of Christians, in harmony with those which Episcopalians cite as evidence that our Lord organized, or provided in the Apostles for the organization of a visible society which, through the Apostolic Succession, has been perpetuated to this day. But we have the advantage of having no difficulty whatever in explaining their texts in harmony with ours.

The texts quoted by Denominationalists against Episcopalians may be divided into two classes, those which are supposed to teach the invisibility of the Church, and such as are believed to support the pretension that there is no body of Christians which can make good an exclusive claim to allegiance. In order to prevent repetition, we shall confine ourselves for the present to the first group, reserving what we have to say about the second for other connections. And in the interest of brevity we shall consider in pairs the texts which have substantially the same import.

"The kingdom of God is within you." "The Kingdom of God is not meat and drink, but righteousness and peace and joy in the Holy Ghost." Denominationalists quote these texts for the purpose of proving that the religion of Christ is subjective rather than objective. If they can make this appear, it follows as a matter of course that the Church is essentially invisible, for, if Christianity be exclusively a religion of the heart, none but God can know who embraces it. Now no one denies that the Church of the Gospels has a spiritual side to which these texts and others like them refer; but, because we recognize this, are we logically forced to the conclusion that Ecclesiasticism is no part of Evangelical truth? Though man has an invisible mind, he nevertheless possesses a visible body. When we speak of the former without reference to the latter, it is not concluded that the person referred to has only a mental existence. Every text which relates to the invisible principles, life, and fruits, of the Christian religion, can be offset by at least a dozen that refer to a visible organization instituted by Christ. There is a universally recognized canon of interpretation which prohibits the construing of one passage of the Scriptures so as to contradict another. Only in so far as this law is ignored, is there any truth in the popular misconception that almost anything can be proved from the Bible. Had this rule not been disregarded, Denominationalists could never have found any Scriptural ground upon which to stand. In order to justify sectarianism, they invented the theory of the invisibility of the Church. This ingenious conceit was rendered plausible by the desperate expedient of interpreting a few texts so as to make them contradictory to the whole tenor of both the Old and the New Testament. Before their interpretation of the isolated passages, upon which they rest their cause, can be accepted, every book of the Bible will have to be rewritten; and not only this, but eighteen hundred years of Ecclesiastical History must be blotted out. It should be remembered, too, that, the authorized translation of the first of these texts is in dispute. Alford insists that it should be "among" instead of "within." The weight of authority inclines to this interpretation, and with good reason. It is inconceivable that our Lord in speaking to the Pharisees should have said "the Kingdom of Heaven is within you," that is, in your hearts; for in no sense was this true of them.

Those who hold that Christ did not found a visible Church, with which He would have every disciple identified, also quote these texts: "For in Christ Jesus neither circumcision availeth anything, nor uncircumcision, but faith which worketh by love." "Christ sent me not to baptize, but to preach the Gospel." As circumcision was a rite of initiation into the Jewish Church, it is argued from these texts that the externalism of the Old Dispensation has been wholly done away in the New. But upon this hypothesis the circumcision of our Lord, and His participation in the synagogue and Temple worship are inexplicable, as are also the facts that He appointed Baptism as the initiatory rite of the Society which He founded, and that the Apostles deemed it absolutely necessary to administer this Sacrament to all converts. Baptism and the Lord's Supper are so plainly required in the New Testament, that even Denominationalists almost universally have felt called upon to administer them. But so long as they maintain the invisibility of the Church, it would seem that consistency requires that, like the Quakers, they should renounce the use of visible ordinances; for by continuing to admit and retain members by their use, they witness against themselves. None of the leading non-Episcopalian Denominations will accept an unbaptized person as a member. This being the case, their representatives cannot consistently quote these texts against us.

With more plausibility Denominationalists make the following citations in support of their invisibility theory of the Church: "The Church of God which He purchased with His blood." "He is the head of the Body, the Church." There can be no doubt that if there be any such thing as an unrecognizable Church composed exclusively of the sanctified, it is here referred to. For surely the "Church of God," the "Church of Christ" includes at least all who are destined to be so happy as to attain Gospel Salvation. There is no difference of opinion between us and Denominationalists on this point. Our contention is upon the question whether or not "the Church," "the Body," has reference to a visible organization containing both good and bad. They argue, with some show of reason, that "the Body" of which Christ is the head, is, and must necessarily be, "a glorious Church, not having spot, or wrinkle, or any such thing, but that it should be holy and without blemish." But this in all probability is not the declaration of an existing fact. It is more likely a prophecy of what the Church will be at the consummation of all things when the tares shall be separated from the wheat.

It is asserted that a "body having corrupt members cannot have an immaculate Head." We reply that God was certainly the head of the Jewish Church which had many unrighteous members; in fact all who belonged to it were more or less so. "Everybody allows," says Mr. Hammond, "that the ancient Jewish Church, the Church before Christ, was a visible Church, and God's Church—God's Church and people, in spite of its many corruptions—and one Church and one body, the communion of the circumcised: every one knows how depraved, how rotten, even that was, and yet every man who knows his Bible also knows that it was not lawful for any man to leave it and found another." The Psalmist declares there is "none holy, no, not one." As in the Old Dispensation, all failed in their efforts to keep the law, so in the New all have fallen short of their high calling in Christ Jesus. Thus if our Lord be the Head of any Church, it must be of a body in which not only some, but all its members are more or less imperfect. If credence is given to their own testimony, it will be admitted that the most eminent Saints in all ages have been far from perfect. And if, as Denominationalists contend "the Church is composed not of the christened, but of the Christlike," then there is not, never has been, and probably never will be, a Scriptural Church on earth. Even the Apostles St. Peter, St. Paul and St. Barnabas would not have been eligible for membership in such a Church. If Churches consist of the "Christlike" only, most of them will be reduced to "me and the meenister" with grave doubts as to the minister! "Let us suppose," says William Law in his letters to the Bishop of Bangor, "that the Church of Christ was this invisible number of people united to Christ by such internal invisible graces. Is it possible that a kingdom, consisting of this one particular sort of people invisibly good, should be like a net that gathers of every kind of fish? If it were to be compared to a net, it ought to be compared to such a net as gathers only of one kind, namely, good fish, and then it might represent to us a Church that has but one sort of members. If anyone should tell us that we are to believe invisible Scriptures and observe invisible Sacraments, he would have just as much reason and Scripture on his side as your Lordship has for this doctrine. And it would be of the same service to the world to talk of these invisibilities if the canon of Scripture were in dispute, as to describe this invisible Church, when the case is with what visible Church we ought to unite."

That the texts do not support the Denominational theory of invisibility is further evident from the fact that one of them, as we see from the context, refers to a Church having "Elders," whom St. Paul exhorts "to feed the Church of God." Now, these Ephesian Elders and the Christians whom they were charged to shepherd were visible. It is impossible otherwise to think of them. In the other text the Church is spoken of as "the Body of Christ." An invisible body is also unthinkable. It is of the essence of a body to be recognizable. The Denominationalists, themselves, do not think of something invisible when they speak of the Congregational, Presbyterian, Baptist and Methodist bodies. These are all visible societies.

There still remains the strongest text quoted by Denominationalists to prove their theory. "We are come," says the writer of the Epistle to the Hebrews, "to the Church of the first born who are enrolled in Heaven." At first sight it would seem as if they must be right in maintaining that such words cannot possibly have reference to a Church composed of both good and bad. The difficulty arises from the mistaken idea that the names of none can be written in the Book of Life, except of those who are in the state of salvation, and destined to remain so to their life's end. It is strange that those who have so much to say about "conversion," and "backsliding," should lose sight of the fact that a name once registered in Heaven may be blotted out. If there be such a thing as falling from grace, no reason can be assigned why the word Church in this passage should mean something different from what it does everywhere else in Holy Scripture.

If, now, we turn for a few minutes to history, we shall see even more clearly than we have seen from our necessarily incomplete examination of the Scriptures, that the society instituted by Christ is a visible organization.

The Sacrament of Baptism, as we already have had occasion to observe, conclusively shows this to be the case; it has been administered from the beginning almost universally. Though there has been some difference of opinion, especially since the Reformation, as to the benefits annexed to this ordinance, all agree that it formally admits the recipient to the society of believers.

Now, a society which makes provision by the administration of a visible Sacrament, for the reception into membership of visible men and women, is certainly a visible organization.

The legislation of this society as manifestly proves it to have been highly organized. The pages of Ecclesiastical History from the beginning to the end are largely occupied with the accounts of the Councils, Synods and Convocations which have borne essentially the same relation to the society founded by Christ as Senates, Parliaments and Legislatures bear to the various civil commonwealths of the world. These Legislative Assemblies of the Church, the first of which met at Jerusalem in Apostolic times, settled disputes; decided which books were Divinely inspired and should, therefore, be regarded as a part of the Bible; formulated the Faith once delivered to the Saints; and passed a great body of laws or canons for the regulation of the Church. The Councils and their acts prove beyond peradventure that the society founded by Christ, was a visible organization, just as much so as is the United States, or any other nation.

The persecutions which the Church suffered during the first four or five centuries prove the same. It was the uniform policy of the civil authorities to smite the Christian Shepherds that the sheep might be scattered. An unorganized society would have had no rulers that could have been singled out from the rest to suffer the terrible vengeance of the law, and obviously an invisible society could not have been persecuted at all.

The fact that the Church has in all ages excommunicated those who have been guilty of great offenses, also proves that she is a visible organization. That part of St. Paul's second Epistle to the Corinthians in which he gives directions concerning the course to be pursued in

the case of a notorious evil liver, and the excommunication of Arius and other notable heresiarchs by the
Councils, are inexplicable upon the Denominational
hypothesis of an invisible Church.

But perhaps the strongest historical argument in
favor of that view of Christ's mission for which we contend, namely, that in addition to the teaching of a new
philosophy of life and illustrating it in a career of self-
sacrifice which ended in the atoning death on the cross,
He organized a new Kingdom, is found in the simple fact
that before the Reformation the Denominational idea
never obtained. For fifteen hundred years it was universally believed that Christ had made provision for the
preservation of the new wine of the Gospel by the creation for it of a new receptacle, the Church. The notion
that the hearts of true believers were to be the only
receptacles, never occurred to anyone, and a suggestion
to this effect would have been ridiculed as preposterous.
How this could have been the case, if the theory of an
unorganized invisible Church be correct, has never been
satisfactorily explained.

In closing our argument in favor of the Episcopalian
conception of the Church, we may venture to call attention to the inconsistency of the great majority of those
who would persuade us that the society instituted by
Christ was not a visible organization. Methodists,
Presbyterians, Baptists, Congregationalists and many
other bodies of Christians have made for themselves
more or less elaborate organizations, and are leaving
no stone unturned which will contribute to their upbuilding. By doing so they virtually profess to be wiser
than Christ; for, according to their representation, He
had not like them the wisdom to perceive the necessity
for a corporate Christianity. They contend that the
Christian religion without organization could not, un-

der present conditions, make progress against opposing
influences in the conquest of the world for Christ. In
this they are unquestionably right. There can be no
doubt that if the various organizations of Christians
were to disband, the cause of Christ would rapidly wane
until Satan could boast of a complete triumph. But
were the conditions of the first centuries more favorable
to Christianity than they have been for the past two
or three hundred years, within which it has been found
necessary to organize several hundred Christian societies? No. On the contrary, the Gospel in our day
would stand a thousand chances to one in our Lord's
time of making its way without the assistance of an
organization. The greatest obstacle now to be overcome is a languid indifference; then the way had to be
fought through a solid phalanx of the most powerful
and persistent opposition. It would be a marvel beyond all comprehension, if the Divine Founder of our
Holy Religion who knew that He would be nailed to the
cross and that His Apostles and their successors for a
long time would nearly all suffer martyrdom, had been
so devoid of foresight as to quit the world without
leaving an organization which would be compact and
vigorous enough to live and grow in spite of all the
organized forces which heathendom, through the
representatives of the Roman Empire, could muster
against it.

St. Augustine, one of the greatest theologians that
the Church has produced, must, therefore, have been
right when, as an able summariser points out, he taught
that "The Kingdom of God was not a mere hope, but a
present reality; not a mere name for a Divine idea, but
an institution, duly organized among men, subsisting
from one generation to another; closely inter-connected
with earthly rule, with definite guidance to give, and a

definite part to take in all the affairs of actual life. To him the Kingdom of God was an actual Polity, just as the Roman Empire was a Polity, too. It was 'visible' in just the same way as the earthly state, for it was a real institution with definite organization, with a recognized constitution, with a code of laws and means of enforcing them, with property for its use, and officers to direct it."

II.

PERPETUATED BY SUCCESSORS OF THE APOSTLES.

THAT our Lord intended His Church or Kingdom to continue through the ages is antecedently probable, because the conditions which made the founding of it necessary, would require its continuation. This generation of sinful men and women needs the regenerating influence of the Church quite as much as that which witnessed its founding. To argue otherwise would be to accuse of partiality Him who was no respecter of persons.

Again it may be inferred, if not positively concluded, from Holy Scripture that the Church was designed to continue through all generations. The numerous prophecies of the Old Testament in which the mission of the Messiah is represented to be that of founding an everlasting Kingdom and universal Dominion certainly favor this conclusion. When our Lord said "upon this rock," the confession of faith in His Divinity, "I will build My Church and the gates of Hell shall not prevail against it;" when He commissioned His Apostles to "Go and teach all nations, baptizing them in the name of the Father and of the Son and of the Holy Ghost; teaching them to observe all things whatsoever

I have commanded;" and when He gave them this promise for their encouragement, "Lo! I am with you alway even unto the end of the world," it is as if he had proclaimed the perpetuity of the Church in almost so many words. Certainly nothing else can be inferred from these texts.

Furthermore, if the Church were to continue, since it could only do so through a succession of officers, it is antecedently probable that the Apostolic College, which after the Ascension, was the visible head of the Church, would not be allowed to die out with the twelve. All other organizations that the world has ever known, have made provision for a succession of their chief officers, and there is no reason to suppose that it was to be otherwise with the Church of Christ. The promise, "Lo, I am with you alway, even unto the end of the world," besides proving that the Church is to endure through all the ages, proves the same of the Apostolic office. The College of Apostles was constituted a moral, corporate personality, which was to continue to the end of the world. Its identity is no more diminished by the perpetual succession of its members, than our individuality is affected by the constant change of the elements that compose our bodies.

The fact that the Apostolate was not limited to the original twelve, justifies the inference that this office was to be perpetuated in an uninterrupted succession. Matthias was elected to take the place of Judas. St. Paul claimed to be an Apostle, not of men, but by the direct appointment of Christ, and his claim was recognized by the other Apostles. James, the Lord's brother, evidently was consecrated by the Apostolic College the first Apostle or Bishop of Jerusalem. Timothy and Titus were made Apostles, respectively, of Ephesus and Crete. St. Jerome, one distinguished even among Saints, himself only a Presbyter, writes: "Immediately after the passion of the Lord, James was ordained by the Apostles Bishop of Jerusalem." "That Timothy was a Bishop," says Bishop Bull, "and Bishop of Ephesus, the metropolis, or chief city of Asia, is so fully attested by all antiquity, that he must be either very ignorant or very shameless that shall deny it, especially there being besides very plain evidence of the Episcopal power and authority, wherewith he was invested, in this very Epistle of St. Paul written to him." St. Jerome calls Titus "Bishop of Crete;" St. Ambrose says, "The Apostle Consecrated Titus Bishop;" Theodoret, that he was "the Bishop of the Cretans;" and so the whole band of witnesses.

When, in addition to what might naturally be inferred, we take into account the fact that in all ages and every part of the world there have been men claiming to be, and universally recognized as, successors to the Apostles, the conclusion that the inference respecting the perpetuation of the Church through Bishops of the Apostolic Succession is correct, can hardly be resisted. As Mr. Haddan points out, "in one sense Apostolic Succession requires a complicated proof; in another it is a palpable fact—as much a matter of moral certainty as is the actual appointment, by the rightful authority, of ministers of the state. No one doubts the fact of the Ordination of the Clergy or Bishops now officiating, although, among some myriads, there may occasionally have been an impostor. Yet this assurance is not founded on personal inspection of legal evidence. It rests upon the overwhelming presumption that the fact would not be as it is, unless the legal evidence were behind it; and this presumption extends back to the beginning as regards the Church." "It is," as Bishop Hugh Miller Thompson says, "merely trifling with words if a man knows, and evidence of incompetency to express an opinion if he does not know, to say, 'you cannot prove that, from any modern Bishop up to the Apostles, there is a continuous succession of Ordainers.' You might as well tell me I cannot prove that the oak tree on the lawn has an unbroken descent from some oak of two thousand years ago! I do not need to prove a self-evident fact in nature, or a self-evident fact in organic society. The oak of to-day proves the oak of twenty centuries ago. The Bishop of to-day proves the Bishop of eighteen centuries ago. They knew oaks then from bramble bushes as well as we do. They knew Bishops just as well as we do, perhaps better, and they knew, too, that Bishops came from Bishops as oaks come from oaks. There is no other way known to man to get either oaks or Bishops. The ground has been gone over so many times, and so carefully and exhaustively, and by such thorough scholarship, that one may rest in peace."

There can be no doubt that, if the Apostolic office were continued in the Church, it would be the center of unity and the fountain of ministerial authority; hence we are right in saying that the Church itself was perpetuated through the Apostles and their successors. They were the representatives of Christ, and after His Ascension, the visible head of the Church. Before He returned to the right hand of the Father to make intercession for us He gave them all power and said: "As my Father hath sent me even so send I you." Nothing, therefore, could be more certain than that the Apostles and their successors were appointed by Christ Himself to be His representatives. As before the Ascension there would have been no Church without Christ as its head, so since then, there can be no true Christian Church without the representative headship of the Apostolate.

We are aware that these inferences will seem new and strange to many, but we submit to the candid reader that they are naturally drawn from the texts which have passed under review. And we are all the more confident as to the correctness of our conclusions, because of the fact that they are in accord with the representations that were made by the early Fathers and the great Doctors of the Church. Let us see what some of them have to say about (1) the perpetuation of the Apostolic office in the Episcopate, and (2) the necessity of Bishops to the existence of the Church.

1. What then do the ancients say concerning the perpetuation of the Apostolic office through the Historic Episcopate?

St. Clement of Rome, A. D. 95, says that "desiring to avoid controversy which they foresaw, the Apostles ordained certain men to the end that, when they should have fallen asleep in death, others of approved character might succeed to their special office." Such were Timothy and Titus.

Irenæus, A. D. 180: "We must obey those who are the Elders in the Church, those who, as we have shown, have the succession from the Apostles; who, with the succession of the Episcopate, have received also the sure gift of truth, according to the will of the Father; but as for the rest, who leave the original succession, and come together wherever it may be, them we must hold in suspicion, whether as heretics of a wrong opinion, or as men who make division through pride and self-pleasing, or again, as hypocrites." "All who wish to see the truth, have it in their power to fix their eyes on the tradition of the Apostles, which is manifested in all the world; and we can recount the number of those, who were appointed by the Apostles as Bishops in the Churches, and their successors down to our own time, who neither taught nor had any knowledge of the wild notions of these men. For had the Apostles known any mysteries which they taught to the perfect in private, and unknown to the rest, they would have delivered them to those surely before all others, to whom they intrusted the very Churches themselves. For they desired them to be eminently perfect and utterly without reproach, whom they left behind as their actual successors, handing on to them their own position of presidency."

Tertullian, A. D., 200, adopts Irenæus' line of argument and enlarges upon it in dealing with Gnostic heretics. He asks them a double question: First, do they hold the rule of Faith? Second, have they an Apostolic Succession? "Let them produce the account of the origins of their Churches; let them unroll the line of their Bishops, running down in such a way from the beginning that their first Bishop shall have had for his authorizer and predecessor one of the Apostles, or of the Apostolic men who continued to the end in their fellowship. This is the way in which the Apostolic Churches hand on their registers. As the Church of the Smyrnæans relates that Polycarp was installed by John, as the Church of the Romans relates that Clement was ordained by Peter, so, in like manner, the rest of the Churches exhibit the names of men appointed to the Episcopate by Apostles, whom they possess as transmitters of the Apostolic seed." "So, now, you who wish to exercise your curiosity to better profit in the matter of your salvation, run through the Apostolic Churches, where the very chairs of the Apostles still preside in their own places—Corinth, Philippi, Thessalonica, Ephesus, Rome. Make it your business to inquire what they have learnt and taught!"

Nor had the Fathers any other thought of Bishops but as successors in the very Office and Order of the

C. A.—12

Apostles. "Irenæus," observes a learned commentator, "regards the Bishops in every Church as succeeding in an especial sense to the Apostles. They represent in every place by Apostolic Succession the Catholic Faith; they have the 'gift of the truth' and the Apostolic authority of government; they are the guardians also no doubt of the grace by which Christians live, of which as much as of the truth the Church is the 'rich treasury.'" And St. Jerome, A. D. 390, commenting on that saying of St. Paul, "Other Apostles saw I none save James the Lord's brother," says: "For by degrees, as time went on, others were ordained Apostles by those whom the Lord had chosen, as that passage to the Philippians proves, saying: 'I supposed it necessary to send to you Epaphroditus, your Apostle.'" "The Bishops," observes Pacian, "are called Apostles, as Paul declareth in speaking of Epaphroditus."

So that as has been well said, "if the words of Holy Scripture be not altogether unmeaning and unsubstantial, if the Church of the Apostles be anything more than a phantom or a vision, if its first rulers, St. James and St. John, Clement and Epaphroditus, Ignatius and Polycarp, were really what they seem to have been, what they claimed to be, and what they were admitted to be, then is it most certain that they, and all their successors after them, were, as universal Christendom believed, Bishops or Apostles in the Church of God."

As the author makes no claim to being a Patristic scholar or an historical authority, a few quotations from the writings of those who have been preëminently such will greatly strengthen his position, and so carry conviction to the reader. Hooker: "Let us not fear to be herein bold and peremptory, that, if anything in the

Church's government, surely the first institution of Bishops was from Heaven, was even of God: the Holy Ghost was the author of it." Bishop Bilson: "Of this [the Apostolical Succession] there is so perfect record, in all the stories and Fathers of the Church, that I must muse with what face men that have any taste of learning, can deny the vocation of Bishops came from the Apostles; for that they succeeded the Apostles and Evangelists in their Churches and chaires may inevitably be proved, if any Christian persons or Churches deserve to be credited." Bishop Sanderson: "The Bishops are the lawful successors of the Apostles and inheritors of their power." Archbishop Bramhall: "The line of Apostolic Succession is the very nerves and sinews of Ecclesiastical unity and communion both with the present Church, and with the Catholic symbolical Church of all successive ages." Bishop Taylor: "Episcopacy relies not upon the authority of the Fathers and Councils, but upon Scripture, upon the institution of Christ, or the institution of the Apostles, upon an universal tradition and an universal practice, not upon the words and opinions of the Doctors; and it hath as great a testimony as Scripture itself hath." Archbishop Laud: "This I will say, and abide by it, that the calling of Bishops is *jure divino*, by Divine right." Canon Liddon: "When we say that Bishops are successors of the Apostles we are not formulating a theory, but stating a fact of history." Bishop Moberly: "The historical fact of an Episcopal Succession, tracing back to the Apostles themselves, is undeniably established." And even John Calvin in writing to a friend who had recently been consecrated to the Episcopate, felt constrained to acknowledge: "Thou hast been appointed a Bishop; with thee is present the authority of the Apostle Paul."

Presbyterians, Lutherans, Methodists and some other bodies of Christians who are without the Historic Episcopate, claim that if there be any ministerial succession coming down to us from New Testament times, it is through the order of Presbyters or elders, not that of the Apostles. They affirm that, after the death of St. John, the Church was governed by colleges of the Presbytery of which, when Christianity had been well established, there was one in every large city. These had jurisdiction over adjacent villages and the surrounding country. Each of them had a Moderator or President who was elected from year to year. In the course of time reëlections became almost the universal rule. As the Moderator-Presbyters were usually men of great force and influence and withal men of ambition, they soon, either by common consent or usurpation, set aside their brother Presbyters and assumed the authority and prerogatives of the Apostolate under the title of Bishops.

In proof of all this they urge the probability that there was an early period of the Church's life when "Bishop" and "Presbyter" were convertible terms. And, it is, indeed, a curious and admitted fact that there is no special name absolutely restricted to the highest Order, on which all others depend, in the New Testament. "But," as Mr. Eagar observes, "whatsoever may be the explanation, the Order of the Episcopate shares this namelessness with even greater things. The second Sacrament has no absolutely distinctive Scriptural name; it may be referred to once as 'the Lord's Supper;' it is called 'Eucharistia,' but that word is employed also in other meanings; our common name of 'Holy Communion' is not to be found in the Bible. The Doctrine of the Incarnation has to go outside Scripture for a name in which to sum up the revealed truths, and we have to employ a word not found in Scripture whenever we speak of the Everlasting God as 'the Trinity.' In all these matters, sensible persons have long ago learned that names count for very little and facts for a great deal; the same observation applies at least as forcibly to the question of the Episcopate." It is probable that in the case of some of the Churches founded by St. Paul, the chief Elder had the oversight of the flock during the Apostle's absence; but there is no evidence that such overseers or Bishops had the power of ordaining, or that they were anything more than the Archpriests, or Archdeacons of later days. But the period of this Presbyterial overseership, if it existed at all, was so brief and confined to such narrow limits; its history was so obscure, and the speedy emergence of the threefold order so universal, that nothing in regard to the permanent constitution of the Church can be built upon the fact of the identity for which our brethren contend. A departure from the universal rule of centuries cannot be justified by a reference to the possible practice of one brief, transitional period of history. If in the Apostolic age Presbyters were sometimes called Bishops, it was only because the highest Order of Church governors to which this title was afterwards reserved, were in the earliest ages generally called Apostles. "The Bishops," says St. Ambrose, "are Apostles;" and St. Cyprian: "The Lord appointed Apostles, that is, Bishops;" and St. Jerome, "Bishops occupy the place of Apostles;" and Pacian, "the Bishops are entitled Apostles;" and Tertullian, "were first ordained by the Apostles;" and St. Irenæus, "are traced in all Churches from the Apostles;" and St. Augustine, "are instead of Apostles;" and, in one word, all the Saints and all Martyrs, all Churches, and all times, declare the same truth—that Bishops are the

Apostles of the Most High; or that, in the words of Hooker: "The first Bishops in the Church of Christ were His blessed Apostles."*

Presbyterians are ever reminding us, also, of what St. Jerome says about the Church at Alexandria. It is, as they say, at least possible to conclude from his account that when the Patriarchal See fell vacant, it was filled by the election of a Presbyter who, by this act, without Episcopal Consecration, became Bishop. To this we reply: (1) St. Jerome nowhere actually says that an Alexandrian clergyman who had received Ordination to the Presbyterial office only, became Bishop simply because of his election to the Episcopate by brother Presbyters. (2) Even if at Alexandria the election was not followed by Consecration to the Episcopate, this departure from the general rule may be accounted for upon the hypothesis that some of the Parochial Clergy had been duly invested with the Episcopal character by the laying on of hands. At a later period this is known to have been the case at Rome, and it probably accounts for the fact that in the early British Church there were so many more Bishops than Dioceses. Of course these possible Bishops of Alexandria could not legally exercise the functions of the Episcopate until they had been canonically elected to a vacant See, but after such election they could, without further qualification, ascend the Episcopal throne.§

As the late Prebendary Sadler, one of the most profound of modern Biblical students, in a tract on Church government, says: "The idea of an Apostolically-ordained Presbyterian, or other such system, following upon the death of the Apostles and existing for any length of time, appears to me to be involved in the greatest difficulties. It seems incredible that a Presbyterate appointed by Knox

* Appendix I. § Appendix II.

and Melville, should have lasted three hundred years, whilst a supposed corresponding system, appointed by St. Paul himself, hopelessly collapsed in half a century." Elsewhere he sums up the case thus: "(1) We have the Lord Himself personally appointing the Apostles and apparently assuring them that their ministry would last till the end of the world. (2) We have in the New Testament the history of the first thirty or forty years of the Church, during the whole of which period the one sole, supreme government is the Apostolic, with the exception of the Church in one city. (3) This exception is the Mother Church of Christendom, which, if St. James be not an Apostle, is under Episcopal as distinguished from Apostolic rule. (4) We have the great Apostle of the Gentiles ruling the Churches committed to him with an hyper-Episcopal oversight, keeping apparently all power of every sort in his own hands. (5) We have the Apostle at the close of his career writing letters to the men through whose means he had exercised his Episcopal control over Churches in all parts of the civilized world, in order to instruct them in the right use of the quasi-Apostolic powers he had made over to them. Then there is a gap of some seventy years at the most, and at the end of this period history presents us with the spectacle of the Christian Church everywhere officered by men possessing the Governmental and Ordaining powers of the Apostolic delegates, though, as was to be expected, with more defined and localized spheres of action. And yet apparently for the one almost avowed purpose of interposing some break, and proving a disconnection between the Apostolic and any later ministry, we are asked to assume the existence of some intermediate Presbyterian or Congregational system, of the constitution of which history has not preserved to us one fragment, and which, if established, must have been established without any principles of permanency impressed upon it, so that, according to the confession of those who conjecture it, its very memory had perished out of the mind of the Church within a hundred years after its appointment."

The obscure but short period between the last of the Apostolic and the first of the post-Apostolic writers, during which, according to the representations of Denominationalists, the Church was governed by a Board of Presbyters, has been compared to a tunnel. We have good light where we have the books of the New Testament to guide us, and again when we come down to the abundant literary remains of the latter part of the second century; but there is an intervening period, here and there faintly illumined by a few documents giving such scanty and interrupted light as may be afforded by the air-holes of a tunnel. If in our study of the dimly-lighted portion of the history we wish to distinguish what is certain from what is doubtful, we may expect to find the things certain in what can be seen from either of the two well-lighted ends. If the same thing is visible on looking from either end, we can have no doubt of its existence. Beyond question the Church, before entering the tunnel, was governed by Apostles and when it came out, by Bishops, claiming to be successors of the Apostles.

We shall conclude this division of our subject with a famous passage from Chillingworth's crushing answer to the representations of Presbyterians: "When I shall see all the fables in the 'Metamorphoses' acted and proved true stories; when I shall see all the democracies and aristocracies in the world lie down to sleep, and awake into monarchies, then I will begin to believe that Presbyterial government, having continued in the

Church during the Apostles' times, should presently after, against the Apostles' Doctrine and the will of Christ, be wheeled about like a scene in a mask and transformed into Episcopacy. In the meantime, while these things are thus incredible and in human reason impossible, I hope I shall have leave to conclude thus: Episcopal government was universally received in the Church presently after the Apostles' times. Between the Apostles and this presently after, there was not time enough for, nor possibility of, so great an alteration; and, therefore, there was not such alteration as is pretended. And, therefore, Episcopacy being so ancient and Catholic, must be granted also to be Apostolic."

2. In reference to the necessity of Bishops to the existence of the Church, it may be said that, since they are the successors of the Apostles, it follows as a matter of course that, as there could have been no Church in the Apostolic days without the headship of "the eleven" and those whom they made partakers with themselves in the Apostolate, so, after their time, there could be none without a Bishop. We see from the Acts that the first disciples "continued steadfastly in the Apostles' doctrine and fellowship." This was, in the nature of things, a necessary condition of membership in Christ's Apostolic Church. As Bishops of the uninterrupted and Canonical succession are nothing less than Apostles, it is, in the nineteenth century as in the first, obligatory upon all professing Christians to be in communion with one of them. At any rate this view prevailed down through the ages until the Reformation.

St. Ignatius, A. D. 107, writes: "Where the Bishop appears, there let the people be, as where is Christ Jesus, there is the Catholic Church." "The Bishop is the center of each individual Church, as Jesus Christ is the center of the universal Church." "He who does anything apart from the Bishop, and the Presbytery, and Deacons is not pure in his conscience." "For as many as are of God and of Jesus Christ, they are with the Bishop." Elsewhere the same Father says: "Do your diligence, therefore, that ye be confirmed in the ordinances of the Lord and of the Apostles, that ye may prosper in all things whatsoever ye do in flesh and spirit in the Son and Father and in the Spirit, with your revered Bishop, and with the fitly wreathed spiritual circlet of your Presbytery, and with the Deacons who walk after God. Be obedient to the Bishop and to one another, as Jesus Christ was to the Father, according to the flesh, and as the Apostles were to Christ and to the Father, that there may be union both of flesh and of spirit."

Irenæus, A. D. 180, gave laconic expression to the conviction which universally prevailed during the first fifteen hundred years of Christianity, when he said: "No Church without a Bishop."

The blessed Athanasius, A. D. 350, writing to one who had fled from the duties of the Episcopal office, for fear of persecution, says, "How wouldst thou have become a Christian, if there had been no Bishops?" And then he proceeds to assert, in the uniform language of the primitive Saints, from the Martyrs Ignatius and Irenæus down to Basil and Ambrose, that the Church is in such sort built upon the Bishops—that is, the Apostles of our Lord Jesus Christ—that the one cannot even be contemplated as distinct from the other; a Church without Bishops being, in the judgment of these ancients, not "defective," or "imperfect" merely, but, as they speak, "no Church at all."

Speaking of the necessity of Bishops to the existence of the Church, the author of "Notes on the Catholic

Episcopate," says: "So constant was this belief among all lands wheresoever the Gospel had been preached, that even those misbelievers who fled out of the ark of the Church, and formed to themselves conventicles apart, never dreamed of setting up any purer or more primitive—nay, or any other—form of government than this, but perpetuated their errors by a succession of Pseudo-Bishops. And, when certain women, 'led away with divers lusts,' and seeking to annul even the distinction between the sexes, ventured to usurp the office of teachers, and to frame a new company of believers, it was by imitating the only order which they had ever heard of, and appointing from their own ranks Bishops, Priests, and Deacons, that they attempted to execute their impious plan."

So far as Holy Scripture is concerned, one passage only has been quoted as leaving an opening for other than an Episcopally ordained ministry in the Church of Christ. "Forbid him not," said our Lord of the man who cast out devils in His name, while not following the Apostles. But an injunction not to forbid work does not necessarily imply its orderliness, or even legality; and what is there, save a very doubtful analogy, to connect this man's actions with the work of the ministry? We should not be at all willing to forbid the work of, say, "The Young Men's Christian Association," or to deny that it is "on Christ's part." But we should be greatly surprised if this were construed into a recognition of any claims that its worthy secretaries might put forth to be a branch of the Christian ministry. It is quite certain, at any rate, that neither in the New Testament, nor in Church History, is there any trace of the followers of this man, or of any like him, as a separate body of Christians. So that one of two things must have happened—either his work absolutely died out, or he found that very work a means of drawing him into the fellowship of the Apostles.

III.

THE APPOINTED ARK OF SALVATION.

THE Church of Christ which has been perpetuated through the Historic Episcopate is the appointed ark of Gospel Salvation, and only by entering it can a person place himself in assured covenant relationship with God. Passing by for the present the difficulties which this statement will suggest to the minds of non-Episcopalian readers, let us first see what reasonably may be inferred from the Scriptures and what light the writings of the Fathers and Doctors throw upon the subject.

It must be evident to every attentive reader of the Bible that it divides the human race into two great classes—those who are in covenant relationship with God, and those who are without the pale of his covenanted mercies. A religious covenant is an agreement which God condescends to enter into with man. Between man and man there are, speaking broadly, two kinds of agreements—the commercial and the beneficent. The former has in view mutual profit, but the latter is of no benefit to the contracting party who takes the initiative except the satisfaction he experiences in the effort to bless. Where a covenant between God and man exists it is of course so far as He is concerned one of grace.

The importance of entering into such relationship with God may be inferred from the fact that the Creator Himself proposes it. He certainly would not do so, if it were a trifling matter. Our falling in with this proposal must, therefore, contribute to our highest eternal welfare and to the great glory of God. The same may be inferred even more clearly from the fact that both the Jewish and Christian Scriptures are called Testaments, a word which in Holy Writ is synonymous with covenant; indeed the titles of Old and New Testaments arose from an inaccurate rendering in the Latin Vulgate of the word meaning covenant by *testamentum.* It would be a decided gain if the correct titles could be used. In the Revised Version of the New Testament the word "covenant" is almost without exception the translation.

Now the title of a book or of a collection of writings is drawn from the chief subject treated of. The fact that the Bible is divided into Old and New Covenants is therefore very instructive. It shows that God not only proposes to enter into covenant relationship with us, but that He makes it the principal topic of His Revelation, which He would not do if it were not supremely important. The Church is the ark of Salvation because only by entering it and by remaining in it, can a person be in covenant relationship with God. That under the Old Dispensation none could establish this relationship except by membership in the Jewish Church is, in the light of the Law and the Prophets, so manifest that I presume it will not be questioned by any; and since membership in the Church of God was so necessary in the Old Dispensation, all will admit that we ought not to conclude without the best of reasons that it is any less so in the New. There is, however, no ground for such a conclusion. On the contrary, all the facts point in the other direction. God does not change; the condition and needs of mankind have remained the same; and Christ expressly declares that He came not to destroy, but to fulfill the Old Covenant Scriptures. These considerations, though falling short of a positive proof that the Church occupies as important a place in the present Dispensation as in the preceding, render it at least highly improbable that the assertion to the contrary is true.

But that which we have seen to be antecedently probable must be apparent, it would seem, to all who have the least familiarity with the Gospels and Epistles. These when taken as a whole, and especially when interpreted in the light of the writings of the Fathers who lived nearest the time of the Apostles, leave no room for reasonable doubt that he who would be in covenant relationship with God and thus make sure that he is an inheritor of Gospel Salvation, must be a member of the Apostolic Church. Those who think that they have made their calling and election sure because they have been converted and are in the enjoyment of experimental religion, that is, have, as they say, the witness of the Spirit that they are saved, will find it difficult to explain satisfactorily many of the most striking passages of the New Testament.

Why, for example, did our Lord in His commission to the Apostles connect Baptism with the preaching of the Gospel and the teaching of obedience? Why was Baptism administered to the three thousand upon whom, on the Day of Pentecost, the Holy Ghost fell; or why to St. Paul who, upon the occasion of his miraculous conversion, was smitten to the ground and made blind by the heavenly light; or to Cornelius who had the assurance of an angel that he was accepted of God? These and many similar questions cannot be answered by those who attach little or no importance to the Ecclesiastical side of the Gospel. The theory that salvation is offered upon the condition of conversion, is one of those half truths which leave a large part of the New Testament unexplained and inexplicable. In the Christian Dispensation as in the Jewish there can be no assurance of salvation outside of the covenant relationship, and this cannot be entered now any more than it could then by faith and conversion alone, but with these through the door of membership in the Church which has come down to us from Christ through Bishops of the Apostolic Succession. Nevertheless baptized Denominationalists as well as Greek, Roman, and Anglican Catholics are regarded as members of this Church, if they be not willfully but ignorantly separatists, because in their Baptism they thought they were uniting with the true Church of Christ and the will is taken for the deed. Baptism may be valid although not regular. To many this will look as if we exalted the Church at the expense of what they call "vital religion." But faith, conversion, and other Evangelical doctrines are not really undervalued in the Episcopal Church. It is not that we make less of these doctrines but more of the Church than Denominationalists do. We think that the Scriptures justify us in this; and to verify the correctness of our interpretation of them to this effect, we appeal to the writings of those who lived nearest to the time of the Apostles.

Ignatius, of Antioch, A. D. 107, as we have just seen, says: "Where the Bishop appears, there let the people be, as where is Christ Jesus, there is the Catholic Church." Again, "He who is within the Sanctuary is pure; he who is outside is impure, that is to say, he who does anything apart from Bishop and Presbytery and Deacons, is not pure in his conscience." "If anyone follows a separatist, he does not inherit the Kingdom of God." So also Irenæus, Bishop of Lyons, A. D. 180: "In the Church God placed Apostles, Prophets, Doctors, and the whole operation of the Spirit, and all who do not have recourse to the Church do not participate in Him, but deprive themselves of life. For where the Church is, there is the

Spirit of God, and where the Spirit of God is, there is the Church and all grace." "God will judge all those who make schisms. No reformation can be wrought by them, which can compensate for the injury of the schism. God will judge all those who are outside the Church." And Cyprian, of Africa, A. D. 250: "Whosoever shall be found without the Church, will be cut off from the number of sons. He will not have God for his Father, who refused to have the Church for his Mother." "To separate from the Church is to deny that Christ came in the flesh; because it is to scatter that which He gathered together in one. This is to be Antichrist!" "If a separatist should lay down his life for the name of Christ, he would die unblest." "The House of God is one, and no man can have salvation except in the Church." He also speaks, as did some copies of the earlier Baptismal Creeds, of "remission of sins, and eternal life through the Church." Origen, A. D. 230, says, "Outside this House, that is to say, outside the Church, no one has salvation."

This language, astounding as it must be to modern Denominationalists, is not as strong as that used by the renowned Augustine, A. D. 398. He spoke as follows of a class of sectaries, who, as respects their doctrinal teaching, were certainly orthodox: "I do not assert that if a Donatist should profess to have suffered any injuries in the cause of his party, or to have endured temporal losses, it would profit him nothing; I say more. I say, that if he should suffer without the pale of the Church, it will be as the enemy of Christ; and if one of Christ's enemies should say to him, being without the Church, 'Offer sacrifice to our idols, worship our gods,' and he, through refusing to worship, should be slain by the enemy of Christ, his blood he may pour out, a crown he cannot receive." "The Holy mountain of God," he says elsewhere, "is His Holy Church. Those who are not in communion with her will not attain to everlasting life." And still more pointedly, "Christ is the head and Saviour of His Body. Outside this Body the Holy Spirit gives life to none." Jerome, A. D. 390: "As from Adam and his wife the whole race of men have sprung, so of Christ and His Church the whole multitude of believers are begotten." He also compares the Church to the Ark. "What the Ark was in the Deluge, that the Church is in the world."

"Clement, A. D. 194, and Origen, A. D. 230," says Canon Gore, "alike endeavored to mitigate this doctrine of exclusive salvation within the Church, so as to bring it into harmony with God's universal purposes, with his recognized equity and good-will towards all, and with the universal presence of the Word to all men. But with all this it is an undoubted truth that they did, like all the other Fathers, regard God's covenant in Christ as made with a visible society, membership in which was of universal obligation, and alienation from which was death."

"It is sometimes argued," observes the same profound author, "that St. Paul could not have believed in Salvation through the Church, because this contradicts his doctrine of the justifying effect of individual faith. But in fact there is no such contradiction. The Christian life is a correspondence between the grace communicated from without and the inward faith which, justifying us before God, opens out the avenues of communication between man and God, and enables man to appropriate and to use the grace which he receives in Christ. There is thus no antagonism, though there is a distinction between grace and faith. Now, grace comes to Christians through social Sacraments, as members

C. A.—13

of one 'spirit-bearing body.' 'By one Spirit we are
all baptized into one body;' 'we being many are one
bread and one body, for we are all partakers of that one
bread.' Thus the doctrine of the Church as the household of grace is the complement, not the contradiction of the doctrine of faith. Faith is no faith if it
isolates a man from the fellowship of the one body, and
the one body has no salvation except for the sons of
faith."

The Patristic doctrine of salvation only in the
Church, harsh as it now sounds to Denominationalists,
is no other than that held by their spiritual ancestors.
The Presbyterian Westminster Confession put forth in
A. D. 1647 speaks of the visible Church as "the house
and family of God, out of which there is no ordinary
possibility of salvation."

IV.

THE DEPOSITORY OF SACRAMENTAL GRACE.

" He, Ransomer from death, and Light from shade,
    Now gives His holy grace, His Saints to aid.
  Approach ye then with faithful heart sincere,
    And take the safeguard of salvation here."

Not only is it necessary to enter the Apostolic Church
in order to establish covenant relationship with God,
but also because she is the depository of Sacramental
grace of which her Ministers are the sole authorized
dispensers. The subjective blessings of valid Sacraments, that is, of Sacraments administered by Ministers
of Apostolic authority, may come to those who receive
them at the hands of an unauthorized ministry; but
the benefits of Baptism, Confirmation and the Lord's
Supper are not wholly of a subjective character any

more than are the benefits of prayer. To those who ask in faith and in accordance with the will of God, prayer, besides giving right direction to inward dispositions, secures to the petitioner spiritual and temporal blessings. In like manner valid Sacraments when received in faith and repentance assure the recipient that he is a child of God and an heir and joint heir with Christ to the life which now is and to that which is to come. Nor is this all. Such Sacraments also remit sins and convey strength to live a life of righteousness.

I am not saying that the Sacraments of non-Episcopalians do not convey these blessings, but that there is no *assurance* that they do; indeed their ministers do not claim to administer Sacramental grace. On the contrary they maintain that the benefits of the Sacraments are purely subjective, and condemn as Romish superstition and error the doctrine which has been taught in every branch of the Catholic Church from the beginning; namely, that the Sacraments are channels of grace. If it be true that the Roman Church teaches that they work by magic or charm to save their recipients, she is in so far clearly unscriptural. Repentance and faith are alway spoken of, or implied, in connection with the administration of Holy Baptism, and, in the sixth chapter of the Gospel according to St. John, in which eternal life and the resurrection are plainly made dependent upon the Sacramental eating and drinking of Christ's body and blood, faith and coming to Christ are also connected with the resurrection and life everlasting.

As in many other particulars, so in respect to her doctrine of the nature and efficacy of the Sacraments of Baptism and the Lord's Supper, it will be discovered upon examination, that the Anglo-Catholic Church of which the Protestant Episcopal Church is a branch,

occupies the middle ground between the Roman Catholic
Church and the various Protestant bodies of Christians.
This position is due to the fact that at the Reformation the Mother Church of England, from which the
American daughter has not departed in any essential
of doctrine or ceremony, returned to the ground that
she had occupied in the earliest and purest ages, while
the Roman Church continued in her Mediæval departures, and the sixteenth century and later Denominations have gone off quite as far in the opposite
direction.

Anglo-Catholics connect salvation with the Sacraments and with faith and repentance. All that is
Scriptural and essential in the Roman and Protestant
views of the efficacy of the Sacraments, we hold. For
with the one we agree that, "the Sacraments are generally necessary to salvation and that they work invisibly in us and do not only quicken, but also strengthen
and confirm our faith in Christ;" and with the other we
hold that the Sacraments "have a wholesome effect
and operation in such, only, as worthily receive the
same by a death unto sin, and a new birth unto righteousness, by repenting themselves truly of their former
sins, by having a lively faith in God's mercy through
Christ with a thankful remembrance of His death, and
by being in charity with all men."

In all ages there have been many who have depreci-
ated the importance of external rites and ceremonies.
This is the tendency of a large element even in the Anglican Communion, and it is so in all the Protestant
bodies about us. Surely those who are inclined to
under-estimate the Sacraments have not well considered
the fact that they were instituted by Christ Himself at a
time when the evil of externalism was at its height
in the Jewish Church. He was familiar with this evil,

and often inveighed against it, and yet He made the
very existence and continuance of His Kingdom to depend upon external observances. This is unaccountable
unless we infer, as under the circumstances we must,
that there is an intimate and vital connection between
divinely instituted externalism and deep piety and genuine spirituality. And that there is such a connection
is further indicated by the constant practice of the
Apostolic and primitive Church. The Apostles, themselves, and those next to them, who lived nearest to the
time of the great Head of the Church, and consequently
knew most about His teaching, unquestionably regarded the external rites of Baptism and the Lord's
Supper as inseparably connected with salvation. We are
willing to grant that they made as much of repentance
and faith as a modern Methodist, but while admitting
this we must insist that the Apostles, Fathers and Doctors attached as much importance to Baptism and the
Lord's Supper as the ancient Jews did to Circumcision
and the Passover. The proof of this is abundant in
nearly every chapter of the Acts of the Apostles, and
on almost every page of the Fathers. All who would be
saved were urged to be baptized without delay, and the
early Christians seldom, if ever, met without celebrating
the Holy Communion. Some of us might make more
of certain doctrines which Denominationalists magnify,
but none can esteem and use valid Sacraments less
without diminishing the aids to holy living.

Before the Ascension it was Christ only, and afterwards the Apostles, or those whom they commissioned,
who dispensed the Bread of Life in the Lord's Supper.
It was as necessary to receive this Heavenly food at
their hands as to continue in their doctrine and fellowship and the appointed worship. We read of the three
thousand, who believed and were added to the Church

by Baptism, that "They continued steadfastly in the Apostles' doctrine and fellowship, and in the breaking of bread and in the prayers." The only way in which Christians of later days can imitate the example of the first Disciples is by adhering to the Bishop of the Apostolic Succession who has been canonically placed over them. At least so taught the Fathers.

"Let no man," wrote the Apostolic Ignatius when on his way to martyrdom, A. D. 107, "let no man be deceived. If anyone be not within the precinct of the Altar, he lacketh the bread of God. For, if the prayer of one and another hath so great force, how much more that of the Bishop and of the whole Church." "Let us, therefore, be careful not to resist the Bishop, that by our submission we may give ourselves to God. And in proportion as a man seeth that his Bishop is silent, let him fear him the more. For everyone whom the Master of the household sendeth to be His steward over His own house, we ought so to receive as Him that sent him. Plainly, therefore, we ought to regard the Bishop as the Lord Himself." "For as many as are of God and of Jesus Christ, they are with the Bishop; and as many as shall repent and enter into the unity of the Church, these also shall be of God. Be not deceived, my brethren, if any man followeth one that maketh a schism, he doth not inherit the Kingdom of God. If any man walketh in strange doctrine, he hath no fellowship with the passion." "Be ye careful, therefore, to observe one Eucharist [that is, the Holy Communion], for there is one flesh of our Lord Jesus Christ and one Cup unto union in His blood; there is one Altar, as there is one Bishop, together with the Presbytery and the Deacons, my fellow-servants." "Let no man do aught of things pertaining to the Church apart from the Bishop. Let that be held a valid Eucharist

which is under the Bishop or one to whom he shall
have committed it. Wheresoever the Bishop shall appear, there let the people be; even as where Jesus may
be, there is the Universal Church. It is not lawful apart
from the Bishop either to baptize or to hold a love-
feast; but whatever he shall approve, this is well-
pleasing also to God; that everything which ye do
may be sure and valid."

"Athanasius," says Canon Gore, "endeavors to recall
a Bishop who in time of persecution had been guilty of
fleeing from his duty, in part by reminding him of
monks who have made good Bishops, but principally
by recalling to his mind the dignity of the Episcopate,
as instituted by Christ through His Apostles and having, therefore, not merely the authority of the Church
but the authority of Christ Himself, and as being the
essential condition of the continuous life of the Church
and the handing down of grace."

V.

OBJECTIONS ANSWERED.

THIS Lecture would be incomplete without some
reply to the principal objections which, judging
from my own experience, must inevitably have
presented themselves to the Denominational reader.
He will, of course, perceive, as I did, that such arguments
tend to unchurch the non-Episcopal bodies; to make it
an imperative duty to go out from them, and to enter
some undoubted branch of the Catholic Church; to
invalidate the ministry and sacraments of non-Episcopalians, and to limit covenanted salvation to the historic Catholic Church. All this, it will be said, is unmit-
igated and intolerable bigotry. In a generation, which,

like ours, glories in its creedless liberality, this apparently well-founded accusation will settle the whole matter in the minds of the great majority, who have been led on by curiosity to follow me thus far.

A long experience in a position which has brought me in contact with great numbers of non-Episcopalians, does not encourage the hope that there is anything to be said which will prevent most of us from parting company at the end of this lecture. Nevertheless, Episcopalians, as might be expected, have their ready answer to these, as to all other objections, that are urged against their Church, which, in each and every case, is so far satisfactory as to clear the way for the continuous procession of intelligent Denominationalists, who are coming into the Episcopal Church at the rate of at least twenty thousand annually. Though this is a great host, all who have completed their Churchward journey believe that it would be far greater, if inherited prejudice and the popular cry against illiberality did not deter many from investigating the claims of the Church. Nine out of every ten who hear and read enough really to understand these claims, sooner or later identify themselves with us. The truth of this statement will be established in other connections.

1. The propositions which we have been considering are objected to, because, if followed to their logical conclusion, they unchurch the various non-Episcopal bodies of Christians. The edge of this objection will be blunted by the explanation that, though we do not recognize a society which was organized by a human agency only three hundred years ago, more or less, as a branch of the Divine Institution of which we read in the New Testament, yet we do admit that all its members, who have been duly baptized with water in the Name of the Father and of the Son and of the Holy Ghost, are

members of the "One, Holy, Catholic Church of Christ," as really as ourselves. The difference between them and us is, that they are living in schism while we are not. Nevertheless, by reason of their Baptism, they are Christians.

If I mistake not there are several of the Denominations whose representatives, if true to the convictions which prevail among them, could not say as much of Episcopalians. Consistency would require them to call our Christianity in question, because we are not united to Christ by a particular form of Baptism or by some special kind of faith and experience. At any rate it cannot truthfully be said that any of the leading and so-called orthodox Denominations are more liberal than we are in the cordial recognition of Christian brethren who are outside of our respective communions. Thus, if we unchurch the Denominations we do not unchristianize their members. According to our understanding, their case is very much like that of those who belonged to the great revolt effected by Jeroboam. "The ten tribes did not cease to be Hebrews. They were still brought by circumcision into covenant with God; they are still addressed as His chosen people. Their Priests are never recognized as the Priests of God; their ministrations are always stigmatized as illegitimate; but the people, being Israelites and being circumcised, are still accounted the elect or chosen people of God, are always recognized as belonging to the one body. Wide as was the breach which Jeroboam made, it did not split the 'commonwealth of Israel' into two. He sinned grievously himself, and he 'made Israel to sin'—in fact, it is beyond all doubt that separation in that age was wholly sinful. But, notwithstanding the schism, the Jewish Church remained one. Not even Jeroboam, the great heresiarch, who carried five-sixths of the congregation of Israel along with him—Jeroboam, whom God appointed to rule over the ten tribes—could found a new Church or people of God."

It has been asked, "But, how do you account for the blessing which has attended the labors of the various Denominations, if they are not true Churches of Christ?" In the same way that we account for the successes of the Young Men's Christian Association or of the Salvation Army. God's abounding grace constantly overflows its channels. God forbid that we should deny for a moment the good and holy work done for Him by the Denominations. Why should we? It is the work of our fellow-Christians, and it is because they are Christians by Baptism or desire and profession, and not because the societies to which they belong are Churches, that God has blessed their preaching and endeavors.

Denominationalists usually justify their separation from the Historic Church of our race upon the ground that they were "kicked out." In proof of this they mention the fact that a large number of self-constituted ministers, who had been intruded into English benefices in the Revolutionary period, were ejected upon the restoration of the monarchy, and that many of the Church of England pulpits were closed against John and Charles Wesley. We answer that even if such ejections and exclusions could be shown to have been wholly unjust and reprehensible, they afford no excuse for the sin of schism. Two wrongs do not make one right. Even, though, for the sake of argument, it be conceded that the Independents and Methodists met with unjust and harsh treatment, yet it cannot be admitted that they were compelled to leave the Church; for many of the leaders of both movements remained in the Church all their days, and died in her communion. Besides, there is really no such thing as "kicking" people out of the Catholic Church. They can be made to endure wrong and cruel persecution, but they cannot be cut off from the Body of Christ of which they were made members at Holy Baptism. Not even excommunication will do this. It may prevent participation in the benefits of the means of grace. But, those, who at various times since the middle of the sixteenth century, have left the English and American Episcopal Churches, were not even excommunicated. They went out of their own accord. If we look at the matter from the standpoint of Denominationalists, the most charitable explanation of their conduct is that they were unwilling to suffer wrongfully for the sake of Christ. In this respect the followers of John Wesley, if the representations respecting the persecutions which he endured are true, did not imitate his example, for, according to many accounts that we have seen, he could not be "kicked out." There is, however, room for doubt whether credence should be given to all that has been published on this subject. Mr. Wesley, himself, never accused the Church of casting him out—least of all in his last days—when, he tells us, he had "more invitations to preach in Churches than he could accept of;" when many of the Clergy were "prejudiced in favor of the Methodists;" when, as his biographer Tyerman says, "he was invited in all parts of the country by Rectors, Vicars, Curates, and others to favor them with his services. An eminent Methodist in a "Contemporary Review" article, has testified that, on the whole, the Bishops treated Wesley better than he could have expected. "So persistent were Wesley's irregularities that it has always seemed to me that great indulgence on the part of the Bishops was exercised, or he would have been, in every Diocese, inhibited with vigor." Those who read history through Anglican spectacles will continue to attribute our unfortunate divisions to the Puritanical Pharisaism and willfulness of the first Separatists. No reflection is here intended upon their descendants. Denominationalists can no more be held responsible for the sins of their ancestors, except in so far as they knowingly and deliberately continue in them, than Episcopalians can be for those of the "fox hunting parson."

Moreover, we must not allow our objectors to forget that, if we unchurch their recently organized voluntary societies, because they have no historic connection with Christ through an Apostolic and Canonical succession of Bishops, we are simply following the example of their ancestors who unchurched us, not only because they insisted that the Presbytery was the only Divinely instituted form of Church government, but also because they maintained that the whole Episcopal establishment was so utterly corrupt that it was not any part of the Church of Christ, but rather the synagogue of Satan. Heylin, who wrote his standard History of Puritanism and Life of Archbishop Laud about the time of the Cromwellian Revolution, thus summarizes the language used by the enemies of the Church in the innumerable pamphlets which in his day were scattered broadcast. "They could find no other title for the Archbishop than Beelzebub of Canterbury, the Pope of Lambeth, the Canterbury Caiaphas, Esau, a monstrous Antichrist, a most bloody opposer of God's Saints, a very antichristian beast, most bloody tyrant. The Bishops are described as unlawful, unnatural, false and bastardly governors of the Church, the ordinances of the devil, petty Popes, petty Antichrists, incarnate devils, cogging, cozening knaves, who lie like dogs, and so on."

When we were thus not only unchurched but also reviled, instead of retorting in kind upon the calumniators of the Church, Hooker, Andrews, Thorndike,

Taylor, Laud and a host of others calmly proved by works that have never been answered that Episcopacy is an essential part of the Church's constitution and that, notwithstanding the sins of omission and commission of which many of her representatives in high places were guilty, the Church of England is a true branch of the Church of Christ. Nor were our scholars and Saints content with writing unanswerable controversial works. They frankly confessed our short-comings and preached the necessity of reformation with a fidelity and vigor that resulted in the purifying of the body Ecclesiastical and in making her confessedly the greatest educational, missionary, and benevolent agency that the world has ever known.

Our Methodist brethren who seem to be the most deeply offended at our alleged uncharitableness towards other Christian bodies and have so much to say about it, may be reminded that after all we simply occupy the ground that John Wesley took in regard to all Separatists from the Historic Church. He never looked upon the association of which he was the head as anything more than a society within the Church. Nor would he listen to any suggestion of separation, but warned his followers against it and prevented it so long as he lived. Dr. Beet, who is perhaps the greatest living scholar among English Methodists, says: "Wesley had no thought of founding a community outside the Anglican Church, and strongly urged his followers to remain in the ancient fold." As is well known John and Charles Wesley both died Priests and communicants of the Church in good standing.[*]

2. Again, it is objected that the propositions which we have been maintaining, logically lead to the conclusion that it is the duty of non-Episcopalians to leave their respective societies and to identify themselves with

* Appendix IX.

some undoubted branch of the Divinely instituted Church. What we really intend to teach is at least capable of statement in the following less objectionable form:—It is the duty of all Christians and of those who would become such, to examine the relative claims of the various religious bodies to their allegiance. Other things being equal, we feel sure that Americans who have any regard for antiquity and for the predominating judgment of Christendom, will feel obliged to ally themselves with some branch of Episcopacy which has come down from the Apostles rather than with any of the various forms of a self-constituted ministry as found in Denominationalism. Until the Reformation practically the whole of Christendom believed the "Historic Episcopate" to be an essential characteristic of the Church founded by Christ, and even now the vast majority of Christians hold to this view. If the teaching or practice of the early Church on any point is unanimous, or nearly so, then it is not safe to draw conclusions contrary to it except upon unmistakable evidences of error. "We require you to find out but one Church upon the face of the whole earth, that hath been ordered by your discipline, or hath not been ordered by ours, that is to say, by Episcopal regiment, since the time that the blessed Apostles were conversant." This is the famous challenge of Hooker, who wrote at the close of the sixteenth century against the Presbyterians. It has never yet been met. Until non-Episcopalians can meet it, they cannot reasonably object to the logic which makes it their duty to be in communion with the canonical Bishop of the region in which they live.

3. It is also objected that the line of argument pursued in this lecture invalidates the Ministry and Sacraments of Denominationalists, that is, makes them of no effect. If we have said or implied anything of this kind,

we take it all back. For the truth is, instead of depreciating their Ministry and Sacraments, we admit not only all for which most Denominationalists contend, but, in the case of Baptism we go beyond their claim for it by acknowledging that it makes the candidate "A member of Christ, the child of God, and an inheritor of the Kingdom of Heaven," which they deny. It must, however, not be understood from this acknowledgment that we concede a Divine Priesthood to Denominational ministries. We can and do acknowledge as much of Baptism administered by ordinary Laymen and Lay-women. But why should they take offense at our refusal to force upon them a character which they, themselves, repudiate? Denominationalists generally deny that their ministers are Priests and that Divine Grace is given through the channel of Sacramental ordinances. According to their view a minister is only a commissioned preacher, and the Sacraments are simply commemorative ceremonies. How can they justly charge us with uncharitableness if we simply take them at their word upon this point?

"It is well to understand," says Bishop Hugh Miller Thompson, "that we have little, if any, difference with the 'Denominations' about their ministry and ordinances. These are valid for all that is claimed for them. They say that their ministers are teachers of religion, duly appointed and authorized by a voluntary society. They are certainly this. They assert that their ministers are not Priests and have no Sacerdotal power or authority. To this assertion we assent. They profess not to have Apostolic Succession. We agree with them upon this point. They state that they administer an Ordinance in which the Body and Blood of Christ are not really present, and are not verily and indeed given, taken, and received; but that it is merely a mode of

recalling to their minds our Lord's death. This statement is quite unobjectionable. About Baptism we
differ somewhat from them, attributing to that Sacrament, as administered by them, a greater effect than
their own faith ventures to hope for. Administered
with water, in the name of the Holy Trinity, we believe
it to regenerate the soul that duly receives it, and to
graft it into the body of Christ's Church. So, we admit
their ministry to be all that they claim it to be; and we
admit their ordinances to be in no case less, and in one
case more, than they, themselves, believe."

And if there be any Denominationalists who claim
that their ministry is a Priesthood and that their Sacraments are the means through which Divine gifts are
received, the irritation caused by our attitude towards
non-Episcopacy may be somewhat soothed by the fact
that they are not alone in being called upon to sustain
the charge of invalidity. Romanists are continually
representing our Ministry and Sacraments to be invalid.
There was a time when Denominationalists also did
this. Bishop Coleman, speaking of the Puritans of
Colonial days, says: "While some were pleased to allow
that a clergyman ordained by an English Bishop required no further credentials to officiate when called to
a society of Congregationalists, others compelled such
to submit to a 're-ordination by the brethren.' This
ceremony was gone through with, for example, in the
case of the Rev. Thomas Hooker, at Newton, afterwards
Cambridge, in the year 1633, and of Master Cotton, at
Boston, in the same year. Episcopal Ordination was
even looked upon as something for which those receiving it must needs apologize, and there seems to be
reason for believing that in some instances they were
obliged to recant it." Such treatment has never wor-
ried us. Whenever occasion has arisen, our writers and

preachers have proceeded to show by unanswerable arguments based upon Scripture and history that our Ministry and Ordinances are valid.

If Denominationalists are sure of their ground, let them, when we call in question their ministry, pursue the course towards us that we do towards Romanists. Unfortunately for them, of those who do this the majority have the experience of good Dr. Wolff, of missionary fame, about whom the following anecdote is related. The Doctor, burning with zeal to preach the Gospel of Christ, was on one occasion traveling in some out of the way region in the Orient. It was in the Diocese of one of the Bishops of the Greek Church; and in the course of his wanderings he fell in with the Bishop. "Who are you?" said the Bishop, looking at him rather suspiciously. "A poor Missionary," said the Doctor. "A what?" asked the Bishop. "A Missionary," repeated Dr. Wolff, pulling out his little black Bible. And those of us who are old enough to have seen Wolff fingering his Bible, will remember how it always seemed to open of itself at the precise text he wanted. "I am come to preach salvation to these people. How shall they call on Him on whom they have not believed? Or how shall they believe in Him of whom they have not heard? Or how shall they hear without a preacher?" "That is all very well," said the Bishop, "but why don't you finish the text?" "How shall they preach except they be sent?" "Who sent you?" "Sent?" said Wolff. "Yes, sent!" replied the Bishop. "My Metropolitan sent me, and his predecessors sent him, and I send my Priests and Deacons. Now, who sent you?" "The Spirit of the Lord," said Wolff boldly; for he was not a man to be put out of countenance. "I hope you do not deny that Christ is able to send His own messenger without human intervention?" "God forbid that I should doubt it for a moment," the Bishop answered, "I know He can. I know that He sent Moses and Aaron, without human intervention, to establish the Aaronic Priesthood; and I know that He superseded this very Priesthood of His own Ordination, by sending also without human intervention the Apostolic Priesthood; and what He did once He can do again. God forbid! that I should doubt that; I should be a Jew if I did. Still I do observe that whenever God does send anyone direct from Himself and without human intervention, He is always graciously pleased to confirm His own appointment to the minds of his faithful servants by signs and wonders. Moses called down bread from Heaven. He and Aaron brought forth water from the rock. And so, also, when God was pleased to supersede that Priesthood, many wonders and signs were wrought by the hands of the Apostles. They did not go upon their own testimony; but appealed to these as witnesses; as, in the case of their Master, Himself, the works which they did testified of them. Now," continued the Bishop, "without at all doubting the possibility that a Wolffian succession may be commissioned to supplant that of the Apostles, where are your witnesses? I suppose you do not expect us to take your word for it. What supernatural powers do you appeal to, in proof of your Heavenly mission?" This was a puzzling question. It had puzzled Mahomet several hundred years before. That false prophet, however, got out of it cleverly, by saying that he had written the Koran, which as everyone thought, was a miracle of itself; but poor Wolff could not say that he had written the Bible; so he fell to thinking. The result was that he came home, I will not say a better man—for a most excellent man he always was—but by many shades a wiser man; and soon afterwards sought for Ordination in the regular way, and was ordained by Bishop Doane, of New Jersey.

Nor has the Greek Bishop been the only one to recognize that miracles are the necessary credentials of him who, without Episcopal and Canonical Ordination, claims to have a sufficient call to preach the Gospel and administer the Sacraments. When the Anabaptists appealed to Luther, "not doubting," as the historian says, "that he who had first preached the liberty of the Gospel would pronounce in their favor," they had certainly some reason to be astonished at a reply which seemed to involve the formal renunciation of one of the first principles of his Reformation. "Let the Senate ask this man," said the Reformer, when giving advice about the ministerial pretensions of their would-be pastor, Muncer, "who called him? and, if he shall answer, 'God,' let them charge him to prove his calling by some manifest sign, which, if he cannot do, let him be repudiated as an impostor." Under the circumstances this was a harsh and inconsistent judgment which must be as great a source of regret and embarrassment to the Lutheran ministry as John Wesley's famous Sermon CXV, on "the Ministerial Office," is to the Methodist Ministry.*

4. Finally, it will be objected that we limit covenanted salvation to membership in the historic Catholic Church. But this is not the same as saying that only members of the Greek, Roman, and Anglican Communions will be saved. As has already appeared by reiterated statements, we acknowledge all who have been baptized in the name of the Trinity to be in covenant relationship with God. Nor is it equivalent to a declaration that all non church members will be lost. I suppose that there is not an Episcopalian to be found anywhere, who believes that God's mercy does not

* Appendix XII.

overflow the Church. But if there were such, Denominationalists should be the last to accuse them of bigotry; for, as we have seen, their ancestors, the Presbyterians, declared in their Westminster Confession of Faith that there is a visible Catholic Church, "the house and family of God, out of which there is no ordinary possibility of salvation."

No, we do not limit salvation to the adherents of the Catholic Church. What we do say is that covenanted or assured salvation is limited to the Church. Nor do we, as our objectors represent, tie God's gifts of grace and mercy to Sacramental Ordinances. Our doctrine is lucidly and concisely set forth in Dr. Seabury's edition of "Haddan's Apostolical Succession," "Without Bishops, no Presbyters; without Bishops and Presbyters, no legitimate certainty of Sacraments; without Sacraments, no certain union with the mystical Body of Christ; without this, no certain union with Christ; and without that union, no salvation. Yet with these necessary provisos at every step, by the very nature of the moral laws and attributes of God: First, that these outward things may be had; secondly, that due allowance be made for ignorance, prejudice, or necessity; thirdly, that the system be regarded as subservient and ministering to a true faith, a living religion, and a hearty love of Christ in the soul."

We recognize the truth, that God is free to grant His blessings through whatever instrumentality He may see fit to use, or directly without any ceremonial channel. But are we justified in concluding that, because God is not bound to the Ordinances which He has instituted as the instruments of our salvation, we are free to disregard them? If God be not limited, we are. Those of us who know His appointments, certainly are not justified in expecting that we can be saved without using them.

We do not, then, make the Church of the Historic Episcopate to be the only way of salvation, or confine the
bestowal of God's Grace to her Ministry and Sacraments. All we claim is that they are the Divinely appointed ark of safety and channels of refreshment. Multitudes, doubtless, will reach Heaven by other ways.
But we contend that it is, nevertheless, required of all
to determine whether or not God has appointed a way,
and if it be found, to walk in it. Moreover, Holy Scripture makes it a duty to search out and to take "the
old paths," rather than the new. "Stand in the ways,
and see and ask for the old paths where is the good
way, and walk therein, and ye shall find rest for your
souls."

These words of the Prophet Jeremiah, addressed to
the perverse and erring people of Judah, are full of instruction for those who desire to serve God acceptably
under the Christian as well as the Mosaic Dispensation.
At all times entitled to the most serious consideration,
they are especially applicable to this age. What this
precept, when applied to the unhappy condition in which
divided Christendom finds itself, requires is that we
should all follow the history of the body with which we
are identified and each Article of its distinctive Creed
back to the place of the parting of ways. There we
shall find *the way* from which all others have diverged
—"the good way" all Christians once pursued, that in
which all, if they will, can walk again in unity and
brotherly love, and by which the hosts of Christ can
progress towards universal conquest. The world will
never be evangelized by a divided Church, and the
Church will never be united so long as Christians continue in the paths of their own choosing. All must
come back to the "old paths." For nearly a thousand
years Romanists have been wandering further and

further from these paths in one direction, and Denomina-tionalists, since their beginning, more than three cen-turies ago, have been doing the same in the opposite course. Both of these must follow the example which the Anglican Communion set at the Reformation, by retracing their steps until they come to "the good way." God grant that the Denominational reader for whom this chapter has been especially written, may be disposed, by the operation of the Holy Spirit, to heed the Prophet's injunction, by asking for "the old paths," "where is the good way?" and having found it, may he walk therein and find rest for his soul.

"For all Thy Church, O Lord, we intercede;
  Make Thou our sad divisions soon to cease;
Draw us the nearer each to each, we plead,
  By drawing all to Thee, O Prince of Peace.
Thus may we all one Bread, one Body, be
  Through Thy blest Sacrament of Unity.

"We pray Thee, too, for wanderers from Thy fold;
  Oh, bring them back, good Shepherd of the sheep,
Back to the Faith which Saints believed of old,
  Back to the Church which still that Faith doth keep.
Soon may we all one Bread, one Body, be,
  Through Thy blest Sacrament of Unity."

The Church for Americans.

LECTURE IV.

THE MOTHER CHURCH OF ENGLAND.

AUTHORITIES.

BRIGHT, Early English Church History.
BRIGHT, Waymarks of Church History.
COIT, Early History of Christianity in England.
COX, Is the Church of England Protestant?
COLE, The Anglican Church.
FRY, Lectures on the Church of England.
GARNIER, CANON, The Title-deeds of the Church of England.
HART, Ecclesiastical Records of England, Ireland and Scotland.
JENNINGS, Ecclesia Anglicana.
JENNINGS, A Manual of Church History. (2 Vols.)
LANE, Illustrated Notes on English Church History. (2 Vols.)
LIGHTFOOT, BP., Leaders in the Northern Church.
PERRY, CANON, Students' English Church History. (3 Vols.)
PRYCE, The Ancient British Church.
ROBERTSON, History of the Christian Church. (8 Vols.)
ROSS-LEWIN, Continuity of the English Church.
SPARKS, The Resistance of the English Church and Nation to the Encroachments and Usurpations of the Bishop of Rome.
STOUGHTON, Ecclesiastical History of England. (2 Vols.)

PAMPHLETS.

GARRETT, BP., Historical Continuity.
GRUEBER, The Church of England and the Ancient Church of the land.
LOWRIE, The Mother Church of England.
NYE, The Story of the Church of England.
NYE, The Right of the Church of England to Her Property.
OLDROYD, The Continuity of the English Church Through Eighteen Centuries.

MISCELLANEOUS.

CHURCH CLUB LECTURES, The Church in the British Isles.
CHURCH CLUB LECTURES, The Church in the British Isles, Post Restoration Period.

THE MOTHER CHURCH OF ENGLAND.

W E have endeavored to show elsewhere* that the
Gospel makes identification with some true
branch of the Apostolic Church of Christ
obligatory upon all. It is now necessary, in order that
the way may be prepared for determining whether or
not a person who unites with the American Episcopal
Church fulfills this obligation, to devote a lecture to the
Mother Church of English-speaking Christianity.

I.

CONTINUITY OF THE ENGLISH CHURCH.

W E shall assume that all, whether they be representatives of Romanism or of Denominationalism, admit that the Church of England, before the Reformation, was a part of the true Church of
Christ. Certainly she was the only form of organized
Christianity then in the land. It is equally certain that
her title to Catholicity was never questioned during all
of the pre-Reformation ages. The impression, however,
prevails that the Church of Rome was the Church in
England up to the time of Henry VIII., and that the
present religious establishment is a new foundation.

The necessity for the dissemination of knowledge concerning the origin and continuous history of the Mother

---

*Lectures I and III.

Church of England, is illustrated by an experience which I had about a year ago upon the occasion of the holding of the first Service in one of the many large towns of Ohio where, as the General Missionary of the Diocese, it has been my duty and privilege to care for the isolated and neglected members of the Church by establishing Missions or occasional Services. At this place, a county-seat, there was not an adherent of the Church to be found, and so, though the congregation was good for a stormy evening, and the Service, considering a number of adverse circumstances, was as satisfactory as could be expected, it did not look as if the result would justify the somewhat unusual expenditure of time, money, and energy which the Service had cost. It was, therefore, a source of encouragement and gratification to me when, as the congregation was disbanding, a middle-aged man with his half grown son lingered to thank me for the Service, and to request permission to accompany me to the hotel for some conversation about "your Church."

When we reached my room he told me the following interesting story: "I am a farmer living twelve miles from town. I saw the announcement of your Service in our county paper, and, having lately become interested in the Episcopal Church, my son and I have driven all the way through the rain and mud to attend it. I have never been at one before, partly, because there has been a lack of convenient opportunity, and partly, because of a deep-rooted prejudice of thirty years' standing against that Church. In times past, as you may remember, there was a great deal more of controversy and bigotry about matters of religion than there is now. The members of the rural congregation to which I belonged would have gone home feeling that they had not received their money's worth unless the preacher had dwelt at some length upon the perfections of their sect and severely criticised its numerous rivals. One of the ministers who stood high in the estimation of us all for learning, because, as I have since concluded, he descanted a great deal concerning matters about which neither he nor his auditors knew anything, used frequently to go out of his way, for there was no parish within fifty miles of the place, to denounce the Episcopal Church. As much of his reputation for learning rested upon his supposed familiarity with history, I did not question his representation that the Mother Church of England owed its existence to Henry VIII. From what he said about that monarch and his Ecclesiastical handiwork, I naturally concluded that I never should go across the road to attend a Church which had such an ignominious origin and between which and the Church of Rome there was nothing but the thinnest and flimsiest paper wall. Though I have since frequently spent more or less time in a city where you have many Churches, and though there has for years been a parish within less than three hours' drive, the resolution formed so long ago has never been broken until this evening.

"This departure from a life-long course is accounted for by the fact that a much-beloved relative, who has long been one of the most respected ministers of the Denomination to which I belong, to the astonishment of everybody, became an Episcopalian a few weeks ago. Shortly after seeing the announcement of the change, I received a copy of the Prayer Book and certain publications containing some account of the Episcopal Church, and answers to popular objections to her. There is, of course, no doubt in my mind as to whom I am indebted for them. Under the circumstances it was natural for me to read them attentively in the hope of discovering the reason for my friend's unexpected action.

Even the cursory examination which I first gave the Prayer Book led me to the conclusion that it was a pretty good book, even if Henry VIII. did make it. The pamphlets put the Episcopal Church, as to its origin, history, and relationship to Rome in a very different light from that in which it was placed by the pulpit orators, from whom my knowledge of Ecclesiastical History has been chiefly derived. After reading them I went back to the Prayer Book and have read much of it over, and over, with an ever-increasing sense of the beauty of its Services—hence my desire to join in their public use as I have had the privilege of doing this evening. And now I have a favor to ask of you. It is that you will outline a course of reading in the history of the English and American Episcopal Churches, and give me the address of a publisher from whom the books may be procured."

It need hardly be said that this request was readily complied with. The next thing that the writer heard of the man was from the Rector of the nearest Church. He and a part of his large family had put in an appearance on a Sunday morning. After the Service he made himself known and requested that he and his house might receive preparation for Confirmation at the Bishop's next visitation. All the family, who have arrived at the years of discretion, are now communicants of the Church. Its head has proved to be a veritable missionary outside of his own household, for he has talked to his neighbors about the Church, and distributed broadcast among them Prayer Books and tracts. So successful has he been that the community, which, owing to the recent construction of a railway and the establishment of a station for its convenience, is developing into a village, has determined to erect a Chapel and request the Bishop to send a Clergyman to minister to them.

There is, indeed, considerable reason for the widespread opinion that Henry VIII. founded the Church of England. Several new organizations were formed during that period. And so many changes were made in her government, doctrine, and worship as to make it very natural for people generally to suppose that the Reformed Church of England was simply one among the new organizations. It was to the interest of the representatives of Romanism on the one hand, and of Denominationalism on the other, to encourage this impression. Both were anxious to make it appear that this Church is a creature born of the Reformation. Romanists desired this because it could then be shown that so far as historic continuity and identity with the Church that our Lord founded are concerned, we are no better off than any of the sects; and Denominationalists, because it puts our Church on the same footing with themselves. This accounts for the fact that history, as it is taught in our common schools, often does us flagrant injustice. The author has heard no less a personage than the principal of a high school, who afterwards became superintendent, tell his pupils that Henry VIII. founded the Episcopal Church.

Episcopalians claim that the present Church of England is identical with that which was in the land before the Reformation. The changes in doctrine, government, and worship, though confessedly great, did not necessarily result in the creation of a new Church. This is because all such changes were merely reformatory and so stopped short of revolution. "I know that some people are to be found," writes Lord Selborne, "who pretend that a new Church of England was set up at that time, and the old Church cast out. For that pretense there is no foundation in law or in fact. A Church does not lose its identity or sameness, as an organized institution, by changes in form or ceremony. In the English Reformation, the organization of the Church, as the Church of England, was not displaced or broken at any single point. And I think it right to add, though it is not my object to enter at all into theological questions, that nothing was then done which made the Church of England really different in any point of substance affecting religious faith or practice from what it had originally been in the days of Augustine, the first Archbishop of Canterbury."

The Reformation left the Church stripped of Roman bondage and corruptions, but this only rendered her, in all important respects, what she had been before the captivity, an independent, pure branch of the Catholic Church of Christ. "An old Gothic tower, founded centuries ago, might, in lapse of time, be so overgrown with ivy, and choked with rubbish, as to have all its original features concealed. If the ivy were pruned away, and the rubbish removed, it would not be a newly-founded tower, but the old one restored. But if the proprietor should build a new one on some other part of his estate, digging new foundations and raising new walls, this would be another tower, however closely it might resemble the old one in its outward features." The point of difference between the Church of England and the various Denominations is seen in the fact that they were not even in existence before the Reformation, while she has come down in unbroken continuity from the Apostles. If, in an evil day, the United States should become tributary to some foreign power from which, after a struggle of, say, three hundred years, our posterity succeeded in freeing themselves, and if they then returned to the full constitutional government which had been in force before, and never more than partially set aside, would not the nation, at the end of the three centuries of subjugation, be historically the same as that which had previously existed? If so, the Church of England was identically the same after the Reformation as before.

"Out of Lake Leman," as our poet Bishop, Coxe, of Western New York, puts it, "comes the 'arrowy Rhone,' beautiful as light from the clear blue sky. You may have stood on the little promontory where the Arve issues forth to meet it—a red torrent from the Alps, once the crystal of melted snows, but now arrayed like a Papal legate. How the purer river writhes and refuses to be tainted! How the red ruffian presses and pushes it to the wall! Still the Rhone keeps up the contest as best he may. For a time he holds his own, but, alas! the red wins, and the sapphire disappears. What is visible to the common eye is no longer the blue Rhone, but only the blood-colored Arve. Is the nobler river lost? By no means. It becomes the Rhone again, and rolls on superbly, through the broad lands, where Irenæus planted the Gospel, under the walls of Lyons and Arles, and so to the sea. Behold a parable that illustrates the Nicene Church in England, in her original glory, and in her restored identity."

That the contrast between the Church of England, immediately before, and after, the Reformation did not necessarily interrupt the continuity of her history, has been aptly illustrated by the celebrated Dr. Hook, in a sermon preached before the Royal Family: "About two years ago," said he, "the very Chapel in which we are now assembled was repaired, certain disfigurements removed, certain improvements made. Would it not be absurd on that account to contend that it is no longer the Chapel Royal? Would it not be still more absurd if someone were to build a new Chapel in the neighborhood, imitating closely what this Chapel was five years ago, and carefully piling up all the dust and rubbish

which was at that time swept from hence, and then pronounce *that*, not *this*, to be the ancient Chapel of the
sovereigns of England? The absurdity is at once apparent; but this is precisely what has been done by the
Roman Catholic or Papist. The present Church of
England is the old Church of England reformed in the
reigns of Henry, Edward, and Elizabeth, of certain superstitious errors; it is the same Church which came
down from our British and Saxon ancestors, and, as
such, it possesses its original endowments, which were
never, as ignorant persons foolishly suppose, taken
from the Church and given to another."

This point has been illustrated also by the washed
face of a besmirched coal miner. The change gives the
appearance of a complete transformation, or of a new
creation; and yet no one believes that the identity has
been changed. "I make not," says Archbishop Bramhall, A. D. 1593-1663, "the least doubt in the world but
that the Church of England, before the Reformation,
and the Church of England, after the Reformation, are
as much the same Church, as a garden before it is
weeded, and after it is weeded, is the same garden;
or as a vine, before it is pruned, and after it is pruned
and freed from luxuriant branches, is one and the same
vine." "Be it known to all the world," said Bishop
Hall, A. D. 1574-1656, "that our Church is only reformed or repaired, not made new—there is not one
stone of a new foundation laid by us; yea, the old walls
stand still."

The identity of the Church of England, which has
been since the Reformation, with that which was before,
is established by a variety of considerations. We shall
here consider five of them.

1. In all essentials of Catholic doctrine, worship, and government there was no change. This observation will, according to our design, receive full proof and illustration in other connections. We shall, for the present, do no more than simply call attention to the fact that our Book of Common Prayer is essentially the same as that which had been in use from the earliest times. During the Dark Ages, many Roman superstitions and corruptions crept into the various liturgical "Uses." The Reformers eliminated these. The first Prayer Book of Edward VI., A. D. 1549, was mainly a simplification of the old Service Books, translated into English, with very little matter added. Indeed, Cranmer offered to prove to all comers that "the Order," or, as we should say, the Prayer Book of the Church of England, as set out by the authority of King Edward VI., was the same as had been used in the Church for fifteen hundred years past—a challenge which was never taken up by any Roman Catholic. None of the revisions of A. D. 1559, 1604, or 1662 seriously altered the character impressed upon the English Liturgy from the first. The Roman Liturgy was never used in England, except in some monasteries of foreign monks, and by the present Italian schism during the last one hundred and fifty years.

2. Those who effected the English Reformation did not intend to abandon the old Church and to found a new one, nor did it even occur to them that they were doing so, in casting off the Roman yoke. They put their house in order, but it was the same dwelling after as before. Mr. Gladstone says: "I can find no trace of that opinion which is now so common in the mouths of unthinking persons, that the Roman Catholic Church was abolished at the time of the Reformation, and that a Protestant Church was put in its place, nor does there

appear to have been so much as a doubt, in the mind of any one of the Reformers, whether the Church legally established in England after the Reformation was the same institution with the Church legally established in England before the Reformation." The fact that the Roman Church was never by any Act of Parliament recognized as the English Church and that the Reformed Church has always been so regarded, notwithstanding there were no Acts of Establishment passed in the reign of Henry VIII. or any of his successors, is in itself sufficient conclusively to establish the claim of Episcopalians that the English Reformers did not intend to organize a new body, and that the Church of England after the Reformation, was, and is, in history and in law, identically the same which was previously the Church of that country.

But while no statute can be cited which suggests that any new organization was effected at the Reformation, many official documents of that period plainly show that there was no intention of breaking the Church's continuity. For example, in the Preface to the First Prayer Book of Edward VI., published at the very crisis of the Reformation, we find this statement: "The Service in this Church of England, these many years hath been read in Latin to the people." It was expressly declared in an Act passed in the year 1533 that "it is not intended to force the Church of England into an uncatholic position, or to change its character as a sound branch of Christ's Holy Church." And when Queen Elizabeth was requested by the German Emperor to permit the Roman Catholics to set up an independent worship, she refused, upon the ground that "there is no new faith propagated in England, no religion set up but that which was commanded by our Savior, practiced by the primitive

Church, and unanimously approved by the Fathers of the best antiquity."

In freeing herself from the Roman yoke and corruptions, the Church of England no more became a new Church, than she did, when, after centuries of liberty and purity, she began to be yoked and corrupted. If the casting off of the Papacy, Indulgences, Mariolatry, and the like, made a new Church in England, then the imposition of them upon a Church that was certainly wholly free of them for five centuries, and practically so, for more than a thousand years, must have created a new English Church. "The Anglican Church," says Bishop Coxe, "was primitive and pure; she became enslaved and defiled; she regained her liberties, she washed, and is clean. But she is none other to-day, as to individuality and identity, than she was when Italians were sent to put chains upon her; when she shook her chains in defiance, as she chafed under them; when she lay down and slept awhile, baffled and degraded; or when, at last, she woke and broke from her fetters, and began to be herself again; until now, God has given her to many nations, and set her footsteps in the seas, and enabled us to say, 'Her sound is gone out into all lands, and her words into the ends of the world.'"

3. Another strong evidence of the historical continuity of the English Church is afforded by the fact that there was no transfer of property. The force of this argument will be felt by all. If the Roman Church had been the Church of England before the Reformation, the Romanists of that land now would have, at least, a moral title to all the Church property that had been accumulated up to the time of Henry VIII. But their own English Bishops are on record as disclaiming any right whatsoever to such property. I have before me a

copy of a very interesting document entitled, "Declaration of the Roman Catholic Bishops, the Vicars Apostolic, and their Coadjutors in Great Britain," the ninth section of which is "On the claim of the British Catholics to the property of the Church established in England." It runs thus: "British Catholics are charged with entertaining a pretended right to the property of the established Church in England. We consider such a charge to be totally without foundation. We declare that we entertain no pretension to such a claim. We regard all the revenues and temporalities of the Church establishment as the property of those on whom they are settled by the laws of the land. We disclaim any right, title or pretension with regard to the same." This declaration proves that even the Pope and his English representatives do not believe that the Church of Rome was the Church of England before the Reformation, otherwise there would be no such article in their pronunciamento.

It has also been decided by the highest Civil Court of England that Rome has no title to English Church property. A nine hundred and ninety-nine years' lease of a piece of land to be used for military purposes was given by the Church to the Crown in A. D. 872. Upon its expiration some twenty years ago, it was adjudged that, according to the laws of the realm, "it reverts to the original owner, the party that gave the lease, namely, the Church of England." This lease was executed over six centuries before Henry VIII. was born. It conclusively establishes the identity of the Church of England in the reign of Queen Victoria, with the Church which existed in the time of King Alfred, thus witnessing to her continuous organic life through one thousand years of history.* But a thousand years, long as the stretch of time is, far transcending the grasp of imagination,

* Appendix XIII.

cover but little over half of the Church's existence in England. Planted by St. Paul or St. Joseph of Arimathea, or at least by some disciple who sat at the feet of the beloved St. John, she has come down through the British, the Anglo-Saxon, the Norman, the Mediæval, the Reformation, and the Revolution periods to the present, looking "forth as the morning, fair as the moon, clear as the sun, and terrible as an army with banners."

It is worthy of note, in passing, that the property at present possessed by the Church of England, speaking broadly, was given her before the Norman Conquest, A. D. 1066, or since the Reformation. The influence of Rome was but little greater in the first of these periods than it has been in the second.

4. The name of the Church after the Reformation is the same as before, *Ecclesia Anglicana*, the Church of England. If the Church of Rome had been the Church of England until the reign of Henry VIII., the name would have borne witness to it, and would have been necessarily changed, but, as it is, the unchanged name bears strong testimony to the identity of the present Church of England with that which was before the Reformation.

5. But a most conclusive evidence of the identity of the present Church of England with that of the pre-Reformation period, is the fact that the whole nation, with scarcely a dissenting voice, consented to the changes which terminated the usurped jurisdiction of the Pope in England, and restored to the Crown its ancient authority over both the temporal and spiritual estates of the realm. It is popularly and erroneously supposed that there would have been no Reformation of the English Church, but for the iniquitous matrimonial projects of Henry VIII., the consummation of which made necessary the repudiation of the Roman supremacy. As a

matter of fact, however, nothing can be more confidently predicated than that the Reformation of England would have taken place very much as it did, and at about the same time, even if the King had seen fit to resist, rather than abet it. ".Revolutions which shake the deepest foundations of society, and destroy old forms of belief; reformations for which a world is anxiously looking, do not take their rise from the will of a single individual. They are the slow growth of time, the outcome and final result of centuries of forgetfulness of duty, and of infinite and wide-spread mismanagement. It is as great a folly to attribute the English Reformation to the will of Henry, as to ascribe the gradual and necessary progress of the Papacy wholly to the False Decretals, or to assert that the French Revolution sprang from a single cause. At the time of Henry's accession, the Reformation was already in existence, silently working and fermenting in the minds of all men. Any occasion might give it birth; at any moment any individual—a monk in Germany, or a King in England — might call it forth, and clothe it with a shape and a name." Henry VIII. was therefore, in reality, to use one of Motley's illustrations, but the gilded hand on the outside of the dial—the hour to strike was determined by the obscure but weighty movements within.

There had been a time when the Roman sway was, upon the whole, beneficial to England, but that time had passed. Adam Smith goes none too far when he says: "During the tenth, eleventh, twelfth, and thirteenth centuries, and for some time before and after that period" [that is to say, during the time of Papal domination in England] "the constitution of the Church of Rome may be considered as the most formidable combination that was ever formed against the authority and security of civil government, as well as

against the liberty, happiness, and reason of mankind."
"In nearly every way," says Dean Farrar, "material
and moral, the Papacy was a curse to England."

Their novel Courts of Appeal, and the usurped power
of appointing to vacant Bishoprics and benefices,
enabled the Popes at will effectually to resist the constitutional legal machinery; to introduce innumerable
corrupting agencies, and more and more to gratify their
insatiable greed for money by a system of extortion so
stupendous and unconscionable as really to amount to
wholesale robbery, the like of which the world perhaps
never witnessed before or since. Some faint idea of the
extent of that stream of gold which, during the Dark
Ages, flowed to Rome from England, may be gathered
from the recorded complaint of the House of Commons,
made as early as the year A. D. 1376. It was maintained on the floor of the house that "the sums paid to
the Pope by those alone, who were indebted to him for
Ecclesiastical preferment, amounted to five times as
much as the taxes of the whole realm, which accrued to
His Majesty, the King, and that there was no monarch
in Christendom so rich as to possess the fourth part of
the treasure which was annually exported from England to Rome." Bishop Grey, who was translated from
Winchester to York in A. D. 1215, was compelled to pay
to the Pope, for receiving the pall, a sum equivalent to
fifty thousand dollars of our money. In the light of
this, how ridiculous it would be were the Pope to make
any serious claim to the property of the Church of England. He impoverished our Mother Church, but did
not put so much as a penny into her endowments and
buildings. The money that went to Rome would have
built and endowed a hundred cathedrals and colleges,
but that which came from thence would not have kept a
single Italian monk from starvation.

The people generally had long been convinced that things could not always go on in this way. And it is a great, though strangely prevalent, mistake, to suppose that Henry VIII. was the first to take steps for the purpose of curbing the rapacity of the Roman potentate. Nothing could be wider from the truth. Indeed, so accustomed were the people to struggle against the encroachments of the Papacy, and so many were the laws which they had in different ages enacted for their self-defense, that, when Henry VIII. found it convenient for more reasons than the one usually assigned, to exercise, even in Ecclesiastical affairs, the prerogative of ruling his Kingdom without interference from the Pontiff—a prerogative which the great majority of his predecessors had exercised—he had but little to do beyond the enforcement of long-existing laws.

The proof of all this is admirably set forth by Dr. Ingram, a London barrister, in his excellent volume, entitled "England and Rome, A History of the Relations Between the Papacy and the English State and Church, from the Norman Conquest to the Revolution in 1668." After a most scholarly and exhaustive presentation of the whole subject in the light of full quotations from the statutes of the realm, it is asked: "What Ecclesiastical jurisdiction did the Pope possess in England at the accession of Henry VII. in 1485," that is, thirty-two years before Luther commenced his reformatory work, and fifty-seven years before Henry VIII. broke with Clement VII.? The answer to this question is to the effect that the Pope was possessed of no such jurisdiction whatsoever. "The Pope could not appoint, translate, suspend, or depose a Bishop, or regular Prelate in England. He could not appoint to an English prebend or benefice; and every Englishman who accepted a preferment at home from the Pope, without the King's leave, was liable to banishment and forfeiture of all his property. A Papal excommunication of itself, had not the slightest effect in England. No one could receive, read, or publish such a document, or any other Papal sentence or process without leave of the King."

It may be conceded that the Popes, during several reigns, practically ruled, and grievously spoiled, the Church of England, notwithstanding the laws of the realm. But it should be remembered that they were permitted to do this by the Kings who found it to their real or imaginary political interest to be on friendly terms with so great a potentate. Not one of them since the Plantagenets, had possessed a strictly legitimate claim to the crown, and they needed the support of Rome to prop up their thrones. Though the people were exceedingly long suffering, yet their spoliations and wrongs sometimes became intolerable. At such times they not infrequently offered effectual protest. The forcing of the Magna Charta from the despicable John in the year 1215, is an illustration in point. This celebrated document provided both in its opening and closing sentences for the recognition and restoration of the ancient liberty of the Church to govern itself.

As we approach the Reformation, we find the nation growing more and more impatient of Papal interferences and exactions. This accounts for the phenomenal success of Henry VIII. in freeing himself and people from the Roman grasp. Romanists and Denominationalists have joined hands in efforts to make it appear that this self-willed and burly King so intimidated his cowering subjects that they espoused his cause against the Pope, though of course their sympathies and prayers were with His Holiness. This view is contrary to the witness of all trustworthy contemporaries who have left on record their impressions concerning the temper of the people. Even Bishop Gardiner, who in the next reign opposed the Reformation, and suffered five years' imprisonment in the Tower of London, and was made Lord Chancellor by "Bloody" Mary, tells us: "All who have been born and reared in England, learned and unlearned, men and women, are agreed upon this point that they have naught to do with Rome." And a correspondent of Cardinal Pole writes: "One thing yet resteth that I thought convenient to advertise you of wherein I do perceive ye be ignorant, which is this: Ye write in one part of your book that ye think the hearts of the subjects of this realm greatly offended with abolishing of the Bishop of Rome's usurped authority in this realm, as if all the people, or most part of them, took the matter as ye do. Wherein I do answer ye be deceived. If, at this day, the King's grace would go about to renew in his realm the said abolished authority of the Bishop of Rome, I think he should find much more difficulty to bring it about in his Parliament, and to induce his people to agree thereunto, than anything that ever he proposed in his Parliament since his first reign." Dr. Ingram says: "It is even absurd to speak of the existence of coercion at a time when the King, the two Universities, the two Convocations, all the Monasteries, Colleges, Chapters, and Hospitals in the Kingdom, and the two Houses of Parliament were of the same mind."

Thus, there can be no question that the Reformation would have come about in England some time in the course of the sixteenth century, when it was taking place in all the surrounding nations, even if Henry VIII. had been content to retain Catherine of Aragon as his wife. So unanimously resolved upon casting off the Papal yoke were the people, that of all their representatives at Parliament, only one Bishop, Fisher, and one

Layman of note, Sir Thomas More, voted against the various constitutional legislative acts which terminated the already illegal Papal tyranny and robbery in England. Of the nine thousand eight hundred Clergy, only one hundred and eighty-six refused to assent to the Reformed Offices in A. D. 1559. Investigation would doubtless show that most of these were foreign intruders. And when the Nation and Church, at the accession of Elizabeth, finally and forever repudiated the usurped authority of the Pope, only one hundred and ninety-two out of more than nine thousand Clergymen refused to subscribe to the Prayer Book, and only eighty of these were Rectors of Churches.*

This unanimity puts the identity and continuity of the present Church of England with that which was before the Reformation beyond the possibility of doubt. The whole nation, not excepting even Fisher and More, for they did not withdraw from the Church, belonged to it after the repudiation of the Pope's authority as they had done before. It was, therefore, the same Church minus the unconstitutional interferences of the Papacy. During long centuries of her early history, the Church of England, notwithstanding her independence of Roman authority, had flourished and been universally recognized as a true branch of the Catholic Church of Christ; and now that she has regained her ancient liberty and purity, she is unquestionably the same Church that she was before and during the period of her captivity and corruption—the Church of England in unbroken continuity from the time of Archbishop Theodore, who about the year 670 consolidated the various Churches of the Heptarchy into one National Church, the Mother of English-speaking Christianity, the rock from which the American Episcopal Church is hewn.

* Appendix XIV.

II.

NOT ORIGINALLY A MISSION OF ROME.

MANY of the facts produced in proof of the identity of the present Church of England with the Church of that country before the Reformation, also prove that the Church of Rome was not the un-reformed Church of England. Unless, indeed, that for which we have been contending be a fiction, the very fact that the present Church of England is not the Church of Rome proves that she never was such. For if this had ever been the case, it must still be so, or else the identity of which we have spoken does not exist. In establishing the historical continuity of the Mother Church, we have, therefore, necessarily established her constitutional independence of Rome; nevertheless, it will be well to make this appear from other points of view.

That the Church of England up to the Reformation was not, as Ultramontanists represent, simply a branch of the Church of Rome is evident from her origin. Just when, and by whom, the Church was planted in England, can probably never be satisfactorily determined. "We see the light of the Word shined here, but see not who kindled it." But that it was very early and not by the Roman Church is certain. One tradition to which many learned men have been inclined to give credence, tells us that St. Paul, himself, preached in Britain. That he visited Northern Europe seems more than probable from his Epistle to the Romans, where he expresses his intention of taking a missionary journey into Spain.

(236)

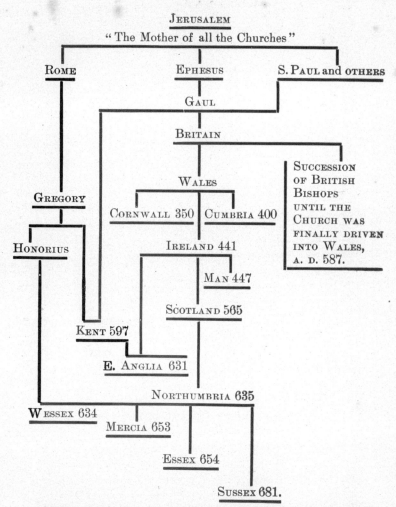

JERUSALEM

"The Mother of all the Churches"

ROME   EPHESUS   S. PAUL and OTHERS

GAUL

BRITAIN

GREGORY   WALES   SUCCESSION OF BRITISH BISHOPS UNTIL THE CHURCH WAS FINALLY DRIVEN INTO WALES, A. D. 587.

CORNWALL 350   CUMBRIA 400

HONORIUS   IRELAND 441

MAN 447

SCOTLAND 565

KENT 597

E. ANGLIA 631

NORTHUMBRIA 635

WESSEX 634   MERCIA 653

ESSEX 654

SUSSEX 681.

Diagram, showing the origin of the British Church to have been independent of Rome. The red type and lines show the descent of the present Church of England, and the black type and lines show the late appearance and meager results of the Roman Missions. They had nothing to do with the conversion of the Anglo-Saxon conquerors of Northumbria, Mercia, Essex and Sussex; and the part taken by them in the conversion of Kent, East Anglia and Wessex is as compared with that taken by the native British Church unimportant, except in the case of Kent.

Thence he might easily have sailed to England. Clement, of Rome, a disciple of St. Paul, and mentioned with commendation by him in his Epistle to the Corinthians, about A. D. 95, thirty years after the death of the Apostle says that in preaching the Gospel, St. Paul "went to the utmost bounds of the West." Now this expression, "the utmost bounds of the West," is the epithet that the ancients ordinarily used in speaking of the British Isles which composed the principal and altogether the best-known part of the most westernly portions of the land that appeared on the maps during the first centuries of the Christian era. Eusebius, A. D. 325, says that one of the Apostles "visited the British Isles," and Theodoret, about a century later, mentions Britain as one place where St. Paul labored. Hore concludes his scholarly summing up of the authorities with the remark: "There can be no reasonable ground for doubting that the British Church was not only of very ancient, but also of Apostolic foundation."

There are some ten traditions respecting the planting of Christianity in Britain. It would be a grave error to consider them as altogether worthless because they are not a certain source of knowledge. "One leading idea seems to underlie them all alike, that the Gospel was preached in Britain at an early date, but that this was effected by different and independent agencies, at different times, from different places, and at different points in the Island."

That the early Church of Britain was not a Roman Mission is certain. For when in A. D. 597 the Bishop of Rome sent Augustine with a band of missionaries to the Island, they found an ancient, regularly organized Church. As Thomas Fuller quaintly expresses it: "Religion came into Britain, not by the semi-circle of Rome, but in a direct line from the Asiatic Churches." The celebrated jurist, Blackstone, says: "The ancient British Church, by whomsoever planted, was a stranger to the Bishop of Rome, and all his pretended authority."

The difference between the two Churches in matters of ceremony, which soon became a source of contention, also shows that the native Church was not one of Roman origin. Evidence to this effect still exists. All the English Cathedrals and old Churches were built with the Chancel to the East, and the main entrance at the West. No such universal respect was paid to the points of the compass in Ultramontane countries. Rome had no Trinity Sunday in her Ecclesiastical year before the end of the fourteenth century, and she still names the Sundays following Pentecost until Advent after that Festival, whereas we name them after the feast of the adorable Trinity. This was the case before the Reformation, as may be seen by reference to the Old Sarum Missal, for example, "The 10th Sunday after the Feast of the Holy Trinity." Thus, as long as one stone remains upon another, and while we adhere to our respective Liturgies, there will remain monumental and documentary witnesses of great antiquity and worth to the independent origin of the English Church.

It has often been represented that the original Celtic population, and with it the native Church of Britain, were all but annihilated by the Angles and Saxons, who in the fifth and sixth centuries frequently invaded the Island and eventually conquered the greater part of it, and that the Roman Mission was so successful in the conversion of the new inhabitants that the date of its establishment may properly be reckoned as the beginning of the present Church of England. If this representation were true, we, as members of the Anglican Communion, would have no interest to serve by calling it in question. For it would be an honorable origin for our Mother Church. During the first six or eight centuries, the Church of Rome was as pure a branch of the Catholic Church as any on earth. But even if Christianity had been planted in England by Rome, her pretended right to be called the Church of England to the time of the Reformation, could not possibly be established. The argument from which it might appear to the unreflecting that such a claim had been made good, would prove quite too much to the thoughtful, namely, that the Church of Rome and Italy should be subject to the Church of Jerusalem and Palestine.

But the representation is not true. The native Church was not annihilated. We read that numerous Synods of the Welsh Bishops were held during the sixth century, at some of which there were as many as one hundred and nineteen Bishops present; this number being doubtless made up chiefly of abbots, monastic Bishops, and the Bishops driven thither from English Sees. The most important of these Church assemblies were held at Brevi, near Lampeter, A. D. 569, and Lucus Victoriæ, A. D. 570, both presided over by St. David, who had been consecrated Bishop by the Patriarch of Jerusalem, thus adding an independent strand in our Apostolic Succession.

Nor was the conversion of the Anglo-Saxon conquerors due to the Roman Mission in any such degree as is popularly supposed. As Mr. Gladstone says: "It was not by the action of Rome that the whole of England was converted. A very large portion of England was converted, not by the action of the Roman missionaries, but from the North." Christianity was really restored to fully nine-tenths of the Island by missionaries, who either went out or received their inspiration from the ancient Celtic Monasteries of Iona and Lindisfarne. To

St. Aidan, founder of the latter, and not to St. Augustine, rightfully belongs the credit of evangelizing the Anglo-Saxons. The foreign missionaries did not succeed in permanently planting the Church beyond the Kingdom of Kent. The remaining six divisions of the Heptarchy were Christianized by the native missionaries. If we illustrate by the hand the relative size of the territories of which Augustine and Aidan were respectively the apostles, we shall see that to the foreigner belongs about as much as is represented by the portion between the ends of the fingers and the first joint, leaving the remainder of the fingers and the palm to represent the territory that was rechristianized by the Celtic missionaries.

And even the credit for the conversion of Kent is by no means wholly due to Rome. Augustine found a powerful and indispensable ally in the Queen, who was a Gallican, that is, French not Romish, Christian. She must at least share equally with the monks, the credit of the King's Conversion, and the wonderful wholesale Baptism of the little kingdom which followed. They began their work of evangelization in her Canterbury Chapel. Pope Gregory himself confessed that "next to God England was indebted to Bertha for its conversion."*

The words of the profoundly learned and accurate historian, Lightfoot, late Bishop of Durham, and his quotation from the French statesman and author, Montalembert, a Roman Catholic, confirm our representation in respect to the relative extent and success of the labors of the foreign as compared with native Missionaries. "Of the triumphs of the Celtic Evangelists," says Dr. Lightfoot, "something has been said already. If we desire to know the secret of their success it is soon

---

* See Frontispiece.

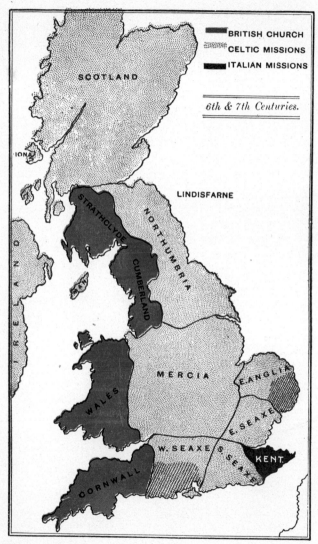

Map, showing the parts taken respectively by the native and Roman Missionaries in the conversion of the Anglo-Saxons.

told. It was the power of earnest, simple, self-denying lives, pleading with a force which no eloquence of words can command. But, whatever may be the explanation, the fact remains. Iona succeeded where Rome had failed." "From the cloisters of Lindisfarne," writes Montalembert, "and from the heart of those districts in which the popularity of ascetic Pontiffs, such as Aidan and martyr kings, such as Oswald and Oswin, took day by day a deeper root, Northumbrian Christianity spread over the southern Kingdoms. What is distinctly visible is the influence of the Celtic Priests and missionaries everywhere replacing and seconding Roman missionaries, and reaching districts where their predecessors had never been able to enter. The stream of the Divine Word thus extended itself from North to South, and its slow but certain course reached in succession all the people of the Heptarchy. Of the eight Kingdoms of Anglo-Saxon confederation, that of Kent alone was exclusively won and retained by the Roman monks, whose first attempts among the East Saxons and Northumbrians ended in failure. In Wessex and in East Anglia, the Saxons of the West and Angles of the East were converted by the combined action of continental missionaries and Celtic monks. As to the two Northumbrian Kingdoms, and those of Essex and Mercia, which comprehended in themselves more than two thirds of the territory occupied by the German conquerors, these four counties owed their final conversion exclusively to the peaceful invasion of Celtic monks, who not only rivaled the zeal of the Roman monks, but who, the first obstacles surmounted, showed much more perseverance, and gained much more success. Sussex still remained heathen; Sussex, the smallest of all but one of the earliest founded; Sussex, the immediate neighbors of the Roman missionaries in Kent; Sussex was at

last stormed and taken. And here again the conqueror
of this last stronghold of heathendom, though an
ardent champion of the Roman cause, was a Northumbrian by birth. Wilfrid had been a pupil of Aidan, and
his missionary inspiration was drawn from Lindisfarne."

III.

ROMAN ENCROACHMENTS AND THEIR RESISTANCE.

BUT it is said that, however it may be in regard to
the planting of the Church among the Britains
and the conversion of the Anglo-Saxon conquerors, the fact remains that from A. D. 596, to the Reformation, the headship of the Pope was as fully recognized in England as in the See of Rome. We have
already had repeated occasions to show the utter base-
lessness of this pretension, but inasmuch as reiteration is necessary to remove the effect of inherited misconceptions, especially when, as in this case, they are
deepened by persistent misrepresentations which have
just enough of truth to give the color of plausibility,
we shall here speak of the resistance, which, at every
step, was offered to the encroachments of Rome upon
the liberties of the Church.

The Italian missionary was not long content with
confining himself to the work of converting the heathen
conquerors of Kent, but felt called upon to meddle with
the worship, ceremonies, and observances of the native
Church in order that they might be conformed to the
Roman usage. It is probable that, but for Augustine's
haughty demeanor, he would have succeeded in persuading the Celts to make some of the desired changes.
In A. D. 603, seven Bishops, accompanied by many

learned men from the famous Monastery of Bangor, met him in a conference. Augustine and his monks, failed to rise and to receive courteously the Bishops and their attendants when they arrived. This slight set the natives against the foreigners. So when Augustine had explained the object of the meeting, and made his demands, it was replied in substance: "We will observe none of your customs, nor accept you as our chief. If you would not rise up to us just now, how much more will you despise us if we begin to be subject to you. We indeed owe fraternal love to the Church of God and to the Bishop of Rome, but we owe no obedience to him whom you call Pope. Besides, we cannot submit ourselves to him or to you, his representative, because we are already subject to the Metropolitan Bishop of Caerleon-on-Usk [now the See of St. David's, Wales], who is, under God, our spiritual overseer." Of the eight Sees of these seven British Bishops and their Archbishop, all of which were in existence at least a hundred years before the coming of Augustine, two, Lan-Patern and Morgan, are extinct; the other six, namely, Hereford, Worcester, Llandaff, Bangor, St. Asaph, and St. David's, have existed continuously from that day to this; a standing visible proof of a Christianity still existing in Britain, that was not brought there by Roman missionaries.*

The conference between Augustine and the British Bishops, marks the first of a series of protests against Roman encroachments that extended through a thousand years, of which we can take notice of only a few, in the briefest words possible.

Toward the close of the seventh century, Wilfrid, Bishop of York, had some difficulty with Theodore, Archbishop of Canterbury. Wilfrid appealed his case to the Bishop of Rome who commanded that he should

* Appendix XV.

be reinstated into his Bishopric. The matter came up
for consideration before the Witan or the Parliament of
those days. "Who," said the rulers of the nation, in
effect, "who is the Pope and what are his decrees?
What have they to do with us, or we with them? Have
we not the right and power to manage our own affairs,
and to punish in our discretion all offenders against
our laws and customs?" So they burned the parch-
ment containing the Pope's directions, and cast Wilfrid into prison. Afterwards, in the National Anglo-
Saxon Synod of Osterfield, Wilfrid reproached the
members with having "openly opposed the Pope's
authority for twenty-two years together."

In A. D. 747, when it was proposed at a Council to
refer difficult questions to the Bishop of Rome, those
present refused to entertain it, and declared they would
submit to the authority of the Archbishop of Canterbury in such matters.

The Anglo-Saxon Church was certainly independent
of Rome down to the Norman Conquest, A. D. 1066.
For when William was making his plans for the subjugation of England, he secured the Pope's blessing and
coöperation upon the representation that he desired to
bring the Church of that country under the dominion of
the Roman See. This was the surest way to gain the
Pope's approval, for, as the historian Freeman says in
his Norman Conquest, "England's crime in the eyes of
Rome—the crime to punish which, William's crusade was
approved and blessed—was the independence still retained by the Island, Church, and Nation. A land where
the Church and Nation were but different names for the
same community, a land where Priests and Prelates
were subject to the law like other men, a land where the
King and his Witan gave and took away the staff of a
Bishop, was a land which, in the eyes of Rome, was more

dangerous than a land of Jews and Saracens." But
William, after his successful conquest, was quite as
loath to give the country over to Papal dominion as
his predecessors had been. In a letter to the Pope he
writes thus: "Thy legate Hubert, Holy Father, hath
called upon me in thy name to take the oath of fealty
to thee and to thy successors, and to exert myself in enforcing the more regular payment of the money which
my predecessors were accustomed to remit to the
Church of Rome. One request I have granted, the other
I refuse. Homage to thee I have not chosen, nor do I
choose, to do. I never made a promise to that effect,
neither do I find that it was ever performed by my predecessors to thine." A word of explanation in regard
to the money referred to in William's letter is necessary
to prevent misunderstanding. It was not an obligatory tribute, but a voluntary gift for the support of a
school at Rome where English youths were to have in
return the advantages of a liberal education. "The
regularity of its payment depended upon the prosperity of the country, and upon the rise and fall of the
Church of Rome in popular esteem."

Early in the twelfth century, Warelwast, Bishop of
Exeter, was sent to Rome for the purpose of bearing
official protestation against the repeated effort of the
Pope to meddle with English affairs, and of explaining
to His Holiness "that the Church and realm of England
occupied a different position from the continental kingdoms and Churches, and had always been independent
of Papal jurisdiction." "There are abundant proofs,"
writes Bishop Coxe, "that the Anglican Church was
everywhere recognized as maintaining an exceptional
position, other than that of the Latin Churches connected with 'the Holy Roman Empire.' At the Council
of Bari, A. D. 1098, when Anselm's spare and modest

figure was hidden from Urban II., at a humble distance from his throne, he cried out, 'Anselm, father and master, where art thou?' When he very meekly advanced, the Pontiff gave him a privileged seat, and added, ' We include him indeed in our œcumene, but as the Pope of another œcumene.' Whatever meaning he may have attached to his almost prophetic words, it is evident that he regarded him as a Patriarch, and as somewhat which others were not."

To this period also belongs the famous correspondence of Pope Pascal II., who wrote to the King and Bishops of England two letters, which, as has frequently been observed, show beyond all doubt that, at the time when the Papal power was at its zenith, the Church of England was a thoroughly self-governing body, possessed of its own system of Ecclesiastical law and administration, and also that the Pope's power of visitorial interference had no existence. The letters are too long for transcription here, but a short extract or two will be sufficient to demonstrate the truth of the above observation. "From the Apostles St. Peter and St. Paul," says the Pope, "the custom has been handed down to us that the more weighty affairs of the Church should be managed or reviewed by our See. But you, in despite of this long-established custom, settle among yourselves the business relating to Bishops, without even consulting us. You will not allow the oppressed to make their appeals to the Apostolic See. You venture without our knowledge to celebrate the Councils and Synods. You even attempt, without our knowledge, to make translation of Bishops, an unwarrantable liberty, as such affairs ought not to be attempted except by our authority. If for the future, you are willing to pay a due respect to the Apostolic See, we will treat you as brothers and sons; but if you per-

sist in your obstinacy we shall shake off the dust of our
feet against you, and deliver you to the vengeance of
God as backsliders from the Catholic Church."

Resistance to the encroachment of the Popes, notwithstanding this threat, was persisted in until the beginning of the thirteenth century, less than two hundred
years before the Reformation, when, through the traitor,
King John, the State and Church were all but given over
as plunder to Rome. But this they did not submit to
long. The Archbishop of Canterbury became the head
of a great popular uprising which left the King helpless
in spite of all that his ally, the Pope, could do for him.
On June 15th, A. D. 1215, John was compelled to sign
the famous Magna Charta. The first provision of this
renowned document runs: "The Church of England
shall be free and hold her rights entire and her liberties
inviolate." After specifying these rights and providing
for the freedom of the subject, and law and order in the
realm, the Charta concludes with a reassertion of its
initial principle: "That the Church of England be free,
and that all men have and hold the aforesaid liberties
truly and peaceably, freely and quietly, and wholly in
all things and in all places forever."

About the middle of the thirteenth century, Robert
Grosseteste, Bishop of Lincoln, successfully resisted attempted Papal interference in the affairs of his Diocese.
In his sermons he boldly connected the misery of the
people with the wickedness of the Popes, whom he char-
acterized as devouring wolves in sheep's clothing. Said
he: "The Roman Pontiff and his Court are the fountain and the origin of all the evils of the Church."

In the year 1307, Parliament protested against the
multiplied forms of Papal exaction, and refused to
allow the Pope's tax-gatherer to leave the country with
money he had collected. Shakespeare was not mistaken

in putting these vigorous words in the mouth of the England of this period :

> "Thou canst not, Cardinal, devise a name
> So slight, unworthy, and ridiculous
> To charge me to an answer, as the Pope.
> Tell him this tale ; and from the mouth of England
> Add thus much more—that no Italian Priest
> Shall tithe or toll in our dominions.
> Though you, and all the kings of Christendom
> Are led so grossly by this meddling Priest,
> Dreading the curse that money may buy out,
> And by the merit of vile gold, dross, dust,
> Purchase corrupted pardon of a man,
> Who in that sale sells pardon from himself,
> Yet I alone, alone do me oppose
> Against the Pope, and count his friends my foes."

Toward the middle of the fourteenth century, tl foreign Clergy were expelled from the country; shi which brought them hither were confiscated, and any who introduced Papal letters or bulls into the land, were condemned to forfeit all their possessions. Soon afterward, the Statutes of Provisors and Præmunire were passed. The first of these ordered that "Kings and all other Lords are to present unto benefices of their own or their ancestors' foundations, and not the Pope of Rome," and the second that "all who should sue for redress in the Papal court should be put out of the protection of the laws of England, and forfeit their goods to the State." It was about this time hn Wyckliffe, "the Morning Star of the Reformatio..., was engaged in his wonderful work of opposing the Romish encroachments, and in translating the Bible into English. This was one hundred and fifty years before the time of Martin Luther.

A little later, in A. D. 1420, "Archbishop Chichele, when censured by Pope Martin V. for not disregarding the English laws which prevented the Pope from appointing to English benefices, told him that he, himself, was the only Bishop in England who did pay any attention to orders from Rome; and when Martin, by way of reply, took away from him his rank of ex-officio legate, and bestowed that title on another Bishop, proceeding further to excommunicate all the other Prelates, and to threaten an interdict, his Bulls were stopped by the government, and the Archbishop appealed at once to a General Council, while the new legate was never suffered to act in that character."

Finally, about a century later, came the Reformation when the Papal yoke of which the whole nation had all long been so impatient was at last cast off.   In March, [1] D. 1534, the Convocation of Canterbury declared that the Roman Pontiff has no greater jurisdiction given to him by God in this kingdom than any other foreign Bishop, and in the following June, the Convocation of York adopted substantially the same resolution.

Even this necessarily rapid and condensed sketch of the resistance of the Church of England to the encroachments of the Papacy upon her liberties, is quite sufficient to justify a passage in one of the earlier writings of Cardinal Manning: "If," said he, "any man will look down along the line of early English History, he will see a standing contest between the rulers of this land and the Bishops of Rome. The Crown and Church of England, with a steady opposition, resisted the entrance and encroachment of the secularized Ecclesiastical power of the Pope in England. The last rejection of it was no more than a successful effort after many a failure in a struggle of the like kind." "Through the long ages of Roman domination," writes Bishop Lightfoot, "the English Church was the least enslaved of all the Churches. Her statute book is a continued protest against this foreign aggression. Her ablest kings were the resolute opponents of Roman usurpation. When the yoke was finally thrown off, though the strong will of the reigning sovereign was the acting agent, yet it was the independent will of the Clergy and of the people which rendered the change possible. Hence there was no break in the continuity of the English Church."

No labored or extended argument is now needed to prove that the Mother Church of England is a true branch of the Catholic Church of Christ. We need only to appeal to the history that has been reviewed, and to the Roman Church itself. For it must be remembered that the English Church continued in communion with the Church of Rome until the promulgation of the Pope's Bull of excommunication in the year 1570, which was thirty-five years after the repudiation by Parliament and Convocation of the usurped Papal Supremacy in England.* During this long interval of a full generation, Anglican Sacraments and Orders were regarded as valid at Rome. And if the English Church retained her Catholicity for so many years after the Reformation, no living man can show why she has not continued to be truly Catholic until the present day. Rome has never questioned the Catholicity of the Anglican Church between the landing of Augustine and the Reformation. She cannot deny the Catholic character of the pre-Augustinian Church in Britain, for the British Bishops had undisputed seats in the great Church Councils. Pope Leo XIII., in his recent declaration concerning the invalidity of Anglican Orders conveniently loses sight of these indisputable facts of history.

In view of all this, we may well ask with a writer in one of the periodicals: Are Romanists sincere when

* Appendix XV.

they allege, as an historical fact, that Henry VIII. was
the founder of the English Church? Alfonso M. Liguori, a Doctor of the Roman Communion, says in his
History of Heresies and Their Refutation, "Mary,
likewise, proclaimed the innocence of Cardinal Pole, and
requested Julius III. to send him to England as his legate *a latere*. He arrived soon after, and, at the request
of the Queen, reconciled the Kingdom again to the
Church, and absolved it from schism. On the Vigil of
St. Andrew, A. D. 1554, he confirmed in their Sees the
Catholic Bishops, though installed in the time of the
schism, and recognized the new Sees established by
Henry. All this was confirmed by Paul IV." In this
proclamation, the Bishops are styled "Catholic," and
the Anglican Church is represented as being in schism,
but no mention of Henry being the founder of the English Church is made, although this would have been the
proper time to have asserted the fact, if such were the
case. Thus the Popes and Roman historians being witnesses, the Church of England is a true branch of the
One, Holy, Catholic and Apostolic Church of Christ.

This apologetic dissertation concerning the Mother
Church of our race would be incomplete without some
fuller reference to two objections which are constantly
urged against her. The first of these is that she was
founded, or at least reformed by the "adulterous" Henry
VIII., and the second, that her reformation was so incomplete that she is still permeated with Romanism.

1. Of course, educated persons know that only the
ignorant or the prejudiced can maintain that Henry
VIII. founded the present Church of England, and so
this objection has no weight with them. They see that
the great Tudor, who lived less than four hundred

years ago, could not have founded a Church that, as an overwhelming accumulation of evidence proves, has had a continuous existence from the present day back through the ages, one thousand seven hundred years, to the very threshold of the time of the Apostles.

It must, however, be admitted that Henry VIII. did have a great deal to do with ridding the Church of Papal interference, and that the part he took would perhaps not have been taken but for his iniquitous matrimonial schemes. But when our objectors go so far as to leave the impression that but for the King's guilty love for Anne Boleyn, there would have been no Reformation in England, and that the Church would have continued under the tyranny of Rome, they take an untenable position. It must be evident to all who have even a cursory knowledge of the drift of events in England, that the rupture could not have been much longer deferred. Henry VIII. was simply the instrument in God's hands for setting in operation and guiding the Reformation, and, except in his determination to get rid of the Pope's usurped authority in England, he was a very unwilling tool of Providence. In view of the fact that the Pope dubbed him "Defender of the [Roman Catholic] Faith" for a tractate which he wrote against the German Reformation, and that he left money for the saying of masses forever for his soul, it is highly ridiculous to attribute the Anglican Reformation to him. If Henry VIII. hanged the men who believed in the Pope, he burned alive those who disbelieved in transubstantiation and auricular confession. His laws would have sent to the stake every Bishop, Priest and Deacon who accepts the Anglican Prayer Book.

If our ancestors could have had the choosing of the instrument, they doubtless would have chosen a more exemplary man, but the choice could hardly have fallen upon a better King. For it is universally conceded that, notwithstanding his moral imperfections, Henry VIII. was one of the ablest and most popular monarchs who ever occupied the English throne, or, in fact, that of any other nation. "He carried the country safely, without massacre and without a general civil war, through the most tremendous crisis that ever existed in England." The uneducated and unprincipled Romanist or Denominationalist who pours contempt upon the English Church and her American Sister because of the domestic faults of Henry VIII. should in justice not altogether lose sight of his regal virtues. Nor must they be allowed to forget that his character compares very favorably with that of some of the great Puritan leaders and is positively respectable in comparison with that of many of the Popes.

So far as Puritanism is concerned, take its great hero, Oliver Cromwell. His memory to this day is held in execration by many in England and especially in Ireland where his ruthless butcheries were such as to be almost without parallel in the annals of inhumanity. He landed in Dublin with an army in A.D. 1649. Several battles were fought, and men, women and children were indiscriminately slaughtered. Houses were pillaged and burned; Churches desecrated, and terror reigned wherever he went. For a long time the Irish would say: "The curse of Cromwell upon you," when they desired an expression of hatred. In view of this, and much more of which it is a piece, the several writers of first rank who denounce him as a bloody tyrant would seem to have truth on their side. Certainly his military cruelties brought more suffering and sorrow to the world than that which resulted from the conju-

gal infidelities of Henry VIII. And as for Romanism,
Pope John XII., was convicted by an Italian Synod of
almost every enormity to be found in the catalogue
of crime. During the tenth century about thirty Pontiffs occupied the Papal chair. Each succeeding one sur-
passed, if possible, his predecessor in abominable crimes.
The mind sickens in reviewing the enormities of these
monsters of wickedness.* Even King Edgar, who, though
not a severe moralist, was a saint if compared with the
Pontiffs of his time, has recorded his testimony against
them. "We see in Rome," he says, "only debauchery,
licentiousness, and drunkenness; the houses of Priests
are the shameful abodes of harlots, and of worse than
these. In the dwelling of the Pope, they gamble by
night and by day. Instead of fastings and prayers,
they give place to bacchanalian songs, lascivious
dances, and the debauchery of Messalina."

It should be remembered also that Henry VIII. was
not the only very imperfect man whom God has been
pleased to use to accomplish His great purposes. Jehu,
one of the greatest reformers among all the Kings of
Israel, fell far short of perfection. "Constantine established Christianity in the Roman Empire and Napoleon
restored it in France, yet who cavils at either of these
great changes on account of the want of personal sanc-
tity in the authors." We have, therefore, in the case of
Henry VIII., only one of many historical instances
which illustrate the truth that God's ways are not
man's ways, and show how he causes the wrath of man
to praise Him, and brings good out of evil.

But really, no country has upon the whole more reason than England to be proud of those who were conspicuous in bringing about its reformation. If the
political part of it was wrought by Henry VIII., the

----

*Lecture II.

doctrinal and spiritual parts were accomplished by such men as Latimer, Ridley, Cranmer, Jewel, Parker, Taylor, Hooker, and a host of the like, who for their piety, and learning, and martyr heroism, shine as bright stars in the Christian firmament. "After all," says the fair-minded Evangelist, Barnes, "rail at her as we will, there is no Church on earth like the Church of England; no holy army of martyrs like to hers; no ritual so pure and uplifting; no giants of theology like hers; no history on the whole so honorable."

2. As to the objection that the English Reformation did not go far enough, we may say that our plan contemplates a fuller answer in another connection than space here permits.* For the present, therefore, we shall content ourselves with an appeal to representative men both within and outside of the Anglican Communion. And first, there are the great English theologians, whose writings are universally acknowledged to be the bulwark of the Reformation, Pearson and Butler—the latter was brought up in non-conformity, but left it—and Barrow, and Bull, and Beveridge, and Chillingworth, and Taylor, and Ussher, and Leighton, and Tillotson, illustrious divines, whose folios form the library to which Denominationalists as well as Episcopalians go for sound doctrine, and for arguments with which to refute Roman controversialists. Then, coming down towards our own time, there are such profound scholars as Arnold, Maurice, Whately, Alford, Lightfoot, Stanley, Vaughan, and many contemporaries of almost equal endowments and learning who were, if we are to believe the representations of Denominationalists, so blind and ignorant as not to perceive that by remaining in the English Church they were casting the weight of their immense influence on the side of

*Lecture VI.

deadly error. Nor will we allow those who accuse us of Romanism to pass over our Laity such as Gladstone, Hatherley, Selborne, Wilberforce, Shaftesbury, Gordon, Salisbury, Hope, and our own George Washington, Patrick Henry, Peyton Randolph, Alexander Hamilton, James Madison, John Jay, John Marshall, and a host of others whose high conscientiousness, taken in connection with their well-known Protestant sympathies, forbid us to believe that they would have clung so firmly and lovingly to the English and American Episcopal Churches if these were, as is affirmed, tainted to the core with Roman and Mediæval corruptions. On the contrary, nothing can be more certain than that, if our critics be right, the great majority of them would have found their way into one or another of the numerous non-Episcopal bodies of Christians.

Moreover, the brightest lights that non-Episcopal Protestantism has produced have given their unqualified indorsement to the English Reformation. The renowned Casaubon of Geneva said: "Unless I am deceived, the most perfect part of the whole Reformation is in England, where the study of antiquity flourishes along with the study of truth." And this is the testimony of the greatest jurist and theologian of the seventeenth century, Hugo Grotius, of Holland: "It is clear to me that the English Liturgies, the custom of the laying on of hands on those arriving at years of discretion in memory of their Baptism, the regimen of Bishops, the Presbyteries composed of Clergy alone, with many other things of the same kind, agree with the customs of the ancient Church, from which we cannot deny that in France and Belgium we have departed." And surely no American will again accuse the Episcopal Church of Romanism after reading the following from the immortal Puritan fathers: "The humble request of his

Majesty's loyal subjects, to the rest of their brethren in and out of the Church of England: We esteem it our honor to call the Church of England, from whence we rise, our dear Mother, ever acknowledging that such hope and part as we have obtained in the common salvation, we have received in her bosom and sucked it from her breasts." But the witness of John Wesley will be even more convincing to many objectors. There is the testimony of his life-long adherence to the Church and his constant refusal to allow the Methodists to separate from her. Besides we have his express words uttered as late as the seventy-seventh year of his age: "Having had an opportunity of seeing several of the Churches abroad, and having deeply considered the several sorts of Dissenters at home, I am fully convinced that our own Church [the Church of England] with all her blemishes, is nearer the Scriptural plan than any other in Europe."

The Faith and worship of the English and American Episcopal Churches are as free from error and superstition as those of any non-Episcopal Denomination. Those who had the greatest influence in the Reformation of the Church of England, had reference in all they did to the ancient, uncorrupted Church. Dr. Jewel, Bishop of Salisbury, a chief reformer, says: "We are come as near as we possibly could to the Church of the Apostles and the old Catholic Bishops and Fathers, and have directed according to their customs, not only our Doctrine, but also the Sacraments and forms of Common Prayer." "I protest," said Cranmer, "that it was never in my mind to write, speak, or understand anything, but what I have learned of the Sacred Scriptures and of the Holy Catholic Church of Christ from the beginning; and also, according to the exposition of the most holy and learned Fathers and Martyrs of the Church."

The guiding principle of Cranmer, Ridley, Hooker, Bull, Thorndike, and all the galaxy of the English Reformation leaders, is also well expressed in the following passage from Bishop Beveridge: "When this, our English Church, through long communion with the Roman Church, had contracted like stains with her, from which it was necessary that it should be cleansed, they who took that excellent and very necessary work in hand, fearing that they, like others, might rush from one extreme to the other, removed indeed those things, as well doctrines as ceremonies, which the Roman Church had newly and insensibly superinduced, and, as was fit, abrogated them utterly. Yet, notwithstanding, whatever things had been at all times believed and observed by all Churches in all places, those things they most religiously took care not so to abolish with them. Hence, therefore, these first reformers of this particular Church directed the whole line of that Reformation which they undertook, according to the rules of the whole or Universal Church, casting away those things only which had been either unheard of, or rejected by the Universal Church, but most religiously retaining those things which they saw equally corroborated by the consent of the Universal Church."

If there were two or more Churches that could make in other respects equally good claims to our allegiance, it would certainly appear to be the will of God that we should identify ourselves with the one whose government, doctrine, and worship are most closely patterned after the Church of the earliest and purest times. As things now are, Americans who choose their Church relationship with reference to the primitive model, must give the preference to the Episcopal Church.

The Church for Americans.

LECTURE V.

THE AMERICAN CHURCH.

I. The Pre-Colonial Church.
II. The Colonial Church.
III. The National Church.

AUTHORITIES.

ANDERSON, History of the Colonial Church. (3 Vols.)

BEARDSLEY, Life and Correspondence of Bishop Seabury.

BENHAM, Short History of the Episcopal Church in America.

BRAND, Life of Bishop Whittingham. (2 Vols.)

COLEMAN, BP., The Church in America.

HAWKS, Contributions to the Ecclesiastical History of the United States of America.

LEONARD, BP., History of the Christian Church.

McCONNELL, History of the American Episcopal Church.

McVICKAR, Professional Years of Bishop Hobart.

PERRY, BP., The History of the American Episcopal Church. (2 Vols.)

SMITH, The Church in the New Land.

STONE, Memoir of Bishop Griswold.

WARD, Bishop William White.

WILBERFORCE, BP., History of the American Episcopal Church.

WHITE, BP., Memoirs of the Protestant Episcopal Church in the United States of America from its organization to the present day.

WORDSWORTH, CANON, Theophilus Americanus.

PAMPHLETS.

PERRY, BP., The Faith of the Framers of the Constitution of the United States.

PERRY, BP., The Faith of the Signers of the Declaration of Independence.

PERRY, BP., Historical Sketch.

ROYCE, Historical Sketches of the Church of England and the Protestant Episcopal Church in the United States.

THE AMERICAN CHURCH.

WE have seen that the Church of England is a branch of the Church of Christ.* A review of the history of the American Episcopal Church will now be necessary in order to determine whether or not the connection between the two is such as to justify the conclusion that in becoming or remaining an Episcopalian, a person will be doing the will of Christ by identifying himself with His Church.

I.

THE PRE-COLONIAL CHURCH.

THIS period extended through the one hundred and ten years from the discovery of the American Continent by John Cabot in A. D. 1497, to the establishment of the first permanent colony in the year 1607. Before the planting of the Jamestown colony the Church had no organized form. It is, however, matter of record that the Cabots, Drake, Frobisher, Cavendish, and others who were the first discoverers, explorers and colonizers of various parts of the North American Continent, were accompanied by Priests of the Church of England, who conducted daily Morning and Evening Prayer whether on ship, or land. In A. D. 1579, on the first Sunday after Trinity, Francis Fletcher, Drake's chaplain, conducted Service, preached and administered the Holy Communion on the

---

*Lecture IV.

shore of a "fayre and good baye," which is supposed to
be Drake's Bay, about thirty miles from San Francisco.
These are the first recorded Christian Services held
within the present limits of the United States. They are
commemorated by the massive and elaborately carved
"Prayer Book Cross" of granite placed in Golden Gate
Park, San Francisco, by the late Mr. George W. Childs,
of Philadelphia.

It is somewhat uncertain when the first Baptism was
administered in this country. The honor is claimed on
behalf of two places and for both Romanists and Anglicans. The child of an Indian chief is said by some to
have been baptized in the year 1570, in Virginia, by
Quiros, a Jesuit — one of a small colony of missionaries
who settled in the wilderness, but after a few years were
all murdered by the natives. Others maintain, with a
greater show of probability, that the converted chief,
Mantéo, and Virginia Dare, the first English child born
in America, baptized, respectively, on the Ninth and the
Tenth Sundays after Trinity, August 13 and 20, 1587,
on the Island of Roanoke, by the chaplain of Raleigh's
second colony, were the first recipients of the Sacrament
of Regeneration. Dr. McConnell confidently asserts:
"These were the first fruits, not only of the Church of
England, but of Christianity in the Colonies."

But there was no continuity in the Church's life for
more than a quarter of a century later. The pre-
colonial Church either came and went with the adven-
turesome seamen, or lingered only while the several
abortive attempts at colonization lasted. So devoid of
stability and the essential equipments was it that calling it a Church is only possible by a very broad application of our Lord's words: "Where two or three are
gathered together in My name, there am I in the midst
of them."

II.

THE COLONIAL CHURCH.

THE American Church may be said to date its organized existence from the establishment of the first permanent colony at Jamestown, Virginia, A. D. 1607. The distinguished honor of making the beginning of this Church is due to the Rev. Robert Hunt who conducted daily Morning and Evening Prayer, preached twice every Sunday, and administered the Holy Communion quarterly. The scene as it is briefly described in the quaint phraseology of the time, presents to the imagination a striking picture of the first American Church edifice and worshipping congregation. "We did hang an awning to the trees to shield us from the sun, our walls were rails of wood, our seats unhewed trees, our pulpit a bar of wood." Here on an equally rustic Altar occurred the first recorded celebration on the Atlantic seaboard of the Holy Eucharist according to the English Liturgy. This was June 21, the Third Sunday after Trinity, five weeks after landing.

The colony was more than once prevented from breaking up by dissension, through the reconciling influence of Mr. Hunt. The Rev. Alexander Whittaker, styled the Apostle to the North American Indian, was Hunt's worthy successor. It was he who baptized the celebrated Pocahontas in A. D. 1611. In the year 1619, the first elective assembly of the New World met in the Jamestown Church. It was opened with a Prayer Book Collect by one of the Church's Clergy. Its first act was

a provision for the protection of the Indian from oppression, and the second for the establishment of a
university. Thus the foundation of our Republican
form of government was laid a year before the famous
"Mayflower" left England with the first of the Pilgrim
colonists. Our Colonial Church was established seven
years before the Holland-Dutch came to New York,
eleven years before the much-belauded Massachusetts
Bay Puritans landed, and twenty-seven years before
Lord Baltimore came with the first colony of Romanists. From all this it will be seen that the Episcopal
Church is justly entitled to the distinction which her
members often claim for her of being denominated "the
American Church," or "the Church." This is not because she is the largest body of Christians in the country, nor because we claim her to be the only true branch
of the Apostolic Church of Christ, but owing to the fact
that she was the first Church to celebrate the Christian
worship and Sacraments on our shores as she was also
the Church of the first permanent settlers within the
limits of the thirteen original states. It must be remembered, also, that, as Bishop Coleman points out,
she was "by charter and law established in the older
colonies; that more than any other Ecclesiastical
organization she had to do with constituting the nation, and, in the period of the Civil War, with its maintenance and reunion; and that, while conservative and
Catholic in her character, she yet is distinctively American in spirit."

But even if our pretension were not supported by
any of these interesting considerations, it would be
abundantly justified by the simple fact that this is an
English-speaking nation, and ours is preëminently the
Church of the English-speaking race. According to
the idea which prevails among us, it is necessary in

order to justify our existence, for us to claim that the Episcopal Church is the Church of the American people. To us it seems to have been plainly the intention of the Master to establish one Church only which was to be continued by the Successors of the Apostles, called Bishops. Each Bishop is, by virtue of his Apostolic authority, conveyed through Canonical Consecration by successors of the Apostles, supreme in his own Jurisdiction. Moreover, the great Ecumenical Councils made provision for the protection of this supremacy. Therefore, there can be only one Bishop in a given Diocese, and one Church in a Nation. If two or more bodies exist with separate officers, only one can be the right and lawful Church of Christ, the others must be usurpers or schismatics. Our claim to be the Church in the United States having the right to exclusive allegiance is canonically justified chiefly by the fact that this country was originally the possession of the English Nation, and that the English tongue and laws were adopted by the common consent of the American people. The Church of England which consecrated and gave us our Bishops, traces its descent from the Apostles of our Lord and possesses the independence that was originally conferred upon Her, and all other National Churches. No civil officer can produce a more legitimate authority than can a Bishop of the Episcopal Church. Therefore this is the American Church.

The Colonial Church was for the most part under the nominal supervision of the Bishop of London. But this was a very unsatisfactory arrangement. It necessitated an expensive and perilous voyage of six thousand miles on the part of candidates for Holy Orders. This kept many from applying at all, and of the few whose consecrated zeal impelled them forward, a large proportion perished by shipwreck, or died abroad by one or another of the pestilential diseases, so common a century

or two ago in all parts of Europe. Under these circumstances it was impossible to secure an adequate staff of
native-born Clergymen. The Church was, therefore,
largely dependent upon recruits from England. And,
unfortunately, of the few who came, some were either
adventurers or persons who had left home to avoid discipline for some misdemeanor. Laws had to be made to
restrain such from even the gross vices of gambling and
drunkenness, and to force them to discharge the duties
they were neglecting. As, however, the Church here was
practically without a head, these unworthy ministers
escaped the penalties and continued to work havoc
wherever they went.

It is related that a clergyman on his way to Maryland, or purposing to emigrate, died. His valet assumed the clerical garb of his master, took possession
of his letters of Orders, his stock of sermons and other
papers, continued the journey to Maryland, and there,
under the name of the dead clergyman, had charge of a
parish for a long time. This outrage also occurred: A
known profligate in Orders obtained, through family
influence, an important parish. The incensed congregation rose up and declared that he should not come
among them. They accordingly barred the windows
and put extra locks on the doors of the Church. But
they had to deal with a resolute man. A window was
forced, and when the good people entered through the
opened door they found their pastor in the desk, his
opened Prayer Book flanked on either side by a pistol,
and he ready to address them as "Dearly beloved
brethren." Having "read himself in," his future concern
was only the taxes collected for the support of religion.

The Northern Clergy were of the most exemplary
character. But they were few, and suffered much persecution from the Puritans, who "assumed the right of

taxing all for the support of their ministers and meeting-houses; and, wherever they could gain over the
local Governor to their persuasion, proceeded to en-
force their claim with signal violence." "With melancholy hearts," a member of the Church at Wal-
lingford, Connecticut, wrote home to complain, "have
divers of us been imprisoned, and our goods from
year to year distrained for taxes levied for the building and supporting of meeting-houses." As late as the
year 1750, an old man, who had been long a member
of the Church, was whipped publicly for not attending meeting. Dr. Peters, a contemporaneous writer of
Colonial History, relates that, in the same year "an
Episcopal Clergyman, born and educated in England,
who had been in Holy Orders above twenty years, once
broke their Sabbatical law by combing a discomposed
lock of hair on the top of his wig; at another time, by
making a humming noise, which they called whistling;
at a third time, by walking too fast from Church; at a
fourth, by running into a Church when it rained; at a
fifth, by walking in his garden and picking a bunch of
grapes; for which several crimes he was complained of
by the Grand Jury, and a warrant granted against him,
was seized, brought to trial, and made to pay a considerable sum of money." At Hartford, one of the judges
of the county court, assisted by the mob, pulled down a
rising Church, and with the stones built a house for
his son. Mr. Morton, a staunch Churchman of Massachusetts, was persecuted violently, all the more because
of the satires contained in his "New English Canaan."
He died in England from the effects of his imprisonment
at Boston.

Owing to the many disadvantages growing out of
the dependence upon a foreign Episcopate, repeated and
persevering efforts were made to secure the Consecration

of Bishops for this country, but without avail. The celebrated English philanthropist, Granville Sharp, used his great influence on behalf of the neglected sheep of the American wilderness, and almost succeeded in bringing about the Consecration of chief shepherds for them. "Twice," says the author of "The Professional Years of Bishop Hobart," "was the goodly plan frustrated when on the very point of completion. In the reign of Charles II., the patent was actually made out, appointing the Rev. Dr. Alexander Murray, a good man, and a companion of the King's exile, Bishop of Virginia, with a general charge over the other provinces; but the scheme fell through by a change of ministry, and what Clarendon had done, the 'Cabal' revoked, though the deeper cause probably was, that the King, himself, had no heart in the matter. A second time, in the reign of Anne, was provision made, a scheme of four American Bishoprics adopted, and certain government lands in the Island of St. Kitts actually sold for their endowment. The death of the Queen cut this short, and although subsequently approved and recommended by the first and ablest men of the Church, by Berkeley, Butler, Gibson, Sherlock, and, above all, by the meekest of Prelates, Archbishop Secker, it was never carried into effect." "At one time," writes Canon Perry, in his "History of the Church of England," "there were two non-juring Bishops in America, namely, Dr. R. Welton, and Dr. J. Talbot, A. D. 1722, the former in Philadelphia, the latter in Burlington, N. J., but they were not allowed to exercise Episcopal functions, except by stealth, and the government soon afterwards interfered with, and put an entire stop to, all action on their part."

The failure to secure the Episcopacy was chiefly due to the political influence of the Puritanical sects. But strange as it may appear, some of the Prelates themselves objected to the giving of the Episcopate to "the New World," upon the ground that there could be no adequate provision made in such a barbarous country for the due support of Bishops in the state and dignity which, according to their conception, properly belong to them. As Dr. McConnell observes: "The idea of a Bishop in the American wilderness was as grotesque to them as now would be the suggestion of a professor of higher mathematics among the Zulus." It is surpassingly strange that their "lordships," who for the most part were really good and learned men, should so far have been blinded by their environment as altogether to lose sight of the simplicity of the Apostolic and primitive Episcopate. But, in view of the unfortunate experience of our fathers, it is even more inexplicable that the multiplication of Bishops to supply the growing needs of the American Church is, at this late date, prevented by the survival of the misconceptions of our English forefathers. Large sections, in many of our states and territories, are at this time deprived of adequate Episcopal ministrations because they have not the ability to make "ample provision" for the support of a chief shepherd. An able editorial critic thus puts the unscriptural and unjustifiable character of the legislation regulating the creation of new Dioceses and Missionary Jurisdictions: "It is the fashion to talk of the Episcopate as distinctively the Missionary Order; and so it ought to be; but the Constitution of the Protestant Episcopal Church forbids it to be so unless on conditions at which the Apostles of Jesus Christ—men who were sent without scrip for their journey, and without gold, silver, or even brass in their purses—would have been amazed."

But having, in accord with their inherited ideas, conceived this objection against responding to the appeal of the Colonial Church, the English Bishops were doubtless confirmed in it by the fact that the Clergy already in the field were paid in tobacco instead of in gold, and that they experienced considerable difficulty in collecting even the scanty amount of that indigenous weed which had been promised. The Clergy often had occasion to complain that the tobacco given them in payment for their salaries was inferior in quality. The stipends were fixed in some Parishes at sixteen thousand pounds of tobacco per annum. This would realize, if the article were of the best grade, the equivalent of between four and five hundred dollars of our money, upon which sum the Rectors are said to have lived, even when married, very comfortably. Why could not a Bishop have done the same?

No wonder that under these circumstances the Church was in an almost hopelessly depressed condition. At the South she was nearly ruined by the irregularities growing out of the want of Episcopal oversight, while to the Northward she was downtrodden and all but crushed out by Puritanism. But there were many notable exceptions among the Southerners, of Clergymen and Laymen who were examples of piety and self-sacrificing devotion. And in the course of time there was also an unmistakable reaction against Northern Puritanism.

This reactionary movement started in the year 1722, among the faculty and graduates of Yale College. Seven of these, all professors, Congregational or Presbyterian ministers, were accustomed to meet together for the purpose of studying and discussing the claims of the Episcopal Church. These meetings grew out of a Prayer Book, which many years before had providentially fallen into the hands of President Cutler, and from the study of certain standard works of the Anglican Divines, contributed by the celebrated Dean Berkeley, to the College library. One of them tells us that not a single path was left untrodden, which seemed likely to lead to fresh sources of knowledge. The best writers on either side of the controversy were carefully consulted, and their arguments deliberately discussed and weighed. As far as temporal ease and prospects were concerned, it would have been a welcome result to these inquirers, had they found the principles of Congregational government to agree, in their judgment, with those of the primitive Church of Christ. Such a conclusion would have retained them in the peaceful discharge of their accustomed duties, and have preserved unbroken the cords of love which bound them to their kindred, friends and country. But the enjoyment of present ease would cease to be a blessing, if purchased at the cost of truth; and come therefore what might, the dictates of conscience were to be obeyed. When, therefore, after long study and many conferences, they had fully made up their minds as to the truth of the Anglican Church's position, they met the trustees of Yale College and astonished them beyond measure by reading the following address:

" *To the Rev. Mr. Andrew and Mr. Woodbridge and others, our Reverend Fathers and Brethren, present in the Library of Yale College this 13th of September, 1722.*

"REVEREND GENTLEMEN:—Having represented to you the difficulties which we labor under, in relation to our continuance out of the visible communion of an Episcopal Church, and a state of seeming opposition thereto, either as private Christians, or as officers, and so being insisted on by some of you, after our

repeated declinings of it, that we should sum up our case
in writing, we do, though with great reluctance, fearing
the consequences of it, submit to, and comply with, it,
and signify to you that some of us doubt the validity,
and the rest of us are more fully persuaded of the invalidity of Presbyterian Ordination, in opposition to Episcopal; and should be heartily thankful to God and man
if we may receive from them satisfaction herein; and
shall be willing to embrace your good counsels and instructions in relation to this important affair, as far as
God shall direct and dispose us to do."

Signed,   TIMOTHY CUTLER,
                        [President of Yale College.]

JOHN HART,
SAMUEL WHITTLESEY,
JARED ELIOT,   } Professors and
JAMES WETMORE,   Ministers.
SAMUEL JOHNSON,
DANIEL BROWN,

When this declaration was made there was only one
of our Clergymen in all Connecticut. In the course of
the next month, at the suggestion of the Governor of
the Colony, there was a public discussion between its
signers and the amazed Puritans. At this debate Presbyterians contended that the Apostles, in the nature of
things, could have no successors, and that the title
Bishop, which Episcopalians restrict to those whom
they conceive to be invested with Apostolic authority,
is used in the Epistles as a synonym of Presbyter or
Elder. It was shown by the converts to Episcopacy,
that the first of these assertions is a misleading half
truth. It is of course true that the Apostles could not
transmit to successors their blessed personal experience
as the privileged Disciples of the Lord, their Pentecostal
illumination and inspiration, their ability to bear the
testimony of eye-witnesses to the Resurrection and their
power to work miracles. But the instances of St.
Matthias and St. Paul prove that the Apostolic office

was not limited as to number, or person, or time, for these were not of the twelve first selected by Christ, and yet they were confessedly none the less Apostles.

It appears, therefore, from Scripture that the Apostles could and did perpetuate their office by delegating their authority to those who should assist and succeed them in the administration of the Church. To argue the impossibility of this, as the Presbyterians do, upon the ground of the supernatural endowments of the Apostles and their close relationship to our Lord, is as inconsistent and contrary to human experience as it would be to insist that kings and princes can have no successors, because they cannot convey their personality to others. Moreover, according to this hypothesis the Elders and Deacons could have no successors, for they also worked miracles. The remark of Hooker expresses the truth respecting this matter: "In some things every Presbyter, in some things only Bishops, in somethings neither the one nor the other, are the Apostles' successors."

The circumstance of Presbyters sometimes being called Bishops in the New Testament and *vice versâ*, does no more prove that there was no distinction in office and authority, than the calling of the Apostles Elders places them upon a level with the Presbytery. They also called themselves Deacons. Are we therefore to conclude that the Apostolate and Diaconate are the same office in the Church of the New Testament? Bishop means overseer or superintendent. The confusion arises from losing sight of the fact that Bishop is a title common to the members of both the Apostleship and Presbytership. These in their respective spheres were rulers. The Presbyter-bishops were local, parochial superintendents. The Apostle-bishops were General, Diocesan or Metropolitan superintendents. The difference

C. A.—18

between the Presbyterian and Apostolic Bishops appears very plainly in what St. Paul had to say to the representatives of both Orders who were stationed at Ephesus. Upon comparing Acts 20: 28-36 with I Timothy 5: 1, 19-22, and II Timothy 2: 2, it will be observed that the duties required of them, respectively, correspond exactly with the requirements of the Episcopal Church from the second and third Orders of her ministry. The Presbyter-bishops were charged with the feeding, protection and correction of particular flocks. The Apostle-bishops were exhorted to seek out and prepare fit men for the Holy Orders; to ordain those who should be found worthy, and to administer discipline to the Clergy who should be guilty of irregular life or heretical teaching. In order to avoid confusion it was not very long before Presbyters ceased to be called Bishops, and the title was reserved exclusively for the successors of the Apostles. This rests upon the testimony of the early Fathers who tell us that "those who in their day were called Bishops were first called Apostles." "It was precisely as if, by the common consent of the American people, springing from gratitude for the services, and veneration for the memory, of Washington, it should be determined, for the future, to appropriate to him alone the title of president; and to all his successors in the presidential office created by the constitution, what is now regarded as the less dignified name of governor. It would not detract one iota from the constitutional privileges and powers attached to the office itself."

Thus the representatives of Presbyterianism at the famous Yale debate found that "their chief argument, from the different uses of the words Bishop and Presbyter in the New Testament, was met by the incontestable evidence from Scripture of the superintendency of

Timothy over the Clergy and Laity of Ephesus, and of Titus over the Church in Crete. The appeal to the history of the first and purest centuries of the Church was made until at length, as Johnson records it, 'an old minister got up and made an harangue against us in the declamatory way to raise an odium, but he had not gone far before Mr. Saltonstall, the Governor, who, himself, presided, got up and said that he only designed a friendly argument,' and so put an end to the conference."

The Puritans regarded this notable defection from their ranks with apprehension and dismay. On the occasion of the celebration of the one hundred and fiftieth anniversary of Yale College, President Woolsey, referring to the event, said: "I suppose that greater alarm would scarcely be awakened now, if the theological faculty of the college were to declare for the Church of Rome, avow their belief in transubstantiation and pray to the Virgin Mary." Nor were they mistaken in the expectation that others would follow. In the ten years subsequent to that memorable declaration more than one in ten of the graduates of Yale, who entered the ministry, followed the example of Cutler, Johnson, Brown and Wetmore—the leaders of the great army of Denominational ministers, who, from that day to this, have been drawn into the Church's service. So many were the accessions to the Church from Congregationalism and Presbyterianism that in the year 1734 the Independents sent a petition drawn up by the famous Jonathan Edwards to the Bishop of London, in which they represented to his lordship that they did not need any more Church missionaries in New England, as they only drew away from their own people into the Episcopal ranks; that there was, however, great need of missionaries in Carolina and New York, and not north of that.

III.

THE NATIONAL CHURCH.

OUR National Episcopal Church is one of the results of the American Revolution. It was not that Churchmen generally preferred to be independent of the Church of England, but that owing to the temper of the times, and the relation of the English Church to the State, it was simply impossible to continue the relationship of a daughter as in colonial times. Henceforth the Church, if it continued at all, must be regarded as an independent sister. But, as a matter of fact, it looked very much as if she would become extinct. Many of her own sons supposed that she was hopelessly prostrate, and despaired of her resuscitation. An anecdote concerning Chief Justice Marshall, related by Bishop Meade, is illustrative of the deep-rooted impression which prevailed that the Episcopal Church could not be revived even in the stronghold of old Virginia. When the Bishop "soon after the establishment of the Theological Seminary of Virginia, was collecting funds for it, he presented the subscription list to Judge Marshall. With his usual kindness and liberality, he set down a handsome amount, but at the same time said he really feared that it was doing an unkindness to the young men of Virginia, thus to tempt them to prepare for the ministry of a Church which could never be revived. He lived, however, to rejoice in seeing the failure of his fears and prophecy."

Even the good, and for the most part, judicious, Dr. William White, of Philadelphia, the first Bishop of

Pennsylvania, saw no hope for the saving of the feeble remnant but in the adoption of the extraordinary measures recommended in his famous pamphlet written at the close of the war. In it he advocated, among other novelties, the creation of a temporary fictitious Episcopate, ordained by Presbyters and Laymen. The proposition was regarded and represented, especially by the few remaining Northern clergymen, as preposterous, and there is reason to believe that Dr. White himself came to regret this production of his pen. At least, on the blank pages in the back of his private copy there was found, in his handwriting, a note of explanation and justification which we quote here, because of its concise description of the condition and prospects of the Church during, and for some time after, the struggle for Independence. "The circumstances," runs the note, "attached to that publication are the following: The congregations of our Church throughout the United States were approaching annihilation. Although within this city [Philadelphia] three Episcopal Clergymen, including the author, were resident and officiating, the Churches over the rest of the State had become deprived of their Clergy during the war, either by death or departure for England. In the Eastern States, with two or three exceptions, there was a cessation of the exercises of the pulpit, owing to the necessary disuse of the prayers for the former civil rulers. In Maryland and Virginia, where the Church had enjoyed civil establishments, on the ceasing of these, the incumbents of the parishes, almost without exception, ceased to officiate. Further South the condition of the Church was not better, to say the least."

Then follows the aged Bishop's explanation of why he thought that the true Apostolic Episcopate could not be secured in time to save the Church from ruin.

But in the Providence of God this was to be another of the many illustrations of the maxim, "Man's extremity is God's opportunity." The Blessed Saviour had promised that the gates of hell or death should not prevail againt His Church. The fact that the Colonial Church did not utterly perish in the dark days which immediately preceded and succeeded the Revolution, is an all but conclusive proof of its Divine and indestructible character. No political revolutions, no bigoted persecutions, no machinations of evil-minded men are sufficient to crush out the Church of the living God.

> "Crowns and thrones may perish,
>   Kingdoms rise and wane,
>   But the Church of Jesus constant will remain."

The Colonial Church had been one, with the Bishop of London as the center of unity, but after the Declaration of Independence the remnant of the Church in each colony became a little feeble National Church. As in the period of the Heptarchy, there were seven independent branches of the Apostolic Church in England, so for some time there were thirteen separate and distinct little Episcopal Churches in America, as there were also thirteen little nations in the country. These were consolidated into one Church and one nation in the same year. And it is noteworthy that in many instances the same men were, under God, instrumental in the unification of both. Two-thirds of the framers of the Constitution of the United States were, by birth, by Baptism, by family association, Churchmen.* Of these nearly one-fifth were deputies in actual attendance upon the early General or State Conventions of the Church. This no doubt accounts for the striking resemblances between the governments of the United States and the Episcopal Church about which we shall have occasion to say more.

---

* Appendix VI.

The unity which was ultimately effected in both State and Church was in part the result of a felt necessity for self-preservation. In the case of the Church it was seen to be necessary in order that sufficient influence might be exerted to secure the Consecration of Bishops by the English Prelates, and to obtain permission from Congress for them to take up their abode in the several States. The Bishops in England were no longer unwilling to consecrate for America, but, under the laws by which their official acts were regulated, they could not proceed without special permissory legislation by Parliament. This, owing partly to piques connected with the outcome of the late war, but principally to the great power of the Puritan enemies of the Church, was exceedingly hard to obtain, and consequently required all the influence that could be exerted by a united effort.

The want of general coöperation accounts for the failure of the Connecticut Clergy to secure Consecration from the English Episcopate for their admirable Bishop elect, Dr. Samuel Seabury. After many months of fruitless negotiations, he was at last compelled to apply to the non-juring Bishops of Scotland, who, having no connection with the State, were free to exercise the functions of their Apostolic office according to discretion. They invested Dr. Seabury with the Episcopal character at Aberdeen in an upper room on November 14, 1784, Bishops Kilgour, Petrie and Skinner being the Consecrators. "This ever-memorable Service was performed," says an eye witness, "in the presence of a considerable number of respectable Clergymen and a great number of Laity."

The Consecration of Dr. Seabury took place about two years and a half after the declaration of peace and the acknowledgment of the independence of the colonies. It was the most important event which had so far happened in the history of the American Episcopal Church. Its immediate and direct influence for good cannot be exaggerated. It destroyed the argument of necessity by which Dr. White, and some Southern Churchmen sought to justify their proposition to abandon temporarily the government of the Church by the Historic Episcopate. There was now a Bishop in the States, and if the canonical number three could not possibly be secured, he could by himself consecrate others, and so perpetuate the succession, and provide for the performance of all the Episcopal offices required at any time. If this unfortunately had been necessary, we should have been as well off as the Mission which the Church of Rome has planted in the United States, for, not to mention other irregularities, its Episcopate is uncanonically derived through one Consecrator. Their first Bishop, Dr. Carroll, arrived in the year 1790, six years after Bishop Seabury. About twenty years afterwards, without regard to Canon law, which requires that there shall be at least three Consecrators, he invested four others with the Episcopal office. Thus Episcopalians have the legal line of the Apostolic succession in this country, while Romanists have not. Morover, we have a decided further advantage in that our Episcopacy was first on the ground. According to Ecclesiastical Law, we therefore constitute the American branch of the Catholic Church, and they are intruding schismatics.

In any case, however, the Episcopal Church would be the only logical and legitimate Catholic Church of the land, because Americans are English-speaking people, and this is the historic Church of our race. The Mother Church of England was established among our British ancestors for centuries before they came into

contact with Romanism through the Mission of Augustine, and she was identified with the English nation for
fifteen hundred years before the birth of the oldest of
the non-Episcopal bodies. Indeed the very existence of
England as a nation and kingdom is owing to this
Church which was instrumental in uniting the seven
tribes into which Anglo-Saxons were divided. Many of
the Bishoprics and other Ecclesiastical foundations are
older than the Kingdom, and have held their lands and
endowments longer than the Crown has possessed its
property. There was an Archbishop of Canterbury
three hundred years before there was a King of England. And not only has she been connected with our
race much longer than any other Christian body, but
she has now, and, in all probability, always will have by
far the greater number of English-speaking adherents.
Moreover, taking it altogether, she is as the foundation
of the English nation and civilization, the most powerful agency for good the world has ever seen. The
Church of England is, therefore, as preëminently the
Catholic Church of our race, as the Church of Rome is
that of the Italians, and the Greek Church that of the
Eastern nations.

Dr. Seabury's success in obtaining the Episcopate,
and his safe return were a great joy to the Connecticut
Clergy. But the Presbyterian ministers appeared to be
rather alarmed, and "in consequence of his arrival assumed and gave to one another the style and title of
Bishop which formerly they reprobated as a remnant
of Popery." Upon one occasion when the Bishop entered the hall where the Yale College commencement
exercises were going on, some one suggested to the
President that he be invited, out of respect to his office,
to a seat upon the stage among other distinguished
persons; to which it was replied: "We are all Bishops

here, but if there be room for another, he can occupy it."

Besides removing the plea of necessity for the creation of a spurious Episcopacy, Dr. Seabury's Consecration by the Scottish Episcopate apparently had the effect of mortifying the English Bishops, and of inducing them to redouble their efforts to secure the requisite Act of Parliament to enable them to consecrate for foreign countries without the administration of the civil oath. In little less than two years and a half, they had not only secured the enabling act, but under it, had duly set apart Drs. Provoost and White as Bishops, respectively, of New York and Pennsylvania; and in A. D. 1790, they Consecrated Dr. James Madison, Bishop of Virginia, and so the canonical number necessary to transmit the Apostolic Succession was at last obtained from England.

Still another direct and important effect of the timely action taken by the Northern Clergy in securing a regularly consecrated Bishop, is seen in the restraint put upon the Southerners, who were for making radical changes in the Prayer Book, and for materially curtailing the ancient rights and powers of the American Episcopate. That such restraint was sorely needed will be sufficiently evident by observing that it was proposed to omit the Nicene Creed from the Liturgy, and to deny our Prelates many of the rights and powers which have been, by common consent, a prerogative of Bishops from the beginning.

For some time after the Consecration of Drs. Provoost and White the thirteen State Churches, without formal action, grouped themselves into two incipient Provinces with the Bishop of Connecticut as the primate of the Northern, and the Bishops of New York and Pennsylvania at the head of the Southern. Owing to the unfortunate difference of opinion respecting the regularity of Dr. Seabury's Consecration, and the Southern prejudice against him, growing out of his Chaplaincy in the British Army, and to the dissatisfaction of the Connecticut Clergy and Bishop with what they regarded as the want of Churchliness in the Southerners, it seemed highly probable that two distinct and separate Episcopal Churches would be perpetuated in America. This to all appearance would certainly have been the case but for the wise management of the Rev. Dr. Parker and Bishop White.

Dr. Parker was a distinguished Boston Clergyman, who in A. D. 1804 was consecrated Bishop of Massachusetts, but died before performing a single Episcopal act. In order to accomplish the union of the Northern and Southern Churches, he contrived to have the Rev. Dr. Bass elected Bishop of Massachusetts, and an application made to the General Convention of A. D. 1789, for his Consecration by Bishops Seabury, Provoost and White. Dr. Bass was not consecrated at that time and it is thought that there was no expectation that he would be, but the election and application led to the unanimous adoption of a resolution in which the validity of Bishop Seabury's Consecration was recognized. At an adjourned meeting of this Convention, held in Philadelphia on September 29, 1789, the Bishop of Connecticut was present with his Clerical deputies. But they would not subscribe to the constitution previously adopted until it had been so far changed as to allow the House of Bishops their ancient vetoing power, and the privilege of introducing new measures. These changes made, the Connecticut delegation affixed their signatures, took their seats in the convention, and so the Northern and Southern Churches were united. At the next General Convention this unity was effectually cemented by the consecration of the Rev. Thomas John Claggett, D.D., as Bishop of Maryland by the Bishops of Connecticut, New York, Pennsylvania and Virginia. Through the first Bishop of Maryland, though his was the only Consecration in which Bishop Seabury took part, all American Bishops subsequently consecrated are able to trace their Apostolic succession along both the Scottish and English lines.

Thus the connection between the Church of England and the American Episcopal Church is such that the Catholicity of the latter cannot be denied if it be admitted of the former. The history of our Church "in a nut-shell" is this: It was founded in Jerusalem, A. D. 30, by Jesus Christ; was planted in England, possibly by St. Paul or one of his pupils; was more or less subject to the usurpations of the Bishop of Rome from the twelfth to the sixteenth centuries, then freed and reformed; was a mission of the Church of England in America until after the Revolution, when it became autonomous and was called "Protestant Episcopal." It therefore possesses authority from Christ Himself, and has continuous existence from the days of the Apostles.

Cardinal Gibbons in his "Faith of Our Fathers" says of us, "The very name you bear betrays your recent birth; for who ever heard of a Baptist or an Episcopal or any other Protestant Church, prior to the Reformation?" To this we reply that the Mother Church has the same name now that she had before the Reformation, *Ecclesia Anglicana*, the Church of England. The French Roman Catholic Dupin, a distinguished Doctor of the famous Sorbonne Faculty and regius professor of Divinity who flourished some two hundred years ago, opens a chapter in his Compendious History of the Church, with the question: "In what state was the Church of England, and what passed there

in the eleventh century?" The Magna Charta which
dates back three hundred and fifty years before the final
breaking with the Papacy, speaks of the Church of England and guarantees her liberty and the independence
of all Ecclesiastical persons. As Dr. Stearns in his
"Faith of Our Forefathers," a crushing reply to Cardinal Gibbons, says: "It was the Church of England
then and it is the Church of England now; it was 'free'
then; it is 'free' now. The 'Episcopal' Church in the
United States is its legitimate offspring, recognized by
it as such. Its name of 'Episcopal,' therefore, does
not 'betray' its 'recent birth;' nor is that birth
'recent' in any other sense than that in which the
birth of every Church, the Roman itself not excepted, in
a recently discovered country is recent."

Of course Roman controversialists proceed upon the
hypothesis that the Church of England was originally a
mission of the Church of Rome. But we have seen that
this is not true, and that even if it were, our right to
independence of Papal dominion would not be affected.
The argument to the contrary, if carried out to its logical conclusions, would prove quite too much for our
adversaries. It would subject Rome to Jerusalem from
which all Churches have directly or indirectly sprung.
Or if they contend that as the child is governed by its
parents rather than the grandparents, so a mission
must be subjected to the Church that planted it, rather
than to the mother of all Churches, we point out that by
this reasoning the Church of Rome should be subject to
the Church of Greece. For it is now a well-established
fact that the Greeks planted Christianity in Rome, and
indeed that the Church there was for more than two centuries confined to a Grecian colony. Bishop Coxe says,
"The local Roman Church was for three hundred years a
mere colony of Greek Christianity." And Dean Stanley,

in his "Eastern Church," writes: "The Greek Church reminds us of the time when the tongue, not of Rome but of Greece, was the sacred language of Christendom. It was a striking remark of the Emperor Napoleon, that the introduction of Christianity itself was, in a certain sense, the triumph of Greece over Rome. The early Roman Church was but a colony of Greek Christians or Grecized Jews; the earliest Fathers of the Western Church wrote in Greek; the early Popes were not Italians but Greeks; the name of Pope is not Latin but Greek, the common and now despised name of every pastor in the Eastern Church; she is the mother, and Rome the daughter." Canon Gore observes that "at an unknown moment, before the middle of the third century, the Church of Rome, which up to that time had been Greek in language—alike in her Liturgy and her theology—a Greek colony in the Latin city, became, perhaps somewhat suddenly, a Latin Church, and in consequence of this change of language so completely forgot her Greek past that in the fourth century she was ignorant of an accident in her life which the coincidences of modern discovery have laid open to our eyes."

The unity so happily effected in A. D. 1789, between the Northern and Southern Dioceses, though often more or less strained, fortunately has never been broken. Its most severe trial was at the opening of our great Civil War. The Southern delegations were, of course, not present at the General Convention which met in the year 1862, but the right of the South to representation was not questioned, seats were assigned them as in times past, and their absence was not recognized by the secretary, who never omitted their Dioceses at the roll call. They had formed a separate General Convention for the Confederate States, but this was dissolved immediately after the war, and all were represented as usual at the first General Convention which met thereafter. This coming together of Churchmen, among whom were many of the most influential leaders on both sides, did much more than is commonly realized to help forward the reconstruction of the Union and Government.

For many years after the foundations of unity and Catholicity had been laid and well cemented, the upbuilding of the superstructure was discouragingly slow. This, in fact, continued to be the case until about thirty years ago. It was due to the operation of a variety of causes.

1. There was, first of all, the inveterate puritanical hatred of the Church, because of those features in her system which were groundlessly denounced as the "rags of Popery."

2. There was also the wide-spread conviction that the Episcopal polity was essentially opposed to the newly-founded Republican form of government, and that consequently its introduction and toleration would be a menace to the recently-acquired liberties. Bishop White says: "I have lived in days in which there existed such prejudices in our land against the name, and still more against the office, of a Bishop, that it was doubtful whether any person in that character would be tolerated in the community." Even as late as the year 1827, when Bishop Chase laid the massive foundations for "Old Kenyon," the people of the region about Gambier had the gravest suspicions that he was building an English fort for the subjugation of the country west of the Alleghanies, and could scarce be restrained from taking up arms against the Bishop and workmen.

It is still periodically represented, to the great prejudice of the Episcopal Church, that she fits in with a

Monarchical rather than a Republican form of government. In a recent widely-circulated attack upon the Episcopal Church by a Congregational minister, it is charged that she cannot make good the claim to be the Church of the United States, because she "has not in history been loyal to Americanism," and "it is not in its government American."

So far as the first of these assertions is concerned, what little foundation there is for it exists in the fact that before the Independence, there being no Bishop in this country, our Clergy either came from England or went there for Ordination, and so their loyalty to the Crown was pledged in the oath required from the English Clergy by the government. But though our ministry was thus embarrassed, our laymen were as free as those of any other communion to govern themselves according to their conviction. It is a mistake to suppose that before the Declaration of Independence, opinion as to the advisability of separating from the mother country was nowhere divided except in the Episcopal Church, and the colonies where she predominated. The Puritans were by no means unanimous for an appeal to arms. In Massachusetts a majority were at first opposed to the war; a bill to sanction it was twice defeated in the Legislature. In Connecticut the opposition was still greater. In New York the parties were so equally divided, that when the Provincial Congress chanced to receive notice upon the same day in 1775 that General Washington was about to cross the Hudson and General Tryon had arrived in the harbor, they ordered the colonel commanding the militia so to dispose his men that he could receive whichever General should first arrive, and wait upon both as well as circumstances would allow. Two-thirds of the signers of the Declaration of Independence were Episcopalians.

One signer from Massachusetts, Elbridge Gerry, afterwards Vice-President of the United States; all but one of the signers from New York; one signer from New Jersey, Francis Hopkinson, a vestryman and warden; all the signers but one from Pennsylvania; all but one from Delaware; all but one from Maryland; all the signers from Virginia; all from North Carolina; all from South Carolina; and all but one from Georgia, were Episcopalians. This immortal document was mainly drawn up by Thomas Jefferson, who was, at least, a baptized member and a professed adherent of the Episcopal Church. He was, to the day of his death, a constant attendant upon her Services.*

Washington, the Commander-in-chief of the armies, and the one, under God, to whom the nation owes more for its independence than any other, was a Communicant, Vestryman, and Lay Reader of this Church, and died in it.§ Robert B. Livingston, who, in A. D. 1764, organized the opposition to the Stamp Act in New York, was an Episcopalian. So was Charles Cotesworth Pinckney, to whom we owe the phrase, "millions for defense, but not a cent for tribute." He was also the author of that clause of the Federal Constitution which provides that no religious test shall ever be required as a qualification for any office in the United States. And there was Patrick Henry, whose famous speech, "Give me liberty or give me death," went so far in deciding Virginia to join her sister colonies in the struggle for freedom. The debt of gratitude which we owe this thrilling Revolutionary orator cannot be appreciated unless we realize how indispensable the help of Virginia was to the patriot cause. Had Virginia stood aloof, or taken sides with England, we should, in all probability, have failed. John Morton, who, as chairman, on July 2, 1776, cast the vote by which Pennsylvania was committed to the

* Appendix V.   § Appendix III.

C. A.—19

Revolution, was an Episcopalian. So was Cæsar Rodney, who did a similar service for Delaware. Richard Henry Lee, of Virginia, called the Cicero of the Revolution, who first proposed the idea of a Congress for all the Colonies, and introduced into Congress a resolution for the Independence of the Colonies, was an Episcopalian. On his motion, and supported by his eloquence, was adopted the recommendation of the Committee which drew up and reported the Declaration of Independence; and in that instrument was embodied by Congress the very words that Lee had used in his original resolution: "That these united Colonies are, and by right ought to be, free and independent States; that they are absolved from all allegiance to the British Crown, and that all political connection between them and the State of Great Britain is, and ought to be, totally dissolved." The declaration of rights adopted by the Virginia Legislature, and embodied in the Declaration of Independence, was written by George Mason, an Episcopalian. The Declaration was first publicly read in the State House Square, Philadelphia, by John Nixon, an Episcopalian. Peyton Randolph, the first President of the American Congress—that very Congress which inaugurated and set on foot the War of the Revolution—was an Episcopalian. So was Robert Morris, whom Congress appointed superintendent of finances, and by whose management of them, and the pledging of his own immense fortune—an act that reduced him to poverty—did so much to raise the necessary means to keep our armies in the field. Benjamin Franklin, whom Congress sent abroad as one of its special envoys, and who, by his tact and persistence, negotiated the treaty which secured for us the aid of France, without which our cause must, to all appearance, inevitably have failed, was nominally an Episcopalian.*

* Appendix IV.

The lanterns which lighted Paul Revere's famous ride to alarm the country of the British movement upon Lexington and Concord were hung in the steeple of "Old Christ's Episcopal Church" by an Episcopalian. The Bishop of Iowa, the learned and painstaking historiographer of the American Episcopal Church, to whose writings I am indebted for many of the facts of this lecture, says truly: "Not a field of battle, from Bunker Hill to Yorktown, was there, but was moistened by Churchmen's willing offering of life-blood for country and freedom." General Sullivan, of New Hampshire; General Cobb, of Massachusetts; General Ward, of Rhode Island; Generals Morgan and Lewis, of New York; General Brearly, of New Jersey; Generals Ross, Cadwallader, and "Mad Anthony" Wayne, of Pennsylvania; Generals Sumpter, Marion, and Moultrie, of South Carolina; Generals Gwynnett, Wymberly Jones, and Walton, of Georgia, were all Episcopalians. So were Generals Montgomery and Mercer, who in turn so gallantly laid down their lives at Quebec and Princeton. Alexander Hamilton and John Laurens, the first of whom commanded, and the other led, the storming party which captured the first British redoubt at Yorktown, where Cornwallis surrendered and where the war was practically ended, were Episcopalians. Nelson, the Governor of Virginia, who called out the militia of the lower part of the State, himself personally giving the State security for the funds to equip them, and who, at the head of three thousand five hundred of them, marched to Yorktown, reaching the scene of action just in time to reinforce the army of Washington and that of our French allies, so that they were enabled to surround Cornwallis and prevent his escape, was an Episcopalian.

James Madison, afterwards President of the United States, who, besides giving the benefit of his great mind to the country during the continuation of the struggle, after its close, when the States were about to fall apart, was mainly instrumental in the formation of our present Constitution, was an Episcopalian. All of these men, together with Monroe, and Jay, and Marshall, and Livingstone, and Rutledge, and King, and the Pinkneys, and the Harrisons, and Edmund Randolph, and Lord Sterling, and "Lighthorse Harry" Lee, and Lillington, and Derr, and Troup, and William Samuel Johnson, and hosts of others, were Episcopalians. Francis Hopkinson, of New Jersey, one of the Episcopalian signers of the Declaration, was the father of Joseph Hopkinson, also a member of the Episcopal Church, who was the author of our National song, "Hail Columbia;" and Francis Scott Key, of Maryland, the writer of "The Star Spangled Banner," was an Episcopalian.

As for our Clergy, when the great crisis came, there were only two hundred and fifty of them in the country. It is true that some of them, including Dr. Seabury, who afterwards became the first Bishop of Connecticut, strongly sympathized with England. These for the most part either left the country or remained neutral. But a goodly proportion of our ministry must be reckoned among the staunchest of patriots. They felt themselves absolved from their Ordination vows. The Rev. Doctors Bass and Parker, both in turn, after the war, Bishops of Massachusetts, refused to read prayers for the King and Parliament and instead prayed for the American cause. Dr. Provoost, of New York, afterwards first Bishop of that State, was an ardent friend to America. The Rev. William White of Philadelphia, who became the first Bishop of Pennsylvania, also Doctors Madison and Smith, the first Bishops respectively of Virginia and South Carolina, took sides with the Colonies. The Rev. David Griffith of Virginia, Rector of the Church which Washington attended, did the same. The Rev. Charles M. Thurston, of Gloucester County, Virginia, went into the army as a soldier, rose to the rank of major and became known as the "fighting parson of Gloucester." The Rev. Peter Muhlenburg, of Woodstock, who had been a soldier before he became a Clergyman, entered the army as Colonel of the 8th regiment of Virginia and afterwards rose to be a brigadier-general.

A graphic account is preserved of the leaving of the pulpit for the field by Mr. Muhlenburg. Having procured a colonel's commission from General Washington, he proceeded on a Sunday to Church, and, after a patriotic sermon, took leave of his congregation in the following words: "There is a time for all things—a time to preach and a time to pray; but there is also a time to fight, and that is now come." He then gave them his benediction, and throwing back his gown discovered to them his military uniform. We may well leave the poet Read to tell the remainder of this dramatic story in the closing verses of one of the most stirring poems in the English language:

> A moment there was awful pause,—
> When Berkley cried, "Cease, traitor! cease!
> God's temple is the house of peace!"
>   The other shouted, "Nay, not so,
> When God is with our righteous cause;
> His holiest places then are ours,
> His temples are our forts and towers,
>   That frown upon the tyrant foe;
> In this, the dawn of Freedom's day,
> There is a time to fight and pray!"
>
> And now before the open door—
>   The warrior Priest had ordered so—
> The enlisting trumpet's sudden roar

Rang through the chapel, o'er and o'er,
 Its long reverberating blow,
So loud and clear, it seemed the ear
Of dusty death must wake and hear.
And there the startling drum and fife
Fired the living with fiercer life;
While overhead, with wild increase,
Forgetting its ancient toll of peace,
 The great bell swung as ne'er before:
It seemed as it would never cease;
And every word its ardor flung
From off its jubilant iron tongue
 Was, "WAR! WAR! WAR!"

"Who dares"—this was the patriot's cry,
 As striding from the desk he came,—
 "Come out with me, in Freedom's name,
For her to live, for her to die?"
A hundred hands flung up reply,
A hundred voices answered "I!"

Mr. Muhlenburg, having led three hundred brave volunteers to the front, remained with the army till the close of the war, and then engaged in civil pursuits until his death in 1807. There was also the patriot, the Rev. Charles Pettigrew, of North Carolina. In South Carolina, where at the breaking out of the war, there were only twenty Clergymen of the Church, it is said that fifteen of them, or three-fourths of the entire number, took sides with America. Six of the Signers of the Declaration of Independence were sons or grandsons of Episcopal Clergymen.

The Rev. Thomas Duché, of Philadelphia, arrayed in full canonicals, offered the first prayer in Congress. The following interesting reminiscence of this event is preserved to us in a letter to his wife from the venerable John Adams. "When the Congress met, Mr. Cushing made a motion that it should be opened with prayer. It was opposed by Mr. Jay, of New York, and

Mr. Rutledge, of South Carolina, because we were so divided in religious sentiments, some Episcopalians, some Quakers, some Anabaptists, some Presbyterians, and some Congregationalists, that we could not join in the same act of worship. Mr. Samuel Adams arose and said, that he was no bigot, and could hear a prayer from any gentleman of piety and virtue, who was at the same time a friend to his country. He was a stranger in Philadelphia, but had heard that Mr. Duché deserved that character, and therefore he moved that Mr. Duché, an Episcopal Clergyman, might be desired to read prayers to Congress to-morrow morning. The motion was seconded and passed in the affirmative. Mr. Randolph, our President, waited on Mr. Duché and received for answer that, if his health would permit, he certainly would. Accordingly next morning he appeared with his clerk, and in his pontificals, and read several prayers in the established form, and then read a psalm for the seventh day of September, which was the 35th Psalm. You must remember this was the next morning after we had heard of the terrible cannonade at Boston. It seemed as if Heaven had ordered that psalm to be read on that morning. After this Mr. Duché, unexpectedly to everybody, struck out into extempore prayer, which filled the bosom of every man present. I must confess I never heard a better prayer or one so well pronounced. Episcopalian as he is, Dr. Cooper himself never prayed with such fervor, such ardor, such correctness and pathos, and in language so elegant and sublime for America, for Congress, for the Province of Massachusetts Bay, especially the town of Boston. It had excellent effect upon everybody here. I must beg of you to read the psalm. ["Plead Thou my cause O God, with them that strive with me, and fight Thou against them that fight against me."] It was enough to melt a heart of stone. I saw the tears gush into the eyes of the old, grave, pacific Quakers of Philadelphia."

Dr. William White, mentioned above, was elected as the first regular Chaplain of Congress. I do not remember ever reading of any Puritan ministers who did more for the cause of liberty than these Clergymen of the Church. None of them, so far as my knowledge extends, took up arms. They may, in some cases, have done more patriotic preaching than our Clergy, but they certainly did not do as much fighting of which record is made.

During the late Civil War, the Northern members of the Episcopal Church surely manifested as much patriotism as those of any other body of Christians. This will hardly be denied in the face of the notable fact that the Bishop of Ohio was sent by the Northern government to England to dissuade the nobility from acknowledging and favoring the Confederacy, and who, by accomplishing a mission so important to the Union, earned the lasting gratitude of his fellow countrymen. Surely the reader will perceive the injustice of charging the Episcopal Church with a lack of patriotism, when he is told that Mc'Ilvaine, Seward, Chase, Stanton, Wells, Blair, Dennison, Columbus Delano, Henry Winter Davis, Edmunds, David Davis, Isaac F. Redfield, Jay Cooke, Fremont, Mead, Schofield, Curtis, Hancock, Porter, Craven, and other distinguished Union patriots, a complete list of whom would fill several pages, were Episcopalians. The authoress of "Uncle Tom's Cabin," a book which, perhaps, next to the daily press, did more than anything else to fire patriotism and the spirit of war in the rank and file of the North, and, by so doing, contributed immeasurably towards preventing the downfall of the Union, was an Episcopalian.* How can a Church which enrolls the above names among her members, names which represent so many pillars of lib-

* Appendix XVI.

erty and union, be justly stigmatized with a lack of patriotism? A regard to that Scriptural precept which requires honor to be given to whom it is due, would surely place the Episcopal Church far up, if not at the very head of American patriot-producing institutions.

The only conceivable ground for the misconception regarding the patriotism of Episcopalians, is found in the fact that the Episcopal Church steadfastly refuses to meddle in politics. Her policy is to leave the government in the hands of those whom God, by the voice of the people, has charged with its awful responsibilities, and to hold up their hands by the loyalty and the prayers of her members. The Church that teaches her adherents, without regard to political and other preferences, to pray at every Service for the President, and all other civil authorities, and appoints a prayer to be said every Sunday during the session of Congress, is essentially a patriotic Church, and what wonder is it that so many of her sons have been among the most noble and distinguished of our patriots.

In reply to the charge that "the Episcopal Church is not in its government American," one of our Clergymen pointed out that our critic was mistaken as to the essential characteristic of the United States government, which is not the individualism that finds free play in Congregationalism, but the representative policy which prevails in the Episcopal Church. "The critic's idea of American government is a town meeting, a little affair in which each individual expresses his opinion and choice directly. Our conception of American government is that of a nation in which the people voice their choice through representative assemblies or persons. Will it be contended that the American government is not a representative government?"

The Episcopal Church is as effectually safe-guarded against Monarchicalism as the United States, if any thing more so. Though our Bishops, because of their exalted position as successors of the Apostles and their personal worth, are greatly honored, yet they do not, as the heads of their respective Dioceses, exercise as much authority as the Governors of our States; nor does our Primate enjoy the vetoing power with which the President of the United States is invested. The Laity are more fully represented in our Diocesan Synods than the Clergy, and the Lower House of our Triennial General Convention is composed of Clergymen and Laymen in equal numbers. These generally vote together, but a representative of either order may at any time call for a division, and so it becomes possible that a measure which has passed the House of Bishops, and also received the majority of clerical votes in the House of Deputies, may yet fail of becoming a law, because among the Lay delegates there is one more against than for it. This is a remarkable departure from the Mother Church, in whose Convocations the Laity have no voice, and can be accounted for only by the fact that in all things of human ordering, the Church's government was modeled by true sons of America.

The principles which prevail in the government of the Church at large are also carried out in our Parishes. Though the Rector is the official head of the parochial organization, his word is not law except when it relates to the Services and Discipline; and even in these matters he is obliged to have reference to the regulations of the General Convention and Diocesan Synods, in which, as we have seen, the Laity as well as the Clergy have a voice. Besides the Layman, who feels that he has a just grievance against his Rector, is always at liberty to appeal to the Bishop. The Vestry, elected by the supporters of the Parish, have charge of the property and finances. In the case of a vacancy in the Rectorship they fill it with the approval of the Bishop.

"While," as Bishop Perry observes, "our Orders are Apostolic and unchangeable, as coming from above—made, as of old the Tabernacle of Israel was, after the pattern given in the Mount—our organization is of human origin and adaptation, and is just such as might be expected from Churchmen who were leaders and framers of government both in Church and State a century ago. Thus is it that we are at once, in structural being and government, thoroughly republican, distinctively American—the Church of the people, the Church for the people. And the work of our Fathers, both in Church and State, has now the approval and indorsement of more than a hundred successful years."

I cannot better conclude this necessarily somewhat lengthy digression for the purpose of answering the charge of un-Americanism than by calling attention to what Henry Clay had to say upon the subject. This great statesman and orator did not identify himself with any form of organized Christianity until late in life. He is reported to have said about the time of his Baptism, that among the considerations which induced him to become a member of the Episcopal Church rather than of any other, was the fact that years of observation and study had led him to the conclusion that the stability of our government depends upon the perpetuation of two institutions. "One of these, and the most important of the two," said Mr. Clay, "is the Episcopal Church, and the other is the Supreme Court of the United States."*

---

* Appendix XVII.

3. Again, the Revolutionary War was especially disastrous to the Church. As we have seen, many of its already very inadequate Clerical force had abandoned the country. In the four colonies of Connecticut, New York, New Jersey and Pennsylvania there were at the close of the war no less than seventy vacant Churches. Those Clergymen who remained, in the majority of cases came out, after eight long years of privation and anxiety, broken in health and greatly impoverished, if not absolutely destitute. The Churches and rectories very generally had been destroyed or desecrated, and allowed to fall into ruins. When the war began, Virginia had one hundred and sixty-four Churches and ninety-one Clergymen. At the end, ninety-five Churches had been destroyed, and only twenty-eight of the Clergy remained. Moreover, the glebe lands and endowments were, after a time, confiscated. The misfortunes which befell Virginia were common throughout the South.

4. About this time the Church was greatly weakened by the creeping in of heresies. King's Chapel, the oldest foundation of the Episcopal Church in Boston, was lost to the Unitarians. This, however, was due as much to the scattering of Churchmen by the Revolutionary storm as to the ravages of heresy.

5. Again, our immigration since the Revolution has been almost wholly from the non-Episcopal and Roman Catholic elements of England, Ireland and Scotland. And from all the hosts that have come to us from continental Europe, we have received no accessions. The principal part of the Roman constituency is of foreign birth. The papers frequently convey the information that one hundred thousand souls have been added to their Communion within a given year. This is astonishing to all that are not aware that about this number

of Romanists have been immigrating to the United States from year to year. But for this, the growth would have been the other way. All the chief bodies of Protestants, except the Episcopal Church, have had thousands and tens of thousands of accessions by immigration. Our adherents are almost wholly American born. The great majority of English immigrants are Dissenters, and so do not contribute to our upbuilding, though, fortunately, their removal weakens the enemies of the Mother Church, who are bent upon disestablishment and confiscation. The fact that this Church has profited so little by immigration is, in itself, almost sufficient to explain our comparatively slow growth.

6. Moreover, we became an independent Church, and started out on our career as such, just about the time of the great Methodist schism, and the beginning of the revival system, which for fifty years swept very nearly everything before it. In the religious excitement, which in one resistless wave after another rolled over the country, the Church was almost submerged and lost sight of, and hundreds of thousands who, under normal conditions, would have remained in this Church, or would have come into it, were floated into one or another of the Denominations.

7. Even the Civil War brought more disaster to the Episcopal Church than to any other Christian body in the land. "The reason," observes a Southern Clergyman, "is plain. The Churchmen of ante-bellum days were the social as well as the political ruling class of the South. The struggle shattered their fortunes, and left many a family of former affluence in comparative penury. Consequently, many rural, and not a few village, Churches, are to-day in ruins, or bearing every mark of poverty and neglect, occasionally sheltering a dispirited

congregation, vainly struggling to repair the waste places of the local Zion."

8. But perhaps the most potent of many causes which operated against the Church's growth, was the timid and apologetic policy pursued for the most part by her representatives, until about fifty years ago. Then the principles of Bishops Seabury and Hobart began to prevail, and the Church was represented by an ever-widening circle in her true character as a veritable branch of the "One, Holy, Catholic and Apostolic Church of Christ." The adoption of this policy by a considerable number of our Clergy, marks a new and brighter era in the history of the American Episcopal Church. This is also true in respect to the English Church in which the movement was started. The contrast between the phenomenal growth of both Churches in every element of strength since the change, and their languishing condition before it, should be a perpetual admonition to Churchmen never again to commit the fatal mistake of allowing the impression to go abroad that the Episcopal Church is simply one of the post-Reformation sects, whose chief distinguishing features are the Prayer Book and surplice.

But for a long time the revival of the doctrines and ceremonies of the Primitive Church was stoutly and persistently resisted by a formidable party in the Church which styled itself "Evangelical." Its representatives were ever loudly lamenting and denouncing what they were pleased to characterize as the Mediæval and Romanizing tendency of those who called themselves Anglo-Catholics. A few of the more radical among them finally grew so desperate that they could no longer defer the secession which for years had seemed inevitable. Accordingly, in December, 1873, under the leadership of the Assistant Bishop of Kentucky, the so-called Reformed Episcopal Church was organized. It was expected on all hands that there would be a general exodus of the "Evangelicals." This expectation was, however, never realized. Only a handful of the Clergy, and in proportion, fewer of the Laity went out, and many of both after a short sojourn returned. It is known that the disappointment and chagrin of Bishop Cummins were very great, and it is generally believed that they caused his premature death to which his followers attribute in great measure the almost complete failure of their ill-advised and unjustifiable schism. Though it was begun with forty ministers, there are now, after twenty years, only one hundred and twenty, not a few of whom are dissatisfied. One of the most distinguished of Bishop Cummins' original adherents deplores the present condition of things, and asks an explanation of its cause. He says that "a portion of our Church has been impressed from the beginning of our present system with its inherent defects."*

As long as the Church was generally believed to be only one among the sects, it was naturally the most despised and least progressive of them all. The real sects flourished while the Church languished; had she continued in this false attitude, she would doubtless be even now an inconsiderable force among the many Denominations in this country. Our ancestors of a hundred years ago beheld with astonishment the progress of modern Sectarianism, which was then in all its marvelous vigor, and they, perhaps naturally enough, jumped to the conclusion that the weak and waning state of the Church was chiefly due to what her enemies ignorantly represented as Popish ceremonies and

* Appendix XVIII.

doctrines. They did not perceive, and under the circumstances could hardly be expected to have perceived, that the conditions of Sectarian and Church growth are essentially different. The sect in all ages, like the cornstalk, shoots up quickly and bears its fruit in a summer; but the Church, resembling the oak in her growth, advances slowly and remains through frost and sunshine, and from generation to generation.

Our growth, since we have recognized and proclaimed the true, Divine and Catholic character of the American Episcopal Church, has been scarcely less remarkable than that of the most prosperous forms of Sectarianism in their palmiest days. In fact, we are outstripping them in various parts of the country where it once seemed as if we could never get a foot-hold. It has been acknowledged that, if the Church continues her present rate of growth for another decade, she will be the strongest body of non-Roman Christians in New England itself. And it has been admitted by distinguished Denominational ministers that the Church throughout the country is, everything considered, making more rapid and substantial progress than any of the Denominations.

In every State and Territory, the percentage of increase for the period covered by the last census, was all that could have been expected, and in the majority of them was astonishing even to those among us who are most sanguine and confident touching the future of the Church.* In forty-two of our forty-nine States and Territories, our increase has been from thirty to more than six hundred per cent. The population of the United States during the same period increased less than twenty-five per cent. And not only has the general

* Appendix VII.

growth of the Church far exceeded proportionately that of the population at large, but it is also greater than that of any other religious body in particular.

Moreover, there is a very general looking towards us with favor. It is said by those who are in a position to know, that in our large cities, where the Church is well represented, out of ten persons who change from one Denomination to another, nine of them come into the Episcopal Church. Among those recently confirmed in thirty of the New York City parishes, there were over four hundred who had been born and educated in the several Denominations. In one of the classes alone there were one Jew, one Baptist, two French Protestants, three Unitarians, three Congregationalists, seven Methodists, nineteen Romanists, twenty-eight Presbyterians and fifty-two Lutherans. This drift is rapidly making us the dominant body of Christians in all large centers of population.

One of the most remarkable and encouraging features of our growth is the number of able ministers from the various Denominations who are coming to us. Our accessions from their ranks now amount to about forty annually, and the rate is increasing from year to year. It is estimated that within the last thirty years fully fifteen hundred Denominational preachers have been received into our ministry. Many of these were the foremost men of their respective Denominations. A number of them have become Bishops among us and Rectors of our largest parishes.

This remarkable drift towards the Episcopal Church is, of course, observed by the Denominational leaders who try to account for it. A Presbyterian writer thinks that it is due to "the attractiveness of the Prayer Book Worship." A Lutheran believes that "the possession of the Historic Episcopate explains it." But a New

York Baptist minister "hits the nail on the head" when, after calling attention to the fact that his Denomination has increased only thirty-six per cent. in the Empire State, while the Episcopal Church has gained one hundred and forty-one per cent. in the same period, he says: "The true explanation is to be found in the confidence, assurance, and courage of the Episcopal leaders. They believe that theirs is '*the* Church,' and are not slow to assert their belief. That very assurance, and the exclusiveness which comes from it, is the tower of their strength. They are not ashamed of their belief; they have the courage of their convictions, and a large part of the world takes them at their own estimate. Here is the secret of their power." In commenting upon these words, the editor of one of our religious papers rightly says: " This is a clear-headed, and, we believe, substantially a true judgment. It goes to prove two things : first, that many thinking people are in search of '*the* Church;' second, that those are hardly true sons of the Church who seek to take away this bulwark by decrying or minimizing her Catholic claims, or by entering into entangling alliances, which would remove the exclusiveness which legitimately results from such claims."

It is popularly supposed that since the Oxford revival, almost as many go from the Episcopal Church to the Roman Communion as come to her from the several Protestant Denominations. And for some time after its beginning there was, it must be confessed, much ground for fear that this would be the case. As Dr. McConnell remarks: "In England, as a direct consequence of the revived Ecclesiasticism, such great names as Newman, Manning, Oakley, Faber, Wilberforce, Palmer, and Ward passed from the Church's rolls to the lists of Rome. In America, Bishop Ives, of North

Carolina, and a group of men of lesser station, but greater character, followed in the same path. But the general apostasy for which many looked did not occur. The facts seemed to point to a different outcome, as the event has shown. The sum total of the losses to the Roman Catholic Church in Great Britain up to A.D. 1888, including Clergy and Laity, men and women, fall below two thousand. That is to say, an average of thirty-five persons per year have left the Church of England for Rome during the last sixty years. One large parish Church would hold them all, living or dead."

Nor is it speaking beyond bounds to say that for every one who went to Rome five have come from her to us. Bishop Perry, of Iowa, says that during his Episcopate of eighteen years, there have been received into the Church in Iowa from the Roman obedience over seven hundred adults who have exchanged, intelligently, and with a full knowledge of what they were doing, a false Catholicity for a true. "In the same time," the Bishop adds, "we have lost to Rome, so far as I can learn, less than half a dozen individuals." The Bishop of Maryland reports that in his average Confirmation classes there are about thirty converts from Romanism and the same number from the Methodists each month. "The tide of return," says he, "appears a steady one."

But increase in numbers does not much more than half tell the story. The growth of the Church must also be measured by her influence upon the Denominations about her. During her prostrate condition Methodism moulded all Protestantism to her own form. But this is no longer the case. Methodism is now herself putting on the external garments of the Church. The general observance of Christmas and Easter by special services and decorations; the responsive readings and

anthems and the growing elaboration of ritual; the
catechising of children, and the reception of them into
full membership at the tender age of twelve years and
even younger; the Gothic architecture, pipe organ and
stained glass—all these things and much more, particularly the decline of the revival system, bear witness to
the fact that the influence of the Church is becoming
more and more dominant.

Even in old Presbyterian, Puritanical Scotland, we
find a remarkable illustration of the growing ascendency of Church ideas. A number of the most prominent
ministers in the established Kirk, including such famous
men as Milligan, Macleod, Lang, Boyd and Cooper
have organized "The Church Society," the special objects of which are "(1) The consistent affirmation
on the same basis of the supernatural life and
Heavenly calling of the Church. (2) The fostering of
a due sense of the historic continuity of the Church
from the first. (3) The maintaining of the necessity
of a valid Ordination to the Holy Ministry, and the
celebration in a befitting manner of the Rite of Ordination. (4) The assertion of the efficacy of the Sacraments. (5) The promotion of the religious education
and pastoral care of the young on the basis of Holy
Baptism. (6) The restoration of the Holy Communion
to its right place in relation to the worship of the
Church, and to the Spiritual life of the Baptized. (7)
The revival of daily Service where practicable. (8) The
observance, in its main features, of the Christian year.
(9) The deepening of a penitential sense of the sin and
peril of schism." "Now it seems to me," says an irate
Scotchman from whom we quote the above, "that
though the promoters of this movement do not say so,
the whole thing smacks of High Churchism. What do
you say to expressions like 'Catholic Doctrine,' 'His-

toric continuity of the Church,' 'Valid Ordination of the Holy Ministry,' 'befitting celebration of the Rite of Ordination,' 'efficacy of the Sacraments,' 'basis of Holy Baptism,' 'Holy Communion in relation to the Spiritual life of the Baptized,' 'revival of daily Service,' 'observance of the Christian year' and 'sin and peril of schism?'"

Romanists sometimes claim that the striking change which has come over Denominationalism is due to the influence of their Church. But there is really nothing in this. Owing in part to the origin and character of the Roman constituency, and also in part to the detestation in which the whole Ultramontane system is still held by Denominationalists, these representatives of the extremes have very little social and less religious intercourse. But Episcopalians and Denominationalists have always mingled freely in all things except religion. And as our members have been a great, if not the dominant, influence in the social, political and commercial world, it is evident that they have had much to do directly and indirectly in bringing about the change under consideration. Take, for example, the striking change in respect to the observance of Christmas and Easter, and even of the Lenten season. There can be no question that it is due to Episcopal rather than Roman influence. This is especially evident in the case of Lent. Though its religious observance is by no means general, yet it receives almost universal recognition in the abandonment of social gaieties. This is accounted for by the fact that during this holy season a large and important section of society withdraws from the social world, and it is, as everybody knows, composed not of Romanists, but of Episcopalians.

Truly we may thank God and take courage. The day of small things and of adversity is being succeeded

by one of rapid growth and great prosperity. The
touching prayer contained in the old poetical version of
the ninetieth Psalm, sung at the Consecration of Bishop
Seabury, is being graciously answered:

> "To satisfy and cheer our souls,
>   Thy early mercies send;
> That we may all our days to come
>   In joy and comfort spend.
>
> "Let happy times with large amends
>   Dry up our former tears,
> Or equal at the least, the term
>   Of our afflicted years.
>
> "To all thy servants, Lord, let this
>   Thy wondrous work be known,
> And to our offspring yet unborn
>   Thy glorious power be shown.
>
> "Let Thy bright rays upon us shine:
>   Give Thou our work success:
> The glorious work we have in hand
>   Do Thou vouchsafe to bless."

THE CHURCH FOR AMERICANS.

LECTURE VI.

OBJECTIONS TO THE EPISCOPAL CHURCH.

AUTHORITIES.

BULL, BP., A Vindication of the Church of England.
CLARKE, Walk About Zion.
CRAKANTHORP'S DEFENSIO ECCLESIÆ ANGLICANÆ.
CURTEIS, Dissent in Its Relation to the Church of England.
GARNIER, CANON, Church or Dissent.
HOPKINS, BP., The Primitive Church Compared with the Protestant Episcopal Church of the Present Day.
KIP, BP., Double Witness of the Church.
SNYDER, The Chief Things, or Church Doctrine for the People.
STALEY, The Catholic Religion.

PAMPHLETS.

SHANKLIN, Some Objections Against the Episcopal Church.

MISCELLANEOUS.

WHY CAN'T OUR MINISTERS PREACH IN YOUR PULPITS.

OBJECTIONS TO THE EPISCOPAL CHURCH.

I N almost every community in which the Episcopal Church is represented, many persons are kept from an examination of her peculiar claims to the allegiance of Americans by certain groundless objections, some of which it is the purpose of this lecture to state and answer. No attempt will here be made to exhaust the subject, because the most weighty of the objections have been or will be considered in other connections, and because many of those which remain are too trifling for serious notice.

It is believed that all the popular objections against the Church may be answered not only to the entire satisfaction of candid persons, but that to such, some of them can be made to appear as reasons why Americans should identify themselves with the Episcopal Church rather than with any other.

I.

PRAYER BOOK WORSHIP.

T HOSE who object to the Episcopal Church because she uses a Prayer Book in her public Services are constantly growing fewer. Indeed, there has been for some time a marked drift towards liturgical forms of worship in all of the leading Denominations. Many of their ablest representatives have been advocating, in their religious journals, and on the floor of their

Conferences and Synods the adoption of precomposed Services, and nearly all of the city congregations have anticipated official sanction by introducing certain features of our Ritual, such as the chanting of Scripture, the responsive reading of the Psalms, the repetition of the Lord's Prayer, and even the Apostles' Creed by minister and people. Nevertheless, there are still some to be found in almost every community who feel that there can be no "praying from the heart," no genuine, acceptable "approach to the throne of grace," except by an extempore worship. Of such let me beg due consideration of the following facts:

First Fact. Our Lord *commanded* the use of precomposed forms of prayer. "When ye pray say, Our Father." He surely would not have given this direction if precomposed prayers tend to promote empty, formal worship more than extempore prayers.

Second Fact. In all ages of the Church, in both the Old and the New Dispensation, the vast majority of the Saints worshipped God by the use of precomposed Services and prayers. Hebrew scholars tell us that the Jews had not only fixed forms, but also a fixed order in their public worship, both in the Temple and in their synagogues. And when the Apostles founded the Church, we are told, at the very outset, that it was one of the four marks of Christian Unity that all joined, not only in prayers, but in "the prayers," that is, certain well-known, appointed prayers. After the time of the Apostles until the Reformation, worship by precomposed forms was the universal and unvarying custom. Justin Martyr, in the second century, speaks expressly of "Common Prayers." A hundred years later Origen and Cyprian speak respectively of the "appointed prayers," and the "customary prayers." These "common," "appointed," "customary" prayers, of course, could not have been extempore prayers. And that they were not such, is put beyond all dispute by the existence of Liturgies, or as we should call them, Prayer Books, which have been used in various parts of Christendom from the earliest times. Such are the Service Book of St. James, the first Bishop of Jerusalem, used in all the eastern Churches; that of St. Peter, used in Rome; that of St. Mark, used in Africa; that of St. Chrysostom, used in Constantinople; and that of St. John, used in Gaul, Spain and Britain.

Third Fact. Not only was public worship, from the Apostles' time to the Reformation, universally conducted according to precomposed forms, but even at this day, out of three hundred and fifty millions of nominal Christians, at least three hundred millions use the ancient and divinely sanctioned method of worshiping God by means of written forms of prayer and services.

Fourth Fact. Public prayer, according to the teaching of Christ, is agreement in asking. But this cannot take place unless those engaged in worship know beforehand what they are to ask. This essential knowledge can exist only when the people, as well as the minister, are aware of what is coming. Hence, a liturgy is indispensable to true congregational devotion.

Fifth Fact. Strictly speaking, there can be no such thing as public worship without the use of precomposed forms. Mr. Spurgeon is credited with the silly remark that he would tolerate but one form of prayer, namely, "From all ready made prayers, 'Good Lord deliver us.'" But he was forthwith answered by an English Dissenter, who pointed out that in his Sunday School Hymn Book the great Baptist preacher of London had unconsciously sanctioned and adopted a large number of "ready-made prayers." All Denominationalists, so far as I know, except the Quakers, use hymns which are, in reality, forms of worship.

> " Critic freely may rehearse
> Forms of prayer and praise in verse;
> Why should Critic then suppose
> Mine are sinful when in prose?
> Must my prayer be thought a crime
> Merely for the want of rhyme? "

Again, the extempore prayer which the ministers of non-liturgical bodies of Christians offer is, so far as the congregation is concerned, a precomposed prayer, just as really as are the prayers to which a congregation of Episcopalians respond, *Amen.* I repeat, public worship cannot be conducted except by the use of precomposed prayers and services. So far as the congregations are concerned, the only difference between, for example, Methodists and Episcopalians is that the members of a Methodist congregation prefer a form of prayer set forth by their minister, while the members of a congregation of Episcopalians prefer one which has been selected from the richest treasuries of devotion, and which has been approved by the whole Church in Council assembled.

Sixth Fact. The use of the Prayer Book in public worship tends to prevent irreverence. There can be no question that the ministers of non-liturgical Churches are constantly in great danger of approaching the Eternal Being in too easy, unceremonious and irreverent a manner. No doubt all of us have witnessed shocking examples of liberty and familiarity in approaches and addresses to the throne of grace. Perhaps we have seen a minister get up before a public gathering with a cane in one hand and his hat in the other, and folding his arms address the King of Kings and Lord of Lords as if he were complimenting a boy in the street for his good behavior. What an abomination in the estimation of those who have in mind the majesty of God whose throne is in the heaven of heavens, is the prayer of which Mr. Gough used to tell: "We pray Thee O God, that the height of the rostrum may not interfere with the comfort of the lecturer, but that he may be able to give us as good a lecture as Thou hast seen in the papers he has given in other towns in the country."

As a distinguished Denominational minister confesses: "In nearly every newspaper you may read some funny story based upon the ignorance or eccentricity or blasphemous familiarity of some extemporizing prayer maker. All of you have been at times shocked or bored by public devotional performances. Nothing of this sort ever occurs in the Episcopal Church. All things are done and spoken decently and in order."

In view of these facts there can be no reasonable objection urged against the Episcopal Church on account of her use of the Prayer Book, unless it can be shown that it is wanting in spirituality or erroneous in doctrine.* It can hardly be defective in either of these respects. From beginning to end the Prayer Book consists of but little more than selections from the Holy Scriptures. It contains the whole Book of Psalms and a large portion of the Gospels and Epistles. These in themselves occupy four hundred and twenty-seven pages of the five hundred and fifty-seven paged edition which I happen to have before me, leaving only one hundred and thirty pages for the various Services, in all about twenty-five in number. Some of these, notably the Morning and Evening Prayer and the Holy Communion, which are most frequently used, are each about two-thirds part a compilation from the Bible, and even the remaining third is composed of prayers, exhortations and confes-

---

* Appendix XIX.

sions in almost the very words of Scripture. And the
Prayer Book as a whole is an inheritance from the
earliest and purest ages of the Church. It has come
down to us from the Apostles, Saints and Martyrs.
Surely a form of worship compiled from the Word of
God by such as these cannot be lacking in either spirituality or soundness of doctrine. "Blame us not, then,
if we value our Liturgy; it embodies the anthems of
Saints; it thrills the heart with the dying songs of the
faithful; it is hallowed with the blood of the Martyrs;
it glows with sacred fire."*

II.

FORMALISM.

UNDER this head we shall consider the objections
urged against the postures used in our worship.

Many people find in the formalities of her worship
an insuperable objection to the Episcopal Church.
"What is the use," they ask, "of changing postures so
frequently? You kneel and stand, say, a dozen times in
the course of Morning or Evening Prayer. Why not
follow the example of other Protestants and remain
quietly seated during the most, if not the whole, of the
Service?" The answer is found in the fact that while the
Services of the various non-liturgical bodies of Christians, if we except the hymns, provide only for a mental
worship, those of this Church make the fullest provision
for the adoration of Almighty God not only with the
mind, but also with the voice and body. It is a curious
thing that those who have the most to say about the
Priesthood's coming between a man and his God, are

---

* Appendix VIII.

the very ones that intrust their worship most exclusively to ministers. Episcopalians leave less of this all-
important duty to the Priest than any other body of
Christians with which I am acquainted. Our Laity re-
serve to themselves the right of taking about half of the
Service. In rendering their part it is necessary that
they should assume different postures in order to suit
the action to the words. All must perceive, the moment
that they begin to reflect, that it would be highly improper for us to confess our sins and pray for pardon
while sitting. The instinct of propriety and reverence
teaches us that we should not sit when we come before
"the King of kings and Lord of lords in his Holy
Temple." We must at least kneel in prayer and stand in
praise. Except for the precept which inculcates mercy
rather than sacrifice, the Church would doubtless forbid
the use of pews or chairs altogether, unless during the
sermon, but out of consideration for physical infirmities
and because weariness would tend to distract the mind,
we are allowed to sit during the reading of the Lessons
from God's Word, except in the case of the Gospel for
the day which is heard standing, because it is regarded
as a special message from the Lord Himself.

But "the getting up and down" to which our Denominational brethren object, is justifiable upon the
ground of helpfulness in worship as well as reverence.
There is an intimate connection between mental and
bodily worship; indeed it is questionable whether the
former can long exist without the latter. At all events
there are many among the more thoughtful and candid
of the non-liturgical Denominations, who feel that worship is rapidly becoming "a lost art" among them.
That there is only too much foundation for this opinion,
is evident from the prevailing motive for assembling
themselves together. In nine cases out of ten it is

avowedly for the purpose of hearing the sermon and music, that is, of being edified and entertained, not in order to worship.

Again, there can be no question that the Scriptures lend their support to the Episcopalian rather than to the Denominational manner of worshipping God. We read of standing, bowing, kneeling and prostration in worship. Not only were these the postures assumed by our Lord and the Saints of the Bible, but also by the primitive Christians and, in fact, by the Church of all ages down to the Reformation. Before that time the custom which now prevails among Denominationalists of sitting during the progress of Divine Service, was utterly unknown. As the learned author of "The Antiquities of the Christian Church" points out, "Tertullian indeed says, there were some superstitious persons in his time, admirers of the book called 'Hermas Pastor,' who made it a matter of conscience to sit down some time when prayer was ended, because they found the example of the pastor in that book to that purpose. For as he sat down upon a bed after prayer, so they thought themselves obliged to do the same in compliance with his example. But this is no proof of their sitting at prayer, but only after prayer was ended; and that, too, grounded upon a very weak and superstitious opinion, that every circumstance of an action or narration, however indifferent in itself, was to be drawn into example and to be made matter of necessary duty, according to which way of reasoning, as Tertullian observes, they must have worshipped nowhere but where there was a bed, nor sat upon a chair or bench because it would have been a deviation from their example. He adds that the heathen only were used to sit after prayer before their idols, and for that very reason it was not fit for Christians to imitate their practice. All which shows that the Christians then were so far from using sitting as a posture of devotion, that they did not think it proper to sit even after prayer in the presence of God, whilst the Angel of Prayer stood by them, and because it looked more like a heathenish than a Christian practice."

It appears then that the formalities to which Denominationalists object in the worship of the Episcopal Church, are justified by reason, Scripture and history, and consequently that their own practice is condemned by these tribunals from which there is no appeal.

III.

VESTMENTS.

THE prejudice of many against the Episcopal Church chiefly grows out of the vestments worn by her Clergy while conducting Divine Service. A representative of this class said to the writer: "There is one thing about your Church which I fear I can never become reconciled to, and that is the wearing of gowns." An effort will now be made to answer this objection to the Church.

It will be remembered that God gave minute directions concerning the attire of the Jewish Ministry which bears much the same relation to the Christian that the bud does to the flower. In Exodus 28: 2, we read: "And thou shalt make holy garments for Aaron thy brother, for glory and for beauty." Dr. Adam Clarke, the great Methodist commentator, speaking on this text says: "The white surplice in the Service of the Church is almost the only thing that remains of those ancient and becoming vestments, which God commanded to be made 'for glory and beauty.' Clothing, as emblematical of office, is of more consequence than is generally imagined." Chalmers, a Presbyterian divine,

C. A.—21

commenting on the same passage, says: "There is here a distinct sanction given to the association of outward splendor with the office of the ministry—if not such as to make it imperative or indispensable, at least as to condemn the intolerance of those who stand opposed to it. In the antipathy to priestly garments, and in the controversies which have been raised about them, I can take no share."

The use of ministerial vestments and insignia of office is also justified by a deep-rooted instinct which in all ages, our own not excepted, has found universal expression. It is this instinct which accounts for the gowns worn by the Judges of the Supreme Court of the United States, the uniforms of our army and navy, and the epaulets of their officers. Even the members and officials of secret orders are distinguished by regalia, scarfs and badges. This being the case, the use of sanctuary vestments cannot reasonably and consistently be objected to. As has been well said: "When objection is made to our Church on this ground, may we not fairly reply that, to be consistent, the objector must insist upon the officer's laying aside his uniform; that he must oppose the badges and regalia of the different orders and societies, and that when he has abolished all these, we shall be prepared to allow his objection some weight, but not until then?" If this book should chance to fall into the hands of some good Methodist objectors to our vestments and Services, the knowledge that through all his life John Wesley regularly used both, may go far towards reconciling such to them. Except in his field preaching, which was never allowed to conflict with the Church's Services, he always wore essentially the same Priestly garments and read the same prayers that are now seen and heard in the Episcopal Church Service.

The sanctuary vestments convey symbolic instruction. Not to go into particulars, the white surplice reminds both minister and people that they should be clothed in righteousness, and the stole, that they must bear the yoke of Christ. But aside from their teaching value, our vestments serve a very practical purpose. So far as appearance in the Chancel is concerned, they place those whose circumstances oblige them to wear "home spun" on the same footing with their brethren who are able to go about in "soft clothing."

In view of the Scripturalness of Ecclesiastical vestments, of their varied usefulness and of the fact that some peculiarity of dress is almost universally adopted as the insignia of office, it seems surpassingly strange that the first English Separatists went out, because the Church did not discard the Bishop's robe and the Priest's surplice and stole which they were pleased to characterize as "the rags of Popery." But this objection, though persistently urged for three hundred and fifty years, at last bids fair to give way before the general reaction towards the Church and her ways. I, myself, have seen Presbyterian ministers in this country attired in black silk gowns—white would have been more appropriate—conducting a liturgical Service. In Scotland where the cassock, gown and bands are more common I heard a "Parson" read our evening prayer with but few omissions, and this in old St. Giles, Edinburgh, where the apocryphal "Jenny Geddes" in the year 1637, cast a stool at the surpliced minister who ventured to reëstablish the Church of England worship.

It may be observed in passing that the clerical suits which most of our clergymen wear, are also justifiable on several accounts. The ability readily to distinguish ministers from laymen is highly advantageous—it tends to make the Clergy so many witnesses for Christ, known to all men; it sometimes renders them useful to strangers who but for the distinctive habit, would not be aware of their high-calling; it often checks improper conversation, profanity, rudeness and violence.*

IV.

LACK OF VITAL RELIGION.

OF course others must be our judges in this delicate matter, and, if this be their just verdict, it is becoming that we should submit without protest, and humbly begin a reformation. And, yet, I trust that I am not going beyond the bounds of propriety in calling attention to the fact that there is a difference of opinion as to whether the possession of "vital religion" is demonstrated by pious profession, or by good works. If, as St. James seems to teach, it consists in the latter rather than in the former, the Episcopal Church will compare favorably with any other body of Christians of equal size. Indeed, the assertion may be safely ventured that in places where we are as well represented as others, none give or do as much for the cause of beneficence. Our contributions to hospitals and other institutions of mercy in New York and Philadelphia, and in most of the principal cities, are much greater than those of any other Christian body. I happen to have at hand a clipping from "The Churchman" of December 24, 1887, which forcibly illustrates the truth of this assertion: "In New York the Hospital Sunday collection is taken in the Churches on the last Sunday of the year, and in the Synagogues on the preceding Saturday. In 1886 the various Denominations were represented as follows: Episcopal, $16,578.12; Presbyterian, $6,458.27; Con-

---

* Appendix XX.

gregational, $3,520.08; Synagogues, $1,602.06; Methodist, $1,402.00; Reformed, $1,262.92; Lutheran, $770.57; Baptist, $368.53; Unitarian, $227.00; Universalist, $122.70; Roman Catholic, $108.13; Swedenborgian, $92.50; Ethical Culture, $92.00; Friends, $60.00; other Churches, $119.42. Total, $32,784.30." Observe that the Episcopal Church gave towards the support of hospitals on Hospital Sunday, 1886, $185.-97 more than half of the whole collection. And there can be but little doubt that this showing is substantially true of every year. Moreover with the possible exception of the Romanists, Episcopalians in all our great cities outnumber the active workers of other bodies in the various fields of charity. We bespeak for these facts a candid consideration on the part of those who think they are justified in alleging that the Episcopal Church is behind other Christian bodies touching "fervent piety" or "vital religion."

Much of the talk about the Episcopal Church's lack in this respect, is due to the erroneous impression that true religion consists in not doing certain things, such as dancing, card playing and attending theatres, and that people who do these things cannot be sincere Christians.* But may not those who do them, ask their critics, "Who art thou that judgeth another man's servant? To his own master [conscience] he standeth or falleth." In the face of the fact that Solomon said there is "a time to laugh" and "a time to dance," and that our Saviour attended the wedding at Cana, where, if this was like other Jewish marriage feasts, and there is every reason for believing that it was, there were feasting, wine-drinking, merry-making and dancing, what Scriptural ground have our accusers for alleging that a Church which does not forbid these things "is lacking in vital religion?"

---

* Appendix XXI.

It is represented that many join the Episcopal Church because she does not forbid amusements; but it would be nearer the truth to say that this Church is the first choice of some because she makes no unreasonable and unscriptural requirements of her members, and allows them to conduct their private and home life in accord with the dictates of conscience and natural preferences of taste, so long as the moral and social law of God is not broken. We admit that we have too much worldliness among us and would not say one word in its justification. But I would respectfully remind those who reproach our Church because of this fault in some of her members, that people who live in glass houses should not recklessly throw stones. The votaries of society are not by any means exclusively Episcopalians. In fact so evenly are the various Protestant Denominations represented, that none should venture to take the mote out of the eye of his brother religionist without first making quite sure that there is not a beam in his own eye.

A Church which stands second to no body of Christians in her contributions of both money and workers to the cause of benevolence; which has preachers of righteousness who shrink not from rebuking sin, even "in high places," which, in every age of the history of the English-speaking race, has produced such Saints as Alban, the Venerable Bede, Dunstan, Becket, Grosseteste, Wyckliffe, Ridley, Cranmer, Latimer, Taylor, Ken, Wesley, Wilberforce, Bloomfield, Bickersteth, Keble, Selwyn, Patteson, Muhlenberg, Hannington, and ten thousand times ten thousand besides, who, though less distinguished, have their names no less surely recorded in the Lamb's Book of Life—a Church, I say, which has produced, and is producing, such philanthropists, such preachers, such Saints, should not be reproached with a want of "vital religion." If "fervent piety" does not exist in the Episcopal Church, will her critics kindly tell us what it is, and where it may be found?

V.

COMPOSED OF THE UPPER CLASSES.

IT is objected that the Episcopal Church is composed of the upper classes to the exclusion of the masses. Granting for the time being that this objection is well founded, I wish to show that it should not, as it certainly will not, permanently prejudice thoughtful people against this Church, but rather attract them to her. For such will readily perceive that the dominant people of a community must have a Church home as well as their poorer and perhaps less cultured neighbors, and that, if it be true that the Episcopal Church furnishes a home for them, it should be cordially welcomed and kindly spoken of by all.

And we are also of the opinion that, if this popular estimation of the Episcopal Church be really true, the day is not far distant when people will begin to inquire, Why is it so? And, if I mistake not, the answer to this question will contribute to account for, and to increase, the Church's rapid growth, which, of late, has been a source of so great encouragement to her members and friends. For the answer must be that this Church is the home of the dominant people of the country, either because she possesses decidedly superior qualities which recommend her to the broader and more intelligent elements of American society, or else that by her more complete system of religious culture she tends to make her adherents dominant. Either of these answers to the inquiry, Why is the Episcopal Church the home in

so many instances of the leaders in the social, political
and commercial world, will, as time goes on, and misunderstanding is corrected, do more to commend than
to condemn her to the thoughtful.

But we will not admit that the Episcopal Church is
composed almost exclusively, or even principally, of the
wealthy and cultivated. In her, as in all bodies of
Christians, the great middle class fortunately pre-
dominates. It is the back-bone and sinew of "the
churches" as well as of the country; moreover, it is
from them that the more highly favored few arise. We
have very little aristocracy by inheritance in the United
States. It is doubtless true that proportionately more
of the sons and daughters of the Episcopal Church than
of any other Christian body rise to the first rank in the
commercial, professional, official, and social life of the
country. One of our most learned and judicious clergymen, who, because of his fairness towards the Denominations, was held in the highest estimation by them,
and was for many years the President of their local
ministerial association, told me in his old age that
the observation of a long life convinced him that the
ability of the Episcopal Church to make the most of her
children amounts to a species of genius which is not
paralleled in any other communion. Speaking of the
parishes of outlying smaller cities and towns, with the
working of which he had an intimate acquaintance, he
said that he had always observed that when a young
couple connect themselves with the Episcopal Church,
they, in a remarkable number of cases, begin to grow
in every form of prosperity, and continue until they
outgrow the place; then they move to some large city
where ultimately they take first rank. He had met with
so many instances of this kind under such varying
conditions, and had seen comparatively so little of it

outside, that he was persuaded that the elevating influence of the Church was one of her distinguishing characteristics. After having my attention called to this
interesting matter, I found that my own, up to that
time, comparatively limited observation tended to cor-
roborate the representation of my aged friend. A
more or less systematic inquiry subsequently instituted,
convinces me that he was right so far, at least, as the
Diocese of Ohio is concerned. As an illustration in point,
I could name a town of less than 10,000 inhabitants
from which fifteen of the young people, a few days before the writing of this passage, started off to various
widely-separated seminaries and colleges of higher education. All, with possibly one exception, came from
the so-called middle class parentage. The majority of
them are sure to better their condition in life. Is it not
remarkable that twelve of the fifteen should be communicants of the Episcopal Church, which is the smallest Christian body of the town, being still a mission
station? Some years ago a layman, in showing me the
village in which he lived, pointed out our little board
chapel, and, by way of apology for its insignificant appearance as compared with other places of worship,
told me that almost every young man who had risen
above mediocrity and made for himself a name, had
gone out from that Sunday School and Church. Two
of the Clerical deputies of the General Convention of
A. D. 1895 were from that little town and congregation.

And as for the very poor I am sorry to say that not
many of them are found in any of "the churches," but
I am glad to be able to testify that so far as my observation goes they are just as welcome in the most fashionable congregations of Episcopalians as they are in
the corresponding congregations of other Christian
bodies. And none are more solicitous—I do not except

Romanists—that the poor shall have the Gospel preached to them without money and without price. In our large cities we have more down-town Churches —Churches which are kept for the poor population— than any other body of Protestant Christians. Before making up the programme for the last Triennial Council of the Congregational body, the committee requested distinguished delegates to suggest topics for consideration. In one of the replies this subject was proposed: "Why is the Episcopal Church above all others successful in attracting to her Communion both the highest and the lowest classes of society?" And that the Episcopal Church has a better title than any Christian body to be called the Church of the English-speaking poor, will be put beyond doubt if we rise to a world-wide view of the subject. The Anglican Communion, including the Church of England, and her colonial branches, and the Episcopal Church of the United States, has about twenty-eight millions of adherents. It is a low estimate to say that two-thirds, or eighteen millions of these belong to the poorer classes. Now the largest of the other bodies, not excepting the Roman, have not fourteen millions of English-speaking adherents, including both rich and poor; and as none of them, except possibly the Roman Church, has a greater proportion of the poor than the Anglican Communion, she is clearly entitled to the credit of being recognized above all others as the Church of the English-speaking poor.*

> "Oh, the poor man's friend is the Church of Christ,
>   From birth to his funeral day;
> She makes him the Lord's, in her surpliced arms,
>   And singeth his burial lay."

---

* Appendix XXII.

VI.

BIGOTED AND EXCLUSIVE.

IN support of this charge Denominationalists affirm that we do not allow their ministers to preach in our pulpits, that we refuse to admit their members to our Communion, and that we do not recognize their organizations as being true Churches. Now, though there is some difference of opinion and practice among us touching these things, yet, upon the whole, candor requires that we should plead guilty to each of the accusations. Therefore, unless we can satisfactorily explain our conduct, it would seem that the charge of bigotry and uncharitableness is sustained.

What then have we to say in justification of our refusal to allow the ministers of the various Denominations to conduct our Services? It should of course be remarked that one of our canons or laws, makes it impossible for us to join in the practice of exchanging pulpits that is common among some of the Denominations—I say *some*, for the custom is not universal among them. The Congregationalists, Presbyterians, Methodists, Baptists, English Lutherans, United Brethren, and a few others are accustomed to more or less frequent interchanges, and to joining in Union Temperance, Thanksgiving and Revival Services. But none of these would exchange with a Universalist or Unitarian, because they do not believe these Denominations to be orthodox.

And right here we touch upon the principal of the reasons why we do not exchange with any of the

Denominations about us. For though as compared with Unitarians they are sound in doctrine, yet the various non-Episcopal Denominations are, in our estimation, unsound touching what we regard as fundamentals. Not to mention other differences between them and ourselves, they believe that any man can found a Church, and, on this ground, justify their separation from the historic Church of Christ and the Apostles, while we maintain that schism is a great sin, and that the attempt to defend it is a grievous error. This being our honest conviction, we certainly should be accorded as much right to exclude them from our pulpits as they exercise in the case of those with whom they do not agree. From the standing point of the Universalists and Unitarians they are as bigoted and uncharitable as we are from theirs.

Those who make the complaint seek to justify it by arguments based upon the goodness and ability of their ministers. We do not question their possession of these qualities, but on the other hand are ready to pay the tribute of highest respect and admiration to many of the Denominational ministers whom we know. If it were a question of personal holiness or of learning and aptness to teach, we should certainly often be found humbly sitting at the feet of some of them. But these virtues have nothing to do with the matter in dispute. If they had, those who rank themselves among the so-called "Evangelical Denominations" would be obliged to admit to their pulpits Unitarian ministers, many of whom are distinguished for their piety and erudition. It is a question of right and wrong—of whether or not we are at liberty to change the Divine order by encouraging division in the Body of Christ through the abandonment of the divinely-instituted ministry of three orders, Bishops, Priests and Deacons. Thus the argument from the moral and intellectual fitness of the Denominational ministers is not pertinent. It is exactly the ground which Korah and his company took against Moses and Aaron, when they wanted to justify their intended usurpation of the Priesthood. They complained bitterly that Moses and Aaron kept the sacred offices to themselves, whereas all the congregation was holy. "No Episcopalian has ever been more berated for his exclusiveness—more reproached with thinking too much of himself and despising his brethren than were Moses and Aaron. 'And they gathered themselves together against them and said unto them, Ye take too much upon you seeing all the congregation are holy, every one of them, and the Lord is among them. Wherefore then lift ye up yourselves above the congregation of the Lord?' Now you will remember that this man, Moses, was the meekest of men. He did not deserve the reproach of thinking his house better than the other families of Israel, for he was but carrying out God's ordinance, 'that no stranger which was not of the house of Levi should come near to offer incense.'"

Is it not possible that our exclusiveness, like that of Moses, is a matter of principle, and not an evidence of pride and bigotry? Certainly there are hundreds of thousands among us who feel that we must stand by the One, Holy, Catholic and Apostolic Church of the English race, and say: "There is no Divine warrant for the Denominational theory; no trace of it is in the Bible or the early Church. It is not the system instituted by our Lord for the evangelization of the world. It can remedy no evil, for it is in itself, by the strife it engenders, and by the uncertainty and disputation in which it involves religious truth and duty, an evil incalculable." Because we feel and say these things are we therefore justly stigmatized as exclusive bigots? No, we should rather be honored for having the courage of our conviction.

But even if there were no principle at stake, we could not as a rule exchange with the Denominational Ministers for the simple reason that they would be unwilling to take our places and incapable of doing so. This practical and well-nigh insuperable difficulty may be aptly illustrated by an actual occurrence which the saintly Bishop Bedell, who certainly could not be accused of uncharitableness towards the Denominations, used to tell to the great amusement of his auditors. The Bishop, as nearly as I can remember, gave the story as follows: I placed a young Deacon in charge of the parish at —————. He soon identified himself with the local ministerial association, and this being contrary to the policy of his predecessors, he became unusually popular. His popularity, however, was not destined to continue long. He came among them in October. In January the Association determined to inaugurate a Union Revival in which all the Protestant ministers should take part. The Methodists, Presbyterians, English Lutherans, Baptists and Episcopalians were represented. All their ministers entered into the arrangement. The Services were to be held on each evening of the week, except Saturday, in the several churches in a prearranged order. It so happened, either by design or accident, that the turn for opening the Episcopal Church to the Revival came last. The Deacon, therefore, went the round of the other churches, and all were pleased by his presence and at the readiness and ease with which he took the various parts of the service that were assigned to him from time to time. Indeed he was rapidly gaining for himself the reputation of being unusually broad-minded and brotherly for an Episcopal Clergyman, and it was even hinted that if he would only let himself down a little in speech and bearing, he might make a first-class Revivalist. But his reputation for liberality was suddenly blasted and their hope of his becoming an Evangelist withered upon the occasion of the holding of the Service in our house of worship. This resulted from a most unexpected and embarrassing hitch. It would seem that the Deacon was either truer to his colors, or else that he was more of a wag than had been suspected. For it was discovered quite too late that he had taken the precaution of providing surplices and Prayer Books for all. As the brethren came straggling through the Church towards the Chancel, where they expected to place their hats and overcoats upon "the Holy Table," and to take their seats to see and to be seen until "the exercises" should begin, they were politely conducted into the vestry-room. When all had assembled, the Deacon, to their utter surprise began to hand out the surplices. Of course there was a chorus of protests. The Deacon, however, calmly, and with dignity, reminded them that all, including himself, had, at the services so far held, respected the customs of the several churches visited, and that he very much desired that there should be no departure from this reasonable and courteous procedure. Of course no satisfactory answer could be made to this argument, and so there was nothing for the parsons to do but to submit. Accordingly, each, with what grace he could, put on a surplice and accepted a Prayer Book. The Deacon having apportioned the Service between them, led the procession into the Chancel to the great astonishment of the congregation, which was composed of Christians of every name. They then went on with the Evening Prayer, taking the part appointed to them, respectively; but they had not proceeded far when they became hopelessly mixed and exceedingly

embarrassed. At the conclusion of each portion of the
Service there was an awkward break until the Deacon
would come to the rescue by finding the place. There
was, as may be imagined, an utter absence of dignity
and solemnity. It is needless to observe that the ministers of the town in which the unique Service took place
never again asked the Deacon, or any of his successors,
to join them in union meetings.

I have related this anecdote at some length because
it well illustrates the practical difficulties in the way of
our exchanging pulpits with Denominational ministers.
There is scarcely one in a hundred of them that can
render our Services, and perhaps fewer still who would
be willing to wear our vestments, and conform to the
customary postures. It is hoped that after this explanation, the Denominational reader will not again accuse
us of bigotry and uncharitableness because we do not
exchange pulpits.

As to the Lord's Supper the Anglican Communion is
no more exclusive to-day than she, with the other Apostolic Churches, has been for eighteen hundred years.
Her law is set forth in the Offices for Adult Baptism
and Confirmation: "It is expedient that every person thus baptized should be confirmed by the Bishop so
soon after his Baptism as conveniently may be; that so
he may be admitted to the Holy Communion;" and
"There shall be none admitted to the Holy Communion
until such time as he be confirmed, or be ready and
desirous to be confirmed." These Rubrics were designed
to maintain the Scriptural position of Confirmation.
Their framers had no thought of excluding any from
the Lord's Supper. The object was rather to indicate
the way of coming. Those who will not take it exclude
themselves. The adherents of other bodies of Christians
do not often present themselves at our Altars, nor

is there as much inter-Communion between the members of the various non-Episcopal Denominations as is commonly supposed. However, when any Baptized but unconfirmed persons present themselves, it may be said to be generally true that our Clergy do not assume the responsibility of denying them. Even those who interpret the rubrical law most rigidly seldom turn such away, because they attribute what is lacking in them for the want of Confirmation to the failure, owing to defective teaching, to apprehend the importance of that Apostolic Ordinance, and hope that they will receive it as soon as they can be taught more perfectly concerning the divinely appointed way.

But it is claimed that there is abundant evidence against us in the alleged fact that we do not regard the various Denominations as being true Churches. As Mr. Gladstone has pointed out, it is no reply to the Churchman's argument to cry out that it "unchurches" Dissenting communions. He reminds them that when the Puritans "contended against the Prelatical constitution of the Church of England by arguing that the entire constitution of the Church was defined in the Word of God, and that that constitution was exclusively Presbyterian," this allegation "was met, not by complaints of its 'unchurching' the Church of England, but an examination of its matter and foundation." However, no official document of this Church can be cited in which we make any declaration in regard to the status of any of the Denominations. Nevertheless it should be admitted that the great majority of our Clergy, and many of our Laity, feel that the unhistorical Denominations are at best defective Churches. It is evident that if we were to entertain such feelings without good and sufficient reasons, the accusation of uncharitableness might justly be made. But in consideration of the fact that all of

the Denominations, concerning which these views are entertained, were organized at least fifteen hundred years
after the time of Christ and the Apostles, and that they
have abandoned certain features both of doctrine and
government which had always been universally regarded
by Catholic Christians as essential to the constitution of
a true Church, and are still so considered by fully nine-
tenths of Christendom, we may justly feel ourselves ag-
grieved at being stigmatized as narrow, exclusive bigots
because we refuse to go contrary to all tradition and to
the conviction of the great majority of living Christians,
by recognizing the organizations of, for example, Luther, Calvin, and Wesley, all less than three hundred and
fifty years old, as Apostolic and Catholic Churches of
Christ.

It is argued that the prosperity which has attended
the organizations which they represent, is an evidence
of God's favor, and of his special recognition of them.
Some, therefore, would have us believe that as St. Paul,
who, having had no connection with Christ and His
Apostles, was specially called out of season to be an
Apostle, so they have been called out of due time to be
Churches. But the analogy is not complete enough to
hold. The claims of St. Paul, because of the miracles
which he performed, were recognized by the rest of the
Apostles. Moreover, he did not found a new Church.
On the contrary he constantly condemned divisions and
illustrated the importance of unity by the strongest
imagery. If God, through the founders of the various
Denominations, had really called new Churches into
existence, He would certainly have caused them to have
been recognized by the undoubted Historic Churches, as
St. Paul's Apostleship was by the original Apostles.
But none of them are in communion with any branch
of the old Church.

Nor will the argument based upon the rapid progress and great size of some of the Denominations, carry
conviction to the thoughtful. The schism in the Jewish Church comprised ten tribes, while only two remained faithful to the old Church which was, nevertheless, the true Church of God. No modern Denomination
has had a more phenomenal growth than Arianism.
In the short space of fifty years it sprang up and
drew almost half of Christendom after it, and numbered
among its millions of adherents, the Roman Emperors
and Rulers. But Arianism was not, therefore, a part of
the Catholic Church of Christ. Granting, however, for the
sake of argument, that the question of Catholicity can
be decided by the number of adherents to a system, the
verdict must be, as matters now stand and have stood
ever since the Reformation, against the pretensions of
the Denominations to Catholicity. For there are certainly not more than fifty millions of them, while there
are three hundred and fifty millions of us. Thus, from
whatever point of view, it is impossible for the Denominations to make good against the Episcopal Church
the accusation of uncharitableness.

But let us now examine this charge of exclusiveness
from another point of view. There are almost always
two ways of looking at such questions. As we look at
it, those who make the accusation are really the violat-
ors of charity. And this because upon uncharitable
grounds they have withdrawn from the Mother Church,
and have fenced themselves in with new conditions of
Church membership, and excluded all, who, for any reason, do not see fit to comply with the novel requirements. Rome and the Denominations are alike in this
respect. The older Sectarian bodies went out from us,

not because we were too narrow and bigoted, but because they themselves were not broad and tolerant
enough to remain in the ancient and spacious fold. We
are well aware that it is often maintained that they
were driven out. It would be an easy task to prove to
the contrary by evidence that might be accumulated
from almost every page of the Reformation histories.
But there is a much shorter cut to the truth. It is by
showing that this way of accounting for the origin of
the first sects proves quite too much. If their with-
drawal was due to the parent's intolerance, what are we
to conclude in the case of the sects which soon sprang
from themselves? The census shows that in the United
States, the Presbyterians have divided and sub-divided
twelve times; the Baptists have done the same thirteen
times, and the Methodists seventeen times. If the original Denominations could truthfully account for their
exodus on the score of illiberality, why may not those
who sprang from them justify their separation on the
same ground? Out of the five or six Denominations of
the Revolutionary period, have come one hundred and
forty-three. Excepting the Episcopal and Roman
Churches, each of these accounts for its existence by attributing intolerance to its Mother. As only three or
four of all the Denominations now in the country are
the direct offspring of the Episcopal and Roman Communions, it follows that about one hundred and forty
of them must be traced, if the theory of the origin of
sects under consideration be correct, to the bigotry
of the Methodists, Lutherans, Baptists, Presbyterians,
Mennonites, Adventists, and the rest of the long list
which is ever growing longer. Thus, if the Episcopal
Church be exclusive, it would appear that none of the
older Denominations are in a position to stone her for
the fault.

But the theory of maternal intolerance is not the true solution of sectarianism. It is due rather to the exclusiveness and bigotry of the child itself. There is of course a sense in which the Episcopal Church is exclusive. She must, as a branch of the Catholic Church, exclude from membership all who do not accept Christ as the Divine Saviour of the world, and from her communion all open and notorious evil livers. She is indeed fenced about by the Catholic Creeds and the Moral Law, but there is nothing of human construction to keep people out. The only fence that exists, was constructed by God Himself through Moses, the Apostles and Ecumenical Councils. But the Denominations did not consider this fence of Divine regulation sufficient. They felt called upon to supplement it by hedges of their own planting. The Presbyterians were determined literally to wall us in with the "Westminster Confession;" the Baptists insisted on surrounding us with a deep moat filled to the brim with water; the Methodists wanted to hedge us about with their peculiar doctrines of saving faith, instantaneous conversion and experimental religion. The Church did not deny her children the privilege of holding the views of Calvin, Williams and Wesley, but she refused to allow these views to become so many barriers to membership and communion. It was held that inasmuch as the Church is a Divine institution, God alone has a right to impose conditions of entrance. And because the rest of the flock refused to be hedged in, the sectaries withdrew, in order that their ideas might be carried out in their own narrow enclosure.

"It strikes one," says Bishop Thompson, "as rather a queer thing that these people should charge the Church with 'exclusiveness;' that they should take their own special sin and lay it on her shoulders. They each had their birth in exclusiveness. The Church was not holy enough nor orthodox enough, and so the sect was created to exclude all but the saints. This is the historic beginning of every sect. It excludes all but itself from the Kingdom of God. With the early Puritans, whatever was outside of Puritanism was of Satan. The Church, especially, was of the evil one. The only body in the land which demands only Christianity as a test of membership, which does not supplement Christianity with some *ism* as an essential to fellowship, is the Protestant Episcopal Church."

Bishop Vail's remarks concerning the comprehensiveness of the Church as compared with Denominationalism are also to the point and equally forcible:

"The Church is founded upon unity and universality;

"Sectarianism is founded upon unity without universality.

"The Church is founded upon law and liberty;

"Sectarianism is founded upon law without liberty.

"The Church is founded upon conformity and compromise;

"Sectarianism is founded upon conformity without compromise.

"The Church in its practical operation produces forbearance;

"Sectarianism in its practical operation produces intolerance."

The comprehensiveness of the Episcopal Church is manifest from the fact that she contains so many different schools of thought. There are among us High, Low, and Broad Churchmen. These differ with each other on as many points and as radically as do the various Denominations, and yet there is as much unity and harmony with us as in any other body of Christians. This is accounted for by the fact that, while Episcopalians are required to adhere to the faith set forth in the

Catholic Creeds and to submit to the government of the Historic Episcopate, they are, in respect to all comparatively indifferent matters of doctrine and conduct, permitted the largest liberty. Under such circumstances men always form themselves into parties. For example, in this "land of the free" we have at present Democrats, Republicans, Populists, and others, each denouncing the rest, but all respecting the Constitution and the powers that be, and so, paradoxical as it may seem in view of our wrangling, we are really one of the most united and harmonious of nations. The opinion prevails with Americans that the country is upon the whole the better for political combinations and agitations. Episcopalians generally feel the same about their divisions into Schools of Churchmanship. It is thought that, if there were a dead level of agreement among us, our Ecclesiastical waters would soon become stagnant.

VII.

LIKE THE ROMAN CATHOLIC.

THIS objection so frequently urged against the various branches of the Anglican Communion, is based upon partly real and partly imaginary resemblances in her system to that of the Roman Church. That there are some striking similarities we are ready enough to admit, but that they are of a character to justify the conclusion that there is no essential difference between the Episcopal and the Roman Church cannot be allowed. For there are many important doctrinal and ceremonial points about which we differ fundamentally. And even where the resemblance is most striking, objectors have always found it impossible to prove that the condemned doctrine or ceremony is contrary to

Scripture or the teaching and practice of the earlier, purer ages.

The objection, in short, is based upon the erroneous idea, that, because the Church of Rome has erred in many points, she has done so in all, and that, therefore, a Church is reformed only in proportion as she has departed from the Roman faith and ritual. This, as an old writer points out, is because "man is a creature of extremes. The middle path is generally the wise path; but there are few wise enough to find it. Because Papists have made too much of some things, Protestants have made too little of them. The Papists treat man as all sense; and, therefore, some Protestants would treat him as all spirit. Because one party has exalted the Virgin Mary to a Divinity, the other can scarcely think of that 'most highly favored among women' with common respect. The Papist puts the Apocrypha into his Canon; the Protestant will scarcely regard it as an ancient record. The Popish heresy, human merit in justification, drove Luther, on the other side, into the most unwarrantable and unscriptural statements of that doctrine. The Papists consider grace as inseparable from the participation in the Sacraments; the Protestants too often lose sight of them as instituted means of conveying grace."

Now, it is the glory of the Episcopal Church, that she has avoided both the extremes of Romanism and Protestantism. The testimony of the objectors from both quarters proves this. For the representatives of each in turn accuse us of being identified with the other. Romanists declare that we are Protestants, and Protestants constantly represent us as Romanists. Their witness, as a whole, therefore proves that we are neither the one nor the other. We are essentially unlike either of these extreme wings of Christendom. We occupy the middle ground between them. Between the Scylla of Roman Catholicism and the Charybdis of Denominational Protestantism, we steer the middle course, having inscribed on our banner the motto:

"Catholic for every truth of God;
Protestant against every error of man."

The fact that we are so far removed from both, accounts for the mistake which each makes in classing us with the other.

It cannot be denied that there is, according to the tastes and preferences of our Clergy and congregations, a more or less striking resemblance between the Roman and Anglican Communions in the non-essentials of ceremonies and ornaments. But, however it may be with Romanists in these things, Anglicans almost without exception stop short of superstition and idolatry. If, indeed, there be any exceptions, they are so few as not to disprove the general rule of the past three hundred years. We do not deny that there are a few among us who prefer the Latin nomenclature and ritual, and indeed persistently use them, although their use is objectionable to the vast majority of the Anglican Communion. But the excessively elaborate ceremonialism that has been adopted by a congregation here and there of which, merely because of its exceptional character, we read so much, is not at all representative of the Episcopal Church as a whole, and there is not the least probability that it will ever become so. After all these years there is not on an average more than one or two of these extremely ritualistic parishes in a Diocese. Our Bishops, Clergy, and Laity, with very few exceptions, will never consent to abandon the dignified position which we occupy as the American branch of the historic Catholic Church of the English race. As such we have our own traditions, customs and forms of worship, which if less elaborate and showy, are more in harmony with the sturdy, sober qualities of the Anglo-Saxon people than anything which has been imported from æsthetic, gaudy Italy. If there must be imitation, let Rome, which, whether from a political or intellectual point of view, is much more likely to be Anglicized than we are to be Romanized, do the imitating. The Anglican Church was compelled to conform more or less closely to the Italian when Rome was "the mistress of the world," but now that the position of the English and Latin-speaking races has been reversed, the Roman Church must in her turn be moulded by foreign influence.

In the Pastoral Letter delivered at the close of the Triennial General Convention held in Minneapolis A. D. 1895, the Bishops speaking of the Roman terminology say that "it involves the manly independence of a Church rooted in the primitive soil of Christianity, to a Church which has no claim upon the allegiance of the English speaking race." Those among us who have been concerned lest "the Ritualists" would ultimately lead the Episcopal Church to forsake its Reformation principles and surrender to Rome, will have their fears allayed by reading that section of the Pastoral which bears upon this subject. It plainly appears from this timely utterance that the few Romanizers among us cannot reckon upon the support of the Bishops, without which the Church as a whole can never be compromised. Though the great majority of the American Episcopate are pronounced high Churchmen and some of them have a strong predilection for extremely ritualistic services, it is understood that there was in the House of Bishops little or no opposition to this part of their Epistle to the Council and Churches.

But the existence in the Church of those who resolutely have turned their faces towards Mediæval doctrine and ritual, is no more to be regretted than the presence of such as persistently fix their eyes upon the barren and disputatious Puritanism of the Reformation period. One has as much right among us as the other, for the doctrines and ceremonies which they respectively represent, are in the main utterly alien to the primitive Catholicity of which the Anglican Communion is an exponent. Our Church claims to be "Catholic." It is true that the word does not appear in the title, but neither does it in the official designation of the English Church which, nevertheless, strenuously insists upon her Catholicity. The word Catholic occurs in our Creeds which to us are of much greater importance than our name, as must be evident to all from the fact that we repeat one or the other of the former at every Service, and seldom use the latter except in some abbreviated form.* As the Church of England is no less Protestant than the Episcopal Church in the United States, though the term has not been officially adopted as a part of her appellation, so the American daughter is no less Catholic than her English Mother, notwithstanding the absence of the word in the name by which she is distinguished from the various Christian bodies of this country. Now if the Episcopal Church is really what it claims to be, the American branch of the Catholic Church, it must make room for all who accept Christ as their Divine Lord and only Saviour, and who engage by God's help to live according to the Gospel rule of life. But it is too much to expect that all who agree in doing this, will be of the same mind about other things. We find among us men and women who look at subjects from very different points of view. Take for example, the Reformation. The Mediævalist warmly contends

* Appendix XXVIII.

that in some respects, especially in the matter of ritual and ornaments, it went too far, while his Puritan brother maintains with equal warmth that it did not go far enough. But, speaking generally, the one is no more inclined to Romanism than the other is to Denominationalism. Both in nine hundred and ninety-nine cases out of a thousand will remain just where they are, disputing with one another about non-essentials while agreeing concerning essentials and communing at the same Altar.

There is, however, some ground for congratulation that there are a few of both these classes of extremists among us. The positions which they respectively occupy, being almost as widely separated as the East is from the West, make manifest to all men the Catholicity of the Episcopal Church. There is no other body of Christians sufficiently comprehensive to include anything like such radical divergences in either doctrine or ceremony. The all-inclusiveness of this Church is incomprehensible alike to Romanists and Denominationalists. They will not tolerate each other, and they cannot understand a Church that is spacious enough to comprehend within the same fold those who look at things from such different points of view. But how could the Episcopal Church make good her claim to Catholicity unless she had room for both? The Mediæ-valists and Puritans who are among us, though given to disputing with each other about what the rest of us regard as nonessentials, are nevertheless orthodox and exemplary enough touching the essentials of doctrine and life. They adhere unswervingly to "the Faith once delivered to the Saints," and persistently endeavor to make the precepts and example of Christ their rule and pattern of life. These few Episcopalian extremists of the right hand and the left are in fact as good Christians as

the average among the host of their conservative brethren or of those in the Roman and Denominational Communions. We cannot, therefore, deny them a spiritual
home among us without excluding true Christians, nor
can we, so long as they remain within canonical and
reasonable bounds, insist upon conformity, on the part
of our Mediævalists and Puritans, to the ideas and ceremonials which prevail among us, without becoming
guilty of persecution. The Episcopal Church cannot,
therefore, reasonably be objected to upon the ground of
ritualism.

Again, it must be remembered that there are also
many ceremonial similarities between Denominational
and Roman worship. Consistency would require those
who object to the Episcopal Church upon the score of
ceremony, to become Quakers, or even to give up public
worship altogether. But their tendency confessedly is
towards an elaborate and ornate worship.

But, say our objectors, the doctrines of the Episcopal
Church are such as to convict her of Romanism, and,
whatever may be said of ceremonials, doctrines are
essentials. Now, it must also be confessed, there are
many doctrinal parallels between the Episcopal and
Roman Churches. The same may, however, be said of
us as compared with the various Protestant Denominations, for much of our teaching is the same as
theirs. So is it, moreover, with Denominationalists
and Romanists. There are more particulars in which
their faith is the same, than will be readily acknowledged by those who have never been at the pains of
making a comparison. And in fact if it were not so,
the Denominations could make no plausible pretension to orthodoxy. For, though the truth of all that

is said concerning the errors and corruption of the Roman Church be admitted, yet no well-informed person will deny that she holds all the essential doctrines of Christianity. Though she has added much to the Faith as outlined by the Councils, she has never subtracted from it. For, not to go into details, she has the Bible, the Ancient Creeds, the Ministry, the Sacraments, and all the Christian Ordinances. Without these, as all must agree, there can be no such thing as a Catholic Church of Christ. Therefore, resemblances to Rome in these and other essentials of Catholicity, do not constitute the Episcopal Church Romish but Catholic. We cannot, with justice, be identified with the Roman Church because we are partakers with her in the distinguishing features of the Church of the Apostles, and of the earliest ages. It is unjust to accuse us of Romanism unless we consent to and teach the errors which are peculiar to the Church of Rome. From these offenses we are as innocent as any body of Christians on earth.

But in condemning and renouncing the Papal additions to the Catholic Faith, with the corruptions growing out of them, we were careful not to follow Denominationalists in subtracting from that doctrine which has been believed always, everywhere, and by the vast majority of Christians. This is the true Catholic Faith which the Anglican Communion, of which the Episcopal Church is a part, holds "whole and undefiled," without the additions of Romanists, or the subtractions of Denominationalists. And because we are neither plus nor minus touching this Faith, Romanists contend that we are Denominationalists, and they, that we are Romanists, whereas we are neither the one nor the other, but true Catholics.

There can be no doubt that both Romanists and Protestants hold to a great deal of truth, but too often it is opposite halves of the same truth; and a half truth, as we all know, frequently has the effect of a whole error. It will usually be found by the candid investigator that the Episcopal Church holds both halves of the truth. Take for example her doctrine concerning the nature and efficacy of the Sacraments of Baptism and the Lord's Supper. Since the Reformation, as in the age of the Apostolic Fathers, Anglo-Catholics connect salvation with the Sacraments and with faith and repentance. All that is Scriptural and essential in the Roman and Denominational views of the efficacy of the Sacraments, we hold. For with the one we agree that: "The Sacraments are generally necessary to salvation and that they work invisibly in us and do not only quicken, but also strengthen and confirm our faith in Christ;" and with the others, we agree that the Sacraments "have a wholesome effect and operation in such only as worthily receive the same by a death unto sin, and a new birth unto righteousness, by repenting themselves truly of their former sins, by having a lively faith in God's mercy through Christ with a thankful remembrance of His death, and by being in charity with all men."

Take also our doctrine about confession and absolution which is such a bugbear to many Protestants within as well as without the Anglican Communion, who have never taken the pains to inform themselves of the fundamental difference between our teaching and that of the Roman Church. Doubtless there are among us those who practically hold the Romish dogma, but the view which prevails with our Clergy and intelligent Laity, and which alone can be justified by our standards, looks very much like a compromise between the extremes of Romanism and Denominationalism, though, as a matter of fact, it is simply that which is taught in the New

Testament. This will appear from the following dialogue between a Presbyterian lady and an ex-Methodist minister friend of mine who had just made application for Holy Orders in the Episcopal Church.

L. "How strange to think that you left the Methodists to become an Episcopalian. Do you believe in the confessional?"

Ex. M. "Why, yes, I believe with the Episcopal Church that it is our duty and privilege to confess our sins to God, and, yet, if any are troubled in their conscience and wish advice concerning any besetting sin or to make any confession to their pastor so as to receive encouragement in the Christian life, I believe they should have the privilege of doing so. But of course I do not believe in the Roman confessional, that is, an obligatory confession of faults and sins in detail as a prerequisite to the reception of the Holy Communion."

L. "Well, I am glad to be set right in this, as in the future I shall feel somewhat more comfortable about the Episcopal Church. No reasonable objection can be offered to such a confession, for in one form or another it obtains to some degree in all Protestant Denominations. But how about Priestly Absolution? Do you believe in that?"

Ex. M. "Yes, I do; and I think that I can also remove your prejudice against the Episcopal Church so far as it is due to a misunderstanding on this point. I believe that our Heavenly Father is always ready to forgive His erring children when they come to Him in true penitence confessing their sins. And He is so anxious to keep this truth before their minds that He has not only caused it to be written in His Word that He is ready to forgive iniquity, transgression and sin, but so great is His love that He has commissioned

His ministers, or Priests, to preach repentance and remission of sins to all men in His name, and to pronounce absolution to all who truly and earnestly repent, that the penitent may have every encouragement to trust Him."

L. "I have no objection to that kind of Priestly Absolution. It is a very different thing from the teaching of the Roman Church, that would deny the penitent the privilege of trusting alone in the promises of God for pardon, and compel him to receive absolution from Priests."

Ex. M. "The fact is, Mrs. ——, that many Protestants, in their efforts to get away from the errors and corruptions of Rome, have gone to the other extreme. It is often said that the Episcopal Church is more like the Roman Church than any other, and there is a sense in which this is true. Those that are least like her are the Quakers. Except the Bible they have thrown away almost everything; the Sacraments of Baptism and the Lord's Supper, Confirmation, an Ordained Ministry, the Creed, and so far as possible all ceremonies are laid aside, and the inner Light is exalted until it is not to be tested or measured either by reason or Revelation; while the English Church aimed only to throw aside the errors and corruptions of Rome, retaining all that was Scriptural, Apostolic, primitive and Catholic in worship. The motto of this Church is 'Prove all things; hold fast that which is good.'"

But let us see how the assertion that we are like the Roman Catholics, can be proven untrue, those who make it being themselves the judges. After making it they usually proceed to tell their auditors or readers about "the ignorant, superstitious, degraded, priest-ridden condition of Romanists." Now I am not called upon to pronounce upon the truth or falsity of this severe indictment of Romanism. I simply direct attention to it in order that the utter inconsistency of those who make it, may appear. For if there be any truth in what they say concerning the resemblance of Episcopalianism to Romanism, their description of the members of the Roman Church ought to apply to Episcopalians. But all the world knows that such a representation of our constituency would be simply ridiculous. In fact, those who pass this judgment upon Romanism are the same who reflect upon the Episcopal Church by representing her as made up almost exclusively of the aristocratic and dominant elements of the country. "By their fruits ye shall know them." Surely those who assert that the Episcopal Church is like the Roman Catholic do not regard this precept. In fact they know and admit, and even emphasize the dissimilarity of the fruit, and yet declare the identity of the trees. "Do men gather grapes of thorns, or figs of thistles?" "Consistency, thou art a jewel!"

The fact that the Episcopal Church is so non-Roman, and has done more than any of the Denominations to correct the errors and weaken the power of the Papacy, while at the same time she has been wise and conservative enough to hold fast to that which is essential to Catholicity, as also to many nonessentials which are nevertheless good and ancient, will, in proportion as prejudice gives place to candor, come to be regarded as one of the chief reasons for identification with this Church rather than with any of the revolutionary Denominations. In the long run sensible men and women may be trusted to perceive the absurd character of objections to our Church based upon mere resemblances

The Church for Americans.

LECTURE VII.

WHY AMERICANS SHOULD BE EPISCOPALIANS.

AUTHORITIES.

Brittan, An Apology for Conforming to the Protestant Episcopal Church, Contained in a Series of Letters Addressed to Bishop Onderdonk, New York.

Clark, Walk About Zion.

Clarke, Christian Union and the Protestant Episcopal Church.

Faussett, The Claims of the Established Church to Exclusive Attachment and Support—Bampton Lectures, 1820.

Hammond, John Wesley "Being Dead, Yet Speaketh."

Heygate, Why I Am a Churchman.

Little, A. W., Reasons for Being a Churchman.

Mines, A Presbyterian Looking for the Church.

O'Neill, Christian Unity.

Percival, The Glories of the Episcopal Church.

Shields, The United Church of the United States.

Vail, Bp., The Comprehensive Church.

PAMPHLETS.

Dudley, Bp., Why I Am a Churchman.

Hopkins, Wm. C., Reasons Why I Am a Churchman.

Meade, Bp., Reasons for Loving the Episcopal Church.

Randall, Bp., Why I Am a Churchman.

Swope, Why I Am an Episcopalian.

Vincent, Bp., An Address on Church Unity.

Wesley, Reasons Against a Separation from the Church of England.

MISCELLANEOUS.

The Good Way, or Why Christians of Every Name May Become Churchmen,

Why Americans Should Be Episcopalians.

EVERY right-thinking person will readily give his consent to the proposition that in the choice of a Church, reference should be had to God's will and the promotion of one's own salvation and that of the world. The object of this lecture is to show that by uniting with the Episcopal Church, Americans will be most likely to accomplish these important ends.

I.

THE EPISCOPAL CHURCH APOSTOLIC.

IF this Church could not historically and doctrinally make good the claim to be a part of Christ's One, Holy, Catholic and Apostolic Church, it would be impossible to show that Americans are under any Divine obligation to identify themselves with her. That the Mother Church of England is a true branch of the Catholic Church, and that the American Church is identical with the parent stalk in all features essential to Catholicity, are propositions which, as we have shown,* cannot be questioned without a total disregard of the most obvious facts of history. The close and vital connection between the two Churches is evident from the mere fact that they are in the most cordial and complete communion. Our Bishops sit with the English and colonial Bishops at the Pan-Anglican Council once in

---

* Lectures IV and V.

every ten years. The Clergy of all ranks exchange ministrations. A communicant in good standing in one
Church is recognized as such in the other. This inter-
communion could never have existed and would not be
maintained, but for the fact that the Church of England
and the American Episcopal Church are substantially
the same in all essentials of government, doctrine and
worship. They are, therefore, manifestly different
branches of the same vine. And that this vine has its
root in Christ, through the Apostles, is evident from the
fact that it can be traced down the ages in unbroken
continuity. Furthermore, representatives of the Church
of England occupied undisputed seats in the early General Councils, and she was universally recognized as a
true branch of the Apostolic Church of Christ down
to the time of the Reformation. And if she was this
until then, she is still the same, for the present Church
of England is identical with that which was before the
Reformation.*

Of course the non-church member who has made up
his mind to obey Christ by identifying himself with His
Kingdom, will be told by the representatives of each of
the Protestant Denominations that their respective
bodies are true branches of the Church of Christ. I do
not feel called upon to go through the long list of three
hundred or more for the purpose of investigating their
claims, nor to pronounce upon them. It is only necessary that the reader should be put upon some short and
plain way of coming to the truth by personal investigation. You will not be deceived into accepting a Church
as Apostolic and Catholic which is not such, if you will
simply trace its history back to the beginning, or
ascertain whether or not it is or ever has been in communion with any unquestioned branch of the historic

* Lecture IV.

Church. If you are advised to join a Church which cannot trace its lineage to the Apostles, or which is not and never was recognized by any Church which indisputably has come down from the first centuries as being a branch of the Apostolic Church, reject it as a human institution that has no Divine claim to your allegiance. The American Episcopal Church can stand both of these proposed tests, and therefore non-church members and members of human religious societies can make no mistake in uniting with her, for so they will certainly be doing the will of God by identifying themselves with a true branch of His Church.

II.

THE CHURCH OF OUR RACE.

BUT some one may ask, why not join the Roman Church and have done with it—why stop midway between Sectarianism and Romanism? We answer because there is absolutely nothing in the way of Catholicity to be gained, while in other respects much would be lost by so doing.

God, by a wonderful Providence, has made this an English-speaking Protestant country. It is true that the first discoverers and some of the settlers of the Western Hemisphere were Italians and Spaniards, but the discoveries and conquests made under the flag of Spain are of very little concern to us. As the Bishop of Iowa has aptly observed: "Our interest as a race and as a nation centers in the discovery of the North American continent on June 24, St. John Baptist Day, 1497, by Cabot sailing under the authority of King Henry VII. of England. It is on the ground of this priority of discovery of the continent that the English Crown and

Commonwealth based their claim to occupy the West. It was in consequence of this discovery of the continent by Cabot, and in pursuance of this asserted right to people the land on which the cross of England's Church had been first planted, and to which the arms of England had been affixed by Cabot, that the great historical fact is due that we, the people of these United States, are neither by discovery, by colonization, by civilization, by race, by institution nor by faith, Spanish or Roman. The Latin race and the Latin Church were granted by Divine Providence the opportunities of planting their colonies and attempting the conversion of the Aborigines of the Western. Hemisphere. God willed it that in this Western World there should be witnessed the struggle between the two races, the two civilizations, the two ideas of liberty, the two faiths, the one of the English Church and State, and the other of the Latin people and belief. It is this struggle for a continent which has determined our origin as a people, the nature of our institutions, our civil and Ecclesiastical liberties, our common laws, our forms and features, our very speech, our present standing and glory among the nations of the earth, our civilization, our culture and our Christianity."

Since the memorable commemoration of the four hundredth anniversary of the discoveries by Columbus, Romanists have been assiduously claiming a large share of the credit for the wonderful development of this country. The unsophisticated would naturally infer from what Leo XIII. says in a recently published encyclical, that Columbus and the Spaniards not only discovered the North American Continent, but also colonized, civilized, and created the United States. The Pope, as one of his caustic newspaper critics points out, seems to have forgotten that it was Englishmen and their descendants, mostly Protestants, who did all this. The truth is that Columbus discovered only some far-away islands of the West Indies and afterwards made his way to a portion of South America; but he went to his grave believing the land he had seen to be a part of Eastern Asia. The attempt of Leo to establish himself on a specially friendly footing among us on the ground that the Spanish bravoes of South America were Roman Catholics, heroes of the faith and Apostles of Christian civilization, will strike the average American Protestant as a rather heavy Papal joke. Americans are not all that they might be, but they have common schools in which they learn a little of the elementary history of their country. If, therefore, Romanists expect the rising generations to accept the dogma of infallibility, they must either induce the Pope to place our school histories on the "Index of books which Catholics are, at the peril of their souls, forbidden to read," or to cease writing encyclicals in which reference is made to historical subjects.

Think of it for a moment. This independent, republican, Protestant country, the fruit of Spanish enterprise and the Roman Catholic religion! Romanists will find it hard to convince us of this. Indeed they can never do it, so long as Mexico, Cuba, and Central and South America are remembered. If there is one lesson written in bold and unmistakable characters over the face of those countries, it is that Romanism has not the power to create great, free, prosperous and intelligent, or even moral nations. The Spanish and Italian Peninsulas are themselves evidence of this. In the words of Motley: "They have had a different history from that which records the career of France, Prussia, the Dutch Commonwealth, the British Empire and the Transatlantic Republic." The cause of this difference is pointed out by "Janus" who was certainly in a position to know whereof he spoke. There is, says he, "a profound hatred at the bottom of the soul of every genuine Ultramontane, of free institutions and the whole constitutional system." He then proceeds to make the truth of this statement manifest by the most conclusive and varied evidence drawn from the history of almost every European country.

We have not in this connection lost sight of the fact that it is claimed, upon what on the surface seems to be good ground, that the Romanists of Maryland were the first to practice toleration in matters of religion. Their descendants of this generation make much of the statute which provides that "no person whatsoever within this province [Maryland] professing to believe in Jesus Christ, shall from henceforth be anyways troubled or molested for his or her religion; nor in the free exercise thereof, nor anyway compelled to the belief or exercise of any other religion against his or her consent." This with the statement of the historian, Bancroft, to the effect that in Lord Baltimore's colony "religious liberty obtained a home, its only home in the wide world," formed the text and burden of the addresses at the Roman Catholic Conference at Baltimore in 1889, and ever since Romanists have quoted them upon almost every occasion of a conversation with a Protestant.

Before proceeding to examine this claim in the light of the facts in the case, let it be observed that, though Maryland may have been the first to secure religious toleration by legislation, she was not the only colony to practice it. Mr. Bancroft whose complimentary remarks concerning them Romanists are naturally fond of citing, also has something to say about the tolerance of the Episcopalians of Virginia: "I find no trace of persecution in the earliest history of the colony."

The following extract from Bishop Coleman's History of the Church in America will show that no more can be said of Maryland. "Churchmen began very early to settle in Maryland, so called in honor of Queen Henrietta Maria, wife of Charles I. They came from Virginia, some time prior to 1634, and made their homes on the Isle of Kent, opposite what is now known as the city of Annapolis. The Rev. Richard James, who had accompanied Sir George Calvert, the first Lord Baltimore, before he became a Roman Catholic, was for a while their minister. Not long afterwards, a Chapel was erected at St. Mary's where lay Services were held. These Church people suffered considerable indignity at the hands of the Roman Catholics, against whom they felt obliged to petition for redress. They styled themselves 'Protestant Catholics.' One complaint was that a prominent Roman Catholic had stolen the key of their Chapel and removed their books. He was made to restore them, and pay a fine of five hundred pounds of tobacco, to be applied to the support of the first Clergyman who should arrive. Before a great while, the proprietary government was overthrown, and Protestants, with religious toleration, were in the ascendency."

In regard to the pretension that Americans owe their religious and civil liberties to Roman Catholics, we desire in the interest of truth to make two or three observations. To begin, the statute of which we hear so much is not quite so liberal as might be supposed from the extracts which Romanists so frequently quote. The part that they always leave out runs as follows: "Any person or persons whatsoever that shall deny our Saviour Jesus Christ to be the Son of God, or shall deny the Holy Trinity, the Father, Son, and Holy Ghost, or the Godhead of any of the three persons of the Holy Trinity or the unity of the Godhead, or shall use any reproachful words, speeches or languages concerning the Holy Trinity, or any of the three said Persons thereof, shall be punished with death and confiscation or forfeiture of all his or her land and goods to the Lord Proprietor and his heirs." And, in quoting from Mr. Bancroft they forget to mention what he says about the composition of the legislative body which passed the statute. He says: "The Protestant Governor, Stone, and his Council of six, composed equally of Protestants and Catholics, and the representatives of the people of Maryland, of whom five were Catholics, at a general session of the Assembly, held in April, 1649, placed upon their statute book an act for the religious freedom which by the unbroken usage of fifteen years had become sacred on their soil." In another place he tells us that "the very great majority of the Maryland people were Protestants."

Thus it looks very much as if the law were a Protestant act for the toleration of Romanists instead of the reverse, as they would have us believe. That this is the correct view of the matter is rendered next to certain by the fact that in A.D. 1648 William Stone, the Governor, an ancestor of our Bishop Stone, of Maryland, took the following oath: "I will not molest, trouble or discountenance any person in this province professing to believe in Jesus Christ, in particular no Roman Catholic." "What does this signify," asks Bishop Coleman, "but that the Roman Catholics were the tolerated and protected?"

"That Roman Catholics," says Dr. McConnell in his History of the American Episcopal Church, "should be claimed as the champions of religious liberty in the seventeenth century, seems sufficiently grotesque to the student of history. The simple truth in the premises is this: The Calverts did believe and practice so; the Roman Church did neither the one nor the other. The settlers of Maryland were too glad to find safety to think of persecution. Not that they would have done so if they could. They should have, ungrudged, their meed of praise; but they must not have all the praise. It must not be forgotten that their new home was given them by a Protestant king, with the hearty advice and approval of a Protestant council, who in so doing waived their own claims in the interest of their misguided but still loved countrymen. They made the gift with their eyes open. English Romanists were utterly discredited as citizens. It was not alone nor chiefly that their religion was abhorrent. By their own declaration they took their political orders from an enemy whom England could not then afford to despise. Romanists in England meant servants to the Papacy and agents of the King of Spain. Despite of this, Prottestant Englishmen gave them that peaceful home in Maryland, which had already been brutally refused them by their French co-religionists in Newfoundland. The founders were of those few in their day who were Catholics rather than Romanists, and Englishmen before either. Such were the Calverts, a noble race with few contemporaries and fewer descendants. They had neither the will nor the power of intolerance. But they laid no claim to toleration as a virtue. They simply recognized existing facts. The first offer of persecution by the Maryland colony would have brought such a storm about them as would have swept them into the ocean. Churchmen and Quakers, Papists and Puritans, would have combined to exterminate the ingrates. They were glad to leave England, and there is serious reason to believe that they were not altogether sorry to be three thousand miles farther away from Rome."

No, we owe our liberty of conscience, civilization and marvelous material prosperity to our English origin and Protestant religion. This being the case, it seems to be a clear indication of God's will that we should be identified with the Church of the English-speaking race. Neither the Roman Church nor any of the Denominations can establish a claim to the recognition and allegiance of Americans upon the ground of being the Church of our race. Romanism and Sectarianism were respectively six hundred and fifteen hundred years too late in coming upon the scene. Whatever the Roman Catholics in England may have to say about the Church of England, they are unable to deny that their own organization in that country is a new one. It has no succession from pre-Reformation times. But the present Bishops of the older Sees are historically and canonically the successors of those who occupied them before the Reformation back to the earliest days of Christianity. The Archbishop of Canterbury was therefore right when some time ago he styled English Romanism the "new Italian Mission." Romanists at first were much exasperated at an expression which so precisely defined their true status. But one of their own number, the Jesuit Father Humphreys, has since boldly avowed: "We are a new Mission straight from Rome." On this point at least, Anglican and Romans are now agreed. An Archimandrite of the Greek Church, residing in England, says: "Roman Catholics, like ourselves [Greek Catholics], are Nonconformists in these Isles. The Ecclesiastical State Church of England we recognize as an important branch of the great Catholic Church."

Thus, whether we act, in the choice of a Church, with reference to God's will, or regard to the future of our race and civilization, we shall choose the Episcopal Church rather than any other.

III.

A VALID MINISTRY.

WE should be induced to identify ourselves with the Episcopal Church rather than with any one of the Protestant Denominations, because her ministry is more certainly authoritatively commissioned. All agree that the validity of a minister's commission must be considered. Some of the Denominations of modern origin attach almost, if not quite, as much importance to this matter as do Episcopalians and other representatives of Historic Churches. We are at unity in the agreement that no man with impunity can take the great honor and assume the awful responsibilities of representing Christ as a proclaimer of the Gospel message and an administrator of the Gospel Sacraments, unless he be divinely called thereto. But we differ as to what constitutes this call which we agree to be essential. A majority of our Denominational brethren think that it consists exclusively in an inward, spiritual call. The minority among them hold that to this call must be added the laying on of hands by Presbyters or elders. But not even the latter of these, though inclusive of the former, is held to be a sufficient commission by any of the branches of the Historic Church of which the American Episcopal is one. Romans, Greeks, Anglicans and other Catholic and Apostolic Communions, comprising together about nine-tenths of Christendom, insist that none are lawful ministers of the Church of God unless they have received Ordination by a Bishop who can trace his spiritual descent and authority to the Apostles by an unbroken succession. Nor are those who contend for the sufficiency of Presbyterian ordination, able to advance and support any argument that is convincing to us, or reassuring to those among themselves who have once become familiar with, and disturbed by, the facts upon which our convictions rest.

Our Bishops can show their connection with the Apostles by at least three independent continuous ancestral lines, namely, that of Jerusalem, Rome and Ephesus. And this they can do by almost innumerable separate strands. Through St. Augustine, first Bishop of Canterbury, St. Patrick, first Archbishop of Armagh, and the British, Irish and Gallican Bishops, they are connected with St. John and St. Paul; through Archbishop Theodore and several of his successors, with St. Paul and St. Peter, and through St. David and the Welsh Bishops, with St. James and the whole college of Apostles. There is not a candid historian in all the world who will question the continuity of the English succession. Thus, in our Ordinations, nothing is wanting that either the representatives of modern Denominationalism or of the various branches of the ancient Catholic and Apostolic Church deem essential.

In view of the fact that the whole of Christendom held to the necessity of Episcopal Ordination during all of the fifteen hundred years preceding the Reformation, and that nine-tenths of the Christian world still hold it, we could never be quite certain about the lawfulness of the Orders of our ministry, if their possession depended wholly upon the inward call, or upon the laying on of hands by the Presbytery, or even upon both of these. On the other hand, if we, who are in the great majority, be wrong, and they, who are in the small minority, right, there will still be no room for misgiving on our part. For if either the inward call or the laying on of hands by Presbyters, or both of them together, be necessary, the validity of the Ordination which our ministers have received, cannot be doubted. They are obliged to answer questions by responses which they could not make if they were not fully persuaded of a Divine call to preach the everlasting Gospel. It is moreover required that at least two Presbyters shall be present to lay on hands with the Bishop. If, therefore, a Church be chosen with reference to the validity of its ministry, there is none which can present a better claim than the Episcopal Church. No ministry is more demonstrably Scriptural and Apostolic than ours.

IV.

SUPERIOR OPPORTUNITIES.

NEXT to finding in history an external indication of God's will as to our choice of a Church, we should have also in view an environment conducive to our growth in Christ-likeness, and to the up-building of ourselves in "the Faith once delivered to the Saints." Indeed to be governed by these considerations is only another way of obeying Him. For certainly it is His will that we should be rooted and grounded in the true doctrine of Christ and the Apostles, and that we should grow into the full stature of Christian manhood and womanhood. The main object in life should be the shaping of our conduct and the moulding of our character by the precepts and example of our Lord and Saviour. In this great work we require help in the way of constant, efficient teaching. In other words, we must be in a good school of Christ. All Churches are, in one of their chief aspects, religious seminaries of learning. And all persons who attend upon Divine Services are students.

In respect to institutions for secular education, it is well understood that there is a wide difference between them, so far as equipment and efficiency are concerned. Parents and students recognize this, and, when their circumstances will permit, feel it their privilege and duty to select the best. Now we hold that there is just as much room, if not more, for preference in religious schools. If in other respects the popular assertion: "One Church is as good as another," be true, it certainly is not so concerning their teaching capabilities. In this particular some are unquestionably better than others.

The efficiency of a school depends upon four things: The proficiency of the teachers, the course of study, the text-books and the apparatus for illustrating and impressing the truths that are taught. We believe that even a cursory examination of the educational system which prevails throughout the Anglican Communion, will lead all candid Americans, who make choice of a Church for the purpose of learning in the school of Christ, to choose the Episcopal Church. Her ministers or teachers will be found to be well qualified for their work. Her course of study covers the whole ground. Her text-books comprise not only the Holy Scriptures, but also the Book of Common Prayer, which has no equal for the light which it throws upon the Word of God, and for the practical way in which it weaves its teachings into our lives. Her ritual, festivals, and fasts are so many impressive object lessons, tending at once to systematize, emphasize and fix the oral teachings of the Services and sermons. See how the most important events of the Christian Dispensation and the doctrines

which they teach pass under review from year to year
through the whole of our lives.

> " Advent tells us Christ is near,
> Christmas tells us Christ is here;
> In Epiphany we trace
> All the glory of His Grace.

> "Those three Sundays before Lent
> Will prepare us to repent,
> That in Lent we may begin
> Earnestly to mourn for sin.

> " Holy Week and Easter then
> Tell who died and rose again,
> O that happy Easter day,
> Christ is risen again we say.

> " Yes, and Christ ascended, too,
> To prepare a place for you.
> So we give Him special praise
> After those great forty days.

> " Then He sent the Holy Ghost
> On the Day of Pentecost,
> With us ever to abide,
> Well may we keep Whitsuntide.

> "Last of all we humbly sing
> Glory to our God and King,
> Glory to the One in Three
> On the feast of Trinity."

But the doctrinal period from Advent to Trinity
covers only half of the course of sacred teaching provided for in the Prayer Book. After that we have six
months of practical instruction. In the words of the
Bishop of Ohio: "The Church gives us twenty-five Sundays of the Trinity season, in which the holy teachings
of our Lord are set forth. The first six months of the
year are occupied with the succinct narrative of His
earthly experience; the next six months are filled with

the result of His holy instructions. Each Sunday has its theme and topic; and these are the fruits, the outgrowth of His own example. Faith, forgiveness, charity, hope, perseverance, patience, these are some of the sacred virtues illumined and set forth — the Christian works, the Christian development, the Christian walk — accentuated by the glowing words culled from the Bible, and grouped in order, to set forth the unmistakable rule of the Christian's daily life and conversation."

As a distinguished Congregational minister, Dr. Thomas K. Beecher, says: "He, who for years has been a Churchman, and remains ill-grounded in Scripture, shows himself to be an unworthy son of a very faithful Mother. By the Lessons, Gospels, Epistles, Psalms and Collects, appointed for special fast or feast days, the events commemorated by that day are wrought into the memory of every worshipper. And by seasons, longer or shorter, of special religious effort and observance, this Church satisfies the same want which other churches satisfy by weeks of prayer, protracted meetings and long revivals. A good school is a dull place to any visitor who rushes in to find sensation and excitement. He will call it dry, poky, stupid. In like manner, many religious sensation-makers and sensation-seekers will promptly vote the Church calendar and all its smooth machinery of pious drill, a very dull substitute for a regular, rousing revival. But, in the long run, the Church that steadily trains and teaches will outlive the church that only arouses and startles. 'If ye continue in My word, then are ye My disciples indeed.'"

The Rev. Dr. Hitchcock, in a paper read before the last Pan-Presbyterian Conference, thus speaks of the value of the Christian year and pleads for its restoration: "I anticipate a revival of the old Christian year.

Clear back, close up to the Apostolic times, we find at least the Passover, Pentecost and Epiphany. Christmas appears not long after. And then the calendar was crowded with festivals which disgusted our Protestant fathers, bringing the whole system into disrepute. As between Puritans and Papists, we side, of course, with the Puritan, but the older way is better than either. Judaism had more than its weekly Sabbath, and Protestant Christendom needs more, and is steadily taking more. Christmas is leading this new procession. Good Friday, Easter and Whitsuntide are not far behind. These, at least, can do us no harm. They emphasize the three grand facts and features of our religion: Incarnation, Atonement, and Regeneration."

By comparison with the Episcopal Church, the Roman educational system is unintelligible and superstitious, and that of the Denominations is wanting in comprehensiveness and thoroughness. Rome gives too much time to legends and traditions, and the Denominations lay too great stress upon emotions and impulses. The former system accepts the decrees of a Pope; the latter follows the idiosyncrasies of enthusiastic leaders. The one tends to exaggerated dependence, the other to unbounded individualism. The one is petrifaction, the other dissipation. The end of both must be a departure farther and farther from the Catholic Faith. I am not claiming that the Anglican or Episcopalian system is faultless, but I insist that it is incomparably better than either the Roman or Denominational. Besides, it stands to reason that the Church which is entwined with the entire history of our race, has in herself those conservative elements and constructive forces which are just what our national fabric requires. The Church's superiority as a religious educator has all along attracted many Americans to her fold, and will continue to do so in increasing numbers as long as men and women choose their Church relationship with reference to the opportunity afforded to them for becoming rooted and grounded in the Faith of the Gospel, and for growing up in the full stature of Christian manhood and womanhood.

Again, we claim that in the choice of a Church, it is a duty to have regard to opportunities of usefulness to your neighbor and to the world at large. The reasons which would induce you to join the Episcopal Church, on your own behalf, are of equal force when you have in view the good of others. For they, as well as you, have need of building up in faith and character. If the Church's system is best for you, it will likewise be so for your family, for your neighbor, and for your countrymen generally. This will appear more satisfactorily if, after agreeing upon the principal religious needs of our time and country, it can be shown that of all the Christian bodies, the Episcopal is the best adapted to meet them. There will be little, if any, dissent from the affirmation that one of our greatest needs is such a presentation of Christianity as will produce the highest type of character.

We have already seen that the educational system of the Episcopal Church is at least theoretically the best. If our theory be true, it should be capable of something approaching to practical demonstration, for "By their fruits ye shall know them." But how shall we, without comparisons which will be apparently uncharitable, demonstrate our theory by the fruit of the system? It will not do for us to be the judge, for so our decision would be rejected as partial and biased. We must, therefore, produce outside testimony. This is found in the most satisfactory directions imaginable. Upon the whole, those who are placed by the suffrages of the people in the most responsible and exalted public offices, will be admitted to have been the picked men of the country. This has not, of course, always been the case, but the exceptions, it must be conceded, do not disprove the general rule. If, then, we can make it clear that an abnormal proportion of the most illustrious of our public servants have been sons of the Episcopal Church, our claim that she should be chosen because she develops the type of character that the country stands most in need of, will have been made good.

Now, it cannot altogether have escaped the attention of any who are in the habit of reading the obituary notices of distinguished personages, that many of the public men who have died in the course of the last ten or fifteen years, have been buried by our Clergy and Service. Of course, this is no proof that the deceased was a Communicant of the Episcopal Church, but it does prove that he was more or less closely connected with her, or, at least, that she was his preference. I am convinced, however, from personal investigation, that inquiry would, in the majority of cases, establish the fact that he was by birth, education, and life-long association, a Churchman.

In September, 1886, I had occasion to make a memorandum of the men who, in the course of the preceding twelve months, had been added to the United States' list of honored dead. It was as follows: Thomas A. Hendricks, Vice President of the United States; George B. McClellan, General, and candidate for the Presidency; Wm. H. Vanderbilt, the richest man the world had ever known; W. S. Hancock, General, and candidate for the Presidency; Horatio Seymour, twice Governor of New York, also candidate for the Presidency; J. H.

Devereux, General, and Railway President; David Davis, Associate Justice of the United States Supreme Court; S. J. Tilden, Governor of New York, and candidate for the Presidency; John W. Stevenson, Governor of Kentucky, and United States Senator; Rufus P. Spaulding, Judge and Scholar. Of these, Tilden was the only one whose obsequies were not performed by one of our Clergymen, and he, Justice Davis and McClellan were the only persons among these ten distinguished American citizens who were not found, upon investigation, to have been actual communicants of the Episcopal Church. This showing is doubtless proportionately as true of the other years back to Revolutionary and Colonial times.

Bishop Perry, the learned and tireless Historiographer of the American Church, has thrown a great deal of light upon the Church relationship of the great heroes and statesmen, whose names will ever be household words with Americans, as, indeed, not a few of them are with all lovers of liberty, and admirers of greatness throughout the civilized world. It appears from his investigations that, notwithstanding the prejudice against the Episcopal Church, and the false charges as to her patriotism in Colonial times, which charges have been fully answered in another connection,* two-thirds of the First Continental Congress held at Philadelphia A. D. 1774, were Churchmen. The same proportion obtained in the Congress which declared our independence. Of the fifty-five actual signers of the Declaration of Independence, thirty-five were Episcopalians; twelve, Congregationalists; four, Presbyterians; three, Quakers; one was a Baptist, and one a Roman Catholic.§ The Resolution offered in the Continental Congress of A. D. 1776, declaring the thirteen colonies

---

* Lecture V., Part III. § Appendix XXIV.

free and independent, was moved by Richard Henry Lee, of Virginia, an Episcopalian and a vestryman. The Chairman of the Committee of Congress, to which this resolution was referred, and by whom the declaration was reported after its discussion, and adoption in "committee of the whole," was Benjamin Harrison, of Virginia, also a vestryman of the Episcopal Church. The author of the Declaration itself, Thomas Jefferson, of Virginia, although in later life regarded as a sceptic, and certainly holding and advocating views quite inconsistent with those accepted by any Christian body, had been baptized and was a vestryman of the Church in Virginia, and to the last of his life was a regular attendant at her Services.

Of the twelve generals appointed by Washington early in the war, eight were his fellow Episcopalians. It is not too much to claim, indeed it was admitted by the Puritan, Adams, that the issue of the struggle for independence, and the history of this country, would in all probability have been very different but for these illustrious Episcopalian patriots. The sons of the Episcopal Church were no less conspicuous and important in the preservation of the Union when threatened by the Confederacy. Seward, Chase, Stanton, Wells, Blair, Dennison, Henry Winter Davis, Scott, Meade, Scofield, Curtis, Hancock, Farragut, Porter, Waite, Columbus Delano, and many others of scarcely less distinction, were Episcopalians. Nor will it at all weaken our argument, so far as it concerns the superiority of the Church's educational system, if we call attention to the fact that the leaders of the Confederacy were also Episcopalians. This is true of Davis, Lee, Toombs, Hill, Johnston, Bishop Polk, Longstreet, Stuart and Wade Hampton. True, these were not patriots from the standpoint of Northerners, but Southerners regarded them as such; and undoubtedly they would have taken first rank with our heroes had their environment been the same.

The late Bishop Robertson, of Missouri, a high authority on American history, in his "Churchman's Answer," says that those, who in this country have borne rule and been representative men, have with a curious unanimity come forth from those whose piety found its best expression in the Prayer Book. Of the Continental Congress from Peyton Randolph, the majority of its Presidents were Episcopalians. Washington, and two-thirds of the Presidents of the United States since his day, have been Episcopalians. The same has been true of three-fourths of all the Secretaries of State. The most eminent and influential of all our Statesmen have been the same: Franklin, Clinton, Jay, Morris, Livingstone, Patrick Henry, Hoffman, Schuyler, Randolph, Duane, Wirt, Cass, Clay, Benton, Webster. To say that the same is true of the commanders of our army and navy, would be to catalogue the names of almost every one who has attained to eminence. The Chief Justices of the Supreme Court of the United States have, with but two exceptions, been Episcopalians.

Now, this is a very remarkable showing, especially so when we consider that the Episcopal Church ranks only seventh or eighth in point of numbers among the religious bodies of the country, and that both Romanists and Denominationalists, who together must represent nine-tenths of our Christian population, have always been deeply prejudiced against us. There is, under the circumstances, only one satisfactory way of accounting for this, namely, by admitting the truth of our claim, that the Episcopal Church, having the best system of religious education, is the best adapted to produce that type of character of which the country stands most in need. Therefore, if a Church be chosen with reference to the opportunities which it affords to promote the good of others and of the country, it will necessarily be the Episcopal.

V.

DOCTRINAL STABILITY.

THE English Church, having freed herself from the Mediæval errors, which were common to the whole of Western Christendom, occupies now the same doctrinal position that she did during the first centuries of the Christian era. Since the Reformation she has remained immovably anchored by her incomparable Liturgy, to the Faith once delivered to the Saints. This is not the case with Romanism or with any of the forms of Denominationalism.

Rome has been adding to the Faith, the articles of the Immaculate Conception of the Virgin Mary and the infallibility of the Pope, to say nothing of the numerous decrees of the Council of Trent, the acceptance of which is made necessary to salvation and to membership in her communion.

No additions have been made to the faith originally held by Denominationalists, but it has been woefully diminished. With the possible exception of the high German Lutherans, between whom and Episcopalians there is, aside from their Presbyterian government and doctrine of Consubstantiation, so much in common, all the chief Denominations have drifted far away from their original moorings. It is impossible for any, but the historian, to realize the extent to which Denominationalists have been driven about by every wind of doctrine, and how many of them have made shipwreck of faith on the shoals of heresy, skepticism and indifference. But those who have not the leisure or books to familiarize themselves with the melancholy history of non-Episcopal Protestantism in Germany, France, England, Holland, the United States, and indeed all countries without any exception, where it has taken root, will perceive the truth of what we have said as soon as their attention is called to the fact, that all the divisions which have occurred since the Lutherans went out from the Roman Church, and the Independents from the Church of England, mark more or less wide departures from the doctrine and discipline of the first Dissenters. In the nature of things there would have been no division without a difference, and no difference resulting in a division without a departure from the tenets of the earliest sectaries. From the standpoint of the first sects, those who went out must have been in each case heretics. Schism and heresy are inseparable. Church history proves that the two invariably go hand in hand. There may be error in doctrine without separation, but not the latter without the former. This being so, the reader will see at once that all the hundreds of Denominations into which the first two or three non-Episcopal bodies have been multiplied, could not have arisen without wide divergences from the doctrinal position of their sectarian forefathers.

Nor is there any reason for believing that the end is yet. True the multiplication of sects is no longer encouraged and justified as it was until lately. On the contrary, many of the choicest Christians of every name are praying, working and hoping for reunion. But nevertheless we now and then read of the organization of a new Denomination. And, it must be remembered that in reality all who are not identified with any form of organized Christianity, because they think that they can be as good Christians outside the Church as in it, are a church unto themselves. There can be no doubt about it, these one-man churches are increasing at an astounding rate. At the Reformation period every man, woman and child in Christendom was identified with some body of Christians, but now untold millions are unattached. So numerous are the outsiders, especially in the United States, that if a man be asked concerning his religious affiliations, no one is surprised if he reply, "O I belong to the big church," from which we are to understand that he is one of the unaffiliated majority. And this church so called certainly has a larger constituency and is growing more rapidly than any other. Now the point I make is this—and certainly there are none so obtuse as not to be able to see it—that every man or woman having no Ecclesiastical relationship, whose sympathies are with Protestantism, is a witness to the departures, and very wide ones at that, from the position occupied by the first Denominationalists.

The most cursory examination of the writings of Luther, Calvin, and John Wesley will convince any candid mind that even those who now profess to be their followers are not so at all. The evidence of this is found in the fact that these illustrious Reformers held and taught many of the very doctrines which are now said to bar their professed spiritual descendants from the Episcopal Church. They believed Episcopacy to be of Divine appointment, or, at least, the best form of Ecclesiastical government; they held the doctrine of Baptismal Regeneration; they regarded Confirmation as a Scriptural ordinance; and maintained that the Body and Blood of Christ are spiritually, though really, received in the Holy Communion. It was upon the urgent recommendation of Peter Martyr and Bucer, disciples of Luther and Calvin, that the Confession and Absolution were introduced into our Daily Morning and Evening Prayer.

And not only have Denominationalists departed from their founders in respect to those points which were originally held in common with the Church of England, but they have, in many cases, renounced the doctrines which differentiated them from the Church. Take, for example, the distinctive dogmas of Calvin. It is unquestionable that during the last fifty years, Calvinistic theology has been generally surrendered by the Baptists, Congregationalists, and even Presbyterians. And yet so thoroughly was Congregationalism once identified with Calvinism, that in England, the Independent Chapel is still sometimes called, in common parlance, the "Calvinistic meeting." If my memory serves me correctly, it was at Chicago, on the floor of the Great Annual Presbyterian Assembly that a delegate, in speaking upon a resolution providing for some change in the "Confession of Faith," electrified the vast assemblage by asserting that there was not in all the Assembly a single minister who believed in infant damnation. I believe the speaker was not contradicted. Be it remembered, it was Calvinism which "divided the English Church, and, indeed, Protestant Christendom, into two hostile camps." This system is now generally given up. After working endless mischief and estrangement, it is quietly disappearing from the Evangelical Creed. And this is to a great degree true of the distinguishing doctrines of Luther and Wesley, and, in fact, of all who have originated divisions in the Body of Christ. So that, strange as it may appear, those who call themselves by the names of sectaries, are not their followers, either in the many doctrines which they held in common with the Church, or in a few wherein they differed from her. The old Faith is still believed by countless millions, but the new doctrines which were thought to be of so great importance as to justify promulgation at the expense of Christian unity, have, for the most part, been repudiated, or at least neglected, even by the descendants of those who separated from the Historic Church, and banded themselves about their leader in order that they might disseminate his peculiar views.

Now I respectfully submit to the Denominational reader that these and other changes of front constitute a sufficient reason for an examination, if not an abandonment, of your present position. The fact that you are not in accord with the doctrinal eccentricities of your fathers, while they were at unity with us touching the doctrines and customs to which you object in the Mother Church, should at least induce you to listen patiently to any explanation that we have to offer. "A part of the old Denominational platform has already given way under your feet; may it not well be suspected that the rest is rickety and untenable? May it not be that objections still entertained—as, for example, to Apostolical succession, to Baptismal Regeneration, to Absolution, and the like, may turn out to be based on misunderstanding and to be propped up by prejudice? You will no doubt protest that this is impossible, but then your forefathers would have protested just as loudly that they could never be reconciled to the surplice, never abandon the 'Five Points,' never tolerate Liturgical forms. To Churchmen patiently looking on and praying that Christians may be one, it seems that 'Mr. Prejudice has fallen down and broken his leg,' and they may not only wish with Bunyan 'that it had been his head,' but may see in his unsteadiness ground for hoping that that will come next."

The Episcopal Church is doctrinally the most conservative of all bodies of Christians. The fact that she
is known and spoken of as the *via media*, the "middle
way" between the extremes of Romanism and Protestantism, in itself proves this. Whoever, therefore, in the
choice of his Church relationship has reference to un-
changeableness of teaching, will identify himself with
some branch of the Anglican Communion.*

VI.

CHRISTIAN UNITY.

"For hearts that have been long estranged,
And friends that have grown cold,
Shall meet again, like parted streams,
And mingle as of old?"

AS a convert to Episcopacy, I have always thought
that one of the chief reasons for membership in
the Anglican Communion rather than in any
other, is the fact that she occupies the only ground upon
which the greatest need of the Christian world, Unity,
can be satisfied.

Of late years the subject of Christian Unity has been
receiving more and more attention, until now it may be
said to have become the "burning question" of the day.
Professor Fisher, of Yale College, a Congregational divine, clearly discerns the rising spirit of Church Unity,
when he says: "The centrifugal age of Protestantism is
closed. The centripetal action has begun." The change
of thought in favor of a united, rather than a divided, Church cannot have escaped observation by any
except a few Ecclesiastical "Rip Van Winkles." They
will wake up one of these fine days to the realization of the fact that the old leaders of thought,
and the whole of the rising generation are regretting

* Appendix XXV.

and deprecating the evils of divisions and are talking, working and praying for unity, and that they are standing alone as the champions of sectarianism.

Christian Unity is a thought which has been in the hearts of many of the religious movements of the Nineteenth Century. The Irvingite movement, the Tractarian and that which has developed into the Denomination of Plymouth Brethren, were all largely influenced by it. The Evangelical Alliance, the Association for promoting the Unity of Christendom, the Bonn Reunion Conferences, and the Home Reunion Society, are all of them fruits of the desire for unity taking different forms. The longing for reunion is now more than ever finding expression in publications, in the organization of societies, in the official declarations of Churches and in the institution of a day of intercession and instruction which gives promise of general observance. By common consent the day fixed upon is Whitsun-Day. It was first appointed in the year 1894, by the Archbishop of Canterbury. In A. D. 1895, the League of Catholic Unity, a society composed of very distinguished ministers representing several of the leading American Denominations, joined the Primate of the Anglican Communion in the request that on this day, annually, prayers be offered, and sermons preached, on behalf of organic Christian Union.

The reasons for fixing upon Whitsun-Day are obvious. It is the birthday of the One, Holy, Catholic and Apostolic Church of Christ. It was on Pentecost, fifty days after Easter, and ten after the Ascension, when the Disciples were all with one accord in one place, that they were baptized with the Holy Ghost, and endued with that miraculous wisdom and power which enabled them to carry out their Lord's plans and directions, by establishing and building up His Kingdom, in spite of every opposition, with marvelous rapidity. And after eight hundred years of division between the Eastern and Western Catholic Churches and three hundred years of Denominationalism in the West, it has come to be realized by Christians of every name that the world can never be brought to Christ by a divided Church. "The world," says Dr. Milligan, a Presbyterian, "will never be converted by a disunited Church." "In our present divided state," writes a veteran missionary, Dr. Alexander Williamson, himself not a Churchman, "we will never Christianize China—never!" "When I asked," says Bishop Selwyn, "one of the most remarkable of the New Zealand chieftains why he refused to be a Christian, he stretched out three fingers, and, pointing to the center joint, said, 'I have come to a point from which I see three roads branching. This is the Church of England, this the Church of Rome, and this the Wesleyans. I am sitting down here doubting which to take.'" "And," adds the Bishop, "he sat doubting at that 'cross road' until he died." The realization of our impotency is pressing upon the hearts and consciences of multitudes of every name the question, how can unity be restored? It is my purpose to answer this inquiry in part by trying to make it appear that the only practicable rallying point is on the ground occupied by the American Episcopal Church.

At the consecration of Dr. Lawrence, Bishop of Massachusetts, the celebrated Greek Archbishop of the Apostolic See of Zante, said truly of us: "You are Protestant, but you are Catholic. As Protestants, you comprehend all the other Protestant bodies, and, on the other hand, you alone can draw the attention of the Catholic Churches. Your Church, sister of the other

Protestant Churches, and sister of the other Catholic Churches, is the center to which all the eminent pastors of Christians will, in the future, cast their eyes, when, by the grace of God, they shall decide to take steps for the union of the Christian world into one Church with one Pastor." The Archbishop is not alone in his opinion. Count Joseph De Maistre, a distinguished Roman Catholic, thought that if ever Christendom is to be reunited, the movement must proceed from the Anglican Communion. He recognized it as the only mediator who can lay hands upon both parties; for, as he says, "with one hand she touches us [Roman Catholics] and with the other the Protestants."

It will be perfectly manifest to all who are familiar with the Declaration of the House of Bishops at Chicago, in A.D. 1886, and of the Pan-Anglican Conference of Bishops at Lambeth Palace, London, in the year 1888, and of the action of the General Convention at Baltimore, in A.D. 1892, that any scheme of Christian unity which cannot be consummated within the limits of the ground now occupied by the American Episcopal Church, must fail so far as including the great Anglican Communion of more than twenty million adherents is concerned.

As actual proof that it is possible for Christians of every name to unite here in one organic body, let me call attention to the notable fact that representatives of all doctrinal and governmental views are now, and long have been, standing upon this ground. We have in this Church some who are, in respect to their views of God's mercy, Arminians, Calvinists, and Universalists. The Roman, Zwinglian, and Lutheran doctrines of the Sacraments have their advocates, or at least would be tolerated among us. The same is true of the distinctive doctrines of the Baptists, Methodists, Adventists, Disciples, and others. Concerning the vexed question of

Church government, we have High Episcopalians, Presbyterians, Congregationalists, and Indifferentists. There is a sprinkling of those who advocate and practice an extreme Ritualism, such as could scarcely be duplicated in Roman usage, and others who, in spirit, and so far as possible in practice, are severe Puritans. There are subjectivists and externalists; literalists and rationalists; the votaries of society and the recluse—all these schools of doctrine, government, worship and conduct are now actually to be found among both the Clergy and Laymen of the Protestant Episcopal Church.

The comprehensive character of the Church is illustrated by almost all our Confirmation classes. A majority of the adult candidates are usually persons who have grown up under other religious influences. I have before me the account of a class of one hundred and two candidates confirmed on Good Friday, A.D. 1894, in St. Andrew's Church, Harlem, New York. There were fifty-seven Americans, twenty-one Germans, nine Swedes, seven Irish and eight English. The class was composed of twenty men, twenty-eight women, twenty-six girls, and twenty-eight boys. Among these, seven were married couples. Ten men and eighteen women represented the heads of families. They were from the following Christian bodies: the Church, 52; Roman Catholic, 4; Universalist, 1; Lutheran, 9; Methodist, 14; Baptist, 5; Hebrew, 2; Quaker, 1; Dutch Reformed, 5; Presbyterian, 6; Congregational, 3.

The idea for which many of the Denominations stand, finds recognition in the Episcopal Church. The Presbyterian will find, upon investigation, that the authority of the Presbytery is duly recognized in the government of the Church and the Ordination of elders; the Congregationalist, that our parishes are sufficiently independent of each other, and that the Laity have enough to say concerning Ecclesiastical affairs; the Lutheran, that the necessity of faith is taught; the Methodist, that the Church in which John Wesley lived and died, lays a great deal of stress upon conversion and sanctification; the Baptist, that he can immerse without let or hindrance, and that though Baptism is commenced in unconscious infancy, it is not completed until Confirmation is received upon an intelligent confession of faith; the Romanist, that the necessity of unity and Catholicity is emphasized; and so on through the whole long list.

It appears, then, that almost any person, no matter what his peculiarity of belief, can find room enough in this Church, providing only that he sincerely accepts the cardinal doctrines of the Catholic Creeds, grammatically and historically interpreted, and will tolerate the eccentricities and whims of others, who, like himself, believe that the salvation of the world depends upon some little pet idea. If a man can make up his mind to live and let live, he can ride into the Episcopal Church on almost any hobby, and remain mounted without fear of molestation during the remainder of life. Hobbyists are never excluded from a truly comprehensive and Catholic Church such as ours. They often exclude themselves because they are too narrow, intolerant and self-willed to remain where others, as well as they, have liberty.

But, notwithstanding all the apparently irreconcilable and conflicting elements to be found in the Episcopal Church, there is as much harmony and brotherly love among us as in any one of all the bodies of Christians. The Rev. Dr. Shields, the Princeton Professor, whose writings upon the subject of Church Unity have attracted so much attention, bears generous testimony to the truth of this. He says: "Differences which have elsewhere issued in sectarianism, are somehow restrained like balanced forces, or blended like discordant harmony. Episcopalians, Presbyterians, and Congregationalists, in their relation as Denominationalists, are in a chronic state of antagonism and irritation; but the very same Christians or others like them, in their relations as Churchmen, holding to the unity of the Church, simply lose all their sectarian rancor without losing their distinctive beliefs. Denominational variety is thus visibly made consistent with Church Unity."

This remarkable unity, in spite of the widest diversity, is accounted for by the fact, that we agree in recognizing the inherited Apostles' and Nicene Creeds as containing the essentials of doctrine, from which there can be no departure, and in allowing almost unbounded liberty of opinion, respecting all matters, that are not touched upon in these summaries of the "Faith once delivered to the Saints." It is also largely due, as Professor Shields points out, to the fact that we have the Historic Episcopate as a center of unity. "It is not," says he, "a matter of speculation. We have before us all the while, the object lesson of a unifying Episcopate."

There is, therefore, nothing which partakes of the character of mere enthusiasm and experiment, much less of bigotry, in our proposition that all Christians should unite upon the ground now occupied by the Protestant Episcopal Church. For, so far as this Church is concerned, unity is impossible upon any other ground, and, as for almost all other bodies that accept the Divinity of Christ, it is possible here.

But in showing that the Episcopal Church is destined to become the all-embracing form of organized Christianity in the United States, we may call attention to the significant fact that she is already dominant in our largest city, and is rapidly becoming so in all great centers of population. In New York, the increase of population in five years has been 15.38 per cent. The increase of Church membership, all Churches except the Episcopal, has been only 3.12 per cent., while including the Episcopal, it has been 13.03 per cent. But the increase of the Episcopal alone was 31.74 per cent., double that of the population, and nearly treble that of all the Protestant Denominations put together.*

There can be no question that in the leading city of the country, the Church is the most powerful of the religious forces. Leaving out of the list the Christian bodies which represent current foreign immigration, her proportionate lead is even greater than it appears from the following full list of houses of worship which the various Denominations of New York City had respectively in the years 1871 and 1894:

	NUMBER OF CHURCHES IN 1871.	NUMBER OF CHURCHES IN 1894.
Episcopalian	74	103
Presbyterian	51	70
Methodist	50	65
Roman Catholic	40	84
Baptist	30	50
Jewish	25	46
Reformed Dutch	20	27
Lutheran	15	21
Congregational	5	7
Universalist	5	3
Unitarian	4	3
Friends	3	2
Miscellaneous	18	41
Totals	340	522

Now it will be admitted by the observing and reflecting that our great cities exercise a moulding influence

* Appendix XXVI.

over the inhabitants of smaller towns, villages and the country. If, therefore, the Protestant Episcopal type of religion prevails at the close of the nineteenth century in New York, it is probable that by the close of the twentieth century it will do so in all the other greater cities —it does so now in Philadelphia—and that it will be the dominant religion of the country in the course of time.

The history of the spread of Christianity plainly teaches that no body of Christians which is losing ground or falling behind in our great cities, however prosperous it may be in smaller centers of population and in the country, can possibly become the Church of the Reconcilation to American Christians. In the Roman Empire the inhabitants of the smaller towns, villages and country were the last to give up their heathen religion and to embrace Christianity. Long after the Christian religion had been dominant in Rome, Alexandria, Ephesus, Antioch and Constantinople, the "pagans" or, to translate the word, the "inhabitants of the country," continued in heathenism. But in time Christianity became the religion of the whole Empire. Hence we argue that, as the Protestant Episcopal type of religion is now dominant in our greater cities, when sufficient time has elapsed for history to repeat itself, this type will also prevail throughout the United States.

Again, a strong argument in support of the claim that our Savior's prophecy, "They shall become one flock and one Shepherd," will be realized in the Anglican Communion, may be founded upon the fact that the English civilization seems destined to become universal, and so the unifier of all the nations of the earth. The marvelous spread of the English language would seem abundantly to justify this assertion, extravagant as it may appear at first sight. It is stated that within the present century the number of those who spoke our tongue at its beginning has been multiplied six times— from 21,000,000 in the year 1800 to 126,000,000 in A. D. 1894. French, in the same period, has not quite doubled; German, a little more than doubled; Russia keeps close pace with Germany, having risen from 30,000,000 to 70,000,000. Of the 162,000,000 people who are estimated to have been using the seven leading European languages in A. D. 1800, the English speakers were less than 13 per cent., while the Spanish were 16, the Germans, 18.4, the Russians, 18.9 and French, 19.6. This aggregate population has now grown to 400,-000,000 of which the English-speaking people number 126,000,000. From 13 per cent., we have advanced to 31 per cent. The French speech is now used by 50,000,000 people; the German by about 70,000,-000; the Spanish by 40,000,000; the Russian by 70,-000,000; the Italian by about 30,000,000; and the Portuguese by about 13,000,000. Thus the English language is now used by nearly twice as many people as any of the others.

In his history of the English People, Mr. Green forecasts the future of the race in these terms: "Before half a century is over, it will change the face of the world. As two hundred millions of Englishmen fill the valley of the Mississippi, as fifty millions assert their lordship over Australia, their vast power will tell through Britain on the old world of Europe, whose nations will have shrunk into insignificance before it. What the issues of such a wide-world change may be, not even the wildest day-dreamer will dare to dream. But one issue is inevitable. In the centuries that lie before us, the primacy of the world will be with the English people. English institutions, English speech, English thoughts will become the main features of the political, the social, the intellectual life of mankind."*

Now we contend that the Anglican Communion will always follow and keep up with the English language, that in proportion as our civilization unifies the political world, our Church will reunite divided Christendom and Christianize heathenism. If it be asked why she, rather than one of the English-speaking Denominations, may aspire to become the Church of the Reconciliation, the ready answer is found in the simple fact that she is the Historic, the Catholic, the Mother Church of our race. For, other things being equal, it is in the nature of things that her children and grand-children should gather around her rather than about any one of themselves. And how much more likely is this to be the case when, as in this instance, the Mother has so many and great advantages, as is evident from the fact that many of her distinctive features, after having been long rejected by her wayward children, are now being commended and adopted. The Church that has been entwined about the very heart of the Anglo-Saxon nation and that of all its colonies through their entire history, is not likely to be abandoned at this late date by such a conservative race as we are, for some one of the many organizations of the last three hundred years, none of which have taken any hold upon our people as a whole. The Anglican Communion always has been, is now, and ever will be, the dominant religious influence with English-speaking people, and there is as much reason for believing that in the course of time it will become all-embracing as for the belief that ultimately ours will be the universal language. Certainly our civilization cannot assume world-wide proportions without the Church doing the same, for she is its foundation.

---

* Appendix XXVII.

In a day when the divisions of Western Christendom are almost universally deplored, and when those whose ancestors went out from the Anglican Communion, represent the "Historic Episcopate" to be almost the only thing which prevents them from returning to the fold of the Mother Church, the fact that the great non-Episcopal Reformers and their co-laborers were Presbyterians from necessity, not preference, should be more generally known than it is. "Our Churches," writes a distinguished Protestant teacher, "did not embrace the Presbyterian discipline from dislike of Episcopacy, or because it seemed to be opposed to the Gospel, or to be less profitable to the Church, or less suitable to the condition of the Lord's true fold, but because they were compelled by necessity." Luther intended simply a temporary departure from the Episcopal *régime*. Calvin made application to the English Episcopate, and John Wesley to a Greek Bishop for Consecration.

It is not improbable that some arrangement would have been made for the granting of Calvin's request, had his letter not fallen into the hands of unprincipled sympathizers with Rome, who forged an insulting rejection of it. Says Archbishop Abbot: "Perusing some papers of our predecessor, Matthew Parker, we find that John Calvin and others, of the Protestant Churches of Germany, and elsewhere, would have had Episcopacy, if permitted, but could not upon several accounts; partly, fearing the other princes of the Roman Catholic faith would have joined with the Emperor and the rest of the Popish Bishops, to have depressed the same; partly, being newly reformed, and not settled, they had not sufficient wealth to support Episcopacy, by reason of their daily persecutions. Another, and a main cause was, they would not have any Popish

hands laid over their Clergy. And, whereas John Calvin
had sent a letter in King Edward VI.'s reign, to have
conferred with the Clergy of England about some things
to this effect, two Bishops, namely, Gardiner and Bonner,
intercepted the same, whereby Mr. Calvin's offerture
perished; and he received an answer, as if it had been
from the reformed divines of those times, wherein they
checked him, and slighted his proposals. From which
time John Calvin and the Church of England were at
variance on several points, which otherwise, through
God's mercy, had been qualified, if those papers of his
proposals had been discovered unto the Queen's Majesty
during John Calvin's life. But being not discovered
until or about the sixth year of her Majesty's reign, her
Majesty much lamented they were not found sooner;
which she expressed before her Council at the same time,
in the presence of her great friends, Sir Henry Sidney
and Sir William Cecil."

It is also worthy of note that our Church in America
to-day stands with the authority of the Presbyterate
fully recognized, precisely as the English Presbyterians
of A. D. 1660 asked that it might be in the Church of England, when they professed that they would be content
with the Anglican Episcopate, provided such place and
such authority were secured to the body of the Presbyterate. "In their celebrated manifesto favoring a
'moderate Episcopacy,' they acknowledge that this
was 'agreeable to the Scriptures and the primitive government, and likeliest to be the way of a more universal concord, if ever the Churches on earth arrive at such
a blessing.' Their idea of a 'moderate Episcopacy'
was precisely that which has been restored in America,
namely, Episcopacy 'conjunct with synodical government;' the Presbytery and the Laity being admitted
to synods."

It is impossible in the light of the constant and uniformly consistent example and utterances of the Wesleys, to believe they ever intended their followers to separate from the Church of England, or that John Wesley intended to be understood as conveying Episcopal authority upon Dr. Coke, when, by imposition of hands, he set this Priest of the English Church apart for the superintendency of the Methodist Societies in America. The Wesley brothers lived and died in the Communion and Priesthood of the Church. That Charles Wesley did this, has never been questioned, and that John Wesley did so, is evident from his own reiterated statement and deathbed prayer. In answer to his followers who wanted to go out, and to his enemies who accused him of meditating an exodus, he always replied to the day of his death: "I never had any design of separating from the Church. I have now no such design, and I declare once more, that I live and die a member of the Church of England, and that none who regard my judgment or advice will ever separate from it." And when his last hour came, he prayed: "We thank Thee, O Lord, for these and all Thy mercies. Bless the Church and King. And grant us truth and peace, through Jesus Christ our Lord forever and ever." We also have the conclusive evidence afforded by the circular letter addressed by the Methodist Conference to the Societies, in which they say: "Our venerable father, who is gone to his great reward, lived and died a member and a friend of the Church of England. His attachment to it was so strong and so unshaken, that nothing but irresistible necessity induced him to deviate from it in any degree."

Methodists claim that Mr. Wesley intended to consecrate Dr. Coke, his brother in the Priesthood, a Bishop, when he blessed him upon his departure to assume the

direction of the American societies. But it is difficult
to reconcile this view with his words as quoted above,
or with his rebuke of Mr. Asbury, when he began to assume the title and exercise the functions of a Bishop,
upon the ground of his ordination by Dr. Coke. "How
can you," said Mr. Wesley, "how dare you suffer yourself to be called a Bishop? I shudder, I start at the
very thought! Men may call me a knave or a fool, a
rascal, a scoundrel, and I am content; but they shall
never, by my consent, call me Bishop. For my sake,
for God's sake, for Christ's sake, put a full end to this.
Let the Presbyterians do what they please, but let the
Methodists know their calling better."

Even if it be granted that Wesley did intend to invest Coke with the Episcopal character, it must be
admitted that he was the only person ordained to the
Episcopate by him, and that Francis Asbury was the
only so-called Bishop ordained by Coke. Methodist
Bishops must then trace their authority to Asbury,
whose Episcopacy was thus earnestly repudiated by the
founder of Methodism, and with it, of course, their own
pretensions to any office higher than the general superintendency which Asbury was permitted to retain. Nor
must we lose sight of the significant fact that, according
to Wesley's letter of instruction, Coke was sent to America to minister to persons "who adhered to the doctrine
and discipline of the Church of England." He was not
commissioned to found the Methodist Episcopal Church.
It is said that there is not at this time a single descendant of the Wesleys in any of the Methodist Communions.
Three grandsons of Charles Wesley have been Clergymen
of the Church of England. In this they were following
the precept and example of their distinguished ancestor.

From this it will appear that there is not a Lutheran,
or a Presbyterian, or a Methodist in the United States

who would not, if he followed the express preference of the man whom he venerates as the founder and pillar of his Denomination, find his way into the Episcopal Church. The same also might be said of Congregationalists, for Brown who led them out, in his old age, returned to the fold and ministry of the Church. "The Baptist, Congregational and Methodist Churches could construct no platform of Church Unity more Catholic, practical and helpful than the Quadrilateral; while the Lutheran, Reformed and Presbyterian Churches could adopt no other without largely ignoring their own standards and history."

In conclusion, let me answer a practical question which every one, who recognizes the evils of a divided Church and desires to do the will of Christ, should ask himself: "What can I do to bring about the visible organic unity among Christians for which our blessed Lord prayed, and upon which He makes the evangelization and salvation of the world to depend?"

As you no doubt have anticipated, my answer to this, the greatest question which a Christian of these days can ask himself, so far as it relates to the sons and daughters of the Protestant Episcopal Church, is: Pray and work for the return of your brothers and sisters of every Denomination to the Mother Church of the English-speaking race. And to those who are living in separation from her, let me say: Study the claims of the Mother Church upon you, and when you have become convinced that they are superior to those of the Denomination to which you belong, return without delay to your ancestral home where a warm welcome awaits you. Then others will follow your example, and others theirs, and so on in increasing numbers, according to the law of natural progression, until the way will be prepared for the return of whole families of the Mother Church's wayward children. It will be hard for you to take the step. In many cases it will require much courage and great sacrifices; but—I speak from personal experience, and there are many others, some of whom are to be found in almost every community, who will bear witness to the same effect—when once you are within the embrace of the dear Mother Church, there will be no regret, but your satisfaction and happiness will find expression in the beautiful poem written by Bishop Coxe, after he had taken the step which I am advising, you to take:

"I love the Church, the Holy Church,
    The Saviour's spotless bride,
And O, I love her palaces,
    Through all the world so wide.

"Unbroken is her lineage,
    Her warrants clear as when
Thou, Saviour, didst go up on high,
    And give good gifts to men.

"Here clothed in innocence they stand,
    Thine Holy Orders three,
To rule and feed, Thy flock, O Christ,
    And ever watch for Thee.

"I love the Church, the Holy Church,
    That o'er our life presides,
The birth, the bridal and the grave,
    And many an hour besides.

"Be mine through life to live in her,
    And when the Lord shall call,
To die in her, the Spouse of Christ,
    The Mother of us all."

THE CHURCH FOR AMERICANS.

APPENDICES AND SUPPLEMENTARY ARTICLES.

I. LIGHTFOOT: APOSTOLIC ORIGIN OF THE THREE-
FOLD MINISTRY.

II. BISHOP GRISWOLD ON THE PRESBYTERIAN HY-
POTHESIS.

III. WASHINGTON A COMMUNICANT.

IV. FRANKLIN AN EPISCOPALIAN.

V. JEFFERSON AN EPISCOPALIAN.

VI. THE CONSTITUTION OF THE UNITED STATES AND
THE FAITH OF ITS FRAMERS.

VII. GROWTH OF THE EPISCOPAL CHURCH.

VIII. NON-EPISCOPALIAN ENCOMIUMS ON THE PRAYER
BOOK.

IX. JOHN WESLEY ALWAYS AN EPISCOPALIAN.

X. POPE PIUS IV. AND THE ENGLISH PRAYER BOOK.

XI. GREEK CATHOLICS AND ANGLICAN ORDERS.

XII. JOHN WESLEY ON THE MINISTERIAL OFFICE.

XIII. THE NINE HUNDRED AND NINETY-NINE YEARS'
LEASE.

XIV. CONTINUITY OF THE ENGLISH CHURCH PROVED
BY THE UNINTERRUPTED SUCCESSION OF HER BISHOPS.

LIGHTFOOT: APOSTOLIC ORIGIN OF THE THREEFOLD MINISTRY.

LECTURE III; PAGE 182.

THE following self-explanatory correspondence, which appeared in the "Church Guardian," of Montreal, and was republished in the "Living Church," of Chicago, will be of interest to many:

LOCKEPORT, N. S., March 1, 1887.

To THE EDITOR OF THE 'CHURCH GUARDIAN:'

SIR: Having been shown a speech by a Presbyterian minister, in which he claimed that Dr. Lightfoot, Bishop of Durham, acknowledged that Presbyterian order was the rule in Apostolic times, I wrote his Lordship, and received from his chaplain the following reply, which may be of much service in refuting the views imputed to the great orientalist, historian and commentator.   S. G.

———

AUKLAND CASTLE.

THE REV. S. GIBBONS.

SIR: The Bishop of Durham finds to his great regret that, owing to the great pressure of work by which he is surrounded, your letter respecting the Christian ministry has remained unanswered.

The Bishop desires me to say that so far from establishing as the fact that 'Presbyterianism was the first form of Church government,' his essay goes to prove that Deacons existed before Priests, and yet no one would contend that Church government by Deacons was the 'first form,' hence the writer's argument, based on priority of time, proves too much for his taste. It is, however, generally allowed that the names of Presbuteros and Episcopos in the New Testament are sometimes synonymous, Acts, 20: 17; I Peter, 5: 1, 2; I Tim., 3: 1–13, where the Apostle passes at once to Deacons from Episcopos, Titus, 1: 5, 7; but even in the times covered by the New Testament writings, we see in the lifetime of the Apostles individuals singled out to preside over certain Churches and to exercise powers of ordination, government and presidency, as Titus at Crete, James at Jerusalem, Timothy at Ephesus; and though the evidence is necessarily limited, we find in Asia Minor Episcopacy pure and simple, appointed and established, no doubt by the influence of St. John, at the date of the Ignatian Epistles, and its institution can be plainly traced as far back as the closing years of the first century.

We see the threefold ministry traced to Apostolic direction, and this bears out the truth of our Prayer Book Preface to the Ordinal, and is the belief of the Anglican community.

I regret that in a brief letter so much must be passed over and so inadequate an account be given of so interesting and absorbing a subject.

But enough has been said to prove that the Presbyterian's deduction from the Bishop of Durham's article is not justified by the facts.   Yours faithfully

J. R. HARMER, Chaplain.

JANUARY 20, 1887.

II.

BISHOP GRISWOLD ON THE PRESBYTERIAN HYPOTHESIS.

LECTURE III; PAGE 182.

"IT is often affirmed but has never been proved, that the ministers of Christ were, at first, all of one grade, and that the Bishops usurped the authority, which, it is acknowledged, they, in the early ages, possessed. But this is absurd, and altogether incredible. It is absurd to suppose that those, now called Bishops, made such a change. Because, if the government of the Church was left by the Apostles in the hands of Presbyters, they, the Presbyters, must have made the change. On this supposition, there were no Bishops to abuse power; the Presbyters usurped authority, and made the change. If a thing so strange and so wicked was done at all, it was done by Presbyterians or Congregationalists. Those who advance this position virtually say, that within one or two centuries at most, after the government was put into their hands, they all, in every country, agreed in changing it to what Christ never intended. They certainly do very little honor to that mode of Church government, by supposing it so defective and inefficient as to be so soon relinquished.

"It must, too, be difficult for us to believe, that, in the first three centuries, men should have been ambitious of the Episcopate, when its worldly advantages were so small, and its sacrifices and perils so great. Martyrdom in those ages might almost be considered as annexed to a bishopric. The general practice of the persecutor was to smite the shepherd, that the sheep might be scattered; the Bishop was usually the first led to tortures and to death. How can we, in reason, believe that under such circumstances, so great a change should be made in the government of the Church? that the holy martyrs of that time, which truly 'tried men's souls,' should either attempt or desire to alter the institutions of Christ? And had such a change by some Churches been attempted, it seems morally impossible that it should have become general. And yet we are sure from all ancient history, that Episcopacy was general from a very early period down to the Reformation. During the first fifteen centuries, it is not easy to name any one part of Christianity, in which all Christians were more generally united than in what we now call Episcopacy. Were we to admit that so great and material a change was made in our religion, without being recorded in history, we might well fear that other great changes were also made; that even the Scriptures were altered. If all the Churches would agree in corrupting one part, why not in corrupting another part? In any part of the first three centuries, it would have been as difficult to produce such a change, as it would be in our day. And to me, certainly such a change, so silent, so peaceable, and so general, without opposition, or any historical record, is a moral impossibility.   Should there be any here who think differently on this point, they will not, I trust, regret having heard what we think on a subject which so much concerns us all.   Nothing will tend more to unite Christians in love, than candidly hearing from each other the hope that is in them.   And, indeed, if differing Denominations of Christians are ever brought to strive together for the faith of the Gospel, it will be by their first uniting in the government, whatever they may decide it to be, which God has set in the Church."

III.

WASHINGTON A COMMUNICANT.

LECTURE V; PAGE 289.

IT is not disputed that Washington was an adherent of the Episcopal Church and a regular and devout attendant upon her Services, but the statement that he was also a Communicant is sometimes questioned.   In an interesting contribution to the "Living Church" of June 29, 1895, the Rev. Wm. E. Hooker settles this question.   He says: "I have in my library this volume, entitled · 'Memoirs of Washington, by his adopted son, George Washington Parke Custis.'   There is as well a memoir of the author, by his daughter, with notes by Benson J. Lossing.   The work was published in 1859.   On page 173, the writer speaks of Washington as a strict observer of the Lord's Day, and of his habit of attending public worship; of his respect for the Clergy; of his friendship for our Bishop White and the Roman Archbishop Carroll of Baltimore.   Then in a foot note, on the same page, is this statement: 'Washington was a member *in full Communion* of the Protestant Episcopal Church and was for many years before and after the Revolution, a vestryman in Truro parish, whose Church, Pohick, built under his supervision, is yet standing.'"   "I have before me," he continues, "the original drawing of the ground plan and elevation of that Church, made by Washington himself. He was also a Vestryman, previous to the Revolution, in Fairfax parish, whose Church, wherein he frequently worshipped, is yet standing in the city of Alexandria. While President of the United States and residing in New York, he attended St. Paul's Church; in Philadelphia, Christ Church." "A member in full Communion" is merely another way of designating a Communicant. And this statement is unqualifiedly made by one of Washington's own family, his son by adoption. Mr. Custis, himself a Churchman, died in 1857.

To this weighty testimony cited by Mr. Hooker, may be added a passage almost equally conclusive to which the late learned Dr. Bolles calls attention in his "Washington, A Centennial Discourse:" "In the twelfth volume of the writings of Washington, Sparks has a remarkable note as follows: 'I shall here insert a letter written me by a lady who lived twenty years ago in Washington's family, and who was his adopted daughter and the granddaughter of Mrs. Washington. The writer of this letter married Lawrence Lewis, the nephew of Washington.' It is dated Woodlawn, February 26, 1833. It is too long for reproduction in these notes. I give some extracts from it, namely: 'My mother resided two years at Mount Vernon after her marriage. I have heard her say that General Washington always received the Sacrament with my grandmother before the Revolution.'"

The Honorable Mr. Sewall of New Hampshire said: "To crown all his virtues he had the deepest sense of religion. He was a constant attendant on public worship and a communicant at the Lord's Table. I shall never forget the impression made by seeing this leader of our hosts bending in this house of prayer in humble adoration of the God of armies and the Author of our salvation."

General Porterfield, his aid, testifies: "General Washington was a pious man, a member of the Episcopal Church. I saw him myself on his knees receive the Lord's Supper at Philadelphia. As brigade inspector I often waited on Washington in the army, and going once, without warning, to his headquarters, I found him on his knees at his morning devotions. I was often in his company under very exciting circumstances, and never heard him swear or profane the name of God in any way."

Major Popham, a Revolutionary officer much with Washington, testifies that, "he attended the same Church with Washington during his Presidency, that the President often communed, and that he had the privilege of kneeling and communing with him."

Mr. Edward Everett in his famous oration on the "Life and Character of Washington," says: "Washington was brought up in the Episcopal Communion, and was a member of the vestry of two Churches. He was at all times a regular attendant upon public worship, and an occasional partaker of the Communion."

The Honorable R. C. Winthrop, who was one of the orators at the laying of the corner stone of Washington's monument, and also at its dedication, gives the following testimony: "True to his friends, true to his country and to himself; fearing God, believing in Christ, no stranger to private devotion, or to *the holiest offices of the Church to which he belonged;* but ever gratefully acknowledging a Divine aid and direction in everything he attempted, and in everything he accomplished. What epithet, what attribute could be added to that consummate character, to commend it as an example above all other characters in human history!"

The learned Historiographer of the American Episcopal Church says: "That Washington was a communicant of the Church previous to the war of the Revolution, admits of no doubt, if any regard is to be paid to the testimony of numerous witnesses who could not have been deceived. That he was not a frequent or regular communicant after the War and while in public office, is equally certain, but the testimony adduced by the celebrated Dr. Chapman, a distinguished Clergyman of the Church, is conclusive as to his occasional reception. Dr. Chapman's words are as follows: "From the lips of a lady of undoubted veracity, yet living, and a worthy communicant of the Church, I received the interesting fact that soon after the close of the Revolutionary War *she saw him* partake of the consecrated symbols of the Body and Blood of Christ, in Trinity Church, in the city of New York."

"Major Popham's testimony 'that he believed without a doubt that they both, President and Lady Washington, received the Holy Communion' at St. Paul's, New York, comes from one who had every possible opportunity to know whereof he affirmed."

IV.

FRANKLIN AN EPISCOPALIAN.

LECTURE V; PAGE 290.

IN a letter addressed to his daughter, under date of November 8, 1754, Dr. Benjamin Franklin writes: "Go constantly to Church. The act of devotion in the Common Prayer Book is your principal business there, and, if properly attended to, will do more towards amending the heart than sermons generally do. I wish you would never miss the prayer days." Bishop Coleman points out that "it was he who, when the Convention of 1787, for framing the Federal Constitution, had made but small progress in its business, proposed that the Clergy of Philadelphia should be invited to say prayers at the morning sessions of the Convention." After the Revolution, Franklin was at the pains of revising the Prayer Book to suit the altered conditions and his own ideas, which, to say the least, were somewhat eccentric. Our

Historiographer says : " Bishop White had this work in his hand when the 'Proposed Book' was in process of preparation by the committee consisting of Provost Smith, of the University of Pennsylvania, William White and Charles H. Wharton, the latter being the first convert from Romanism to the faith of the American Church."

V.

JEFFERSON AN EPISCOPALIAN.

LECTURE V; PAGE 289.

A CORRESPONDENT of "The Churchman" recently communicated to that paper the following extract from Dr. John Stoughton's "History of Religion in England:" " Bishop Wilberforce, in his 'American Church,' p. 175, calls him the 'Deist Jefferson,' but I have before me an autograph letter by Jefferson, dated August 10, 1823, in which, replying to some application for pecuniary aid, he says :

'The principle that every religious sect is to maintain its own teachers and institutions is too reasonable, and too well established in our country to need justification. I have been, from my infancy, a member of the Episcopalian Church, and to that I owe and make my contributions. Were I to go beyond that limit in favor of any other sectarian Institution' I should be equally bound to do so for every other, and their number is beyond the faculties of any individual. I believe, therefore, that in this, as in every other case, everything will be better conducted if left to those immediately interested. On these grounds I trust that your candor will excuse my returning the inclosed paper without my subscription ; and that you will accept the assurance of my great personal respect and esteem.   'Th. Jefferson.' "

The publication of this letter, says Bishop Perry, elicited from the granddaughter of Jefferson, Sarah N. Randolph, who was engaged in preparing a complete edition of her ancestor's works, a letter under date of May 19, 1888, confirmatory of the statement made in the text. The closing paragraph of this letter is as follows :

"It may interest you to know that I have Mr. Jefferson's little pocket Prayer Book, which he used in his constant attendance at the Episcopal Church, in Charlottesville. For a long time, too, there was in the possession of my family a little folding chair or camp stool of his own invention, so made that it looked, when it closed, like a stout cane. This he carried in hand, though on horseback, and used as his seat in Church. Pardon this long letter with which I have presumed to inflict a stranger, and believe me to be,

Yours respectfully,   SARAH N. RANDOLPH."

VI.

THE CONSTITUTION OF THE UNITED STATES AND THE FAITH OF ITS FRAMERS.

LECTURE V; PAGES 278-292.

IN his little publication, "The Faith of the Framers of the Constitution of the United States," the Bishop of Iowa gives a most interesting account of the Church relationship, so far as it can be ascertained by the most painstaking investigation, of those who in Convention assembled formed our Constitution and affixed their signatures to this all-important national document. I give the result of Dr. Perry's investigation without the proofs:

New Hampshire — John Langdon, Congregationalist; Nicholas Gilman, Congregationalist.

Massachusetts — Nathaniel Gorham, Congregationalist; Rufus King, Episcopalian.

Connecticut — William Samuel Johnson, Episcopalian; Roger Sherman, Congregationalist.

New York — Alexander Hamilton, Episcopalian.

New Jersey — William Livingstone, Presbyterian; David Brearly, Episcopalian; William Patterson, Presbyterian; Jonathan Dayton, Episcopalian.

Pennsylvania — Benjamin Franklin, Episcopalian ; Thomas Mifflin, Episcopalian ; Robert Morris, Episcopalian ; George Clymer, Episcopalian ; Thomas Fitzsimons, Roman Catholic ; Jared Ingersoll, probably Episcopalian. His descendants are Episcopalians, and have been so for several generations. James Wilson, Episcopalian ; Gouverneur Morris, Episcopalian.

Delaware — George Read, Episcopalian ; Gunning Bedford, Jr., Presbyterian ; John Dickinson, originally a Quaker, but in later life inclined toward the Episcopal Church. He was a liberal contributor to the funds of the Church Corporation for the relief of the widows and orphans of our Clergy. Richard Bassett, originally an Episcopalian, but later in life a Methodist ; Jacob Brown, Episcopalian.

Maryland — James McHenry, Presbyterian ; Daniel of Jenifer, Episcopalian ; Daniel Carroll, Roman Catholic.

Virginia — George Washington, Episcopalian ; John Blair, Episcopalian ; James Madison, Jr., Episcopalian.

North Carolina — William Blount, Episcopalian ; Richard D. Spright, Episcopalian ; Hugh Williamson, Presbyterian.

South Carolina — John Rutledge, Episcopalian ; Charles C. Pinckney, Episcopalian ; Charles Pinckney, Episcopalian ; Pierce Butler, Episcopalian.

Georgia — William Few, Episcopalian ; Abraham Baldwin, Congregationalist.

This list, as Bishop Perry observes, shows that about two-thirds of those who framed and attested by their signatures the Constitution of the United States, were connected with the Episcopal Church. He gives the names of some ten or twelve more or less distinguished members of the Convention who were Episcopalians, but who, owing to necessary absence at the time of the completion of the work, did not affix their signatures to the Constitution. Surely it must be conceded that the learned Bishop is right when he says : "No other religious body in the land, if judged in the light of history, has any claim to be compared with, or to be regarded as the American Church." *

---

* See Appendix XXIV.

VII.

GROWTH OF THE EPISCOPAL CHURCH.

Lecture V; Page 304.

OUR growth during the ten years covered by the last census, 1880–1890, has been indeed phenomenal as will appear from the following tabulated statement of communicants:

	1880	1890	Per cent. of increase.
Alabama	3,955	6,196	56+
Arkansas	1,010	2,200	117+
California	4,323	11,239	159+
Colorado	1,758	4,366	154+
Connecticut	20,953	27,374	30+
Dakotas (two)	1,746	3,680	110+
Delaware	2,026	2,943	45+
Florida	1,789	4,409	146+
Georgia	4,536	5,975	31+
Illinois	11,320	20,040	76+
Indiana	3,830	6,126	59+
Iowa	4,203	6,526	55+
Kansas	2,187	3,072	40+
Kentucky	4,295	7,079	64+
Louisiana	3,782	5,256	38+
Maine	2,170	3,080	41+
Maryland and Dist. of Columbia	23,573	30,956	31+
Massachusetts	18,076	29,487	63+
Michigan	10,749	18,482	71+
Minnesota	5,243	10,973	109+
Mississippi	2,386	3,281	37+
Missouri	5,413	9,356	72+
Montana	575	1,514	163+
Nebraska	1,926	4,274	121+
Nevada	315	576	82+
New Hampshire	2,066	2,894	40+

	1880	1890	Per cent. of increase.
New Jersey	16,632	29,821	78+
New Mexico and Arizona	175	696	297+
New York	87,364	131,437	50+
North Carolina	5,836	8,410	44+
Ohio	11,693	18,057	54+
Oregon	737	2,265	207+
Pennsylvania	39,251	58,875	44+
Rhode Island	6,821	10,388	52+
South Carolina	4,686	5,737	22+
Tennessee	3,500	6,044	72+
Texas	4,388	7,379	68+
Utah	385	767	99+
Vermont	3,488	4,244	21+
Virginia	13,951	19,042	37+
Washington	339	2,585	662+
West Virginia	1,945	3,109	59+
Wisconsin	7,133	10,609	48+
Wyoming and Idaho	371	1,733	367+

VIII.

NON-EPISCOPALIAN ENCOMIUMS ON THE PRAYER BOOK.

LECTURE VI; PAGE 318.

THE following passages bearing testimony to the unrivaled excellency of the Book of Common Prayer, are collected from the writings of representatives of nearly all the chief bodies of Christians, or from what unbiased literary critics have to say about our Liturgy. The first quotation shall be from Taine's " History of English Literature." The author of this famous work, by common consent the best upon the subject, was, I suppose, a French Protestant. I give what he has to say somewhat at length, because of his extracts from the Prayer

Book which will enable those not acquainted with it, to form something of an independent estimation of its merits.

"This Prayer Book is an admirable book, in which the full spirit of the Reformation breathes out, where, beside the moving tenderness of the Gospel, and the manly accents of the Bible, throb the profound emotion, the grave eloquence, the noble-mindedness, the restrained enthusiasm of the heroic and poetic souls who had rediscovered Christianity, and had passed near the fire of martyrdom. 'Almighty and most merciful Father, we have erred and strayed from Thy ways like lost sheep. We have followed too much the devices and desires of our own hearts. We have offended against Thy holy laws. We have left undone those things which we ought to have done; and we have done those things which we ought not to have done; and there is no health in us. But Thou, O Lord, have mercy upon us, miserable offenders. Spare Thou them, O God, which confess their faults. Restore Thou them that are penitent, according to Thy promises declared unto mankind in Christ Jesus our Lord. And grant, O most merciful Father, for His sake, that we may hereafter live a godly, righteous, and sober life.' 'Almighty and everlasting God, who hatest nothing that Thou hast made, and dost forgive the sins of all them that are penitent, create and make in us new and contrite hearts, that we worthily lamenting our sins, and acknowledging our wretchedness, may obtain of Thee, the God of all mercy, perfect remission and forgiveness.' The same idea of sin, repentance, and moral renovation continually recurs; the master-thought is always that of the heart humbled before invisible justice, and only imploring His grace in order to obtain His relief. Such a state of mind ennobles man, and introduces a sort of impassioned gravity in all the important actions of his life. Listen to the Liturgy of the deathbed, of Baptism, of marriage; the latter first: 'Wilt thou have this woman to thy wedded wife, to live together after God's ordinance, in the holy estate of Matrimony? Wilt thou love her, comfort her, honor, and keep her in sickness and in health; and, forsaking all other, keep thee only unto her, so long as ye both shall live?' These are genuine, honest, and conscientious words. No mystic languor, here or elsewhere. This religion is not made for women who dream, yearn, and sigh, but for men who examine themselves, act and have confidence, confidence in some one more just than themselves. When a man is sick, and his flesh is weak, the Priest comes to him, and says: 'Dearly beloved, know this that Almighty God is the Lord of life and death, and of all things to them pertaining, as youth, strength, health, age, weakness and sickness. Wherefore, whatsoever your sickness is, know you certainly, that it is God's visitation. And for what cause soever this sickness is sent unto you; whether it be to try your patience for the example of others, or else it be sent unto you to correct and amend in you whatsoever doth offend the eyes of your heavenly Father; know you certainly, that if you truly repent you of your sins, and bear your sickness patiently, trusting in God's mercy, submitting yourself wholly unto His will, it shall turn to your profit, and help you forward in the right way that leadeth unto everlasting life.' A great mysterious sentiment, a sort of sublime epic, void of images, shows darkly amid these probings of the conscience; I mean a glimpse of the Divine government and of the invisible world, the only existences, the only realities, in spite of bodily appearances and of the brute chance, which seems to jumble all things together. Man sees this beyond at distant intervals, and raises himself out of his mire, as though he had suddenly breathed a pure and strengthening atmosphere."

The "North British Review," a Scottish Presbyterian periodical, contained an article some time ago from which this is quoted: "The Liturgy is the choicest selection of what has proved to be best during a long lapse of time. Its Litanies and its Collects are the fruit of the most sublime piety, and the noblest gifts of language, tested by long sustained trial.

No single generation could have created, or could replace the Liturgy. It is the accumulation of the treasures with which the most diversified experience, the most fervent devotion, and the most exalted genius, have enriched the worship of prayer and praise during fifteen hundred years. Who, then, can overestimate its influence in perpetuating the sacred fire of Christian love and Christian faith among a whole people, or exaggerate its power in conserving the pure and Apostolic type of Christian worship."

Dr. Doddridge, an English Independent divine and expositor says of the Prayer Book : "The language is so plain as to be level to the capacity of the meanest, and yet the sense is so noble as to raise the capacity of the highest."

Rev. Albert Barnes, the great commentator among American Presbyterians, says : "We have always thought that there are Christian minds and hearts that would find more edification in the forms of worship in that Church than in any other. We have never doubted that many of the purest flames of devotion that rise from the earth, ascend from the Altars of the Episcopal Church, and that many of the purest spirits that the earth contains, minister at those Altars and breathe forth their prayers and praises in language consecrated by the use of piety for centuries."

Another Presbyterian, Professor Shields, of Princeton University, writes : "The English Liturgy, next to the English Bible, is the most wonderful product of the Reformation. The very fortunes of the book are the romance of history. As we trace its development, its rubrics seem dyed in the blood of martyrs ; its offices echo with polemic phrases ; its canticles mingle with the battle-cries of armed sects and factions ; and its successive revisions mark the career of dynasties, states and Churches. Cavalier, Covenanter and Puritan have crossed their swords over it ; scholars and soldiers, statesmen and Churchmen, kings and commoners, have united in defending it. England, Germany, Geneva, Scotland,

America, have, by turns, been the scene of its conflicts. Far
beyond the little island which was its birthplace, its influence
has been silently spreading in connection with great political
and religious changes, generation after generation, from land
to land, even where its name was never heard. At first sight,
indeed, the importance which this book has acquired, may
seem quite beyond its merits, as the Bible itself might appear,
to a superficial observer, a mere idol of bigotry and prejudice.
But the explanation is in both cases somewhat the same. It
is to be found in the fact that the Prayer Book, like the Sacred
Canon, is no merely individual production, nor even purely
human work, but an accumulation of choice writings, partly
Divine, partly human, expressing the religious mind of the
whole ancient and modern world, as enunciated by Prophets
and Apostles, Saints and Martyrs, and formulated by councils,
synods and conferences, all seeking heavenly light and guidance. Judaism has given to it its Lessons and Psalter; Christianity has added its Epistles and Gospels; Catholicism has
followed with its Canticles, Creeds and Collects; and Protestantism has completed it with its Exhortations, Confessions and
Thanksgivings. At the same time, each leading phase of the
Reformation has been impressed upon its composite materials.
Lutheranism has molded its Ritual; Calvinism has framed its
Doctrine; Episcopalianism has dominated both Ritual and
Doctrine; whilst Presbyterianism has subjected each to thorough revision. And the whole has been rendered into the
pure English and with the sacred fervor peculiar to the
earnest age in which it arose; has been wrought into a system
adapted to all classes of men, through all the vicissitudes of
life, and has been tested and hallowed by three centuries of
trial in every quarter of the globe. It would be strange if a
work which thus has its roots in the whole Church of the past,
should not be sending forth its branches into the whole Church
of the future; and anyone who will take the pains to study
its present adaptations, whatever may have been his preju-

dices, must admit that there is no other extant formulary which is so well fitted to become the rallying-point and standard of modern Christendom. In it are to be found the means, possibly the germs, of a just reorganization of Protestantism, as well as an ultimate reconciliation with the true Catholicism, such a Catholicism as shall have shed everything sectarian and national, and retained only what is common to the whole Church of Christ in all ages and countries. Whilst to the true Protestant it offers Evangelical doctrine, worship and unity, on the terms of the Reformation, it still preserves, for the true Catholic, the choicest formulas of antiquity, and to all Christians of every name opens a liturgical system at once Scriptural and reasonable, doctrinal and devotional, learned and vernacular, artistic and spiritual. It is not too much to say that were the problem given, to frame out of the imperfectly organized and sectarian Christianity of our times a liturgical model for the Communion of Saints in the one universal Church, the result might be expressed in some such compilation as the English Book of Common Prayer."

Some of the Methodists pronounced the Prayer Book Services to be "chaff" and so incapable of sustaining spiritual life. These received this contradiction and rebuke from John Wesley: "The prayers of the Church are not 'chaff;' they are substantial food for any who are alive unto God." In his preface to the "Sunday Service for the Methodists in America" which is simply an abridgment of the Prayer Book for convenient use in missionary fields, he says: "I believe there is no Liturgy in the world, either in ancient or modern language, which breathes more of solid, spiritual, rational piety than the Common Prayer of the Church of England." Elsewhere he says: "I hold all the doctrines of the Church of England. I love her Liturgy."

Dr. Adam Clarke, the most learned commentator among Wesley's followers, says: "It is the greatest effort of the Reformation, next to the translation of the Scriptures into the

English language. As a form of devotion it has no equal in any part of the Universal Church of God. It is founded on those doctrines which contain the sum and essence of Christianity, and speaks the language of the sublimest piety, and of the most refined devotional feeling. Next to the Bible it is the book of my understanding and of my heart."

Dr. Watson, another choice spirit of Methodism, the well-known author of the Theological Institutes, said: "Such a Liturgy makes the Service of God's house appear more like the business of the Lord's Day; and besides the aid it affords to the most devout and spiritual, a great body of Evangelical truth is, by constant use, laid up in the minds of children and ignorant people who, when at length they begin to pray under a religious concern, are already furnished with suitable, sanctifying, solemn and impressive petitions. Persons well acquainted with the Liturgy are certainly in a state of important preparation for the labors of a preacher, and their piety often takes a richer and more sober character from that circumstance."

Robert Hall, one of the brightest lights that ever shone among the Baptists, and one that would have been bright in any firmament, confesses that "the Evangelical purity of the Prayer Book, the chastened fervor of its devotions, and the majestic simplicity of its language, have combined to place it in the very first rank of uninspired compositions."

The following is from the memoirs of the learned Congregationalist, Professor Phelps: "The Liturgy of the Episcopal Church has become very precious to me. The depth of its meaning, it seems to me, nobody can fathom who has not experienced some great sorrow. We have lost much in parting with the prayers of the old Mother Church; and what have we gained in their place? I do not feel in extemporaneous prayer the deep undertone of devotion which rings out from the old Collects of the Church like the sound of ancient bells. I longed for, and prayed for, and worst of all, waited for, some sublime and revolutionary change of heart; and what that was, as a fact on a child's experience, I have not the remotest idea. If I had been trained in the Episcopal Church, I should at the time have been confirmed, and entered upon a consciously religious life, and grown up into Christian living of the Episcopal type."

This is the testimony of another gifted Congregationalist of this country, the Rev. Thomas K. Beecher: "The Episcopal Church offers for our use the most venerable Liturgy in the English tongue. The devotional treasures of the Roman Catholic Church are embalmed and buried in Latin. But in English there are no Lessons, Gospels, Psalms, Collects, Confessions, Thanksgivings, Prayers—in one word, no religious form book that can stand a moment in comparison with the Prayer Book of the Episcopal Church in the two-fold quality of richness and age. The proper name, because truly descriptive, for this Church would be the Church of the Prayer Book. As is the way with all other Churches, so here, the Church champions and leaders have many wise things to say about the Church and her prerogative. But the pious multitudes that frequent her courts are drawn thither mostly by love of the prayers and praises, the Litanies and Lessons of the Prayer Book. And, brethren of every name, I certify that you rarely hear in any Church a prayer spoken in English that is not indebted to the Prayer Book for some of its choicest periods. And further, I doubt whether life has in store for any of you an uplift so high, or downfall so deep, but that you can find company for your soul and fitting words for your lips among the treasures of this Book of Common Prayer. 'In all time of our tribulation; in all time of our prosperity; in the hour of death and in the day of judgment, Good Lord deliver us.' No transient observer can adequately value this treasure of a birthright Churchman; to be using to-day the self-same words that have through the centuries declared the faith, or made known the prayer, of that mighty multitude, who, 'being now delivered from the burden of flesh, are in joy and felicity;' to be baptized in early infancy and never to know a time when we were not recognized and welcome among the millions who have entered by the same door; to be confirmed in due time in a faith that has sustained a noble army of confessors, approving its worth through persecutions and prosperities, a strength to the tried and a chastening to the worldly-minded; to be married by an authority before which kings and peasants bow alike, asking benediction upon the covenant that, without respect of persons, binds by the same words of duty the highest and the lowest; to bring our newborn children as we were brought, to begin where we began, and to grow up to fill our places; to die in the faith, and almost hear the Gospel words soon to be spoken over one's own grave as over the thousand times ten thousand of those who have slept in Jesus. In short, to be a devout and consistent Churchman, brings a man through aisles fragrant with holy association, and accompanied by a long procession of the good, chanting, as they march, a unison of piety and hope until they come to the holy place where shining Saints sing the new song of the redeemed. And they sing with them."

The distinguished brother of the author of the above eulogium, Henry Ward Beecher, was quite as enthusiastic in his praise of our form of worship. He wrote thus in a letter from Scotland after attending a Church Service : "The services began. You know my mother was, until her marriage, in the Communion of the Episcopal Church. This thought hardly left me, while I sat, grateful for the privilege of worshipping God through a Service that had expressed so often her devotions. I cannot tell you how much I was affected. I had never had such a trance of worship, and I shall never have such another view until I gain the gate. I am so ignorant of the Church Service that I cannot tell the various parts by their right names; but the parts which most affected me were the prayers and responses which the choir sang. I had never heard any part of a supplication — a direct prayer sung by a choir — and it seemed as though I heard not with my ear, but with my soul. I was dissolved, my whole being seemed to me like an incense wafted gratefully towards God. The Divine Presence rose before me in wondrous majesty, but of ineffable gentleness and goodness. Throughout the Service, and it was an hour and a quarter long, whenever an Amen occurred, it was given by the choir, accompanied by the organ and the congregation. Oh, that swell and solemn cadence yet rings in my ear. Not once, not a single time, did it occur in that Service without bringing tears from my eyes. I stood like a shrub in a spring morning, every leaf covered with dew, and every breeze shook down some drops. I trembled so much at times, that I was obliged to sit down. Oh, when in the prayers, breathed forth in strains of sweet, simple, solemn music, the love of Christ was recognized, how I longed then to give utterance to what that love seemed to me. There was a moment in which the heavens seemed opened to me, and I saw the glory of God! All the earth seemed to me a storehouse of images, made to set forth the Redeemer, and I could scarcely keep still from crying out." No wonder that Mr. Beecher before his death arranged with an Episcopal Clergyman to officiate at his funeral, using the Church's Burial Service. The marvel is that both he and his scarcely less brilliant brother did not, like their sisters, Miss Catharine Beecher and Mrs. Harriet Beecher Stowe, find their way back to the Church of their maternal ancestors.

Want of space compels us to conclude these quotations with an extract from one of Mr. Edmund Clarence Stedman's lectures on Poetry, delivered at Johns Hopkins University and published in the "Century Magazine." Mr. Stedman stands in the front rank of living poets and critics. He is not a member of the Church, but few if any of her sons have a higher appreciation of her worship than he, and I know of none who have spoken more eloquently of it. "Let me refer," says he, "to a single illustration of the creative faith of the poet. For centuries all that was great in the art and poetry of Christendom grew out of that faith. What seems to me its most poetic, as well as the most enduring, written product is not, as you might suppose, the masterpiece of a single mind—the 'Divina Comedia,' for instance—but the outcome of centuries, the expression of many human souls, even of various peoples and races. Upon its literary and constructive side I regard the venerable Liturgy of the historic Christian Church as one of the few world-poems, the poems universal. I care not which of the Rituals you follow, the Oriental, the Alexandrian, the Latin, or the Anglican. The latter, that of an Episcopal Prayer Book, is a version familiar to you of what seems to me the most wonderful symphonic idealization of human faith— certainly the most inclusive, blending in harmonic succession all the cries and longings and laudations of the universal human heart invoking a Paternal Creator. I am not here considering this Liturgy as Divine, though much of it is derived from what multitudes accept for revelation. I have in mind its human quality; the mystic tide of human hope, imagination, prayer, sorrows, and passionate expression; upon which it bears the worshipper along, and wherewith it has sustained men's souls with conceptions of duty and immortality throughout hundreds, yes, thousands of undoubting years. The Orient and the Occident have enriched it with their finest and strongest utterances, have worked it over and over, have stricken from it what was against the consistency of its import and beauty. It has been a growth, an exhalation, an apocalyptic cloud 'arisen with the prayers of the Saints,' from climes of the Hebrew, the Greek, the Roman, the Goth, to spread in time over half the world. It is the voice of human brotherhood, the blended voice of rich and poor, old and young, the wise and simple. This being its nature, and as the crowning masterpiece of faith, you find that in various and constructive beauty—as a work of poetic art—it is unparalleled. It is lyrical from first to last with perfect harmonious forms of human speech. Its chants and anthems, its songs of praise and hope and sorrow have allied to themselves impressive music from the originative and immemorial past, and the enthralling strains of its inheritors. Its prayers are not only 'for all sorts and conditions of men,' but for every stress of life which mankind must feel in common—in the household, or isolated, or in tribal or national effort, and in calamity and repentance and thanksgiving. Its wisdom is forever old and perpetually new; its calendar celebrates all seasons of the rolling year; its narrative is of the simplest, the most pathetic, the most rapturous, and most ennobling life the world has known. There is no malefactor so wretched, no just man so perfect, as not to find his hope, his consolation, his lesson in this poem of poems. I have called it lyrical; it is dramatic in structure and effect; it is an epic of the age of faith; but, in fact, as a piece of inclusive literature, it has no counterpart, and can have no successor."

But it may be asked, if the Book of Common Prayer contains a form of worship so superior to the extempore use which prevails with Protestants, how is it that this superiority is appreciated by comparatively so few among us? We answer this question by asking another. Why is it that in the world of art the vast majority are not able to distinguish the inferior from the superior, and in nine cases out of ten prefer a trifling ditty to an oratorio, a daub to a masterpiece, or a doggerel to a poem? It is simply because their education is deficient.

"There must be, in ordinary circumstances," writes one who came to the Episcopal Church from Presbyterianism, "not only a taste, but an educated and cultivated taste, to appreciate beauty in a landscape, grace in a statue, refinement in manners, elegance in literature, force in eloquence, melody in music, purity in morals, and, to come to the point in hand, perfection in worship. Time, or opportunity, at least, must be allowed to correct and adapt the taste. It is impossible to rise at a bound from the impression that the sermon is the *summum bonum* for which we turn our feet towards the sanctuary, into the feeling — not new, I apprehend, to the heart of the veriest worldling among the Episcopalians — that when we 'go within thy gates, O Zion,' it is to worship God. It is not possible, from the heavy, dull commonplaces of an extemporaneous prayer, which it is enough to have heard once, to rise, by a single effort, to the dignity of a Liturgy, which, to be adequately admired, must be heard a thousand times. It is impossible to settle down, from the fitful, feverish and momentary flights of the revival and the camp-ground into the chastened and life-long fervor of the incomparable Liturgy."

Moreover, but for inherited prejudices, many would recognize the superiority and appreciate the beauties of the Prayer Book, who now inveigh against it. A curious illustration of the force of prejudice is related of the parishioners of the famous Bishop Bull, who, during the Commonwealth, when the use of the Liturgy was prohibited, committed to memory the various Services of the Prayer Book, and made them the channel of the public devotions of the people in the parish of which he was then minister. "The consequence of which was," says the biographer; "that they who were most prejudiced against the Liturgy did not scruple to commend Bishop Bull as a person that prayed by the Spirit, though at the same time they railed at the Common Prayer as a beggarly element, and as a carnal performance."

IX.

JOHN WESLEY ALWAYS AN EPISCOPALIAN.

LECTURE III; PAGE 205.

IN order to feel the force of the following quotations from Mr. Wesley's works, it will be necessary to bear in mind that he was born in the year 1703 and that he died A. D. 1791, at the extreme old age of 88 years. The extracts from his writings cover the latter half of his life, the first being passed over because it is never claimed that he was anything except a Churchman during the earlier part of his career.

1746: "I dare not renounce Communion with the Church of England. As a minister I teach her doctrines; I use her offices; I conform to her Rubrics; I suffer reproach for my attachment to her. As a private member, I hold her doctrines; I join in her offices, in prayer, in hearing, in communicating." Vol. VIII, p. 444.

1747: "We continually exhort all who attend on our preaching, to attend the offices of the Church. And they do pay a more regular attendance there than they ever did before." Vol. VIII, p. 488.

1755: "We began reading together — 'A Gentleman's Reasons for His Dissent from the Church of England.' It is an elaborate and lively tract, and contains the strength of the cause; but it did not yield us one proof that it is lawful for us, much less our duty, to separate from it." Vol. II, p. 328.

1758: In this year Mr. Wesley wrote his "Reasons Against a Separation from the Church of England;" and in writing to Miss Bishop in 1778, he says: "These reasons were never yet answered and I believe they never will." The Rev. Charles Wesley says of this tract: "I think myself bound in duty to add my testimony to my brother's. His twelve reasons against our ever separating from the Church of England are mine also. I subscribe to them with all my heart. My affection for the

Church is as strong as ever; and I clearly see my calling, which is to live and die in her Communion. This, therefore, I am determined to do, the Lord being my helper." Vol. XIII, p. 199.

1759 : " I received much comfort at the old Church in the morning, and at St. Thomas' in the afternoon. It was as if both the sermons were made for me. I pity those who can find no good at Church! But how should they, if prejudice come between them? An effectual bar to the Grace of God." Vol. II, p. 478. "I had appointed to preach at seven in the evening at Bradford, but when I came, I found Mr. Hart was to preach at six, so I delayed till the Church Service was ended, that there might not appear on my part, at least, even the shadow of opposition between us." Vol. II, p. 516.

1761 : " We had a long stage from hence to Swadale, where I found an earnest, loving, simple people, whom I likewise exhorted not to leave the Church, though they had not the best of ministers." Vol. III, p. 61.

1763 : "I then related what I had done since I came to Norwich first, and what I would do for the time to come, particularly that I would immediately put a stop to preaching in the time of Church Service." Vol. III, p. 152.

1766 : "I see clearer and clearer none will keep to us, unless they keep to the Church. Whoever separates from the Church separates from the Methodists." Vol. III, p. 260.

1767 : " I rode to Yarmouth, and found the Society, after the example of Mr. W——p, had entirely left the Church. I judged it needful to speak largely upon that head. They stood reproved, and resolved, one and all, to go to it again." Vol. III, p. 272.

1768 : "I advise all, over whom I have any influence, steadily to keep to the Church." Vol. III, p. 337.

1770 : " We had a poor sermon at Church. However, I went again in the afternoon, remembering the words of Mr. Philip Henry: ' If the preacher does not know his duty, I bless God that I know mine.' " Vol. III, p. 401.

1772 : "I attended the Church of England Service in the morning, and that of the Kirk in the afternoon. Truly, ' no man having drunk old wine, straightway desireth new.' How dull and dry the latter appeared to me, who had been accustomed to the former." Vol. III, p. 463.

1775 : "Understanding that almost all the Methodists, by the advice of Mr. ——, had left the Church, I earnestly exhorted them to return to it." Vol. IV, p. 64.

1777 : "They, the Methodists, have read the writings of the most eminent pleaders for separation, both in the last and present century. They have spent several days in a General Conference upon this very question : 'Is it expedient, supposing, not granting, that it is lawful, to separate from the Established Church?' But still they could see no sufficient cause to depart from their first resolution. So that their fixed purpose is, let the Clergy or Laity use them well or ill, by the grace of God, to endure all things, to hold on their even course." Vol. VII, p. 428.

1778: "The original Methodists were all of the Church of England, and the more awakened they were, the more zealously they adhered to it in every point, both of doctrine and discipline. Hence we inserted in the very first Rules of our Society: 'They that leave the Church leave us.' And this we did, not as a point of prudence, but a point of conscience." Vol. XIII, p. 134. "I believe one reason why God is pleased to continue my life so long is, to confirm them in their present purpose, not to separate from the Church." Vol. VII, p. 278. "I dare not separate from the Church; I believe it would be a sin so to do; I have been true to my profession from 1730 to this day." Vol. VII, p. 279.

1785: "Finding that a report had been spread abroad that I was just going to leave the Church, to satisfy those that were grieved concerning it, I openly declared in the evening that I had now no more thought of separating from the Church, than I had forty years ago." Vol. IV, p. 320.

1786: "Whenever there is any Church Service, I do not approve of any appointment the same hour; because I love the Church of England, and would assist, not oppose it, all I can." Vol. XIII, p. 55. [This is taken from a letter to the Rev. Freeborn Garretson, of the Methodist Society in America, and clearly shows that in no instance did he suffer anything to be done to oppose the Church of England, whether in the States or at home.]

1787 : "I went over to Deptford, but it seemed I was got into a den of lions. Most of the leading men of the Society were mad for separating from the Church. I endeavored to reason with them, but in vain ; they had neither sense nor even good manners left.　At length, after meeting the whole Society, I told them : 'If you are resolved you may have your service in Church hours; but remember, from that time you will see my face no more.'　This struck deep, and from that hour I have heard no more of separating from the Church."　Vol. IV, p. 357.　"Few of them, those who separated, assigned the unholiness of either the Clergy or Laity as the cause of their separation.　And if any did so, it did not appear that they themselves were a jot better than those they separated from."　Vol. VII, p. 183.

1788 : "This is the peculiar glory of the people called Methodists.　In spite of all manner of temptations, they will not separate from the Church.　What many so earnestly covet, they abhor.　They will not be a distinct body."　Vol. XIII, p. 232.

1789 : "Unless I see more reasons for it than I ever yet saw, I will never leave the Church of England, as by law established, while the breath of God is in my nostrils."　Vol. XIII, p. 238.　In this year, two before his death, Mr. Wesley wrote "Seven more reasons against separating from the Church."

1790 : "I have been uniform, both in doctrine and discipline, for above these fifty years, and it is a little too late for me to turn into a new path, now I am gray-headed."　Vol. XII, p. 439.　"The Methodists in general are members of the Church of England.　They hold all her Doctrines, attend her Services, and partake of her Sacraments."　Vol. XIII, p. 119.

X.

POPE PIUS IV. AND THE ENGLISH PRAYER BOOK.

LECTURE II; PAGE 130.

AN interesting letter upon this subject, from Dr. W. D. Wilson, has recently appeared in the New York *Churchman*, under the heading, "The Pope and the English Liturgy: A New Confirmation of the story."　It is substantially as follows : In A.D. 1568–70, the Pope offered to accept the English

Liturgy, and allow it to be used in England, if only Elizabeth would acknowledge that she had received it from him, and used it with his consent and in subordination to his authority. This story is commonly repeated as resting on the authority of Lord Coke, who is reported to have said that he had seen the letter. But Coke does not say, in his charge at Norwich, that he had seen it. What he does say is : " I have oftentimes heard it avowed by the late Queen, in her own wordes, and I conferred with some lordes that were of greatest reckoning, who had seen and read the letter." Of course, therefore, there was such a letter written. But, within a short time past, it has been found that in the "Calendar of State Papers," there is a dispatch from Lord Walsingham, who was then in France, to Lord Burleigh, dated June 21, 1571, in which it appears that there were some negotiations going on in regard to a marriage between Queen Elizabeth and the Duke of Anjou, in which Walsingham says that an " offer was made by the Cardinal of Lorraine, that the Pope would have allowed and confirmed as Catholic the English Liturgy and other offices, so the Queen, my mistress, would have acknowledged the same as received from him." This was written while the negotiations for the marriage were pending. But after they had failed, and Elizabeth had refused to accept the Pope's offer, he issued his famous bull of excommunication. But this statement of Walsingham proves that such an offer was made, and this confirms the statement made by Lord Coke some thirty-five years afterwards. Now, although this statement of Walsingham does not prove that such a letter was sent, as Coke's statements do, it proves that such an offer was made, and throws an important light on the motives and reasons for it.

C. A.—28

XI.

GREEK CATHOLICS AND ANGLICAN ORDERS.

LECTURE II; PAGE 144.

Though Anglican Orders have not been officially pronounced upon by the Greek Church, there can be no doubt that, if occasion for formal action should ever arise, their validity would be recognized. Romanists try to make it appear to the contrary by representing that when the Greek Church receives one who is in Anglican Orders he is reordained. They give no instance, and we do not remember to have seen the account of any. Even if their representation respecting the attitude of the Greeks towards our Orders be correct, it avails them nothing, for the Roman Clergy must also be reordained before they are allowed to minister at Greek Altars. But we are inclined to doubt the correctness of their representation. It is not long since we saw it stated that a "faddy" Anglican Clergyman persuaded a Russian nobleman to try to arrange for his reordination by the Metropolitan of St. Petersburg. But the theological professsor there wrote to the Procurator: "Take care what you are about, for the Greek Church has never disowned the Orders of the Church of England." The matter was looked into and the Anglican Priest returned home without being reordained. The subject was then given as the thesis for the theological degree in the academy, and all the students came to the conclusion that our Orders were valid. The statement, that at the Bonn Conference the Greeks voted against the acceptance of our Orders, has been shown by Canon MacColl to be contrary to fact. "The chief Greek Churchman present was Archbishop Lycourgus, and he accepted their validity."

Some years ago, the Patriarch of Jerusalem invited the Archbishop of Canterbury to send a Bishop to overlook the Anglican Church there. He has allowed our congregation the use of the Chapel of Abraham in the church of the Holy Sepulchre and has often invited our Clergy to go with him to sacred Functions, and has placed them in the Chancel among his Clergy. A short time ago, the Russian Bishop of California, at the invitation of the Bishop of Iowa, was present in his Cathedral, and sat vested in his Chancel. At the Consecration of the Bishop of Massachusetts, the Archbishop of Zante, who came to represent the Eastern Churches at the World's Fair Parliament of Religions, was present in the Chancel during the Function, and preached a brief sermon. He was in attendance at the opening of the Diocesan Convention of New York, and received the Holy Communion at the hands of Bishop Potter. He also made an address at the Missionary Council in Chicago.

In June, 1887, the Patriarch of Alexandria wrote to the Archbishop of Canterbury in the following terms: "Most Reverend Archbishop of Canterbury, Exarch of all England, my Lord Metropolitan Brother, Beloved in Christ, my Lord Edward, we embrace your reverence in the Lord, and in gladness address you."

In a correspondence which took place in A. D. 1896 between the Ecclesiastical head of the Russian Church and that of the Anglican Communion the former addressed the latter as follows: "Palladius, by Divine mercy, Metropolitan of St. Petersburg and Ladoga, Archimandrite of the Lavra of the Holy Trinity and St. Alexander Nevsky, Presiding Member of the Most Holy Governing Synod of all the Russias, unto Edward, Lord Archbishop of Canterbury, Primate of All England and Metropolitan, greeting in the Lord."

Lycourgus, late Archbishop of Syra and Tenedos, in a speech at Ely, in A. D. 1870, said, "When I return to Greece I will say that the Church of England is a sound Catholic Church, very like our own."

To the foregoing expressions of kindly feeling toward the English Church may be added the utterances of an Archimandrite in the course of a correspondence in the columns of the *West London Observer :* "Permit me, as a member of the oldest branch of the great Catholic Church, namely, the Greek Church, to state that all right minded Catholics agree so far with the writer of the letter signed 'An English Catholic,' as to freedom of speech. It is a great pity that discussion on religious subjects is not liked by the Roman Catholic section, who are really, like ourselves, Nonconformists in these Isles. The State Church of England we recognize as an important branch of the great Catholic Church, which was established prior to the Roman Mission. The Pope, or Bishop of Rome, is only head of that portion of the Catholic Church which adheres to the Roman doctrines of the Council of Trent, and has no authority over the Greek, English, or any other Catholics. Shakespeare said, 'There is no ignorance but darkness,' so let all branches of the Catholic Church for the future be allowed free ventilation of religious subjects."

XII.

JOHN WESLEY ON THE MINISTERIAL OFFICE.

LECTURE III; PAGE 211.

THE following is extracted from John Wesley's Sermon No. CXV. on "The Ministerial Office." The text is, "No man taketh this honour unto himself, but he that is called of God, as was Aaron."—*Hebrews V:4*. It was delivered at a Conference of Methodist preachers held in the city of Cork, May 4, 1789. This, it is important to remember, was only two years before the death of Mr. Wesley and five years after his reputed ordination of Dr. Coke to the

Episcopate. The utterance is noteworthy on several accounts. It shows that Wesley up to that late date did not
intend to found a Church; that he did not understand his
Service and laying on of hands in connection with Dr. Coke's
departure for America as a setting apart to the office of a
Bishop; that he did not feel constrained to depart from the
Church of England in any essential feature of doctrine or
discipline, and in fact did not do so, even in non-essentials,
much if any further than such societies as the Brotherhood of
St. Andrew have done in our day; and that he did not regard
the preachers whom he appointed over the Methodist societies, as standing on the same footing with the Clergy of the
Church. It is difficult to see how any modern Methodist in
the light of these quotations can regard himself as a follower
of John Wesley.

"Many learned men have shown at large that our Lord
Himself, and all His Apostles, built the Christian Church as
nearly as possible on the plan of the Jewish. So the great
High Priest of our profession sent Apostles and Evangelists
to proclaim glad tidings to all the world; and then Pastors,
Preachers, and Teachers, to build up in the Faith the congregations that should be founded. But I do not find that ever
the office of an Evangelist was the same with that of a Pastor,
frequently called a Bishop. He presided over the flock, and
administered the Sacraments; the former assisted him, and
preached the Word, either in one or more congregations. I
cannot prove from any part of the New Testament, or from
any author of the first three centuries, that the office of an
Evangelist gave any man a right to act as a Pastor or Bishop.

"But may it not be thought that the case now before us
is different from all these? Undoubtedly in many respects it
is. Such a phenomenon has now appeared as has not appeared in the Christian world before, at least not for many
ages. Two young men sowed the Word of God, not only in
the Churches, but likewise literally 'by the highway side;'
and indeed in every place where they saw an open door,
where sinners had ears to hear. They were members of the
Church of England, and had no design of separating from it.
And they advised all that were of it to continue therein,

though they joined the Methodist society; for this did not imply leaving their former congregation, but only leaving their sins. Not long after, a young man, Thomas Maxfield, offered himself to serve them as a son in the Gospel. And then another, Thomas Richards, and a little after a third, Thomas Westell. Let it be well observed on what terms we received these, namely, as Prophets, not as Priests. We received them wholly and solely to preach, not to administer Sacraments.

"In 1744 all the Methodist Preachers had their first Conference. But none of them dreamed that the being called to preach gave them any right to administer Sacraments. And when that question was proposed, 'In what light are we to consider ourselves?' it was answered, 'As extraordinary messengers, raised up to provoke the ordinary ones to jealously.' In order hereto, one of our first rules was given to each Preacher, 'You are to do that part of the work which we appoint.' But what work was this? Did we ever appoint you to administer Sacraments; to exercise the Priestly office? Such a design never entered into our mind; it was the farthest from our thoughts. It was several years after our society was formed, before any attempt of this kind was made. The first was, I apprehend, at Norwich. One of our Preachers there yielded to the importunity of a few of the people, and baptized their children. But as soon as it was known, he was informed it must not be, unless he designed to leave our Connexion.

"Now, as long as the Methodists keep to this plan, they cannot separate from the Church. And this is our peculiar glory. Methodists are not a sect or party; they do not separate from the religious community to which they at first belonged; they are still members of the Church; such they desire to live and to die. And I believe one reason why God is pleased to continue my life so long is to confirm them in their present purpose, not to separate from the Church.

"But, notwithstanding this, many warm men say, 'Nay, but you do separate from the Church.' Others are equally warm, because they say I do not. I will nakedly declare the thing as it is. I hold all the doctrines of the Church of England. I love her Liturgy. I approve her plan of discipline, and only wish it could be put in execution. I do not knowingly vary from any rule of the Church, unless in those few instances, where I judge, and as far as I judge, there is an absolute necessity. For instance (1) As few Clergymen open their Churches to me, I am under the necessity of preaching abroad. (2) As I know no forms that will suit all occasions, I am often under a necessity of praying extempore. (3) In order to build up the flock of Christ in faith and love, I am under a necessity of uniting them together, and of dividing them into little companies, that they may provoke one another to love and good works. (4) That my fellow-laborers and I may more effectually assist each other to save our own souls and those that hear us, I judge it necessary to meet the Preachers, or, at least, the greater part of them, once a year. (5) In those Conferences we fix the stations of all the Preachers for the ensuing year. But all this is not separating from the Church. So far from it, that, whenever I have opportunity, I attend the Church Service myself, and advise all our societies so to do.

"I wish all of you who are vulgarly termed Methodists would seriously consider what has been said. And particularly you whom God hath commissioned to call sinners to repentance. It does by no means follow from hence, that ye are commissioned to Baptize, or to administer the Lord's Supper. Ye never dreamed of this for ten or twenty years after ye began to preach. Ye did not then, like Korah, Dathan and Abiram, 'seek the Priesthood also.' Ye knew 'no man taketh this honour unto himself, but he that is called of God, as was Aaron.' O contain yourselves within your own bounds; be content with preaching the Gospel; 'do the work of Evangelists;' proclaim to all the world the loving kindness of God our Saviour; declare to all 'The Kingdom of Heaven is at hand; repent ye, and believe the Gospel!' I earnestly advise you, abide in your place; keep your own station. Ye were at first called in the Church of England; and though ye have and will have a thousand temptations to leave it, and set up for yourselves, regard them not. Be Church-of-England men still; do not cast away the peculiar glory which God hath put upon you, and frustrate the design of Providence, the very end for which God raised you up."

The Rev. L. H. Wellesley Wesley, Rector of Hatchford, England, an aged and erudite descendant of the same family of which John and Charles Wesley were members, in an article recently published in *The London Church Bells*, is represented as insisting upon the fact that the founder of the original Methodist Societies was loyal to the Church of which he lived and died a member. "How," said he, "the Wesleyan ministers can call themselves 'Rev.' and their chapels 'churches' in the teeth of John Wesley's teaching, I cannot understand. He always called the chapels 'preaching houses' and the ministers 'preachers.'"

XIII.

THE NINE HUNDRED AND NINETY-NINE YEARS' LEASE.

LECTURE IV; PAGE 228.

THE statement of this passage having been called in question I wrote to the learned author of "The Continuity of the English Church through Eighteen Centuries," the Rev. A. E. Oldroyd, Vicar of Oundle, England, requesting him to be good enough to investigate the matter and let me know the result. In a letter bearing date June 8, 1896, he gives the following extracts from two of the answers to his inquiries:

"'St. Paul's Chapter, 9 Amen Court, London, E. C., Mar., 18, 1896. I cannot tell what is intended by the passage which you cite. It can have no reference to Tillingham, for this was given to the Cathedral by Ethelbert, and has been in our possession ever since: one of the most interesting cases of continuous possession to be found. This is no case of a 999 years' lease, but a case of unbroken ownership from the days of Ethelbert who died, you will remember, in 616. Some estates in London, notably the Finsbury estate, have lately fallen in after a rather long lease, but not such a lease as that of which you speak.'

"'St. Nicholas Vicarage, Tillingham, Maldon, Essex, Mar. 1896. The Manor together with the lands attached thereto granted by Ethelbert, King of Kent, who began to reign in 565, to Mellitus who was consecrated Bishop of London by

St. Augustine of Canterbury 604, for the endowment of his monastery of St. Paul in London, still remains the property of the Dean and Chapter of St. Paul's."

"I have tried," says Mr. Oldroyd, "in various quarters, but the above is the best result of my investigations. If not the basis of the 999 years' lease paragraph, the Tillingham inheritance of St. Paul's Cathedral Chapter, London, is at any rate quite as strong on the continuity of the Church of England."

It seems probable that this nine hundred and ninety-nine years' lease was first written or spoken of as something conceivable and quite in accord with what might have happened, and that afterwards some one with an imperfect memory related it as an actual fact which, being so plausible and interesting, naturally received wide publication and general acceptance.

XIV.

CONTINUITY OF THE ENGLISH CHURCH PROVED BY THE UNINTERRUPTED SUCCESSION OF HER BISHOPS.

LECTURE IV; PAGE 235.

THERE were Bishops in England who carried on the canonical jurisdiction as well as the Apostolic Succession through the reigns of Henry VIII., Edward VI., Mary, and into the reign of Elizabeth. For example, Kitchin remained Bishop of Llandaff through all the changes from A.D., 1545 to the year 1563. But the point we wish to make is this: all the old English Sees are at this time occupied by Bishops who are the successors in unbroken continuity of all who have preceded them in those Sees back to the time of the first incumbent. This is not true of the Succession of any other religious body. The only one to which some might suppose this continuity appertained, the Roman Church, is entirely without it, for there is not a single Roman Bishop in England who has an Ecclesiastical predecessor in any Bishop of the English Church, either of the pre-Reformation or the post-Reformation period. The Roman Church in England of to-day laid its corner stone in A.D. 1570, and its Bishops and Priests have been imported in most cases from across the Channel, and when not thus derived, their Orders have come from thence. There is no succession of the English Roman Catholic Hierarchy which goes back further than September 29, 1850, when Dr. Wiseman became the first Cardinal Archbishop of Westminster. We thus have (1) The identity of the pre-Reformation with the post-Reformation Church of England, for its Orders are unbroken from the beginning to the present time. As Beard in his "Herbert Lectures" says, "It is an obvious historical fact that Parker was the successor of Augustine as clearly as Lanfranc and Becket." This being true of the first post-Reformation Archbishop of Canterbury, it is of course equally so of the present incumbent. As for the other Sees no attempt has ever been made to raise a doubt as to whether an uninterrupted succession has been maintained. On this point see "Spiritual Succession and Jurisdiction in England," by John W. Lea. (2) The Roman Church in England at present time is a schismatic sect, dating from A.D. 1570, and has no identity or organic connection with the Church of England before or after the Reformation.

It must of course be granted that the corporate life of the Church of England, which, as we have shown conclusively, has existed without interruption from the Apostles, does not absolutely prove the spiritual identity of the post-Reformation with the pre-Reformation Church. If, for illustration, the American Episcopal Church at the next General Convention were to exchange the Bible for the Koran, to deny the doctrine of the Trinity, and adopt Mohammed as its supreme prophet, then, even, if not a man were changed there would be no spiritual identity between the Episcopal Church after the Convention of A.D. 1898 with that which had existed before. But surely none will contend that anything of this

kind took place in the Church of England. No one undoubted Catholic doctrine, practice or institution was abolished at the Reformation, nor were there any novel doctrines,
practices or institutions imposed at that time or since.

XV.

THE ENGLISH CHURCH DID NOT SECEDE FROM ROME.

LECTURE IV; PAGE 250.

ROMANISTS in England were enjoined by the Papal Bull
of A. D. 1570 to withdraw from the Church of England.
Many of the English Laity and some of the Clergy obeyed
this summons and organized another religious body, separate
and distinct from the English Church. This was a schismatic
procedure by the Roman element, for it deliberately left the
regular Church of England and formed a new body in opposition thereto. Truth and justice require it to be made plain
even at the risk of frequent reiteration that the first division of
English Christians was effected by a few sympathizers with the
Papacy in obedience to the mandate of Pius V. The English
Catholics and patriots, now commonly called Churchmen or
Episcopalians, continued on as usual without withdrawing
themselves from any one. The vast majority of the inhabitants remained in the old *Ecclesia Anglicana* which still continues and always will remain preëminently the Church of
that country and our race. The following brief and accurate
account of the beginning of the Roman schism in England
is extracted from Palmer's Church History : "The accession
of the illustrious Queen Elizabeth was followed by the restoration of the Church to its former state. The Clergy generally approved of the return to pure religion, and retained
their benefices, administering the Sacraments and rites according to the English Ritual. *There was no schism for
many years in England, all the people worshipped in the*

same Churches, and acknowledged the same pastors. At last, in 1569, Pius V. issued a bull, in which he excommunicated Queen Elizabeth and her supporters, absolved her subjects from their oaths of allegiance, and bestowed her dominions on the King of Spain. *This bull caused the schism in England;* for the Popish party, which had continued in communion with the Church of England up to that time, during the past eleven years of Elizabeth's reign, now began to separate themselves. Bedingfield, Cornwallis, and Silyarde, were the first Popish recusants; and the date of the Romanists in England, as a distinct sect or community, may be fixed in the year 1570."

Cardinal Manning was once of the opinion that the schism of A. D. 1570 did not proceed from the English King and Church, but from Rome, and as logical deductions from historical facts do not vary with a change of Ecclesiastical relationship, his words are here quoted : " The Crown and Church of England with a steady opposition resisted the entrance and encroachment of the secularized Ecclesiastical power of the Pope in England. The last rejection of it was no more than a successful effort after many a failure in struggles of the like kind. And it was an act taken by men who were sound, according to the Roman doctrines, in all other points. There is no one point in which the British Churches can be attainted of either heresy or schism. She, the Anglican Church, has rejected, what the Eastern Churches rejected before, the arrogant pretense of a universal pontificate rashly alleged to be of Divine right, imposed in open breach of Apostolical traditions and the canons of many councils. The Churches of the East are not schismatical for their rejection of this usurpation; neither are the Churches of Britain. But they are guilty of the schism that obtrude this novelty as the condition of Christian communion."

XVI.

HARRIET BEECHER STOWE.

LECTURE V; PAGE 296.

THERE seems to be some room for dispute as to the Church relationship of Mrs. Stowe. The statements of this book, which were based upon what appeared to be trustworthy testimony, having been called in question by an esteemed correspondent, an effort was made to ascertain the truth of the matter. After putting together all the facts that conveniently could be collected, it was concluded that what had been written might as well remain unaltered. For, while it appeared that she had never been confirmed and was during all her life nominally a Congregationalist, her attachment for and interest in the Episcopal Church were such as to lead people generally, and even members of her own family, to suppose that she was an Episcopalian in body as well as at heart. The following interesting passage from the "Reminiscences of Harriet Beecher Stowe," by Elizabeth Stuart Phelps Ward, shows which way the wind blew as far back as her Andover life, A.D. 1852–64 :

"I dimly suspected then, and I have been sure of it since, that the privilege of neighborhood was but scantily appreciated in Andover, in the case of this eminent woman. Why, I do not know. She gave no offense, that I can recall, to the peculiar preferences of the place. The fact that she was rumored to have leanings towards the Episcopal Church did not prevent her from dutifully occupying with her family her husband's pew in the old chapel. It was far to the front, and her Ecclesiastical delinquencies would have been only too visible, had they existed. A tradition that she visited the theatre in Boston when she felt like it, sometimes passed solemnly from lip to lip; but this is the most serious criticism upon her which I can remember."

In the Life of Mrs. Stowe, edited by her son, the statement is made that she had joined the Protestant Episcopal Church, some time before A. D. 1867. But the Clergyman who was the Rector of the little Parish at Mandarin, Florida, her winter home, informs me that this cannot be true, because in the year 1882 she told him that she had not been confirmed, and was thinking seriously of receiving the Apostolic Rite of the laying on of hands. "Mrs. Stowe," says this Clergyman, who was her pastor for several years, "did not believe in Episcopacy as the only form of Church Polity, but she did believe the Anglican Church to have the best system of worship and teaching. Her three daughters were all thorough Church-women." One of these in a letter bearing date September 3, 1896, speaking of her mother's failure to come to Confirmation, says: "Her reason for this she never told me, but I always supposed it was because of a feeling of loyalty and allegiance to her husband. I can say to you with full assurance of the truth of the statement, that at heart she was warmly and sincerely an ardent Episcopalian." In another letter she says: "From the time of the removal of my father and mother from Andover to Hartford in 1864, my mother attended regularly the Episcopal Church, going to the Communion as well. Trinity Church was the last Church she ever attended, and there she took her last Communion. That the Episcopal Church was the Church of her choice and her heart, there is in my mind no room for doubt." The Rev. Storrs O. Seymour, in a communication to the *Living Church* dated Litchfield, Connecticut, September 5, 1896, says: "While the Rev. Charles E. Stowe was pastor of the Windsor Avenue Congregational Church in Hartford, Conn., his mother generally attended the services of that Church. After his resignation she attended Trinity Church, frequently expressing to the Rector the satisfaction and pleasure which the Church Service afforded her. She was especially delighted with the vested choir."

Mrs. Stowe was counted among the most deeply interested and active Church workers in the Diocese of Florida. In A. D. 1866 she wrote to her brother, the Rev. Charles Beecher, a letter in which she says : "The Episcopal Church is undertaking, under direction of the future Bishop of Florida, a wide embracing scheme of Christian activity for the whole State. In this work I desire to be associated." In 1867 she wrote him in another letter, as follows: "I am now in correspondence with the Bishop of Florida, with the view to establishing a line of Churches along the line of the St. John's river, and if I settle at Mandarin, it will be one of my stations. Will you consent to enter the Episcopal Church, and be our Clergyman? You are just the man we want. If my tastes and feelings did not incline me toward the Church, I should still choose it as the best system for training immature minds, such as those of our negroes."

The winter of A. D. 1883–1884 was the last one spent by her at Mandarin, which, largely through her efforts, had been provided with a pretty little Episcopal Church, to which was attached a comfortable rectory. In January of that year she wrote : "Mandarin looks very gay and airy now with its new villas and our new Church and rectory."

Upon one occasion, when consulted by some neighboring resorters, among whom were representatives of several bodies of Christians, about what had better be done in regard to the establishment of religious services, Mrs. Stowe strongly recommended them to request the Bishop to send a Missionary to the community because, aside from the superiority of her Services, the Episcopal Church was the only one comprehensive enough to include them all.

It is believed that in view of the above showing, no reasonable exception can be taken to the representation that the authoress of "Uncle Tom's Cabin" was an Episcopalian.

It may be observed by the way that Miss Catherine Beecher, Mrs. Stowe's elder sister, to whose excellent school she owed so much, was also a staunch Episcopalian. In some of her writings Miss Beecher expresses regret that her mother, after marriage, saw fit to leave the Episcopal Church and become a Presbyterian in order that she might be with her husband. She thought that the father sooner or later would have followed the mother into the Church, whose Liturgy and system of religious culture would have furnished the family with a much needed balance-wheel, and saved it from its checkered religious history.

We agree with Miss Beecher that the idea of a wife being obliged to follow the husband in the matter of religious affiliation, or *vice versâ,* is all wrong from whatever point of view. As the well-instructed Episcopalian looks at it, no consideration will justify a person in leaving the Catholic Church of his race and country. And in the eyes of a consistent Denominationalist, division being a good thing, it ought to seem desirable or at least allowable that every member of a household should belong to a different body of Christians.

XVII.

HENRY CLAY.

LECTURE V; PAGE 299.

THE following letter from the Rev. Dr. E. H. Ward, Rector of Christ Church, Lexington, Kentucky, was published in *The Pacific Churchman* of June 15, 1896. As the editor in his prefatory note remarks, it furnishes ground for the inference that Mr. Clay might have used the remarkable language attributed to him, but does not establish the fact that he actually did make the statement quoted. However, it appears, by the mouth of two reliable witnesses, that the words were really expressive of his thought :

"EDITOR OF *The Pacific Churchman:*

" Bishop Dudley some weeks ago referred to me a letter

from ———, of ———, in regard to a quotation from Henry Clay. It was the one in which Mr. Clay said that his hope for the future of the United States was in the Supreme Court and the Episcopal Church. I have asked some of Mr. Clay's grandchildren about it, but they can give me no information upon the subject.

"Judge Richard Buckner, who is now past four score, and before whom Mr. Clay often appeared as an advocate, is not able to locate the quotation ; but he said to me that it was so in line with Mr. Clay's thought that it might have been spoken at any time, and on almost any occasion.

"The late Mr. James O. Harrison, who was at one time Mr. Clay's law partner, and who was also his executor, said to me essentially the same thing. So then if we cannot locate the saying, the testimony of these two gentlemen is sufficient to assure us that it was in keeping with Mr. Clay's thought, and so we have a right to use it.

"As I have lost Mr. ———'s address, I take this method of answering his question, hoping that it may be of interest to others besides him.   E. H. WARD."

"Lexington, Ky., May 25, 1896."

Upon reading this correspondence it occurred to me that it had grown out of the passage of this book indicated above. I had heard the statement made in an interesting address delivered by the Bishop of Delaware at the laying of the corner stone of St. Mary's Chapel, St. Mary's, Ohio, in the year 1889. After reading Dr. Ward's letter in *The Pacific Churchman*, I inquired of Bishop Coleman concerning the source of his information. In a letter bearing date, Bishop-stead, Wilmington, Delaware, July 3, 1896, he says : " I cannot now possibly give you my authority for the reported saying of Henry Clay. But I am still satisfied that the authority was such as made and makes me confident to repeat the statement. The Clergyman who baptized Henry Clay, and to whom it might be well for you to write, is the Rev. Edward F. Berkley, D.D., St. Louis, Missouri." In a conversation with the Rev. Dr. Ward he told me that his letter to *The Pacific Churchman* was in response to an inquiry

concerning the grounds for what was said about Mr. Clay in
"The Church for Americans," and that he had heard the late
Judge Sheffy in a speech at a General Convention of the
Church make the same statement. The Doctor regretted that
in his letter he had not remembered to add this important
testimony to that of Judge Buckner and Mr. Harrison. He
thought it probable that the Bishop of Delaware had also
either heard Judge Sheffy make the statement in question or
read it in the *New York Churchman's* report of the Convention.

In accordance with Bishop Coleman's suggestion, I wrote to
the Venerable Dr. Berkley, now in his eighty-third year, who
replied in the following letter, which is a valuable contribution
to the biography of one of the most prominent and interesting
figures of American history :

"PITTSBURGH, PA., July 15, 1896.
"REVEREND AND DEAR BROTHER :
"You ask a simple question about a sentiment attributed
to Henry Clay. I give you the answer, but a statement from
your book which you quote moves me to say something
about his religious character. You have referred to me for
information about an expression of opinion on his part 'that
the stability of our government depends upon the perpetuation of two institutions, to wit, the Episcopal Church, and
the Supreme Court of the United States.' This is very like
him, and he may have expressed this sentiment to others, but
never to me. Although so much younger, as his Pastor, I
was in intimate intercourse with him for fourteen years of his
life, from 1838 to the time of his death in 1852. He often
spoke of the dignity and beauty of the Church Service, and of
its adaptability to strengthen the struggling infirmities of a
'poor sinner.'

"This expression leads me to notice another statement
made in your book, and which you quote in your letter, 'this
great statesman and orator did not identify himself with any
form of organized Christianity until late in life.' A religious
vein ran through his nature, and more than once he said in a
public speech, 'I am not a Christian, but I hope to give evidence of my faith in the excellence and Divine authenticity of

Christianity before I die.' His family were Baptists, but I believe he felt a strong interest in the Church from his early life.

"And here let me say even with the fear of wearying you by going so far aside from your letter, that he did not talk seriously of Baptism until he had taken leave of the Senate, and as he supposed retired from public life. He feared that if he made the sacred promises of Baptism, and the ordinances following, he might in his relations to public life do something that would compromise his Church and his profession. When he was seventy years old in June, 1847, I administered the Rite of Baptism to him and a daughter-in-law, with three or four of her children, in the parlor at Ashland, and not, as the Baptists proclaim to this day, 'in one of the beautiful ponds of Ashland.' I was familiar with the surroundings of that lovely country home, but I never saw any beautiful ponds. He came to the Communion on Sunday the Fourth of July after, and was confirmed by Bishop Smith within a week or two.

"He was afterward sent back to the Senate, pending the then absorbing question of the Missouri Compromise, where his burdened mind and forensic efforts killed him. He died in Washington city on the fifth anniversary of his Baptism, June 28, 1852, and was consigned 'to earth, ashes and to dust' in Lexington Cemetery on the 10th of July.

"To a Churchman I ought to say, that he was baptized in his house, because we were then building a Church, in which he manifested great personal interest, and I had no better place for the Service.

"I could write much in detailing reminiscences of this wonderful man, but if you have interest enough in this great character to endure what I have already said, I shall be gratified. I am cordially yours,

"REV. WM. M. BROWN." ED. F. BERKLEY."

XVIII.

REFORMED EPISCOPALIANS.

Lecture V; Page 303.

I HAVE learned recently to my great surprise that Reformed Episcopalians are often guilty of the grossest misrepresentations in their efforts to persuade our members and those who have their faces turned towards the old Catholic and Historic Episcopal Church to identify themselves with the modern sect known as the "Reformed Episcopal Church." They say that the two Churches properly may be regarded as twin sisters ; so that by becoming a member of either of them a person connects himself with the great Church of the English speaking race. The distinguishing characteristics of these sister Churches are represented to be that the sympathies of her, who is denominated "Reformed Episcopal," are wholly with Protestantism, while those of the "Protestant Episcopal" are centered in Romanism. They commonly speak of their body as, "Low Church" and of ours as "High Church."

Though I had heard from persons who seemed to know whereof they spoke, that these reprehensible tactics were being used by the Reformers, I could not believe that it was generally the case until assured of its truth by their members and publications. Their senior and most distinguished Bishop, Dr. Cheney, of Chicago, speaking of the origin of the Reformed Episcopal Church, says : "The roots of the plant which has seemingly sprung up in the soil of the United States of America and in the last third of the nineteenth century are imbedded in that fertile age, the Reformation of the sixteenth century. From that hour the Church of England rose to that place of influence which she has held through three hundred years, it might have been justly said of her as of Rebecca of old, 'Two nations are in thy womb, two manner of people shall be separated from thy bowels.'" Again he compares the relationship of the body to which he belongs and the Episcopal Church to two chestnuts lying peacefully in the same bur; but in A. D. 1873 the shell burst and the chestnuts went in opposite directions. Elsewhere he maintains that "in one sense this Church is not a new Communion, but the old Episcopal Church." In his sermon at the Consecration of Dr. Cheney, Bishop Cummins declared, "We claim to be the old and true Protestant Episcopalians of the days immediately succeeding the American Revolution."

The fallacy involved in this position would seem to be sufficiently obvious. It lies in the mistaking of a party in the Church for a coördinate branch of the Church. The analogy of Rebecca's twins is not quite apt, for, notwithstanding their differentiating characteristics, they were equally able to perpetuate a posterity of the same organic kind: whereas the conception of heretical doctrines and their promulgation by contentious and schismatical individuals is not a thing of the same kind as the continuity of organization. When certain members of the Low Church party separated themselves from the American branch of the Anglican Communion they severed all connection with that body and organized a new one having no more continuity with the old than the society of Presbyterians, or Baptists, or Methodists. The fact that their secession was headed by a Bishop did not alter its character, for it was nevertheless a going out of individuals from a preëxisting and continuous body. Dr. Cummins held his Bishopric solely for use in the Catholic Church and not outside of or against it. There was no preëxisting organic unity between him and his followers making them in any sense a Church or a constituent part thereof sharing with her her inherent self-perpetuating power. They were simply an aggregation of persons who organized themselves into a body which hitherto had no corporate existence of any kind. This argument is equally applicable to Dr. Cheney's "chestnuts!"

We think that any one who will candidly investigate the subject in the light of history and Canon law cannot escape the conviction that if an American would join the Catholic and Apostolic Church of our race, there is no way of doing so except by entering the Protestant Episcopal Church. Residents of the British Empire must unite with the Mother Church of England or one of her Colonial branches. By joining the Reformed Episcopalians a person no more becomes a member of the Anglo-Catholic Communion than if he were to join the Methodist or Presbyterian body. There is in fact practically no essential difference between the Reformed Episcopal Church and the various sixteenth century and later Denominations; at least there is none which they admit. It might at first sight seem that this statement needs modification, so far as the ministry is concerned, for their Orders are traced to Bishop Cummins, who had been duly Consecrated a Bishop in the American branch of the Apostolic and Catholic Church of Christ. But, aside from the fact that his Consecration of Dr. Cheney was a schismatic and unlawful act, Bishop Cummins was afterwards Canonically deposed. It should also be remembered that Dr. Cummins was only the assistant Bishop of Kentucky, and as such he had no jurisdiction except what was delegated by his superior. He was expressly forbidden by his Diocesan, who was at the time also the executive head of the House of Bishops, to Consecrate Dr. Cheney. Nevertheless he proceeded, and this in spite of the fact that in doing so he violated his Ordination vows which constitute one of the most solemn oaths which a man can take. If, therefore, the Reformers claim that they share the Historic Episcopal Succession with the Anglican Communion, we answer yes, but so far only as the mere laying on of hands is concerned; you have no jurisdiction, and you would not have the tactual succession but for the perjury of him who gave it. His schism and deposition historically and legally separated him from the Anglican Communion. If to this it be replied that the Church from which the American Episcopal body is sprung was also schismatic, the reader is referred to Appendix XIV., which conclusively shows to the contrary.

It is a curious fact that, though the "Reformed" body make a great deal of the Historic Episcopate when competing with Episcopalians for members, in their efforts to commend themselves to non-Episcopalians, they deny that Episcopacy is a Divine institution, and that there is such a thing as Apostolic Succession. The action of their late General Council in forbidding the reordination of Denominational ministers was, therefore, much more consistent than the stress which they put upon the Historic Episcopacy as a distinguishing feature between them and other sectarians. If, for the sake of argument, we admit — what would probably not be conceded by any great Canonist — that this body possesses a valid Historic Succession, it is, nevertheless, difficult to see how such of their congregations as are without an Episcopally ordained Clergyman, and there are several of them, can derive any profit from the Succession. Paradoxical as it may seem, there are probably scores among the Reformed Episcopalians who have never received the Holy Communion at the hands of any minister who has received Episcopal Ordination.

The Reformed Episcopalians are nothing more or less than Prayer Book Methodists. At a Methodist Conference held in Baltimore, Bishop Cummins declared that he and his followers were enveloped with a very thin Episcopal shell which only had to be broken to reveal the full fledged Methodist. They went out from us because we refused to revise our Liturgy so that its doctrine concerning the Ministry and Sacraments would conform with the ideas which prevail among Denominationalists. It is very easily shown that the objections to the Episcopal Church which they made the basis of their schism apply quite as much to the Bible as to the Book of Common

Prayer. This will be apparent upon the mere mention of the passages in our Liturgy to which they took exception. The italicised words and phrases in the following quotations were their great stumbling-blocks : (1) "Receive the Holy Ghost for the office and work of a *Priest* in the Church of God." (2) "Hath given power and commandment to His ministers to declare and pronounce to His people being penitent the *Absolution* and *remission* of their sins." (3) "Seeing now, dearly beloved, that this child is *regenerate* and *grafted* into the body of Christ's Church, let us give thanks unto Almighty God for these benefits." And "it has pleased Thee to *regenerate* this child with Thy Holy Spirit." (4) "Almighty and everliving God we most heartily thank Thee for that Thou dost vouchsafe to feed us, who have duly received these holy mysteries with the spiritual food of the most precious *Body* and *Blood* of Thy Son our Saviour Jesus Christ."

1. Great exception is taken to the word "Priest;" but it should be remembered that this is the general name for ministers of religion in all ages and countries. It occurs many times in the Old and New Testaments ; in the latter it is generally translated "Elder." That the Christian Church was to have Priests in the Old Testament sense appears both from prophecy and early history. Christ was "A Priest for ever after the order of Melchizedek." The word "order" implies more than one, a succession. The Church of Christ therefore, has a succession of Priests of which He is the Head. We have the writings of some of the immediate successors of the Apostles, such, for example, as the epistles of Ignatius, A. D. 107 and Polycarp, A. D. 108, in which the Ministry of the Christian Church is represented as constituted of Bishops, Priests and Deacons. I turn to the short letter of the Martyr Ignatius, written to the Magnesians, and find that the word "Priest" in its uncontracted form, Presbyter, occurs at least five times.

2. It is also very certain that the Prayer Book has no more

to say about Ministerial Absolution than the Bible. Christ said to the Apostles, and through them to their successors and delegates: "Whosesoever sins ye remit, they are remitted unto them; and whosesoever sins ye retain, they are retained."

3. The Prayer Book doctrine of Regeneration furnishes the Reformers their greatest pretext for schism. But our Lord said : " Except a man be born of water and of the Spirit he cannot enter into the Kingdom of God." Much confusion arises from the failure of Methodists and Reformed Episcopalians to distinguish birth from the beginning of life. These are by no means the same thing. In fact birth presupposes the existence of life ; it is therefore the transition from one state of existence to another. This is also true of the regeneration or new birth which Catholic Christians in all ages have connected with Holy Baptism. The recipient of the Sacrament is thereby transferred from the natural relation established by creation to the covenant relation established by adoption. The change in the spiritual life of an infant is somewhat as the natural birth is to the physical life. Baptism is therefore properly called the new birth, and the Reformers in making and maintaining a schism chiefly because of our Prayer Book doctrine concerning Regeneration disregard both Scripture and reason.

4. The teaching of our Liturgy regarding the spiritual reception of Christ in the Bread and Wine of the Holy Communion is also clearly Scriptural. For, on the night in which He was betrayed, "Jesus took bread and blessed it and brake it and gave it to the Disciples and said, Take, eat, this is My Body. And He took the cup and gave thanks and gave it to them, saying, Drink ye all of it for this is My Blood of the New Testament which is shed for many, for the remission of sins." The Reformed Episcopalians are very much like those Jews who strove among themselves saying, "How can this man give us His Flesh to eat ;" but Jesus said unto them, "Verily, verily, I say unto you, except ye eat the Flesh of the Son of Man and drink His Blood ye have no life in you.

Whoso eateth My Flesh and drinketh My Blood hath eternal life, and I will raise him up at the last day, for My Flesh is meat indeed and My Blood is drink indeed. He that eateth My Flesh and drinketh My Blood dwelleth in Me and I in him. As the living Father hath sent Me, and I live by the Father, so he that eateth Me, even he shall live by Me. This is the Bread which came down from Heaven : not as your fathers did eat manna, and are dead : he that eateth of this Bread shall live forever." And St. Paul says, " The Cup of blessing which we bless, is it not the Communion of the Blood of Christ? The Bread which we break, is it not the Communion of the Body of Christ? "

The Princess Elizabeth's famous reply to her Theological inquisitors is true of the old Prayer Book of our Catholic and Apostolic Church, not only so far as its doctrine concerning the Holy Communion is concerned, but likewise, in principle, of all essential points in which the Reformers and other Denominationalists depart from it.

> " Christ is the Word that spake it,
> He took the bread and brake it,
> And what the Word did make it,
> That I believe and take it."

The Rev. Dr. Wm. C. Hopkins, of Toledo, heard Dr. Newton, of Philadelphia, a leader of the Low Church party, say, in a public address, that Bishop Cummins had expressed to him deep regret for starting the Reformed Episcopal Church, and acknowledged that his doing so was a great mistake. Many other low Churchmen in refusing to follow his lead said that all that the Reformed Episcopal Church affirmed was already abundantly affirmed by the old Church and all that was denied is already abundantly denied by the Denominations ; so that no new organization was needed for either the affirmative or negative. They said also that the old Church already allowed all the liberty of opinion that the lowest Churchman could ask, in proof of which they called attention to the fact that for years many of them had freely denied Apostolic Succession and Baptismal Regeneration, and yet continued their ministry without let or hindrance. So that this was the most causeless of all the schisms, and ought to be the first to be healed, and we look forward with hope to the day when the little band of separated brethren will return to the fold, and of them and us there shall be, indeed, "one fold and one Shepherd."

XIX.

EXTEMPORE PRAYER AND EXPERIENCE MEETINGS.

LECTURE VI; PAGE 317.

THERE are many who have derived a great deal of blessing and support from the Prayer and Experience Meeting. Not a few of these are almost if not quite persuaded that, being English speaking people, they ought to be in communion with the Historic Catholic Church of their race. But they hesitate in transferring their allegiance because they fear that her Liturgical Services would not meet their spiritual wants. Such will be glad to know that there is no law to prevent Episcopalians from meeting together to join in extempore prayer and to strengthen themselves and encourage one another by the relation of their religious experience. The regular Services of the Church are of course stereotyped, but they are scarcely more so than those of the various non-liturgical Denominations. So far as general public worship is concerned it does not in any body of Christians take the place of the Prayer and Experience Meeting. There is, however, no Denomination in which it comes so nearly doing so as in the Episcopal Church. The Laity take more part in our regular Sunday services than they do in those of any other religious body. They confess their shortcomings and sins; pray for forgiveness and help ; make a profession of Christ; and, in the Psalter, even tell their religious experience. True they do this by conforming to the postures and joining their voices with the rest of the congregation, but we trust that the prayers, confessions, professions and experiences which Episcopalians say in concert, are no less helpful than those of the hymns which all Christians are accustomed to sing together.

It is true that taking part in precomposed Services does not afford so much of an opportunity to individuals for taking up their cross, but what is lost in this respect is more than compensated for by the removal of a stumbling-block which accounts for a large element in our non-church member population. So much importance has been attached to the class meeting that taking part in it has come popularly to be regarded as a prerequisite to Church membership in good standing, and the degree of spirituality is judged of by the ability to pray and talk in public. In every congregation there are some whose piety is over-estimated, because of the ease with which they meet these requirements ; while that of others is unjustifiably discounted, owing to the lack of fluency and self-assertion which puts them at a disadvantage. The representatives of the latter of these classes who in many cases exhibit the choicest fruits of Christianity, regard the cross which they are called upon to take up as being too heavy for them to bear. The great majority of these would gladly make use of the means of grace which Christ and the Apostles instituted for their admittance to the Church and upbuilding in righteousness, but they cannot meet the requirements of, say, John Wesley and his followers, and so to their regret they feel that they must remain unaffiliated with any body of Christians. All such will find the Apostolic Church of the English speaking race the place for them.

This great historic Communion does not put a yoke upon the humble and shrinking which they are not able to bear. Baptism, of which Confirmation is the completion, and the Holy Communion, are the Gospel ordinances for the confession of

Christ. The reception of these upon the simple conditions imposed in all ages by the Catholic Church, namely, a public promise by God's help to renounce the Devil and all his works; to believe all the articles of the Apostles' Creed; and to keep God's holy will and Commandments, is all that any person or society has a right to require of those who desire to identify themselves with the Savior and His Kingdom.

But if there be any Episcopalian who finds that the regular institutions and worship of his Church do not meet his spiritual needs, he is at perfect liberty to resort to extemporary prayer. And if the use of it in his closet and the relation of his experience in private conversation with his household and particular friends will not suffice, there is no reason why he should not organize a class of any who sympathize with him. This is what John Wesley did. In view of this representation, we trust that none who are convinced of this Church's superior claims to their allegiance will hesitate to identify themselves with her, because her regular public worship is liturgical.

XX.

VESTMENTS — A LAYMAN ON.

LECTURE VI; PAGE 324.

AFTER reading the section concerning the use of Ecclesiastical Vestments a thoughtful Layman was good enough to give me the following excellent criticism:

"You might have added that the vestments form not only a fitting attire, placing the Clergyman in harmony with the underlying spirit of the Service, but they also 'conceal the varying fashions of men' and are a great protection to the Laity against the personal kinks of their Rector. The latter may wear a sack or a dress coat, but whichever it is the overlying cassock and surplice hide it. If — as a minister in a religious body not Episcopal was said to have done — he comes into the Church with his pants tucked into the top of boots, the fact that he does this is not manifest ; but, in the case just alluded to, the congregation were helpless and would have been so if he had worn a green coat. The vestments insure respect for the dignity of worship, as well as for the rights of the Laity, and does this without trespassing upon the liberty of the Clergy."

XXI.

DANCING, CARD PLAYING AND THEATRE GOING.

Lecture VI; Page 325.

AT a Mission held in one of the county-seats of the Diocese of Ohio, where the Church had been newly established, the Missioner encouraged the people to ask questions about points concerning which they would like to know more. Freedom of inquiry was secured by the placing of a box near the door into which unsigned questions might be deposited. One evening, among other inquiries, it contained this : "You say that in order to become a member of the Episcopal Church a person has to 'Renounce the Devil and all his works, the pomps and vanity of this wicked world and all the sinful lusts of the flesh.' Query: Do dancing, card playing and theatre going fall under any of these heads? If so, why are not Episcopalians who indulge in them excommunicated?"

In his answer, which in that community silenced much caviling at the Church, the Missioner, as nearly as I can remember, said : "I confess to a little surprise at this question. Indeed, if it were not for some things which have come to the surface in the course of certain conversations which I have had since my coming among you, I could hardly believe that it is asked in the right spirit. To one raised as I have been it seems almost incredible that any person should seriously contend that professing Christians who participate in these amusements merit the extreme penalty of excommunication. But in view of what I have heard, there seems to be a necessity for treating this inquiry with the same respect that others which appeared more reasonable received.

" People are so constituted that they must have a little recreation. There is a proverb to the effect that all work and no play, if long continued, will inevitably have a bad effect upon both body and mind. The universal recognition of this accounts for the fact that no body of Christians forbids all diversions to its adherents. The only difference therefore between Episcopalians and their criticisers is in the matter of regulation. One resorts to legislation, while the other leaves it to the conscience of its members.

" The Episcopal Church of course expects all her adherents to keep their Baptismal vows. But so far as adults are concerned she treats them as men and women, and not like children, and so she allows them to determine for themselves what are to be included among the things which they have promised to renounce. As for the boys and girls she leaves their parents and spiritual masters and teachers to determine what amusements they shall enjoy.

" Now where such liberty of conscience is allowed there is of course always more or less of diversity in opinion and practice. This accounts for the fact that there are Episcopalians who from conscientious scruples do not dance, play cards or attend theatres. Some of our ministers openly discourage these things, and even those who see no harm in them strongly recommend moderation. However, they also do this in respect to all amusements which are likely to absorb too much time and attention.

" The character of one's amusements when he is at liberty to choose for himself, is largely a matter of taste. I am sorry to say that my parents were not professing Christians and that I was not a Church member until after I had reached the estate of manhood. I therefore felt perfectly free to dance, play cards or attend the circus — there was no theatre or opera in the town near the rural community where I lived. I also frequented the inevitable Church social and joined without compunction of conscience in the various romping and kissing games. I will not say that I did not enjoy them, but I always contended, and I have not up to date seen any reason to change my mind, that if I had a sister I should rather have her go to a select dancing party or the circus — opera much preferred if there be any — than to attend the old time Church social or mite society.

"If some of the Churches which expressly prohibit dancing, card playing and theatre going were to excommunicate all those of their membership who disregard the law, there would be many empty pews in their places of worship. The members of the Episcopal Church are by no means the only professing Christians who take part in the amusements against which the writer of the question seems to be so deeply prejudiced. In fact I have often observed that the various bodies of Christians are generally pretty evenly represented at such parties and entertainments, and that Episcopalians are not always the ones who are most carried away by them. On the contrary, the conduct of those who do these things regardless of the regulations of the Denomination to which they belong, often furnishes an illustration of the truth of the proverbial saying, 'Stolen waters are sweeter than any other.' "

XXII.

THE EPISCOPAL CHURCH THE CHURCH OF THE POOR.

LECTURE VI; PAGE 330.

THIS is the testimony of the Rev. Dr. Jackson, the eloquent and candid Pastor of the Wesleyan Chapel, Columbus, Ohio.

"If time permitted I would like to speak at length in praise of the work of the Episcopal Church among the poor,

Although that Communion has perhaps the highest percentage of wealth per member of any Church in this country, yet the poor have they always with them. To the solution of the problems of poverty they have given much of their best thought and energy. Although numerically among the smallest, yet they lead among the Protestant Churches of America in the erection of hospitals, the foundation of charities, and in the organization of various sisterhoods, guilds, brotherhoods and the like, for the alleviation of human distress. Their Parish and Cathedral system for our great cities, with their Parish Houses, is the only sensible and practical plan yet devised for bringing the whole force of the Church to bear for the relief of our over-crowded tenement house population. The Methodist Episcopal Church, while theoretically the best organized, next to the Catholics, for united attack upon the evils of our great cities, is yet, practically, owing to our compulsory system of pastoral change by the almanac, and the ruinous competition encouraged between our congregations, weakly and criminally negligent and utterly inefficient."

The custom of fashionable dressing in all " the churches " has done more than anything else to exclude the poor from public worship, but this is the misfortune of the Denominations also, and its correction is a problem only partially solved by our various City Missions. One thing is certain that all respectable poor people faithfully attending the Episcopal Church are sure of a warm and permanent welcome.

> "Our Mother, the Church, hath never a child
>   To honor before the rest,
> And she singeth the same for mighty kings
>   And the veriest babe on her breast;
> And the Bishop goes down to his narrow bed
>   As the ploughman's child is laid,
> And alike she blesseth the dark-brow'd serf,
>   And the chief in his robe arrayed.
> She sprinkles the drops of the bright new-birth,
>   The same on the low and high,
> And christens their bodies with dust to dust,
>   When earth with its earth must lie."

C. A.—30

XXIII.

FERMENTED COMMUNION WINE.

LECTURE VII; PAGE 355.

SINCE the publication of the First Editions of this book, I have met with some excellent people who, after connecting themselves with a newly organized Mission, had compunction of conscience about coming to the Holy Communion because the Church requires fermented wine to be used in its administration. This led to considerable conversation and inquiry, which convinced me that the law regulating this matter is a stumbling-block to many whose total abstinence pledge forbids them the use of wine except for medicinal purposes. There are doubtless some of these in almost every community. In view of the gigantic evils growing out of the use of alcoholic drinks, those who do what they can to stem the tide of degradation and sorrow by observing the precept to "touch not, taste not" and "handle not," and by inducing others to follow their example, must command the profound respect of all thoughtful men and women. Can such receive the Holy Communion in the Episcopal Church without doing violence to their noble conscientious scruples? It would be a matter for great regret if this question could not be satis. factorily answered in the affirmative. How then can any one who is pledged to total abstinence justify himself in receiving the Holy Communion in a Church that uses fermented wine and does not permit anything else to be substituted?

In our answer to this question we would call attention to the fact that those who have signed total abstinence pledges generally feel at liberty to use wine or even pure alcohol for medicinal purposes. And surely if the pledge may be set aside by a human physician's prescription in the case of bodily sickness, it may be done by the prescription of the Divine Physician for our spiritual illness. But, it will be asked, did our Lord prescribe fermented wine by using it at the institution of the Holy Communion on the night of His betrayal? We think that there can be no reasonable doubt that He did.

In the General Convention of A. D. 1886, the House of Bishops passed a resolution declaring that the use of unfermented wine was "unwarranted by the example of our Lord, and contrary to the custom of the Catholic Church." The Lambeth Conference of A. D. 1888 more strongly affirmed the same position in the following resolution: "That the Bishops assembled in this conference declare that the use of unfermented juice of the grape or any other liquid other than true Wine diluted or undiluted, as the element in the Administration of the Cup in Holy Communion, is unwarranted by the example of our Lord and is an unauthorized departure from the custom of the Catholic Church."

In an editorial on the first Lord's Supper *The Congregationalist* thus admirably sums up the reasons why we must accept it as a fact that the wine used was fermented:

"The Jews had no scientific knowledge intimating the fermentation of bread and wine to be identical. The Jerusalem Talmud distinctly orders the Passover service to be celebrated with red wine, which is necessarily fermented. The Talmud limited the quantity to such a degree as clearly to show the prevention of drunkenness to be the object. Vinegar was used at the Passover table, showing that vinous fermentation was not prohibited. To this may be added the opinions of Dr. Edersheim, a Christian of Jewish lineage and an eminent graduate of Oxford, singularly familiar with the Talmuds and the entire Hebrew literature, who says: 'The contention that this was unfermented wine is not worth discussion.' All the testimony of the most eminent Jewish Rabbis of our day is also in this direction."

Those who have total abstinence vows resting upon them

may therefore come to the Lord's Supper in the Episcopal Church, because in doing so they will be rendering obedience to the Great Physician of their souls. As the late Bishop of Pennsylvania said to one who hesitated, because of a pledge, to receive the Communion, and sought his Godly advice and counsel: "Our Blessed Lord used the ordinary wine of the country at the institution of the Lord's Supper. In His Divine omniscience He looked through all the future, and saw every possible consequence of such an act. Yet He deliberately chose the 'blood of the grape,' when He would symbolize the Blood of the Cross, and, in His infinite wisdom, which can do no wrong, ordained that it should be used in all places and ages, and among all conditions of men as the one Divine way of celebrating the Lord's Supper. To hesitate at taking a small sip of wine from the Chalice, because it is used by others for intoxicating purposes, is to reflect on our Blessed Lord's wisdom and goodness and love and purity, and to affect to be purer and holier than He. The Lord Jesus, if you take the wine in His strength and at His command, will keep you from any evil consequence to yourself and others; whereas, disobedience to His command dishonors Him, insults Him; sets up your judgment against His, and will put your own self-will above the positive command 'drink ye all of this.'"

One of the persons with whom I conversed about this matter argued that it was wrong to use fermented wine, because newly converted men who had fallen into the drinking habit would have their almost irresistible cravings for intoxicants revived by the taste of it. But I happened to be able to cite an instance from my own pastoral experience which goes to show that there is not much in this. He was an attractive young man, for whom his parents and lovely wife had a great deal of anxiety. After much hesitancy due to fear that he would bring reproach to the Church, he finally yielded to the persuasion of one of his companions who was a Churchman and was confirmed. There were some misgivings about the result of his coming to the Holy Communion, but it did not occur to me or to any one else to use unfermented grape juice or some other substitute for wine. The friend who induced him to come into the Church afterwards asked him whether he thought that there was any danger connected with the taking of the Sacramental wine, to which he confidently replied, no. He then went on to explain why he had no fear. In the first place, he went to the Altar for help to enable him to overcome his besetting sin and he did not go in vain. Moreover, there was scarcely any resemblance in taste between the light diluted wine received from the Chalice and the strong drink which overcame him, for the latter contained a large percentage of alcohol, while the former has scarcely any.

XXIV.

THE DECLARATION OF INDEPENDENCE AND THE FAITH OF ITS SIGNERS.

LECTURE VII; PAGE 378.

SIGNERS of the Declaration of Independence:
New Hampshire — Josiah Bartlett, Congregationalist; William H. Whipple, Congregationalist; Matthew Thornton, Congregationalist.

Massachusetts — John Hancock, Congregationalist; John Adams, Congregationalist; Samuel Adams, Congregationalist; Robert Treat Paine, Congregationalist; Elbridge Gerry, Episcopalian.

Rhode Island — Stephen Hopkins, Quaker; William Ellery, Congregationalist.

Connecticut — Roger Sherman, Congregationalist; Samuel Huntington, Congregationalist; William Williams, Congregationalist; Oliver Wolcott, Congregationalist.

New York — William Floyd, Presbyterian; Philip Livingstone, Episcopalian; Francis Lewis, Episcopalian; Lewis Morris, Episcopalian.

New Jersey — Richard Stockton, Quaker ; John Witherspoon, Presbyterian ; Francis Hopkinson, Episcopalian ; John Hart, Baptist ; Abraham Clark, Presbyterian.

Pennsylvania — Robert Morris, Episcopalian ; Benjamin Rush, Episcopalian ; Benjamin Franklin, Episcopalian ; John Morton, Episcopalian ; George Clymer, Episcopalian ; James Smith, Presbyterian ; George Taylor, Episcopalian ; James Wilson, Episcopalian ; George Ross, Episcopalian.

Delaware — Cæsar Rodney, Episcopalian ; George Read, Episcopalian ; Thomas McKean, Presbyterian.

Maryland — Samuel Chase, Episcopalian ; Thomas Stone, Episcopalian ; William Paca, Episcopalian ; Charles Carroll, Roman Catholic.

Virginia — George Wythe, Episcopalian ; Richard Henry Lee, Episcopalian ; Thomas Jefferson, Episcopalian ; Benjamin Harrison, Episcopalian ; Thomas Nelson, Jr., Episcopalian ; Francis Lightfoot Lee, Episcopalian ; Carter Braxton, Episcopalian.

North Carolina.— William Hooper, Episcopalian; Joseph Hewes, Episcopalian; John Penn, Episcopalian.

South Carolina.— Edward Rutledge, Episcopalian; Thomas Heyward, Jr., Episcopalian; Thomas Lynch, Jr., Episcopalian; Arthur Middleton, Episcopalian.

Georgia.— Button Gwinnett, Episcopalian; Lyman Hall, Congregationalist; George Walton, Episcopalian.

Signatures were affixed to the Declaration on July 4 and August 2, 1776. Several members of Congress who voted for, or while present strongly favored the Declaration did not, for one or another good reason, have an opportunity of signing it. Among such there were five Congregationalists, one Presbyterian, one Dutch Reformed, one Quaker and thirteen Episcopalians. The members of the Episcopal Church of whom this is true are : John Alsop, John Jay, James Duane, Robert R. Livingston, Jr., Henry Wisner, Edward Biddle, Thomas Willing, Robert Goldsborough, John Hall, Matthew Tilghman, Thomas Johnson, Jr., John Rutledge and Archibald Bullock.

In view of this showing and that of Appendix VI., page 413, it is surpassingly strange that Congregationalists, on the one hand, and on the other, Romanists, try to make it appear that the credit of laying the foundations of our Independence and Republican Government is due chiefly to their sons. But, surely, if the representatives of either of these bodies of Christians had any ground for their pretension, Episcopalians would not have predominated so greatly among the makers and signers of the Declaration of Independence and the Constitution of the United States. The first of these instruments was signed by twelve Congregationalists and one Roman Catholic, and the second by five Congregationalists and two Roman Catholics. But thirty-six Episcopalians had the imperishable honor of subscribing their names to the first of these documents and twenty-seven to the second.

As of late years Romanists have been making such astounding claims, we are justified in going a little out of our way to call especial attention to a fact which must be humiliating to them, namely, that Charles Carroll, the only one of their faith whose name appears among the signers of the Declaration of Independence, was a pew renter and an attendant of the Episcopal Church.*

XXV.

PERPETUITY: AN ADDITIONAL REASON FOR BEING AN EPISCOPALIAN.

LECTURE VII; PAGE 386.

ONE of the considerations which will induce many to identify themselves with the Episcopal Church rather than with any other body of Protestant Christians, grows out of the fact that the long continuance and present condition of this Church are a guarantee of her perpetuity. There is a strong desire on the part of most thoughtful men to ally themselves with the permanent and to avoid the ephemeral. The Scriptural proverb "no man also having drunk old wine straightway

---

* See appendix VI.

desireth new, for he saith the old is better" expresses a deep-rooted and far-reaching instinct, which as time goes on will tell more and more upon the growth of the Episcopal Church. Of two or more institutions claiming the allegiance of men and women, the one which gives the greatest promise of durability will, other things being equal, in the long run gain the day. In view of what has been said in other connections it cannot be denied that the Episcopal Church is at least as Scriptural, as pure and as useful as any other Christian body. This being the case, if she can be shown to be more enduring than her rivals, that, in itself, will, in the case of multitudes, settle the question touching the superior claims of allegiance.

Now the very fact that this Church has existed for eighteen hundred years,* certainly proves that she has marvelous qualities of endurance. Nor does she yet show the slightest signs of decay. On the contrary she never was more vigorous in every part of the English speaking world than at this time. Those who identify themselves with the American branch of this Communion will therefore be morally certain that their influence and work and gifts will go towards the upbuilding of an institution which will continue as long at least as the English civilization lasts. It may be that some of the other Protestant bodies will also continue through many centuries to come, but the history of sectarianism is against the probability of any of them doing so.

Of all the sects that arose in the course of the first one thousand years of the Christian Dispensation, none has survived. If Arianism, the greatest of them all, may be said to be an exception, its feeble condition as seen in the Unitarian body will afford no encouragement for hope that the Denominations which have sprung up since the Reformation, though they be ever so flourishing at this time, will be in existence three hundred years hence. Where are the sects that made such a stir in pre-Reformation times, the Donatists, the Novatians, the Arians, the Cathari? If these have all long since

---

*See Continuity of the English Church p. 217.

died out, what guarantee of perpetuity can any post-Reformation Denomination offer? Many of them have had their little day already, and not a few others have not much more than a name to live. Even the most flourishing among them are comparatively no more enduring than some of the early sects. Their growth has not been any more rapid or substantial.

There is therefore no reason why the history of the pre-Reformation sects should not repeat itself in those of the post-Reformation period. The probabilities are entirely on the side of the conclusion that in the comparatively near future Lutheranism, Congregationalism, Presbyterianism, Baptistism, Methodism and all forms of Denominationalism will be things of the past. But while this in the light of history is the outlook of sectarianism, the prospects are that the Historic Church of the English speaking race will, as the centuries come and go, grow more powerful and useful until her children shall be in numbers as the sand by the seaside, for multitude, and her blessing shall cover the whole earth.

Thus, if Americans choose their Church relationship with reference to the probabilities of perpetuity, there is nothing for them to do but to become Episcopalians.

XXVI.

NEW YORK STATISTICS OF THE CHIEF BODIES OF PROTESTANT CHRISTIANS IN 1895.

LECTURE VII; PAGE 393.

Disciples	493
Evangelical	800
United Presbyterian	900
Congregationalists	2,763
Reformed	8,936
Lutheran	11,632
Methodist	14,657
Baptist	15,110
Presbyterian	22,813
Episcopalian	43,689

THESE figures are furnished by the New York city *Mission Monthly*, a Presbyterian publication. The following is its comment:

"It will be noticed that the Episcopalians far outnumber any other denomination in their membership. Their relative growth also surpasses all others. In A. D. 1878 the Presbyterian membership in this city was 17,704, while the Episcopalian was 20,984. Now the Episcopalians almost double the Presbyterians in the matter of Church membership."

XXVII.

STATISTICS OF ENGLISH SPEAKING BODIES OF CHRISTIANS IN THE WORLD.

LECTURE VII; PAGE 396.

THE following estimates by M. Fournier de Flaix, published in the "Quarterly of the American Statistical Association" of March, 1892, are the latest that have been made by a competent authority:

Episcopalians	28,500,000
Methodists of all descriptions	18,250,000
Roman Catholics	15,250,000
Presbyterians of all descriptions	11,175,000
Baptists of all descriptions	9,000,000
Congregationalists	6,000,000
Free Thinkers	4,500,000
Lutherans	2,000,000
Unitarians	2,500,000
Minor Religious Sects	5,000,000
Of no particular religion	15,000,000
English speaking population	117,175,000

The overshadowing preponderance of Episcopalians in the English speaking world will appear still plainer when it is remembered that she is one great, closely-knit Communion, while the various other bodies, except the Roman Catholics, are broken up into many rival sects. For example, there are in America alone seventeen Denominations of Methodists, which to all practical purposes are as separate and distinct from each other as Congregationalists and Baptists. The largest by far of these Wesleyan bodies reports a membership of less than two millions. It is therefore very misleading, when comparing the Anglican Communion with the followers of Wesley, to say that the former has twenty-eight million five hundred thousand, and the latter eighteen million two hundred and fifty thousand. The same is quite as true of Presbyterianism. So far as numbers are concerned, the Romanists really come much nearer to us than any of the Protestant Denominations, but even they are numerically not much more than half as strong; while in other elements of strength, such as social, political, and commercial influence, they fall behind much further.

Moreover, there is no probability that either Romanism or Denominationalism will ever overshadow the Historic Catholic Church of our race. There have been periods since the Reformation when it seemed as if there were ground for fear first that the one and then the other might do so ; but this is far from being the case now. The great Anglican Communion is rapidly recovering from the prostrate and pitiable condition to which she was brought by the coöperation of her powerful Papal and Puritanical enemies, who after abandoning her in great numbers used their immense political power to keep her in the dust. But though they were for a long time successful, she finally recovered her feet, and now it may be said of her : " God even thy God hath annointed thee with the oil of gladness above thy fellows."

That this is true of the English branch of our Communion, appears from the following extract from the Schaff-Herzog Encyclopædia :

" During the century the vigorous life of the Church has been further shown by the restoration of Cathedrals and construction of Churches, in the creation of new Episcopal Sees at home and the rapid extension of the Church and Episcopate in the Colonies. At no time in its history has it been stronger and more vigorous than now ; more alive with Theological discussion and achievement ; more competent to cope with infidelity ; more solicitous to relieve the poor and fallen ; more munificent in its gifts for the conversion of the heathen, or more adapted to secure the esteem and gain the respect of the Anglo-Saxon people."

That the same is true of the American branch of our Communion appears from what a writer in *Harper's Weekly* says :

"The Episcopal Church has now for many years weighed far more in public estimation than is indicated by its very moderate array of Communicants and Clergy in the United States. The Church in America stands not alone, but is a Province of the world-wide Anglican Communion, and borrows as well as lends importance by reason of that association and kinship. It derives dignity and gathers influence from its roots in the past, from its mediatory position between the great Protestant bodies and the historic Churches, from its steadfastness among winds of doctrines, from its venerable order, from its sobriety of taste, from its grave splendor of public worship, from its widespread and devoted work among the poor, and from its great strength at centres of thought and influence."

Nor is our unparalleled growth in the British Empire and America the only evidence of renewed life and vigor. We have become the greatest Missionary agency of Christendom. There are at this time nearly one hundred of our Missionary Bishops and four thousand other Missionaries in the field. "They are in every part of Europe, Asia, Africa, South America and in the Isles of the Sea. Many of these Bishops have now established strong Churches which are themselves sending out Missionaries. For instance, the Bishop of Sierra Leone has an entire corps of black Clergy and they are not only self-supporting, but they have sent twenty-eight Missionaries into the interior of Africa."

Nothing can be more certain than that, so far as the English speaking race is concerned, the prophecy "They shall become one flock and one Shepherd" is destined to be fulfilled in the Anglican Communion. It will not be until after the English civilization has run a much more remarkable course than that of Rome, that a New Zealander "in the midst of a vast solitude shall take his stand on a broken arch of London

Bridge to sketch the ruins of St. Paul's." In the meantime some one who is a more reliable prophet and historian, if not a more brilliant rhetorician than Lord Macaulay, will record the collapse of the Papacy and the names of defunct Denominations which are now flourishing.

XXVIII.

CATHOLIC.

LECTURE VII; PAGE 347.

" I WEAR the name of Christ, my God,
    So name me not from man!
And my broad country Catholic,
    Hath neither tribe nor clan:
Its rulers are an endless line,
    Through all the world they went,
Commissioned from the Holy Hill
    Of Christ's sublime ascent."

Both Romanists and Denominationalists object to our use of the word "Catholic." This is because the former persistently claim, and the latter practically concede, the designation to be the exclusive property of the Roman Church. Romanists call themselves "Catholics," and the body to which they belong the "Catholic Church." Denominationalists and not a few thoughtless Episcopalians in both their spoken and written utterances often politely allow this usurpation. It is said that in China courtesy requires a man to use disparaging words in speaking of anything belonging to himself or with which he is connected, so that if he were asked of what religion he was, it would be proper for him to answer: The miserable superstition to which I an addicted is so-and-so. There is a large and increasing element in the Episcopal Church who cannot conscientiously carry their politeness to such an extreme. We feel that consistency with our profession of faith and a regard for truth, require that we should rather protest against the exclusive appropriation by Romanists of what belongs to us quite as much as to them.

We profess to be Catholics, for in one of the Creeds we say, "I believe in the Holy Catholic Church," and in the other, "One Catholic and Apostolic Church." One of the Creeds is repeated at every regular Service and often on less formal occasions. If the Episcopal Church is not really Catholic so far as the Faith is concerned, and Apostolic in respect to her origin and government, we should cease to repeat the Creeds.

Catholic is a Greek word, which literally means general or universal, but this is not its entire significance in the Creeds. It has reference there to the doctrine and government which were universally believed and accepted by the Orthodox during the early ages of Christianity. The Catholic doctrine was defined by the Great Ecumenical Councils, and consists of the twelve articles which were first condensed into the Apostles' Creed and afterwards expanded into the Nicene. During the Conciliary period, which closed with the year 680, there was a great deal of dispute about matters of doctrine, but there was practical unanimity concerning the form of Ecclesiastical Government, and so the Creeds contain comparatively little upon the subject, in fact the older form contains nothing while the other has simply the word "Apostolic." This is however enough to abundantly justify the conclusion that no organization which was not founded by the Apostles and is not governed by Bishops, who are their legitimate successors in Office, has a right to call itself a "Catholic" Church.

Romanists and Denominationalists define the term "Catholic" very differently. The former makes it exclude all bodies of Christians except the Papal Communion and include all the Roman additions to "The Faith once delivered to the Saints." According to the latter, it embraces all Denominations that acknowledge the Divinity of Christ and look to Him for Salvation, whether they adhere to the whole of the Ecumenical Creeds and discipline or not. But "can any one," asks Mr. Labagh, " be so demented as to suppose that when the Primitive Christians repeated the Apostles' Creed and said, 'I believe in the Holy Catholic Church' or the Nicene Creed and said, 'I believe one Catholic and Apostolic Church' they embraced in that language the whole brood of Sectaries that either then existed or might at any future time arise, and at the present time flourish." Both Romanists and Denominationalists agree that "Catholic" is a synonym for universal ; but the one applies it to the doctrines and government that are peculiar to the Roman Church, while the other contends that every sect has as much right as the Church of Rome to stamp its peculiarities with the imprint of " Catholic."

Episcopalians agree with Denominationalists in this conclusion, but we say that neither is right in supposing that the word "Catholic" in the Creeds has any reference whatsoever to their respective peculiarities. On the contrary, it is not a justification, but a condemnation of them. We glory in the fact that, if judged by the Ecumenical Creeds, our Church has no uncatholic peculiarities, none whatsoever. This is true of her both in respect to doctrine and government. Romanists and Denominationalists boast of their doctrinal and governmental peculiarities, we of our freedom from them. Peculiarities are not notes of Catholicity but rather evidences of sectarianism. The dogmas of Transubstantiation, the Immaculate Conception, the Infallibility of the Pope, and Papal Jurisdiction, come perilously near to converting the Roman Church into a mere sect. Many think that so long as that Church persists in these and her many other peculiar heresies she has no title to be regarded as anything more than a sect. The names of Denominationalists, such, for example, as Presbyterian, Baptist, Methodist, Congregationalist, Seventh-day Adventist, usually mark their heretical peculiarities and bear witness to their sectarian character.

That the Episcopal Church is the only Christian body in this country to which the word "Catholic" as used in the Creeds is applicable, appears from the fact that she has no peculiarities and that her teaching and government are the same as those which always have prevailed. The remarkable fact cannot be made too plain that at this time our Communion neither teaches nor practices any essential thing which is peculiar to herself. If this statement, which no Romanist or Denominationalist would dare to make of the communion to which he adheres, be doubted, let him who calls it in question name so much as one doctrine of this Church that is not to-day taught by the majority of Christians. He who undertakes to do this will enter upon an interesting trend of investigation which will ultimately bring him into the Episcopal Church; for not only will the truth of our representation be confirmed, but the attractiveness of a Church devoid of peculiarities will become irresistible.

> "Ancient prayer, and song liturgic,
>   Creeds that change not to the end,
> As His gifts we have received them,
>   As His charge we will defend."

REFERENCES TO QUOTATIONS.

THE Lectures in their original form were written for the class room, not for publication; and even when, after the lapse of several years, the work was prepared for the press, there was no expectation that it would be read by Clergymen and learned Laymen, who might want to verify and use its statements in their articles and books. Hence it was decided to omit the localizing foot-notes which increase and disfigure the pages of more pretentious volumes and are passed over by the ordinary reader. Accordingly no record of quotations was kept. The compiling of this Index has been therefore no little undertaking, and it was found to be practically impossible to make it entirely complete. However, special pains have been taken to trace to their source all quotations which are likely to prove of any value to those who have represented that a list of references would be helpful to them and others.

104, 3rd line, See Smith's Anglican Orders; Whence Obtained, p. 10.
104, 26th line, Denny, Anglican Orders and Jurisdiction, p. 143.
110, 4th line, " Janus," The Pope and the Council, p. 217.
110, 25th line, Robins, On the Claims of the Roman Church, p. 244.
110, 29th line, Willis' Pope Honorius, p. 26.
110, 35th line, Willis' Pope Honorius, p. 26.
111, 16th line, " Janus," The Pope and the Council, p. 324.
111, 25th line, Salmon's Infallibility of the Church, p. 456.
112, 23rd line, Littledale, Plain Reasons Against Joining the Church of Rome,
        p. 90.
113, 22nd line, Salmon's Infallibility of the Church, p. 284.
114, 2nd line, Littledale, Plain Reasons Against Joining the Church of Rome,
        pp. 208-209.
114, 29th line, Littledale, Plain Reasons Against Joining the Church of Rome,
        p. 209.
115, 5th line, Ross–Lewin, Continuity of the English Church, p. 49.
115, 14th line, Ross–Lewin, Continuity of the English Church, p. 49.
115, 19th line, " Janus," The Pope and the Council, p. 147.
115, 33rd line, " Janus," The Pope and the Council, p. 289.
116, 10th line, " Janus," The Pope and the Council, p. 289.
116, 26th line, Bp. Coxe, Institutes of Christian History, p. 176.
117, 2nd line, Robertson, The Growth of the Papal Power, p. 181.
118, 10th line, Salmon, Infallibility of the Church, p. 102.
118, 19th line, Pretended Speech of a Bishop in the Council — The Vatican
        Council, p. 193.
120, 8th line, Marshall's Cyprian, part II., p. 263.
121, 32nd line, Wilson, W. D., The Church Identified, p. 123.
122, 19th line, Smith, J. B., English Orders; Whence Obtained, p. 12.
123, 18th line, Courayer on English Ordinations, p. 292.
123, 35th line, J. H. Hopkins, Monsignor Capel, p. 39.
124, 11th line, J. H. Hopkins, Monsignor Capel, p. 39.
125, 8th line, Dixon, History of the Church of England, vol. I., p. 58.
125, 28th line, Denny's Anglican Orders and Jurisdiction, p. 155.
126, 16th line, Seabury's Haddan's Apostolical Succession, p. 105.
126, 31st line, Hussey, On the Rise of the Papal Power, p. 63.
127, 4th line, Hussey, On the Rise of the Papal Power, p. 64.
127, 24th line, M. R. Butler, Rome's Tribute to Anglican Orders, p. 39 and 40.
127, 30th line, Lee, Validity of the Holy Orders of the Church of England,
        p. 186.
128, 23rd line, Gore, Roman Catholic Claims, p. 147.
129, 12th line, Courayer on English Ordinations, p. 285.
129, 26th line, In Courayer on English Ordinations, p. 318.
129, 33rd line, In Courayer on English Ordinations, pp. 319-320.
131, 30th line, The Living Church, May 19, 1894.
132, 16th line, Decree of Leo XIII.
135, 13th line, Lee, The Validity of the Holy Orders of the Church of England,
        pp. 488-506.
137, 10th line, Lee, Validity of the Holy Orders of the Church of England, ch.
        XXVI., p. 297.
138, 15th line, London Church Times, September 25, 1896, p. 297.
139, 5th line, Church Eclectic, January, 1895, p. 931.
140, 25th line, London Church Times, September 25, 1896, p. 292.
141, 28th line, London Church Times, September 25, 1896, p. 292.
143, 30th line, Report of the Proceedings of the Reunion Conference at Bonn in
        1874, pp. 50, 51.
150, 3rd line, The Christian Union, 1894.
151, 15th line, Bp. Leonard, Witness of the American Church to Pure Chris-
        tianity, p. 15.
151, 28th line, Bp. H. M. Thompson's The Kingdom of God, p. 3.
156, 11th line, The Christian Union, 1894.
160, 7th line, Jewish and Christian Messiah, p. 218.
160, 12th line, Firminger's Attitude of the Church of England to non-Episcopal
        Ordinations, p. 33.
160, 33rd line, Simcox, pp. 62, 63.
162, 21st line, The Christian Union, 1894.
166, 16th line, Hammond, What Does the Bible Say About the Church, p. 23.
166, 34th line, Hammond, What Does the Bible Say About the Church, p. 12.
167, 5th line, Hammond, English Nonconformity and Christ's Christianity
        p. 150.

PAGES

PAGES

257, 13th line, Hammond, What is Christ's Church, p. 126.
257, 25th line, See Sanford's Bampton Lectures, 1861, p. 49.
257, 30th line, Sanford, Bampton Lectures, 1861, p. 49.
258, 4th line, Anglo Catholic Library, Oxford, vol. XI., p. XXIII., sec. VI.,
     Prœmium to "Codex Canonum Ecclesiæ Primitivæ."
262, 24th line, Dr. McConnell, History of the American Episcopal Church, p. 15.
263, 12th line, See Bp. Coleman's Church in America, p. 8.
264, 23rd line, Bp. Coleman, The Church in America, p. V.
266, 35th line, Bp. Wilberforce, History of the American Church, p. 109.
267, 4th line, Bp. Wilberforce, History of the American Church, p. 109.
267, 13th line, Dr. Peters' General History of Connecticut.
268, 6th line, McVickar, Professional Years of Bishop Hobart, pp. 82–83.
268, 25th line, Canon Perry, History of the Church of England.
269, 7th line, Dr. McConnell, History of the American Episcopal Church, p. 67.
271, 28th line, Bp. Perry, History of the American Episcopal Church, vol. I.,
     p. 247.
273, 17th line, Hooker, Eccl. Pol. VII., sec. 4.
274, 21st line, Chapman's Sermons on the Church, p. 76.
274, 32nd line, See Bp. Perry's History of the American Church, vol. I., p. 251.
275, 14th line, Bolles, Connecticut and Bishop Seabury, p. 9.
276, 17th line, Bp. Meade, Reasons for Loving the Episcopal Church, p. 11.
278, 12th line, Hymnal.
281, 35th line, Beardsley, Life and Correspondence of Bp. Seabury, p. 237.
284, 24th line, Stearns, The Faith of Our Forefathers, p. 41.
284, 34th line, Dupin, Compendious History of the Church, Century XI., ch.
     VII.
285, 7th line, Stearns, The Faith of Our Forefathers, p. 41.
285, 34th line, Institutes of Christian History, Bp. Coxe, p. 22.
286, 1st line, Bp. Coxe, Institutes of Christian History, p. 23.
286, 13th line, Gore, Roman Catholic Claims, p. 97.
288, 5th line, The Cincinnati Tribune, October 21, 1895.
291, 8th line, Bp. Perry, The Relations of the Church and the Country, p. 26.
293, 17th line, Bp. Coleman, The Church in America, p. 182.
294, 35th line, Description on an engraving entitled "The First Prayer in Con-
     gress."
297, 29th line, The Cincinnati Tribune, October 21, 1895.
299, 7th line, The Church Standard, September 14, 1895, p. 587.
299, 32nd line, See Appendix XVII.
306, 31st line, Dr. McConnell, History of the American Episcopal Church, p. 340.
308, 15th line, Church Standard, July 8, 1893, p. 19.
308, 31st line, Church Standard, July 8, 1893, p. 19.
310, 5th line, Hymnal.
315, 30th line, British Weekly, January 17, 1890.
316, 3rd line, Hammond, English Nonconformity and Christ's Christianity,
     p. 227.
317, 11th line, Thos. K. Beecher, What a Congregationalist Can Say of the Prot-
     estant Episcopal Church, p. 10.
318, 7th line, Mines, Looking for the Church, p. 29.
320, 15th line, Bingham's Antiquities of the Christian Church, vol. I., ch. VIII.
321, 26th line, Barrett, The Churchman's Scrap-Book, p. 36.
322, 1st line, Barrett, The Churchman's Scrap-Book, p. 36.
322, 19th line, Barrett, The Churchman's Scrap-Book, p. 35.
324, 26th line, The Churchman, December 24, 1887, p. 733.
333, 8th line, Tracts for Missionary Use, No. 3, p. 8.
336, 23rd line, Rubric in the Prayer Book.
337, 20th line, Hammond, English Nonconformity and Christ's Christianity,
     p. 10.
342, 14th line, Bp. Vale, The Comprehensive Church, p. 62.
344, 8th line, Cecil's Remains, quoted by Bp. Kip in "Double Witness."
345, 5th line, Labagh, Theoklesia, p. 173.
346, 18th line, Bishops Convention Pastoral, 1895.
351, 13th line, Article XXV.
355, 17th line, Anecdote related by Bp. J. S. Johnston, of Texas.
364, 3rd line, "Janus," The Pope and the Council, p. 18.
364, 14th line, Stearns, The Faith of Our Forefathers, p. 256.
364, 21st line, Dr. McConnell, History of the American Episcopal Church, p. 50.
365, 3rd line, Bp. Coleman, The Church in America, p. 24.
365, 32nd line, Stearns, The Faith of Our Forefathers, p. 257.
366, 25th line, Bp. Coleman, The Church in America, p. 60.

PAGES

366, 31st line, Dr. McConnell, History of the American Episcopal Church, pp. 50–52.

368, 20th line, M. R. Butler, Rome's Tribute to Anglican Orders, p. 44.

373, 3rd line, Miller's Parish Note Book, p. 49.

373, 31st line, Bp. Leonard, The Witness of the American Church to Pure Christianity, pp. 51–52.

374, 11th line, Thos. K. Beecher, What a Congregationalist Can Say of the Protestant Episcopal Church, p. 13.

374, 35th line, Miller's Parish Note Book, p. 52.

380, 6th line, Bp. Robertson, The Churchman's Answer as to the History and Claims of the American Episcopal Church, pp. 25–26.

384, 24th line, Hammond, What is Christ's Church, p. 119.

385, 19th line, Hammond, What is Christ's Church, p. 119.

386, 9th line, The Churchman, January 12, 1895, p. 46.

386, 24th line, Shields, The United Church of the United States, p. 47.

388, 6th line, Hammond, What is Christ's Church, p. 10.

388, 8th line, Hammond, What is Christ's Church, p. 10.

388, 11th line, Speech at the Wolverhampton Church Congress.

389, 11th line, Bp. Coxe, Institutes of Christian History, p. 283.

391, 33rd line, The Churchman, April 7, 1894, p. 404.

392, 19th line, The Churchman, April 7, 1894, p. 404.

395, 25th line, History of the English People, J. R. Green.

397, 9th line, Marshall's Notes on the Catholic Episcopate, p. 286.

397, 24th line, Marshall's Notes on the Catholic Episcopate, p. 314.

398, 26th line, Bp. Coxe, Apollos, or the Way of God, p. 244.

399, 16th line, Hammond, " John Wesley ' Being Dead, Yet Speaketh,' " p. 14.

399, 21st line, John Wesley's Works, Third London Edition.

399, 27th line, Hammond, " John Wesley, ' Being Dead, Yet Speaketh,' " p. 43.

400, 5th line, John Wesley Works, XIII., 58.

401, 6th line, The Churchman, April 14, 1894, p. 432.

402, 14th line, Hymnal.

405, 5th line, Firminger's Attitude of the Church of England to non-Episcopal Ordinations, pp. 65–66.

406, 22nd line, Bp. Griswold, The Apostolic Office, quoted by Clarke in "A Walk About Zion," pp. 90–92.

408, 15th line, Living Church, June 29, 1895.

408, 29th line, Living Church, June 29, 1895.

409, 15th line, Bolles, Washington: A Centennial Discourse to Young Men, p. 19.

409, 27th line, Bolles, Washington: A Centennial Discourse to Young Men, p. 18.

409, 34th line, Bolles, Washington: A Centennial Discourse to Young Men, p. 19.

410, 9th line, Bolles, Washington: A Centennial Discourse to Young Men, p. 19.

410, 14th line, Living Church, June 29, 1895.

410, 22nd line, Bolles, Washington: A Centennial Discourse to Young Men, p. 20.

410, 31st line, Bp. Perry, The American Church and the American Constitution, p. 5.

411, 4th line, Bp. Perry, The American Church and the American Constitution, p. 5.

411, 10th line, Bp. Perry, The American Church and the American Constitution, 5. p.

411, 16th line, Bp. Coleman, The Church in America, p. 74.

411, 21st line, Bp. Coleman, The Church in America, p. 74.

412, 1st line, Bp. Perry, The American Church and the American Constitution, p. 7.

412, 14th line, Dr. John Stoughton's History of Religion in England.

413, 3rd line, Bp. Perry, The American Church and the American Constitution, pp. 4–5.

413, 21st line, Bp. Perry, The Faith of the Framers of the Constitution of the United States, pp. 2–10.

414, 34th line, Bp. Perry, " The Faith of the Framers," p. 2.

417, 3rd line, Taine, History of English Literature, pp. 251–252.

418, 30th line, Shanklin, Some Objections to the Episcopal Church Considered and Answered, p. 18.

419, 11th line, Mines, Looking for the Church, p. 30.

419, 15th line, Mines, Looking for the Church, pp. 29–30.

419, 25th line, Shields, The United Church of the United States, p. 25.

421, 23rd line, The Good Way; or, Why Christians of Whatever Name May Become Churchmen, p. 16.

421, 27th line, Shanklin, Some Objections to the Episcopal Church Considered and Answered, p. 17.

PAGES

421, 31st line, Wesley's Sermons, No. CXV.
421, 34th line, The Good Way; or, Why Christians of Whatever Name May Be-
    come Churchmen, p. 18.
422, 8th line, The Good Way; or, Why Christians of Whatever Name May Be-
    come Churchmen, pp. 18–19.
422, 22nd line, Mines, Looking for the Church, pp. 30–31.
422, 27th line, From the Memoirs of Professor Austin Phelps.
423, 8th line, Thos. K. Beecher, What a Congregationalist Can Say of the Prot-
    estant Episcopal Church, pp. 9–11.
424, 25th line, Mines, Looking for the Church, pp. 177–178.
427, 29th line, Mines, Looking for the Church, pp. 32–33.
428, 25th line, Anderson's History of the Colonial Church, vol. III., p. 392.
429, 8th line, Works of John Wesley, Third London Editon.
432, 31st line, New York Churchman, August 4, 1894, p. 129.
434, 17th line, Church Eclectic, December, 1894, p. 816.
434, 25th line, Church Eclectic, December, 1894, p. 816.
435, 18th line, Butler, Rome's Tribute to Anglican Orders, p. 53.
435, 26th line, London Church Times, July 31, 1896.
435, 33rd line, Butler, Rome's Tribute to Anglican Orders, p. 53.
436, 4th line, Butler, Rome's Tribute to Anglican Orders, p. 55.
437, 16th line, Wesley's Sermons, vol. III., p. 261.
443, 23rd line, Palmer's Church History, p. 163.
444, 17th line, Ingram, England and Rome, p. 183.
445, 18th line, McClure's Magazine, June, 1896, pp. 3–4.
446, 29th line, Living Church, September 19, 1896, p. 586.
447, 4th line, Living Church, September 19, 1896, p. 586.
447, 8th line, Living Church, September 19, 1896, p. 586.
447, 21st line, Living Church, September 19, 1896, p. 586.
448, 29th line, The Pacific Churchman, June 15, 1894.
452, 22nd line, Cheney, What is the Reformed Episcopal Church? p. 2.
453, 7th line, Cheney, What is the Reformed Episcopal Church? p. 14.
453, 10th line, Cheney, What is the Reformed Episcopal Church? p. 14.
456, 4th line, Prayer Book, "The Form and Manner of Ordering Priests."
456, 6th line, Prayer Book, "Evening Prayer."
456, 8th line, Prayer Book, Baptismal Office.
456, 11th line, Prayer Book, Baptismal Office.
456, 12th line, Prayer Book, Communion Office.
457, 3rd line, St. John, 20: 23.
457, 7th line, St. John, 3: 5.
457, 26th line, St. Matthew, 26: 26–28.
457, 32nd line, St. John, 6: 52–58.
458, 9th line, I. Corinthians, 10: 16.
458, 18th line, Lane, Illustrated Notes on English Church History, vol. II., p.
    75.
464, 28th line, Ohio State Journal, Monday Morning, February 10, 1896.
465, 27th line, Quoted in Kip's Double Witness, pp. 215–216.
467, 13th line, Confraternity of the Blessed Sacrament, "Altar Wines," p. 1.
469, 17th line, Perry, Bp., The Faith of the Signers of the Declaration of Inde-
    pendence.
474, 14th line, The Oklahoma Churchman, June, 1896.
475, 27th line, Psalm XLV., 8, Prayer Book Version.
475, 32nd line, Schaff Herzog Encyclopædia, vol. I., p. 729.
476, 9th line, Church Life, August, 1896, p. 9.
476, 27th line, Barrett, Nineteen Questions About the Protestant Episcopal
    Church, p. 4.
477, 6th line, Quoted in Kip's Double Witness, p. 237.
480, 18th line, Fry, Lectures on the Church of England, p. 17.

INDEX.